# DATE DUE

# From Television
# to the Internet

# BOOKS BY WILEY LEE UMPHLETT

*The Sporting Myth and the American Experience: Studies in Contemporary Fiction* (Bucknell University Press)

*Mythmakers of the American Dream: The Nostalgic Vision in Popular Culture* (Bucknell University Press)

*The Movies Go to College: Hollywood and the World of the College-Life Film* (Fairleigh Dickinson University Press)

*Creating the Big Game: John W. Heisman and the Invention of American Football* (Greenwood Press)

*The Visual Focus of American Media Culture: The Modern Era, 1893–1945* (Fairleigh Dickinson University Press)

*American Sports Culture: The Humanistic Dimensions,* ed. (Bucknell University Press)

*The Achievement of American Sport Literature: A Critical Appraisal,* ed. (Fairleigh Dickinson University Press)

# From Television to the Internet

## Postmodern Visions of American Media Culture in the Twentieth Century

Wiley Lee Umphlett

Madison • Teaneck
Fairleigh Dickinson University Press

Associated University Presses
2010 Eastpark Boulevard
Cranbury, NJ 08512

The paper used in this publication meets the requirements of the American National Standard for Permanence of Paper for Printed Library Materials Z39.48-1984.

Library of Congress Cataloging-in-Publication Data

Umphlett, Wiley Lee, 1931–2005
    From television to the Internet : postmodern visions of American media culture in the twentieth century / Wiley Lee Umphlett.
        p.   cm.
    Includes bibliographical references and index.
    ISBN 0-8386-4080-X (alk. paper)
    1. United States—Civilization—1945–   2. Mass media and culture—United States—History—20th century.   I. Title.
E169.12.U47   2006
302.230973'0904—dc22                                                    2005023494

PRINTED IN THE UNITED STATES OF AMERICA

# THE POSTMODERN ERA OF SOCIOCULTURAL FRAGMENTATION

From newsprint to radio transmission to television programming, mass culture has been the dominant culture of the 20th century and, especially since the 1960s, has crossed all lines of genre, nationality, media and taste.

—James B. Twitchell, *Adcult USA:*
*The Triumph of Advertising in American Culture*

[T]he erosion of the older distinction between high culture and so-called mass or popular culture . . . is perhaps the most distressing development of all from an academic standpoint, which has traditionally had a vested interest in preserving a realm of high or elite culture against the surrounding environment of philistinism, of schlock and kitsch, of TV series and *Reader's Digest* culture.

—Fredric Jameson, "Postmodernism and Consumer Culture"

It is . . . entertainment that is arguably the most pervasive, powerful and ineluctable force of our time—a force so overwhelming that it has finally metastasized into life.

—Neal Gabler, *Life the Movie:*
*How Entertainment Conquered Reality*

# Contents

# Preface and Acknowledgments

IN COVERING THE YEARS FROM THE LATE 1940S THROUGH 2000, THIS book's sociocultural focus is on the visual impact of momentous developments in American media culture—particularly as they have reflected postmodern change and the social fragmentation of American life. Thus, this book complements and expands on the commentary and conclusions of my initial inquiry into the modern era of media-made culture (see *The Visual Focus of American Media Culture in the Twentieth Century*). That work, in dealing with the years from the watershed public event of Chicago's Columbian Exposition in 1893 to the end of World War II, traced the sociocultural influence of revolutionary technological advances that were instrumental in forging new visually oriented forms of media-made or "mediated" origins.

The 1890s was a seminal decade when the modernist milieu of industrialization and urbanization induced a rising middle class, the working-class poor, and newly arrived immigrants to seek out available escapist venues to help counter the alienation of urban life. Fortunately, the times were favorable for creative-bent individuals, enterprising entrepreneurs, and daring opportunists to capitalize on proliferating breakthroughs in communications technology. In doing so, they not only exploited existing media forms but introduced new kinds of entertainments designed to appease the populace's escapist desires. As factors in the ongoing democratization of American culture, both their efforts and the media-made images of new celebrity types planted the seeds for a gradual blurring of the lines between fantasy and reality as well as a narrowing of the divide between the elite and mass cultures.

My first book, in surveying these developments during the twentieth century's first half, explored how the communications media and the related areas of theater, sporting events, fashion, and the advertising messages of a growing consumer culture assumed a communal posture in looking to alleviate

9

the demands that modern capitalism imposed on the individual. How this process was reacted to and reflected in the arts and literature and even such an ephemeral form as the daily comic strip was also examined. This end developed naturally from my premise that the works of both mainstream and popular creative forces are natural reflectors of cultural change as well as the sociological and psychological effects of a time's escapist preoccupations.

To function as a unifying device for my analysis of media-made culture's impact on democratization in the first half of the twentieth century, I formulated a collective metaphor referred to as the *mediated vision*. Emblematic of the sociocultural effect the media generated in providing ways to transcend the wide gulf between dream and reality in everyday life, this way of "seeing" accounted in large part for the origin of the various venues that offered temporary escape from present discontent. During the century's first half, most Americans were acclimated to the mediated vision through media-made forms of communal appeal that either recalled the memories of a nostalgic past or anticipated the realization of a utopian future. Because the increasingly complex sociocultural, economic, and political issues and concerns of the larger society were no respector of class, the escapist pursuits of the well-to-do, or so-called leisure class, served as fantasized social events that demanded media attention, particularly its sporting activities. Some of these, such as golf and tennis, would soon be sufficiently democratized by the media-made culture to welcome widespread participation. Thus, the mediated vision cultivated an egalitarian outlook, cutting across the social fabric of class, gender, age, and race to unite all citizens in a common desire for the solace of escapist experience.

A touchstone literary work my earlier book referred to to illustrate the mediated vision's escapist posture toward present discontent is Theodore Dreiser's *Sister Carrie* (1900). Its story of a small-town young woman naively looking to fulfill her personal dreams in the big city of Chicago at the novel's beginning centers on the character of Carrie Meeber and her time's attraction to urban life. As such, it is a paradigm text that dramatizes the mediated vision's refusal to accept the considerable distance between illusion and reality in life. Carrie's symbolic role also presages the increasingly assertive stance that characterized the New Woman of the twentieth century, a development that would have wide-ranging socio-cultural impact in the postmodern era. Thus my present book updates this ongoing social transition by noting the various reincarnations of Carrie Meeber's persona, particularly during the counterculture movement of the 1960s, the sexual revolution of the 1970s, and in the 1980s' new educated class of young urban professionals who compromised the antimaterialism of the 1960s' hippie culture through the primary goal of making money to enhance a self-indulgent lifestyle.

From the early 1900s, through the 1920s, on to the Depression and World War II years, the communal focus of the mediated vision demanded mainly idealized images and romanticized interpretations of life. But, as my first volume summed up, the communal imperative, as it was affected by evolving social change, harbored the seeds of its own disintegration. The sociocultural uprooting of another World War, the anxieties attendant to the atomic age, and two later sociopolitically divisive military conflicts culminated in the societal upheavals of the 1960s and an increasingly problematic, bureaucratized, and fragmented nation.

This second book, then, also relies on my visual metaphor as it relates to these later developments in a still evolving media culture. But my main focus here is on how its visually oriented communications forms have influenced and contributed to the origin of varied subcultural sectors in the postmodern era, extending from the appearance of television in the late 1940s to the advent of the Internet near the end of the century. As early as the prosperous postwar years, where this narrative begins, the mass-mediated forms of the culture began to display the characteristics of postmodernism in the undermining of traditional values and the breakdown of the hierarchical division between the elite and mass cultures—a major theme of this book. Thus, my attention to the media-made forms of the twentieth century's second half reveals how the postmodernist affinity for fantasizing reality transformed the escapist dreams of the mediated vision into transient subcultures of special interests that sought to make the present more tolerable by intensifying the escapist experience. By century's end, then, American media culture, in fantasizing reality itself, would become a pervasive sociocultural force whose main intent was to offer escapist solace from the anxieties of postmodern life.

The development of this second book, which completes a

two-volume project about an extremely complex subject area, was made easier by my accessibility to the multitude of recent books and articles that support my book's thesis. For their supplemental ideas and thoughts, then, I owe a debt of gratitude to the authors of the works identified in my notes and bibliography. They lend valid support to the notion that the undertaking of an extensive project like this one is truly a cooperative enterprise. In this same light, once again I'd like to thank the staffs of Fairleigh Dickinson University Press and the Associated University Presses editorial department for their constructive criticism in seeing my manuscript through the maze of hurdles on its way to becoming a credible publication.

On a more personal level, toward the end of writing this book, I was diagnosed with cancer. The remedial treatment I had to undergo was made a lot easier for me to bear through the support of my associates. So I take this opportunity to thank all those who empathized with my situation, particularly John Dixon, Ed Woolam, Josh Gash, and Charles Koons. One of these, Mike Feenker, was supportive in another way, too: through his computer expertise in helping me produce an acceptable manuscript for the editing process. Through it all, my wife Joyce, my best friend, has been a steady force in helping me stay the course. For this reason I owe her my most sincere and loving thanks.

◻

As this book's subject matter pertaining to the evolution of twentieth-century media culture ended with the year 2000, the consequences of the tragic events of 11 September 2001 did not fall within its scope. But in their immediate wake, I note that a return was predicted to such dormant mainstream social relationships as connecting with the family and assuming communal responsibility; and that the media culture would reflect their revival. Yet, in retrospect, it appears that my argument for the media as the predominant sociocultural forces of our time has been substantiated by their ongoing role as an escapist buffer against the multiple ills of the postmodern age, including terrorism's ominous threat to the nation's tenuous sense of well-being. While the niche productions of postmodern media that responded to their segmented audiences continued to proliferate, the real world, from which the most popular mass-media forms of fiction, movies, and television mainly derived their subject matter, came across not so much as "real" as it was these forms' fantasized interpretation of reality. Perhaps, then, the major function of media culture, as it existed at the beginning of the twenty-first century, was to continue circumventing the harsh realities of the real world by fantasizing them.

# Prologue: Shifting from the Modern to a Postmodern Milieu

> A dramatic change took place in our economy when GIs returned from World War II. The late '40s saw unmatched demand for new housing, new automobiles, and innumerable consumer goods—and the start of the "baby boom." A postwar depression, predicted by all the intellectuals, academics, and newspaper pundits, never materialized. By 1950, the fifty-year boom was on its way.
> —Jacket blurb for Robert Sobel's *The Great Boom, 1950–2000*

WITH THE WAR OVER AT LAST, MOST AMERICANS OPTIMISTICALLY saw the future as now. Indeed, from a consumer's point of view, the mediated vision had never before looked upon a present that boded so well for the future. After the drastic economic downturn of the Depression and the material privation and social separation of the war years, the overall mood of the nation generated a rejuvenated feeling of economic togetherness. By the 1950s it would evolve into a conformist way of life when undreamed-of prosperity saw most everyone living alike, playing alike, and relishing the fruits of a thriving postwar economy.

In 1946 the movies enjoyed their biggest box-office year, and just as they had reflected social trends and mores since the 1920s, the latest films also mirrored the country's state of being. Those with inspirational themes, such as *The Yearling* and *It's a Wonderful Life*, and nostalgic musicals like *The Jolson Story* and *Till the Clouds Roll By* still revealed Hollywood's penchant for escapist moods. But some films hinted at the uncertainties underlying a seemingly placid social scene. If most war movies had been obligated to present patriotic themes, those of the postwar era were more concerned with dramatizing the grim, nonheroic side of the war, as *A Walk in the Sun* (1946) did in focusing on the personal combat reactions of a platoon of soldiers. In the same year appeared the

15

Oscar-winning picture *The Best Years of Our Lives*, which
centered on the adjustment to civilian life of three returning
veterans. Although this film's plot moved toward a positive
resolution of their problematic situations, an undercurrent of
doubt about what their immediate future might hold lurked
just below the surface. In the film noir genre, more ominous
signs foreshadowed a shift from the movies' traditional manner of fantasizing life as the mediated vision would have it. In
fact, by the end of the 1940s, moviegoers had experienced the
last decade in which the Hollywood studios collectively celebrated the idealized values of the American Dream.

The successor to Franklin Roosevelt's presidency, Harry S.
Truman, a man from America's heartland whose success
story was a composite of the nation's most cherished values,
was both a calming and an unsettling influence on postwar
life. During his administration a new era of prosperity
bloomed with the resurgence of industry and big business,
despite a series of strikes and signs of inflation. But his decision to send troops to Korea in 1950 resulted in growing international tensions and sociopolitical divisions within the
nation. While legislation had established the Servicemen's
Readjustment Act, or GI Bill of Rights, which allowed veterans to earn a college education at government expense, both
the Veterans Administration and the Federal Housing Authority now made it possible for them to buy a home under
the lowest possible mortgage rates. Such unprecedented developments helped change the sociocultural face of postwar
America.[1]

To rectify the housing shortage problem that had persisted
throughout the war years, developer William Levitt utilized
specialized assembly methods to create Levittown, a vast
tract of suburban homes outside New York City. It would provide a ready answer to many servicemen's postwar dream of
owning their own home upon marriage. This planned community with its functionally designed houses that featured the
popular ranch and Cape Cod styles appeared to be the realization of the utopian visions of the 1930s' world fairs. But at
this time the dream of home ownership was only to be realized by whites who began to shun the old neighborhoods of
the city for the patterned life of the suburbs, leaving the inner
cities to the blacks who had migrated there for wartime jobs.
The racist posture of white culture predominance in urban
life that had prevailed since the 1890s would continue to per-

vade the public sphere into the second half of the twentieth century until black power would become a social force to be reckoned with.

Ominous signs of divisive problems began to appear on the international scene as well. Despite the creation of the United Nations in 1945, the cold war between Russia and the West continued unabated during this era. Compounded by the threat of a nuclear conflict after Russia gained access to the atomic bomb in 1949, this situation ignited the fear of a Communist conspiracy infiltrating the United States. It and China's conversion to Communism not only led to the war in Korea but, later, another in Vietnam. In responding to the intent of the Truman Doctrine, both conflicts were dedicated to contain the spread of Communism in Southeast Asia but ultimately at the cost of thousands of American military lives and growing sociopolitical dissension at home. Ironically, the years of peace between 1945 and the outbreak of war in Korea in 1950 were but a prelude to a lifestyle known as "living on the brink"—a time when the mediated vision was again coerced into looking for escapist ways to avoid or fantasize the pressing realities of the present.

Among the most visibly indulgent ways in which the nation realized the consumer promise of the postwar era was through automobile ownership. Having deferred the purchase of a new car since 1942, American consumers, now with sufficient savings and disposable income, were so eager to acquire a new car that even the small retro models that began rolling off the assembly lines in 1945 were quickly snatched up. Soon, though, the big corporations—General Motors, Ford, and Chrysler—began to produce larger models whose advertising promised to show off their owners in terms of who they were or who they wanted to be. Thus, by the 1950s, cars were longer, sleeker, and more powerful than ever, displaying, in fact, more of everything: automatic transmission, air conditioning, power steering, and radio as standard equipment, to cite a few of the more desirable features.

To the mediated vision, though, the most mesmerizing feature of the new cars was their aerodynamic design, set off by a chrome finish, ornamental grills with air scoops, and tail fins, most popularly represented in the 1957 Bel Air Chevrolet. It was a look that suggested the essence of mobility in terms of speed and personal freedom—in effect, the visual encapsulation of the future in the present. To young males in particular, driving a new car not only represented this end but an extension of their masculinity, a message often reinforced in advertising come-ons such as Buick's "makes you feel like the man you are." To please fashion-conscious women, color was emphasized as a significant factor in enhancing overall design, and Ford, recognizing feminine taste as highly instrumental in a family's decision to purchase a new car, was especially sensitive to addressing this feature in its advertising. While the standard automobile of the '50s was the family car (quite often a roomy station wagon), ads began to promote the advantages of a personal car, particularly those directed toward the youth market, whose purchasing power was on the rise. By 1964, Ford, having learned a lesson from the unappealing design of the 1957 Edsel, was promoting the race-car look of the Mustang as the first affordable sports car for young-thinking motorists. Overall, the automobiles of this era were hybrid products of engineering advances and fashion design, both highly instrumental components in enhancing the mediated vision's ongoing love affair with the automobile.

But these futuristic-looking machines were also notorious gas guzzlers, and even though a gallon of gasoline could be purchased for pocket change, alternative measures to save on fuel consumption were being considered by many would-be car owners, a portent of the 1970s' gas shortage. A viable alternative showed up in 1949 in the German-made Volkswagen. Not only was it more economical on gas, its $1,300 price tag was considered an exceptional bargain, pointing out that bigger was not necessarily better. The popularity of the foreign-car imports, particularly those of the Japanese, was also a sign of the rapid economic recovery of both the nation's wartime foes.

During the early postwar years when many Americans were indulging their ready access to travel as escapist adventure, the great influx of more and bigger cars on the roads demanded that existing highways be improved or expanded and that new ones be built. In response to the demand, the Interstate Highway Act of 1956 allowed for the construction of 41,000 miles of divided expressways connecting major cities in a nationwide network. By the time of its completion, the Futurama vision of the 1939 New York World's Fair would become a reality, changing the nation's geographic face and, with its standardized signage system, providing motorists their most mobile opportunity yet for nationwide travel. Indeed, as the automobile's potential for personal mobility facilitated decisions as to where one worked and played, more and more Americans would continue to move around the country, particularly toward the area dubbed the Sunbelt South where new job opportunities as well as a warmer climate beckoned. The automobile also narrowed the sociocultural divide between rural and urban life, minimizing the mediated vision's sense of travel distance, as anyone with a car could take off on a moment's notice to any place in the country as well as Mexico and Canada. With the resultant demise in passenger train service, the railroads converted their new diesel engines to transporting freight to compete with the trucking industry.

Breakthroughs in aeronautical technology provided even more dramatic opportunities to travel in an ever-shrinking world. In 1959, transcontinental air travel was cut to less than five hours, while the appearance of the Boeing 707 passenger plane inaugurated the era of the "Jet Set." Now, the opportunity for both tourists and businessmen to engage in international air travel naturally brought them and other cultures closer together, resulting in a familiarity with their patterns of social behavior. Then, pursuant to the first satellite transmissions in 1962, communications scholar Marshall McLuhan prophesied that the immediacy of the televised event viewed simultaneously by a worldwide audience would create what he termed a "global village," presaging the internationalization of American media culture.

In America in the 1950s, television's role as a socializing force was already evident in its portrayal of suburban lifestyle and the corporate world's dedication to providing the consumer means to perpetuate the so-called "good life." Ironically, in emphasizing the acquisition of material possessions to appease the self, it would result in an ongoing erosion of the nation's traditional values. But, as the following chapters reveal, youth's rebellion against those values, growing minority unrest, deviant social behavior, and revolutionary social change would characterize the sociocultural temper of a fragmented mediated vision during the century's remaining years. It was a milieu both mirrored in and affected by the ever-evolving media culture, most preeminently at first in the ubiquitous medium of television.

# From Television
# to the Internet

# 1

# 1946–1963—Living the American Dream in a Time of New Uncertainties

> Within the first postwar decade television will be firmly planted as a billion-dollar U.S. industry. Its impact on U.S. civilization is beyond present prediction. Television is more than the addition of sight to the sound of radio. It has a power to annihilate time and space that will unite everyone here in the immediate experience of events in contemporary life and history.
>
> —*Life*, 4 September 1944

IN HER PERCEPTIVE ANALYSIS OF TELEVISION'S CULTURAL IMPACT on life in the 1950s, Karal Ann Marling observes how the things and events of the decade were "tailored to the visual sensibility," concluding that because of television's influence on them, "seeing is absolutely central to the meaning of the 1950s."[1] Yet when limited network programming first appeared in 1947, not many could have foreseen the extent of sociocultural impact that the medium would have on its viewers in the years ahead. By the 1950s both adults and children were devoting a great deal of time to watching television, and the popularity of its kind of escapist entertainment was attested to by the astronomical number of TV sets purchased by this time.[2]

## THE RISE OF TELEVISION AS A SOCIOCULTURAL FORCE

Initially, TV programming paralleled radio's formatted way of presenting entertainment, some of it even harking back to vaudeville. The variety shows of Milton Berle, Ed Sullivan, and Sid Caesar contained elements of both, while from the late '40s into the early '50s, situation comedies such as

23

*The Goldbergs, Amos 'n' Andy*, and the *George Burns and Gracie Allen Show* derived directly from their radio counterparts. Even before it became a series, the early variety show segments of Jackie Gleason's *The Honeymooners*, in their satirical take on working-class married life, were patterned after the radio sitcom format.

By the mid 1950s the nuclear family sitcom was the most widely watched TV genre, due mainly to its portrayal of the way the mediated vision expected family life to be.[3] Formulaic series like *Leave It to Beaver, The Adventures of Ozzie and Harriet*, and *Father Knows Best* mirrored an all-white, idealized suburban world of social conformity in which the family was central. Whatever problems there were had a humorous flavor to them and were not so insurmountable that they could not be resolved by a show's end. Indeed, the family sitcom seemed to imply, as the canned laughter accompanying it insistently reminded viewers, that life in the suburbs was too enjoyable for any kind of problem to get one down for long. Starting out in 1951, the most popular show of this type was *I Love Lucy*, which cast former movie star Lucille Ball and her bandleader husband Desi Arnaz in a long-running series. Centered around Lucy's slapstick escapades, the show's perennial popularity has been attested to since its end in 1957 by an endless round of reruns, serving as nostalgic reminders to viewers of how things were during this show's heyday.

With Lucille Ball's success as television's first female superstar came other popular family sitcoms structured around real-life entertainers, such as Danny Thomas in *Make Room for Daddy*. By the 1960s, the genre was featuring the movies' Andy Griffith as a small-town sheriff whose long-running show celebrated the populist values of a simpler time and place, and Dick Van Dyke in his own groundbreaking show whose plots were structured around the workplace and realistic social themes.[4] But by this time, the sitcom had splintered into such fantasized favorites of viewers as *The Beverly Hillbillies*, about a zany rural family suddenly made oil rich, and *Mr. Ed*, with its talking-horse title character, was the epitome of the 1960s' rage for fantasy.

Initially, every radio genre that found new life on television soon became a regular viewing habit. Among the more popular were the talent show format of Ted Mack's *Original Amateur Hour*, a panel show like *What's My Line?*, the weekly popular song ratings of *Your Hit Parade*, the *Lawrence Welk*

*Show*'s dance band music, the variety show format presented by Jack Benny, Bob Hope, and Red Skelton in their own shows, and the daily soap-opera problems depicted in *The Guiding Light*. As in the soaps, the real world also infiltrated prime-time television drama in the popular hospital series *Medic*, the detective/police action of *Dragnet*, whose lead characters affected the terse talk of real policemen, and in the courtroom drama series *Perry Mason* that presented the lawyer in a rare heroic light. And while *Naked City* revealed the seamy side of New York's underworld, *The Untouchables'* documentary style returned viewers to the 1920s and the G-men's war against the crime lords of Chicago.

In a pervasively subtle way, television drama's realistic approach was conditioning the mediated vision to a more visually immediate kind of fantasy than that of the 1930s' gangster movies whose lawless violence had introduced moviegoers to a new kind of escapism. Realism also characterized the television Western that became popular in the mid 1950s, yet another sign of the frontier myth's lingering appeal to the mediated vision. Former radio show *Gunsmoke*, destined for a long TV run, attributed its success to the in-depth characterization of its major roles, and a number of other adult-oriented series followed suit. While the protagonists of *Maverick* and *Have Gun, Will Travel*, for example, boldly countered any antagonist as a measure of their character, these two shows were never as popular as *Bonanza*, which originated in 1959. Through a soap-opera flavor that endeared its lead characters to viewers, this series enjoyed a long run, topped only by that of *Gunsmoke*.

Other realistic dramatic series like *Lights Out!* had roots in radio suspense programs. Both the bizarre stories of *Shock Theater* and *Alfred Hitchcock Presents* inclined toward the surprise ending, but *The Twilight Zone*, created by writer Rod Serling in 1959, soon became television's most watched series of this type. Its metaphorical title suggested the fear of the unknown that pervaded the show's scenarios in their response to the mediated vision's ongoing quest for fantasized escapism, now tempered by Serling's reality-inspired sensibility.

Television, too visually flexible an entertainment medium to remain beholden to radio's limited kind of programming, was experimenting early with live offerings that provided clues to its future entertainment role. In 1949 the medium's affinity for informality was exploited in *Arthur Godfrey and His Friends*, which featured its laid-back star bantering with his guests. In 1950 the first late-night variety show appeared as *Broadway Open House*, which also introduced TV's first sex icon—a tall, bosomy blonde named Dagmar. Though her role was confined mainly to appearing in a strapless evening gown, she was the show's major attraction to male viewers. However awkwardly produced, it was the model for NBC's *Tonight Show*, which started out in 1954 with the versatile Steve Allen heading up a colorful lineup of zany comics. Having introduced this format the previous year on an independent New York station, Allen had actually invented the concept of the informal late-night talk show on which celebrity guests appear. In 1957 the moody Jack Paar continued the tradition, but Johnny Carson brought the format to new heights after he took over in 1962. In taking on celebrities as well as unknowns who had special qualifications for appearing, Carson brought a humanizing manner to television that had natural appeal—undoubtedly a major reason for his thirty-year tenure. To viewers, the *Tonight Show*'s guests, under the off-guard, subtly risqué questioning of Carson, often came across as down-to-earth as their host. Such interaction made for a highly entertaining viewing experience that offered the mediated vision a fresh perception of celebrity culture. Indeed, by revealing celebrities as real, socially interactive people, the talk show enticed viewers into becoming part of the show themselves, thus helping them transcend the ordinariness of their daily lives.

In its immediate way of relating to people, then, live television readily invited informal interaction among its performers. Acutely aware of this situation, Groucho Marx turned his quiz show *You Bet Your Life* into an interview of the contestants, in which he utilized his acerbic wit at their expense. Even the formal interview, which came into its own in the late 1950s, called for more of a personally revealing approach, resulting in styles as different as the brash manner of the *Mike Wallace Interview* and the gently insightful probing of Edward R. Murrow's celebrity interviews on *Person to Person*. While both programs looked ahead to the tawdry talk shows of daytime TV near the end of the century, *Candid Camera*, which caught ordinary people responding to prearranged set-ups unbeknownst to them, presaged reality-based TV of this later era.

Television also transformed relatively unknown hosts into well-known personalities. A gourmet cooking program made Julia Child a household name, Ernie Kovacs's highly original approach to visual comedy proved his skills as a TV innovator, and the urbane manner of Alistair Cooke seemed exactly right for the elitist variety show *Omnibus*. Even the emcees of the ever-popular quiz shows got in the act. Hal March directed contestants through a maze of questions in the attempt to win riches on *The $64,000 Question*. Bill Cullen had housewives, along with competing studio contestants, guessing the prices of displayed consumer products to win prizes on *The Price is Right*, and Monte Hall welcomed tackily attired competitors from the audience in a similar game show called *Let's Make a Deal*.

However, when the news broke in 1959 that the prime-time quiz show *Twenty-One* had been rigged, host Jack Barry and the contestants who had been provided the answers to questions found themselves involved in a scandal that threatened the quiz show's very existence. Despite the black eye it gave television, the longtime appeal of the quiz show genre, coupled with the mediated vision's fantasized preoccupation with the acquisition of instant wealth, was too strong to incur its banishment. So with regulatory controls enacted, the quiz show format went on promoting consumer products and offering even more opportunities for momentarily famous contestants to win big rewards while viewers played along with them in a vicarious intent to enrich their lot in life.

Right from the start, children's series programs also created instant celebrity for those who performed in them. William Boyd, whose career as movie cowboy Hopalong Cassidy seemed finished by the late 1940s, introduced this character to a new generation and, in the process, realized a bountiful windfall from numerous spin-offs of games, toys, and related character merchandise. When Clayton Moore as the Lone Ranger and Duncan Renaldo as the Cisco Kid brought their televised exploits to youthful audiences, they also generated a big demand for their characters' spin-offs. While the trend continued with the appearance of George Reeves as comic book hero Superman, the reign of fantasized heroes extended also to science fiction, inspiring popular series like *Captain Video* and *Tom Corbett Space Cadet*, whose adventures anticipated a timely new escapist realm for children, as the real-life exploration of space would soon be under way.

In 1947, an influential show that marketed products to children appeared. Organized around a puppet named Howdy Doody and a colorful cast of supporting characters led by genial host Buffalo Bob Smith, it cultivated a loyal following of "baby boomers," even allowing for a live audience of them. Along with home viewers, they would retain fond memories of the show over the years. But another warmly remembered children's show aimed at product marketing was *The Mickey Mouse Club*, which started up in 1955 as an hour-long afternoon program. Featuring a talented youthful cast called the Mouseketeers, it took on the semblance of a variety show with something for every child's interest.

Recognizing its promotional potential, Walt Disney first jumped into the television medium in 1954 with *Disneyland*, a prime-time weekly anthology that included both his classic cartoons and educational subject matter. Its miniseries about frontier hero Davy Crockett was so popular it sparked a national mania among children for spin-offs, particularly for the title character's celebrated coonskin cap. Whether looking to the past in the program's segment of Frontierland or the future in that of Tomorrowland, *Disneyland*, as a family show, cut across age differences to attain high ratings[5]. It also helped publicize Disney's California theme park of the same name that opened in 1955. Dedicated to recapturing the spirit of the past while projecting the promise of the future, it was a monument to the inherent escapist desires of the mediated vision in changing times. (The park's sociocultural impact is discussed later in this chapter.)

## Television's Early Approach to Reality Programming

That television's sense of visual immediacy had the power to transform even the most serious subject matter into a form of entertainment was demonstrated in its presentation of news reportage and those who figured in it, either as newsmaker or reporter. From the intensive fifteen-minute evening news coverage of Douglas Edwards and John Cameron Swayze in the late 1940s to the thirty-minute time slots of NBC's low-keyed Chet Huntley–David Brinkley team and the authoritative voice of future CBS icon Walter Cronkite in the 1960s, their reports became an early evening ritual, supplemented by a local network station's look at area happenings.

Attempting to capture the early morning viewing audience, NBC introduced a news/entertainment format in 1952 called *Today*. With Frank Blair, the first in a long line to report the news, and affable Dave Garroway hosting the show, this prototypal program went a long way toward conditioning early risers to the concept of news as a form of entertainment.[6]

That the television camera was an unblinking, immediate witness to reality was evidenced by its coverage in the early '50s of both the war in Korea and a congressional committee's investigation of organized crime. By 1954 the fear of Communism had reached such a pitch that television coverage of Senator Joseph McCarthy's hearings dealing with supposed Communist infiltration into the army hooked many viewers. They were especially intrigued with the witch-hunt methods employed by Senator McCarthy to identify those who had supposedly been affiliated with the Communist cause. Ironically, such brazen tactics upstaged the senator's patriotic zeal, turning the hearings' original intent into a kind of travesty that resulted in his downfall.

Realizing television's power to dramatize reality, radio news pioneer Edward R. Murrow turned his attention to its natural documentary bent in a CBS series called *See It Now* that introduced viewers to the medium's immediately visual style of investigative journalism. Murrow also inaugurated another TV first by conducting informal interviews with famous personalities on *Person to Person*, usually within the setting of their own dwellings. To viewers this early experience with reality TV was akin to having celebrities enter their own living rooms. Despite its obviously anachronistic approach, *You Are There* saw the versatile Walter Cronkite conducting interviews with long-dead historical figures involved in momentous events. This series' title was a reminder in itself of television's natural intent to bring the remote nearer. In 1952 the not-so-distant past also came alive in the real-life film footage of the most watched TV documentary about World War II—*Victory at Sea*. This honored series attracted viewers through both its compelling narrative and stirring musical sound track composed by Richard Rodgers. As the movies had, television also discovered how music could function as visual enhancement.

From the 1950s on into the '60s, investigative documentaries abounded, dealing with such serious topics as mental illness, the population explosion, and the plight of the poor. To explore such matters, special program series were inaugurated, in particular *CBS Reports* and NBC's *White Paper*. Never before had the mediated vision been so directly exposed to the problems of contemporary life as now, when such dire concerns were being projected into the sanctity of the nation's living rooms.

The controversial issues that political leaders either represented or were embroiled in played a significant part in TV's political programming, as evidenced by fixtures like *Meet the Press*, appearing since 1947, and *Face the Nation*. Politicians' live reactions to pointed questioning served not only to humanize them but revealed to viewers their capabilities, or lack of, for leadership. Accordingly, many a voting decision was made after the 1960 presidential campaign debates between Richard Nixon and John Kennedy, in which the latter came across as the more self-assured and photogenic of the two. The visual upshot of these debates was such that Russell Baker concluded that they caused image to supplant "the printed word as the natural language of politics."[7] Though Harry Truman and Dwight Eisenhower were no strangers to the TV camera, Kennedy as president presented the most appealing image of the three. Young, handsome, and supremely confident in his demeanor, he established a natural rapport with the press in his televised conferences that his successors would strive to emulate. Even during the low point of his brief administration—the Bay of Pigs fiasco that precipitated the Cuban missile crisis in 1962—Kennedy was the star of his own TV drama. But one event on the heels of Kennedy's tragic assassination in 1963 revealed just how powerful a visual force television had become, for the on-camera murder of the president's suspected killer came across as an act of such visual immediacy it transformed reality into theatrical drama and clinched television's role as the prime conduit for it.

While television was evolving into a national theater for the staging of public affairs and political events, it was also doing the same for sports, infusing them with an aura of visual immediacy they had never known. Though baseball, football, basketball, and hockey attracted ever-expanding legions of followers into the 1960s, football, more accommodative to the penetrating gaze of the TV camera, would eventually surpass baseball as the more popular televised sport, particularly the professional game. As the escapist milieu of the bar/tavern scene grew increasingly hospitable to televised sports, many male customers began to linger over drinks until a game's outcome was decided. Focusing on the color and pageantry of college football, the television camera capitalized on its special power to involve viewers in the emotional drama of a big game. By the 1960s, televised sports as escapist entertainment were involving the viewer to a degree that "no spectator at a game could ever grasp," according to Jeff Greenfield. Television, he averred, offered "a much more intimate glimpse of sports than the 'real' event could," resulting in a visual experience that "was beyond reality."[8]

Televised sports coverage was expansive enough, too, to respond to a broad range of tastes, as it demonstrated in the mock-heroics of professional wrestling, whose coiffured image of Gorgeous George was the most outlandish example of the sport's exhibitionism at the time; the unladylike exploits of women skaters in the Roller Derby; the legalized brutality of boxing; and the high drama of special events like the 1954 race between four-minute milers Roger Bannister and John Landy. But TV sport's most momentous sociocultural contribution was the role it played in introducing the black athlete to a national audience. The televised triumphs of superathletes Willie Mays in baseball, Jim Brown in football, and Bill Russell in basketball helped dispel the myth of the black athlete as incapable of performing at the top level of sports. In gradually conditioning the public to view organized sport as a social institution that afforded all comers the opportunity to participate on an equal basis, television functioned as a highly visible showplace that not only revealed sport's new sociological mission but its role as a viable escapist retreat for the mediated sports fan.

## TELEVISION'S ROLE IN DEMOCRATIZING HIGH CULTURE

Although the medium was lambasted by many as a cultural wasteland, television, as radio had, performed a key role in introducing the mediated vision to many of Western culture's most monumental achievements in drama and music as well as to notable figures in these fields. By fostering a readily accessible venue for appreciating and popularizing cultural events, the TV networks were another force in helping merge the seemingly irreconcilable tastes of the elite and mass cultures. During the 1950s, for example, television show host Ed Sullivan, whom David Halberstam called the "Unofficial Minister of Culture in America," was an unlikely catalyst in this cross-cultural process by using his Sunday evening show as a stage for performers who ranged as far apart as rock and operatic singers.[9] Even in its beginnings, television had functioned as a natural medium for dramatic productions, from the most revered classic to the unabashedly melodramatic. Sponsored series like the *Philco Playhouse*, *Studio One*, *Kraft Television Theatre*, and the *Hallmark Hall of Fame* even dared to present "live" plays, at a time when the videotaping process was some years away. Even though these productions were subject to acting miscues and technical blunders, by and large, many were highly acclaimed, offering viewers productions like *Hamlet*, *Victoria Regina*, and *Cyrano de Bergerac*. There were also award-winning plays written especially for TV, such as Paddy Chayefsky's *Marty*, Reginald Rose's *Twelve Angry Men*, and Rod Serling's *Requiem for a Heavyweight*, all destined to become well-received films.

In addition to TV's flair for dramatic productions that appealed to a wide range of viewers, musical programs were scheduled that responded to a broad spectrum of musical tastes. Radio's original *Voice of Firestone*, which featured conductor Howard Barlow and his orchestra presenting a program of perennial favorites and semiclassical selections, enjoyed a surprisingly long life from 1948 to 1963. That a supportive TV audience existed for strictly classical music was proven in 1949 when renowned conductor Arturo Toscanini and the NBC Symphony Orchestra made the transition from radio. Helping foster an appreciation for classical music, composer/conductor Leonard Bernstein began appearing on the BBC-inspired program *Omnibus* in the 1950s. His articulate, personable manner in explaining the intricacies of classical compositions made him a natural for the later *Young People's Concerts* series. In 1958 Ed Sullivan maintained his "Minister of Culture" title by devoting an entire program to the Moiseyev Dancers from Russia. In the same year, dance master Fred Astaire appeared in a highly acclaimed "special" in which he displayed the same mesmerizing skills he had in his movie musicals. That the television screen could accommodate itself to the musical theater format, too, showed up in adaptations of such long-running Broadway productions as

*Peter Pan* with Mary Martin in the title role and *Wonderful Town*, starring Rosalind Russell.

## THE SOCIOCULTURAL IMPACT OF TELEVISION ON THE MEDIATED VISION

In attending to both the elite and popular sectors, then, television functioned as a cultural bond between the socially disparate elements of the country to create a new, more egalitarian kind of media culture. Although TV's immediate way of perceiving the real world provided the mediated vision a more realistic take on life, it also gave it a more accessible way of escaping from it while revealing a great deal about viewers according to the programs they watched. So compared to radio's dramatic power to stimulate the imagination, television offered a ready-made substitute for social experience by watching others engage in it. Then, too, its addictive nature intensified the desire for ever more fresh escapist experiences, evidenced by rapid program turnovers as a result of continually changing popular tastes. Such a transition marked the brief careers of the many personalities who came to television, only to fail in sustaining the instantaneous celebrity bestowed upon them by the TV camera.

The ritualized manner of home viewing habits that developed during these years was reinforced by the mass-produced TV dinner, introduced by the Swanson frozen-food company in 1954. Serving this product on a portable tray prompted family members to forsake the dining room table to eat near wherever the TV set was located and continue viewing a program in progress. That the viewing area was arranged with television as the focal point denoted the key social role it had come to play in the household. Accordingly, the TV dinner's popularity inspired other fast-food imitations that reflected the evolving informal eating habits of the American people long after its original purpose had been long forgotten.

By the 1960s, color sets with larger screens were being marketed to accommodate ongoing advances in programming technology. Whereas the "live" close-up presentations of TV drama's early days were confined to staged settings in New York studios, the networks were now locating in the Hollywood area to initiate outdoor film production and realize its larger sweep of movement. By this time, too, as the movies were demonstrating, explosive violence had become more of a promotional feature to attract audiences. Ironically, Hollywood, which had considered television a mortal enemy since its inception, now realized a way to make a comeback through extending its resources to the expanding needs of television programming. During this time, then, the mediated vision found itself the target of both television's relentless growth and the movies' search for alternative ways to reassert their faltering image.

## The Movies and Theater Go on the Offensive

While television was superseding the original entertainment role of radio, compelling it to survive in a culturally different format, both the movies and the legitimate theater were motivated to counter this serious threat to their longstanding status as major forms of entertainment. As TV stations sprang up across the country and thousands of TV sets continued to be purchased, hundreds of movie houses were forced to shut down due to declining attendance. With fewer movies now being made, Hollywood recognized that a viable way to cope was by producing big, highly publicized films. As a prelude to Hollywood's greatest period of the spectacular Technicolor musical in the 1950s, the late '40s responded to the mediated vision's fascination with the past in the themes and settings of such big MGM musicals as *Good News* (1947), *Easter Parade*, and *Summer Holiday* (both 1948). The tradition of dramatizing the lives of popular entertainers and composers inspired Warners' *Night and Day* (1946), about Cole Porter; MGM's *Words and Music* (1948), on the collaboration of Rodgers and Hart; and Columbia's *Jolson Sings Again* (1949), a sequel to the earlier film about Al Jolson's life. Hollywood now seemed sold on nostalgia as an essential musical ingredient to keep moviegoers coming back, and the trend continued on through the '50s with the blockbuster musicals of MGM: *An American in Paris*, featuring the music of George Gershwin; *Show Boat* in its third remake; *The Great Caruso*, with Mario Lanza in the title role (all 1951); *Singin' in the Rain* (1952), a delightful spoof of the movies' early days in the sound era; *High Society* (1956), the musical remake of 1940's *The Philadelphia Story*; and the late nineteenth-century Paris setting of *Gigi* (1958), which, in winning nine Academy Awards, brought this era to a fitting close.

During this time, the most dependable source for the Hollywood musical was Broadway, whose productions' upfront publicity helped sell tickets for their movie versions. Broadway producers also felt a kinship with the moviemakers in that they too were experiencing television's impact on dwindling audiences. The film versions of their shows, then, were a valid way to publicize the Broadway musical as an enduring force in the theater's longtime tradition of creating quality entertainment, as evidenced by the large number of productions that were made into movies. In the wake of the highly successful *Oklahoma!* (1943), Richard Rodgers and Oscar Hammerstein turned out a string of classic hits that included *South Pacific* (1949), *The King and I* (1951), and *The Sound of Music* (1959). All three productions gave American music many of its perennial song favorites. Irving Berlin's *Annie Get Your Gun* (1946) and *Call Me Madam* (1951) proved that his status as a master of melody was still intact, while Cole Porter's debt to Shakespeare's *Taming of the Shrew* as *Kiss Me, Kate* (1948) demonstrated that his special way with both words and music was still as proficient as ever. Newcomers to the Broadway scene helped build on the conventions begun with *Show Boat*, as Alan J. Lerner and Frederick Loewe's *Brigadoon* (1947) and the long-running *My Fair Lady* (1956) presaged the success of *Camelot* (1960). Ironically, *The Fantasticks*, an off-Broadway production, would become the longest-running musical ever, playing from 1960 to 2002.

As *South Pacific* had touched on the problem of racism, so there were other signs that elements of social realism as well as unlikely subject matter were beginning to show up in the Broadway musical. The team of Leonard Bernstein and Stephen Sondheim demonstrated in *West Side Story* (1957) that the improbable subject of rival street gangs could provide apt material for the musical genre. Lyricist Sondheim also collaborated with songwriter Jule Styne on *Gypsy* (1959), based on the burlesque career of stripper Gypsy Rose Lee. Despite any difference in themes or subject matter, all these musicals had one thing in common: in becoming popular movies, they were testimonials to the ongoing symbiotic relationship that had long existed between Broadway and Hollywood.[10]

Accordingly, Hollywood also looked to Broadway's dramatic productions for film property, mainly because the theater's traditionally liberal approach to controversial issues and reality-based subject matter assured their box-office appeal. Even though censorship restrictions were still stringent during the 1940s–50s, Hollywood envisioned good returns on the films of long-running plays like *Death of a Salesman* and *A Streetcar Named Desire*, due mainly to the new realism's cultivation of a more sophisticated audience.

Although Eugene O'Neill was into the waning years of his life, in 1946 he produced what many considered one of his finest works—*The Iceman Cometh*. In it, the illusions his pipe-dreaming characters harbor about life are revealed through their earthy dialogue in the escapist haven of a saloon. In confronting the realities of life by effectively depicting illusion as a form of consciousness that makes life endurable, O'Neill remained a powerful force in American drama, and many of his works appeared as films. His open exploration of his own family's obsessions and repressions resulted in three of his plays produced posthumously during this era: *Long Day's Journey into Night* (1956), *A Moon for the Misbegotten* (1957), and *A Touch of the Poet* (1958).[11]

By the late 1940s, though, new voices were coming onstage, young playwrights with compelling approaches to dramatizing the realities of life and their characters' ways of either confronting or escaping from them. Starting with *All My Sons* (1947), Arthur Miller drew on the era's growing sense of communal loss to expose the dark transgressive side of American experience. *Death of a Salesman* (1949), the best known of his plays, centered around the illusions its central character resorts to to avoid his commitments to family and even life itself. One of the most prolific dramatists of the 1950s was William Inge, whose midwestern background served as a nostalgic catalyst for culturally familiar settings that endeared him to Hollywood and the mediated vision. Despite the wide appeal of such plays as *Come Back, Little Sheba* (1950), *Picnic* (1953), *Bus Stop* (1955), and *The Dark at the Top of the Stairs* (1957), their strong but troubled characterizations seemed intent on revealing that American life at midcentury was not as rosy as it was made out to be.

The die-hard illusions people cling to were clearly a central focus of Tennessee Williams's plays, whose daring subject matter and eccentric protagonists stirred up a great deal of controversy in the predominantly provincial 1950s. From *A Streetcar Named Desire* (1947) and *The Rose Tattoo* (1950) to

*Cat on a Hot Tin Roof* (1955), *Sweet Bird of Youth* (1959), and *The Night of the Iguana* (1961), Williams's haunted characters are in constant self-denial about their situations, preferring to retreat from life rather than confront it. His fearless approach to the Freudian ramifications of sexual desire and repression that O'Neill had introduced gave rise to other playwrights' interpretations of a once taboo subject area. Chief among them was Edward Albee, who in *Who's Afraid of Virginia Woolf?* (1962) turned the conventional situation of marital strife into a penetrating examination of the conflict between illusion and reality, not only in its central characters' relationship but in the play's references to the larger realm of postmodern life. The explicit language of the performers, an integral part of Albee's method, was certainly no illusion as audiences were exposed to some of the rawest exchanges yet between characters on the Broadway stage, prefiguring the theatrical license that Hollywood would soon look to adopt.

While this was a period whose dramatic productions ranged as far apart in theme and subject matter as Thornton Wilder's obeisance to the nostalgic past in *The Matchmaker* (1954) and Archibald MacLeish's biblical parallel of the Job story in *JB* (1958) to Lorraine Hansberry's portrayal of the rising social consciousness of blacks in *A Raisin in the Sun* (1959), the acting style of the time inclined toward the self-reflexive manner of method acting and its focus on psychological characterization. The center for this kind of training was Lee Strasberg's Actor's Studio in New York, which graduated such dramatic presences as Julie Harris, Maureen Stapleton, Eli Wallach, and Marlon Brando. Making his debut in *A Streetcar Named Desire*, Brando, in the role of the brutish Stanley Kowalski, was the exemplar of the method actor who exuded male sexuality. Along with director Elia Kazan and playwright Tennessee Williams, Brando was a major force in the rebellion against the acting conventions of the traditional theater. Many performers who acclimated to the Actor's Studio style—among them, Charlton Heston, Paul Newman, Rod Steiger, James Dean, Kim Stanley, and Shirley Booth—took their unique talents to television's live dramatic series of the time. But with an increasing number of Broadway's dramatic productions being transcribed to the screen, Hollywood was beckoning even more enticingly.

## THE MOVIES AND THE NEW REALISM

Although many films of the last half of the 1940s still abided by Hollywood's formulaic happy-ending resolution and were therefore considered suitable for family viewing, an underlying rebellious mood, as noted earlier, reflected a gradual shift to more reality-derived, controversial subject matter. Anticipating television's dramatic series, which would dwell on the darker side of life, Hollywood started producing films dealing with sociological themes, such as anti-Semitism in *Gentlemen's Agreement* (1947), mental illness in *The Snake Pit* (1948), juvenile delinquency in *Knock on Any Door*, racism in *Intruder in the Dust*, and political abuse in *All the King's Men* (all three 1949). Despite these films' avoidance of the escapist element to center on real contemporary problems, the mediated vision adjusted its focus to view them as Hollywood's latest attempt to entertain.[12]

Certain crime-oriented films popular during the war years, such as *The Maltese Falcon* (1941), *This Gun for Hire*, and *The Glass Key* (both 1942), had set the tone for new extremes of visual violence. As forerunners of the film noir genre, after the kind of dark world they depicted, these movies focused on the deceptive means that certain unsavory individuals engaged in for personal gain. It was a world in which moral corruption played a dominant role, until the corrupted received their comeuppance in the end. From 1946 on to the mid 1950s the genre's nighttime urban scene was rendered in the dim focus of black-and-white photography in such films as *The Big Sleep* (1946), *Out of the Past* (1947), *Kiss Me Deadly* (1955), and *While the City Sleeps* (1956). A number of expatriate directors tried their hand at this form, of which Billy Wilder had created a seminal example in 1944's *Double Indemnity*. The clandestine conniving of its principals, Fred MacMurray and Barbara Stanwyck, epitomized film noir's rebellion against the movies' conventional code of honor and moral integrity. Stanwyck's role, in particular, reflected the time's more open posture toward characterizing unprincipled women, which had been evolving since the 1920s. *Double Indemnity*, through its ironic denouement involving the Stanwyck and MacMurray characters, had prepared the mediated vision for a veritable onslaught of similar productions. It also established a model to show filmmakers how to skirt the Production Code and justify violence and sex when integral to a film's dramatic context.

As noted in my preceding book, sex had always been one of Hollywood's most reliable ploys to promote its movies in spite of society's moral stance and the Code's edicts. Now there were obvious signs that the barriers to sexual content were falling. In the controversial wake of *The Outlaw*, which endured numerous cuts before it appeared in 1943, two other films were released in which the role of sex was aggressively promoted—*Duel in the Sun* (1946) and *Forever Amber* (1947). Based on sensationally publicized novels, both movie versions were initially subjected to the censor's scissors but were ultimately approved. That they were passed was indicative of the Code's slipping role as a watchdog force in the production process.

From 1946 into the 1960s Hollywood produced numerous mainstream films directed toward adult audiences. For example, *The Postman Always Rings Twice* (1946) was another but more sex-exploited take on *Double Indemnity*. *A Place in the Sun* (1951) dealt with a premarital pregnancy that results in a murder conviction. *From Here to Eternity* (1953) centered on an adulterous affair. *The Man with the Golden Arm* (1956) offered an inside look at drug addiction. *Peyton Place* (1958) was based on the sensationalized novel's exposé of small-town moral deviancy. *Anatomy of a Murder* (1959) focused on a rape/murder trial. *Butterfield 8* (1960) was structured around the sexual trysts of a New York model. *Lolita* (1962) was based on Vladimir Nabokov's controversial novel about a pubescent girl's relationship with an older man. And *Tom Jones* (1963) came on as a sexually provocative version of the racy eighteenth-century classic novel. Having gathered momentum year by year, the movies' intent to adapt subject matter to mature tastes would ultimately result in a rating system to categorize both adult and family fare. The upshot would be a segregated mediated vision respecting the kinds of films adults and children could see.

This era also saw a number of Broadway's controversial productions produced as films. As expected, those by Tennessee Williams were promoted for their sensational elements, especially *A Streetcar Named Desire* (1951), *Baby Doll* (1956), and *Cat on a Hot Tin Roof* (1958). Although these films were toned down from their stage versions, they nevertheless played a big part in tempering the mediated vision's growing receptivity toward accepting the aberrant side of life as entertainment.

## THE MOVIE INDUSTRY'S REACTION
## TO REAL-WORLD PROBLEMS

Overall, though, these were difficult years for the movie industry, beset as it was by the proliferating appeal of television. In the late 1940s the government's charge that the major studios' network of exhibition theaters comprised a monopoly and therefore had to disband brought an end to the old studio system. Accordingly, the gradual shutdown of both the downtown chain and neighborhood theaters helped serve the cause of television in several ways: TV viewing became a substitute for the habit of attending the local movie house several times a week; with a slowdown in the production of B movies, TV carried on the B-movie tradition through a surfeit of program series; and to help fill TV's insatiable demand for programming, studios began selling their old movies to television, providing it with a stockpile that would last indefinitely.

In 1947, unexpected problems resulted from the witch-hunting tactics of the House Un-American Activities Committee (HUAC) assigned to investigate the supposed Communist conspiracy of the moviemakers. Even though Hollywood's public image suffered from the hearings, it went on to produce many of its most honored films, as attested to by a number of those cited above. Seemingly reacting to the charges of HUAC, certain movies appeared whose plots revolved around the courageous stand of a solitary individual against entrenched forces. The renaissance of the realistic Western such as *Red River* (1948) and *The Gunfighter* (1950) led to the creation of a timely metaphor in the lone Western hero pitted against formidable adversaries in *High Noon* (1952) and *Shane* (1953), as well as a contemporary counterpart in *Bad Day at Black Rock* (1955). The individual up against conspiratorial foes also found expression in films as far apart in subject matter as director Elia Kazan's *On the Waterfront* (1954), whose story centered on corruption in the longshoreman union, and Alfred Hitchcock's *North By Northwest* (1959), a suspense thriller in which Cary Grant finds himself unwittingly involved in the sinister machinations of Communist spies. Both Kazan and dramatist Arthur Miller had been implicated by the HUAC's investigation of Communism in the film industry, but Miller reacted against this infringement on his creative freedom with a powerfully implicit statement in *The Crucible* (1953). Ostensibly about the seventeenth-century Salem witch trials, the play's parallel with Senator Joseph McCarthy's witch-hunt methods was especially obvious to theatergoers at the time.

This real-world milieu even infiltrated the fantasized science-fiction (SF) genre in such B films as *The Thing from Another World* (1951) and *The Invasion of the Body Snatchers* (1956). By depicting sinister alien entities seeking to infiltrate the social order, they also suggested the era's paranoid fear of an outside force like Communism taking over the American system. Compounded, too, by the worldwide sightings of unidentified flying objects (UFOs) and the threat of a nuclear holocaust, such uncertainties resulted in a deluge of B movies in the 1950s in which science and technology, the traditional symbols of progress, were ironically characterized as inducing a doomsday mind-set.[13] While the theme of invasion from outer space was the focus of *Red Planet Mars* (1952) and *Not of This Earth* (1957), that of science gone awry and the attendant appearance of menacing giant insects also held sway, as evidenced by the special effects of *Tarantula* (1955) and *The Deadly Mantis* (1957). More graphically realistic than the movies themselves was their promotional poster art, particularly that created by Reynold Brown, whose pulp magazine vision captured the mass panic and paranoia that the SF films dramatized. But even while the movies depicted the aberrations of science running amok, Hollywood itself was looking to unique technological developments to help resolve its ongoing problem with dwindling audiences.

## THE MOVIE INDUSTRY'S NEW PROMOTIONAL TACTICS

Convinced now that the best way to attract moviegoers was to give them not so much better as bigger pictures, Hollywood followed up on the all-enveloping visual experience of Cinerama in 1952 with such technical innovations as CinemaScope, Vista-Vision, and Panavision, whose wide-screen dimensions were aurally enhanced by stereophonic sound. Capitalizing on a resurgent interest in religion in the '50s, blockbuster films like *The Robe* (1953) as the first CinemaScope produc-

tion, *The Ten Commandments* (1956), and *Ben-Hur* (1959) offered audiences highly spectacular visual/aural experiences
that television could not compete with. Or so Hollywood
thought.[14] With cinematic innovation at floodtide by the mid
'50s, producer Mike Todd's *Around the World in 80 Days*
(1956) tried to outdo the other visual technologies through his
Todd-AO process and was rewarded with an Oscar for best
picture. Of course, film versions of Broadway musicals like
*Oklahoma!* and *Carousel* (both 1956) were naturals for wide-
screen treatment, as well as dramatic films of epical novels
like *Giant* (1956) and *Mutiny on the Bounty* (the 1962 remake)—all of which were promoted through colorful ad campaigns highlighting their special cinematic techniques.

A trend among the blockbuster movies of epic sweep was
filming them on location after the manner of *Lawrence of Ara-
bia* (1962), whose exotic setting played an integral part in its
promotion. In over fifty years of looking at the movies, the
mediated vision had never had its escapist tendencies responded to on so grandiose a scale. However, another visual
innovation of the '50s was not so well received. Three-dimensional (3-D) movies, which presented viewers the illusion of
in-depth perception through the aid of special glasses, turned
out to be more of a fad than anything else. Following the
highly publicized appearances of *Bwana Devil* (1952) and
*House of Wax* (1953), then, 3-D productions soon faded from
the movie scene. Despite all these new visual enticements,
though, going to the movies would never again have the same
cultural impact it had in the more communally escapist milieu that the theaters of the 1930s and '40s cultivated.

Ironically, by the mid '50s television itself was having an
effect on moviemaking techniques, as demonstrated in the
film versions of original TV dramas. Both *Marty* (1955) and
*Twelve Angry Men* (1957) projected individualized portraits
after the manner of early television's intimate camera interplay between a drama's lead characters. Once again an older
media form profited from the innovations of a newer one.

By this time, too, movie sound tracks had begun to incorporate music that reflected social trends in the contemporary
scene, particularly among the young. While *Blackboard Jungle* (1955) asserted that the American public school system
was being undermined by a spreading wave of juvenile rebellion, the reception of its sound track featuring bandleader Bill
Haley's big hit "Rock Around the Clock," alerted film produc-

ers to the potential of youth as a large untapped audience. The upshot of rock music's mediated relationship with the movies would provide alienated teens a sense of social identity that would last the century.

Although established recording artists like Bing Crosby, Frank Sinatra, Rosemary Clooney, and Doris Day were big draws in a number of movies during this era, the popularity of a young Southerner named Elvis Presley, whose singing style appealed mostly to youth, soon earned him lucrative recording and movie contracts. While ballad singer/movie actor Pat Boone struck a more wholesome image in the eyes of parents alarmed by the erotically suggestive movements of Presley's black-inspired performances, Presley proved the more durable of the two, not only as a recording artist but through his starring roles in numerous movies during the 1950s–60s, thus making him Hollywood's last big musical star.

In addition to their attraction to rock music, teens' cultural tastes in the 1950s rarely rose above the level of the B movies showing at a local drive-in theater. Attendant to the increased mobility afforded by the automobile, some 2,000 drive-ins opened up between 1947 and 1950. Supplanting the function of the fading neighborhood movie house to entertain the new suburbanites, drive-in theaters were originally designed to cater to family audiences. But it was the teenage sector who soon began to dominate, packing into cars and heading for the fringes of large suburban areas where the drive-ins were located. For couples on their own, the drive-in acquired the nickname of "passion pit," where the privacy of a car enabled them to indulge in sexual adventure while a seemingly endless parade of B movies played on into the night.

As to the kind of movie fare showing at the drive-ins, it was all basically of a mold, typified by the exploitative science-fiction and horror films that producer/director Roger Corman turned out for American-International pictures. With exploitative titles like *The Day the World Ended* (1955), *War of the Satellites* (1957), *Teenage Caveman* (1958), and his series of horror films loosely based on the works of Edgar Allan Poe, beginning with *The Fall of the House of Usher* (1960), the drive-in crowd found these films hard to resist. A major reason for their popularity was Corman's feel for what he knew his youthful audience wanted to see in a movie. By capitalizing on the pervasive uncertainties of the era, he graphically demonstrated that the threat of nuclear destruction, raging mutants on the loose, and the shock violence of the horror film could provide endless sources of escapist entertainment. Theorizing, too, that filming terror is "really the re-creation of childhood fantasies" derived from a fear of the dark and strange sounds, Corman contended that the function of his films was to expose the fears of childhood and "show they are baseless."[15] Thus, the dramatization of Corman's thesis had great escapist appeal to drive-in audiences in that it helped rationalize the larger uncertainties of the time.

Many of the old movie theaters that had succumbed to the popularity of TV and the antitrust action against the big studios found new life catering to "Adults Only" audiences as either "art" houses showing foreign films or all-night grind houses, whose main bill of fare was the "sexploitation" film. In it the tradition begun in the 1930s appeared in a variety of forms by the late 1940s, particularly voyeuristic features centered around burlesque queens like Lili St. Cyr and a spate of jungle pictures showcasing nude native women purely for sensational effects. But it was fearless producer Russ Meyer who came up with the most ingenious ways to exploit the female anatomy for commercial purposes. With *The Immoral Mr. Teas* (1959), for example, he initiated his version of soft-core pornography in which gimmicks, such as the title character's visual power to see through women's clothes, were devised as tantalizing ploys that responded to male fantasies.

The focus on women as sex objects not only contributed to a longer life for the old movie theaters but also the drive-ins. And by the late '50s teens as well as older patrons found them awash with sex-oriented movies with titillating titles like *Girl's Town, High School Confidential*, and *Vice Raid* (all 1959). The allure of such seductive sex symbols as Mamie Van Doren and Jayne Mansfield paralleled the kind of provocative image that became an integral ingredient in other films on a higher plain. The deceptively innocent but sexually tantalizing aura that Marilyn Monroe projected, for example, from *The Asphalt Jungle* (1950) to *The Misfits* (1961), made her the American female sex symbol of this entire era. Although at this time, sexual activity in both the A and B films of the 1950s was more a suggested experience than an actually realized one, it nevertheless conditioned the mediated vision to a more open view toward the graphic depiction of sexual activity that would soon be invading the movie screen.

If the 1950s period of American social history is seen as predominantly conformist and lacking in individual expression, Hollywood was apparently doing its best to undermine such an assessment in the kinds of movies it produced. To it, a positive antidote to cold war jitters, the mundane routine of life, and even sexual repression was the laughter that comedy generated in films as diverse as *Born Yesterday* (1950), *Monkey Business* (1952), *Pillow Talk* (1955), *The Girl Can't Help It* (1956), *Auntie Mame* (1958), and even the zany antics of the Dean Martin–Jerry Lewis movies. In the eyes of Hollywood producers the comic experience still retained its time-honored place as a reliable means of offering escape from the harsh demands of an imperfect world.

A subtle force in paving the way for the social acceptance of sex in the movies was screwball-type comedy. By laughing at what straight drama treated in a serious light, the comedic approach could get away with a lot more with respect to sexual innuendo. Controversial signs of things to come were evident in the movie version of a Broadway sex farce titled *The Moon is Blue* (1953). As a prime example of comedy's special way with treating matters of a sexual nature, its characters uttered words of sexual innuendo never heard before by film audiences, such as "virgin," "pregnant," and "mistress." With his wife out of town, the implications of Tom Ewell's sexual fantasies in *The Seven Year Itch* (1955) hardly needed any explanation concerning his attraction to Marilyn Monroe as the lone tenant in the apartment upstairs. Questionable subject matter as wide-ranging as transvestism in *Some Like It Hot* (1959), the philandering activities of married businessmen in *The Apartment* (1960), and prostitution in *Irma La Douce* (1963) lured moviegoers into a receptive posture toward such unconventional fare, tempered by the comic roles that Jack Lemmon played in these films.

Another significant force that contributed to Hollywood's growing liberal approach to sex as a promotional feature was the invasion of the foreign films with their more uninhibited take on sexuality. Film critics, in their appraisal of these daring films as "art," helped immensely in popularizing them. Consequently, cinema art houses sprang up across the nation, many in college towns where they played to supposedly sophisticated audiences more tolerant of controversial subject matter. Such Code-defiant imports as those from Italy, featuring amply built sex goddesses like Sophia Loren and Gina

Lollobrigida, peaked with director Federico Fellini's *La Dolce Vita* (1959), publicized as a film so sensational it even shocked European critics.

But it was the French who unleashed their version of female sexuality incarnate in the person of Brigitte Bardot in a 1956 film titled *And God Created Woman*. With her girlish features and mature woman's body Mademoiselle Bardot was an immediate sensation whose unbridled behavior in this movie made a lasting impression on not only viewers but the movie industry itself. In fact, a sociocultural survey of the "Adults Only" film contends that "history will show that Brigette Bardot was a far more influential force [than Marilyn Monroe] in changing attitudes toward cinematic sex."[16]

By revealing the nude female body for the first time to mainstream American movie audiences, *And God Created Woman* also revealed how far the movies had come since the early days of censorship. At that time, the Supreme Court had denied film the protection of free speech, determining that it was a profit-motivated entertainment medium with the power to influence viewer's morals. By 1957 the Court's increasingly liberal stance led to Justice William J. Brennan's majority opinion that "redeeming social importance" should be the main criterion in deciding whether a creative work would be ruled obscene or not. Although this decision resulted in much confusion over a valid definition of pornography, it would pave the way for movies to dramatize sex in a manner heretofore deemed improbable. Not only did films begin to appear of literary works long considered pornographic, but independent producers would make films that outright defied the Court's ruling on redeeming social value by showing explicit sex purely for its own sake.

## CHANGES IN MOVIE THEATER PROGRAMMING

By the advent of the blockbuster film aimed at countering television's competition, then, the standard movie program had undergone a marked transformation. The newsreel had now given way to the immediacy of daily TV coverage; the so-called "selected short subjects" were gone; the serial, whose fading popularity peaked with the appearance of Superman and Batman in the late 1940s, braved it until 1956 when Columbia's two Westerns were the serial genre's last; and once-popular series like *Andy Hardy, Charlie Chan, Dr. Kildare,* and *Hopalong Cassidy* disappeared in the late '40s, while *Blondie* and *The Bowery Boys* made it into the '50s. Television now assumed the role of introducing series characters in both sitcom and dramatic programming to new waves of fans. Iconic heroes like Tarzan and Sherlock Holmes would continue to show up in the movies from time to time, but mature audiences were now conditioned to expect a new kind of series hero. In 1963 he appeared in the person of undercover agent James Bond in his first film, *Dr. No.*

Based on the popular Ian Fleming novels, the Bond character, convincingly played by Sean Connery, was a British subject whose assignments involved him in highly perilous predicaments from which he always managed to escape. Invariably, Bond's scrapes with danger were assuaged by the endless round of beautiful women he encountered on his ventures, a significant factor in the ongoing popularity of the Bond films to come.[17] While their combination of sex and violence was in direct response to the mediated vision's updated escapist fantasies, they also reflected a new self-styled freedom of expression that presaged the ensuing kinds of movies that would keep customers buying tickets.

## THE ANIMATED FILM TAKES ON NEW DIRECTIONS

In the '50s, that other staple of the movie program, the animated cartoon short, was enduring so much competition from television it had to experiment with innovative techniques to survive. In 1948 the most innovative graphics style yet in animation had appeared when United Productions of America (UPA) began creating cartoons in a minimalist manner. The result was an unlikely popular character in the nearsighted Mr. Magoo and an Academy Award in 1951 for "Gerald McBoing Boing," inspired by a Dr. Seuss story. The revolutionary look of a UPA cartoon ranged from the simplistic manner of its adaptation of James Thurber's "The Unicorn in the Garden" to the abstract style used for Edgar Allan Poe's "Tell-Tale Heart." Though the 1950s saw the Warners studio, with animators Tex Avery, Bob Clampett, and Chuck Jones at the helm, still relishing the popularity of the ongoing feuds between such characters as Tweety and Sylvester as well as Wile E. Coyote and the Road Runner, even their audience appeal was not enough to overcome the onslaught of television; thus Warners finally closed shop in 1963. After the MGM studio ended its reign in 1956, Joseph Barbera and William Hanna, creators of the long popular Tom and Jerry team, saw the future and took their talents to television. That UPA's minimalist manner had a big influence on TV animation was evidenced in the output of these two, particularly in the *Huckleberry Hound* series and the first prime-time cartoon show, *The Flintstones* (1960). As far as this new approach to animated humor was concerned, the movies' loss was television's gain, as in this new format the appeal of the animated cartoon to children continued unabated.[18] Some, like *Rocky and His Friends* (1959), even found adult fans. The minimalist style of TV cartoons may not have aspired to the polished manner of the Disney studio, but they nevertheless complemented the fast-paced medium they were made for.

By the 1950s Walt Disney had turned away from the production of cartoon shorts to deliver mainly animated feature films, which proved to be an expedient move, for it prefigured the real future of Disney animation. Though *Song of the South* (1946), based on the moralizing tales of Joel Chandler Harris, utilized both animation and live action, some critics termed the role of Uncle Remus as stereotyped and demeaning. A perplexed Disney then turned to producing wholly animated features and other projects to win back his earlier acclaim. *Cinderella* (1950) was a high mark in this transition, while *Alice in Wonderland* (1951) was a disappointment to many. In spite of other low points, the Disney magic came through in such warmly received productions as *Peter Pan* (1953), *Lady and the Tramp* (1955)—the first animated feature produced in CinemaScope—and *One Hundred and One Dalmations* (1961). By the 1960s the Disney organization concluded that its greatest appeal to the mediated vision lay in its ability to reaffirm traditional values and ideals in the forms of both the live-action film and feature cartoon—a mission it would find increasingly difficult to adhere to in the years ahead, due mainly to the changing mores of a fast-moving world.[19]

## THE CINEMATIC VISION OF BEST-SELLING FICTION

Of course, the movies had always found rich source material in best-selling fiction, but now, conveniently enough,

more works were being published whose cinematic orientation seemed ready-made for film. The 1950s, in fact, saw a
proliferation of popular novels whose visual qualities saw
them soon appear as movies, for example, *The Caine Mutiny*,
*The Old Man and the Sea*, *Night of the Hunter*, *Peyton Place*,
*Anatomy of a Murder*, and *Exodus*, to name some of the more
noteworthy. While many others were readily adaptable to cinematic transcription, some lost a great deal of their literary
flavor as film.

To capitalize on the promotional aura of a renowned author's name or a novel's critical reputation, Hollywood also
assumed that the film version of a well-received book would
be sufficient to attract moviegoers. Thus, in the movies' attempt to merge elite and popular tastes, audiences were afforded the opportunity to view an acclaimed literary classic
like Fyodor Dostoevsky's *The Brothers Karamazov* and a sensationalized work such as *God's Little Acre* (both 1958). That
it took Erskine Caldwell's 1933 novel twenty-five years to
reach the screen was evidence in itself of the censorship
problems it had faced. Ironically, this now more liberal time
helped sensationalize the film version of *God's Little Acre* as
much, if not more, than the novel itself had been.

Although censorship did not present book publishers the
extent of problems moviemakers had confronted, it remained
a difficult obstacle to deal with until the Supreme Court initiated its series of opinions starting in 1957 intended to distinguish obscenity from protected speech. Accordingly, the
decision concerning a work's redeeming social value as a
major determining factor in adjudging obscenity would soon
see D. H. Lawrence's long-suppressed novel *Lady Chatter-
ley's Lover* on the book market. Previously, the critically
praised first novels of Norman Mailer and James Jones dealing with military life—*The Naked and the Dead* (1948) and
*From Here to Eternity* (1951) respectively—had been weakened by the edict against the earthy, off-color language that
enlisted men typically use. Nevertheless, the bloody combat
description of Mailer's novel was tolerated, while Jones got
by with depicting his characters' liaisons with prostitutes and
graphically described scenes of brutal violence. Both movie
versions softened their novels' impact, even though *From
Here to Eternity*'s focus on an adulterous relationship was
considered sensational for its time.

In circumventing the threat of censorship, some war novels, like Thomas Heggen's *Mr. Roberts* (1946) and Herman Wouk's *The Caine Mutiny* (1951), centered on strong characterizations whose conflict with military bureaucracy took on a kind of ironic contemporary appeal during this socially conformist time.[20] Similarly, James Michener, whose war fiction bridged the time between World War II and the Korean conflict, assumed a personalized point of view in depicting how the exigencies of war impacted on the lives of his characters. Starting out on his long prolific writing career with *Tales of the South Pacific* (1947), Michener saw its World War II background inspire the long-running Broadway musical *South Pacific*, whose movie version appeared in 1958. His Korean War–related novels, *The Bridges at Toko-Ri* (1953) and *Sayonara* (1954), were also made into popular films. In fact, the humanized posture inherent in the war fiction of both Wouk and Michener was a strong factor in popularizing their novels' movie versions.

While the movies of this period produced some heartwarming films, such as *All the Way Home* (1963), based on James Agee's *A Death in the Family* (1957), or even an appealing romance like *Breakfast at Tiffany's* (1961), loosely based on Truman Capote's 1958 novella, Hollywood was mainly seeking to exploit the topically sensational, as though this were the missing ingredient to win back audiences. Most of the time it found what it was looking for in the time's best-selling novels. Though Ayn Rand's *The Fountainhead* was published in 1943, the 1949 film version's thematic conflict between idealism and corporate power presaged the novels centering on the postwar industrialist/businessman. They ranged in kind from Cameron Hawley's *Executive Suite* (1952), filmed in 1954, to Sloan Wilson's *The Man in the Gray Flannel Suit* (1955; film, 1956). While the former focused on a boardroom power struggle for corporate leadership, the latter's symbolic title epitomized the conformist ways of the commuter businessman as indicative of suburban life's demands on material success.[21] Cinematic treatment was also accorded the political novel in such films as the 1949 adaptation of Robert Penn Warren's *All the King's Men* (1946), which centers on the machinations of a Southern demagogue; the 1958 version of Edwin O'Connor's *The Last Hurrah* (1956) and its candid look at the devious side of Boston politics; and in 1962, Allen Drury's *Advise and Consent* (1959), which did the same for Washington politics. To entertain while exposing the corruption at the heart of corporate and political life seemed to be the driving force behind all these novels and their film versions.

The sensational aspects of criminal activity helped promote numerous works that ultimately became movies during this time. Based on the *Leopold v. Loeb* case of the 1920s, Meyer Levin's *Compulsion* (1956; film, 1959) recreates a murder scheme carried out for thrills. Crime/suspense thrillers by Cornell Woolrich and Robert Bloch provided director Alfred Hitchcock the sources for two of his biggest box-office hits— *Rear Window* (1954) and *Psycho* (1959). The film version of Henry Farrell's *Whatever Happened to Baby Jane?* (1960; film, 1962) brought together old stars Joan Crawford and Bette Davis to start a new horror film trend based on reality rather than fantasy. As for the lonely old house genre, Shirley Jackson's *The Haunting of Hill House* (1959), filmed as *The Haunting* in 1963, revealed the movies' ongoing preoccupation with the psychological effects of horror as more terrifying than anything the old Universal monster films had contrived.

During the paperback publishing explosion in the late '40s, another visually intense kind of fiction came on the scene when Mickey Spillane introduced his vigilante detective Mike Hammer. Reminiscent of the terse descriptive style and dialogue of the pulp era's hard-boiled fiction, such novels as *I, the Jury* (1947), *My Gun is Quick* (1950), and *Kiss Me, Deadly* (1952), with their melodramatic emphasis on sex and violence, were all made into popular movies in the 1950s. The formulaic pattern in both their fiction and film versions had Mike Hammer enforcing his own system of justice on those who transgressed it. In the process, he came across to the mediated vision as very much his own man in a socially conformist era, which probably explains the real reason for this character's wide popularity at the time.

Novels with an epic sweep, like Edna Ferber's *Giant* (1950; film, 1956) and John Steinbeck's *East of Eden* (1952; film, 1955), continued to have high priority in Hollywood's eyes. Both film versions were immortalized for their casting of the ill-fated James Dean in rebellious roles that turned him into a cult hero of the 1950s' youth movement, especially after his tragic death in a car crash at the age of twenty-four. Epical stature was also accorded a Western like Alan Le May's *The Searchers* (1954; film, 1956), in which director John Ford cultivated an antiheroic image for John Wayne in contrast to his roles personifying the mediated vision's traditional values. Like their fictional sources, all these films, from the crime/ suspense genre to the Western, sought to entertain through vividly realistic cinematic techniques.

As another sign of changing times, cinematic realism finally began attending to the unavoidable problem of racism. Connoting what it is like to be black in America, the complex metaphorical implications of Ralph Ellison's critically acclaimed *Invisible Man* (1952) eluded film production. But Richard Wright's *Native Son* (1940), his embittered novel based on the experiences he endured as a young black man, was filmed in 1951 with himself in the lead role.[22] Ironically, two novels by white Southerners in which the ingrained racist posture of their region is central to plot development were made into successful films: William Faulkner's *Intruder in the Dust* (1948; film, 1949) and Harper Lee's *To Kill a Mockingbird* (1960; film, 1962). Through the realistic modes of both fiction and film, the American conscience would be gradually sensitized to the necessity for social change concerning the system's disregard of its black citizens' rights.

During this era, too, a new generation of mainstream fiction writers was establishing itself, revealing an acute awareness of society's problems and a candid, cinematic sensibility in describing them. Perhaps the biggest obstacle the new writers faced in making the complexities of the American scene appear real to readers was attributable to what Philip Roth asserted in 1961: "the American writer in the middle of the 20th century has his hands full in trying to understand, and then describe, and then make *credible* much of the American reality. It stupefies, it sickens, it infuriates, and finally it is even a kind of embarrassment to one's meager imagination. The actuality is continually outdoing our talents."[23] Nevertheless, the "American reality," or "actuality," which the mediated vision had mostly sought to avoid through escapist fiction, provided much of the subject matter for many writers' best-received works. Among them, for example, were J. D. Salinger's testimonial to the pain of adolescence, *The Catcher in the Rye*; William Styron's contemporary tragedy, *Lie Down in Darkness* (both 1951); Flannery O'Connor's version of Southern gothic, *Wise Blood* (1952); Jack Kerouac's picaresque tale of life in the '50s drug culture, *On the Road*, Bernard Malamud's story of suffering and atonement in *The*

*Assistant* (both 1957), and John Updike's *Rabbit, Run* (1960), the first of four novels to chronicle the life of its central character as representative of middle-class America in the century's second half. If these works' pessimistic explorations of contemporary life contributed to a generally depressing reading experience, they nonetheless compelled readers to realize the cathartic power of such writing through vividly narrated revelations of their central characters' problems.

## The Ongoing Popularity of Nonfiction and Its Fictive Offshoots

As television's sense of immediacy helped generate renewed interest in nonfiction, this genre provided highly entertaining reading experiences, especially that dealing with notable historical figures. Although *Lust for Life*, Irving Stone's best-selling book about artist Vincent Van Gogh, had first appeared in 1934, its popularity was revived with the release of the 1956 film based on it. As a Technicolor production, it presented viewers a spectacular take on Van Gogh's inimitable uses of color in his paintings. Stone's compelling way of rendering the life of a famous artist was also evident in *The Agony and the Ecstasy* (1961), his monumental work on the career of Michelangelo. But the much-hyped 1965 film version fell short of capturing the artistic significance of this high-culture figure for an audience mostly unfamiliar with his achievements.

The attraction to nonfictional elements was now becoming a feature in the works of authors noted mainly for their fiction output. As a writer of both historically oriented fiction and nonfiction, for example, James Michener proved himself a most revered author in the eyes of the mediated vision, as evidenced by the numerous best sellers he turned out in both areas over a fifty-year span. Ever since the publication of *Hawaii* (1959; film 1966), his sprawling, panoramic saga about America's fiftieth state, Michener was a tireless producer of impressive works that exhibited his flair for merging historical fact and fiction into momentous reading experiences. In alternating between fiction and nonfiction, his prolific output seemed characterized by an inherent compulsion to instruct as well as entertain, undoubtedly a major reason why Michener's books were so widely anticipated and appreciated by his many readers.

While John Steinbeck was more renowned for his best-selling fiction, he occasionally ventured into the realm of nonfiction as he did in 1962 with his well-received *Travels with Charlie*. Roaming about the country in a pickup-truck camper with a dog as his only companion, Steinbeck related his experiences in a visually conceived narrative whose purpose was to reassess the nation's status in the wake of its great economic progress and social change since *The Grapes of Wrath* appeared in 1939. But in another sense, Steinbeck's pilgrimage was inspired by the challenge to be, as he says, "any place away from any here," that same old lure to the mediated vision to "see" what the open road might hold in store.

Reacting to the conformist ways of the time, the sociological critiques of C. Wright Mills in *The Power Elite*, William H. Whyte Jr. in *The Organization Man* (both 1956), and Vance Packard, whose *The Status Seekers* (1959) was a best seller, saw American individualism as a dying force and with it the mediated vision's old-time faith in a progressive future. Fear of what the American society's future might hold was the central focus of J. Edgar Hoover's *Masters of Deceit* (1958), that is, if the nation failed to stem the imminent threat of Communism. Indeed, the director of the Federal Bureau of Investigation (FBI) contended that the purpose of his book was to inform the American citizen "about the menace which threatens his future, his home, his children, the peace of the world."[24] Other similarly motivated works were also intended to warn the public that the problems of the present were escalating. The need for conservation regulations was explicit in Rachel Carson's plea for a ban on chemical pesticides in *Silent Spring* (1962). That married women were growing dissatisfied with their conventional role as homemakers was voiced in Betty Friedan's feminist tract *The Feminine Mystique* (1963), a significant omen of the coming social revolution in women's quest for more proactive roles in society.

But the most socially unsettling sign of all was the revelation that the moral code regulating sexual behavior in American life was hardly being adhered to as most thought, at least according to a study by Indiana University professor Alfred C. Kinsey. His *Sexual Behavior in the Human Male* (1948), known popularly as the Kinsey Report, was the result of thousands of interviews with a broad sampling of American males. The responses to Kinsey's pointed queries about sexual activities, which ranged from normal to what the time considered abnormal practices, would help revolutionize Americans' puritanical notions about sex. Heretofore most had never dared reveal anything about their private sex lives for fear of being branded perverts. Now, this 800-page book, replete with extensive compilations of statistics to support its findings, revealed such startling information as the high percentage of married men who had committed adultery, how many had consorted with prostitutes, and even the number of those who admitted to homosexuality. More shocking was what readers discovered about women in the 1953 report sequel, *Sexual Behavior in the Human Female*, as it revealed that American women had apparently been sexually emancipated for some time. By breaking down the Victorian myths surrounding the underground topic of sexual behavior, Kinsey was unwittingly preparing the mediated vision for the sexual revolution that started up in the late 1960s, signs of which had begun to appear in the movies, stage productions, and novels cited above.[25]

Countering the considerable negative reaction to the Kinsey reports as well as the general puritanical posture toward sexual matters, the legal team of Eberhard and Phyllis Kronhausen argued for a more tolerant attitude toward the role of sex in life and the arts in their *Pornography and the Law* (1959). In it they contend that "both erotic realism and pornography, each in their own way, fulfill certain functions and answer basic needs in the human psyche which have been recognized by many societies and periods," and that such works are "especially welcome at a time when automation, push-button housekeeping, mass production, and progressive eradication of individual differences make everybody's search for identity a matter of spiritual survival."[26] But not all would have agreed that erotic literature and art were the answer to one's "spiritual" or self-identity needs, as certain other literary trends of the time revealed.

In 1948 Dale Carnegie produced another timely self-help book, *How to Stop Worrying and Start Living*, further testimony that the era's anxieties were urging people to seek remedies beyond themselves to cope with the pressures that an atomic age imposed on them. To the more speculative, the hope of future reincarnation seemed to offer an answer, as reported in a popular 1956 book, *The Search for Bridey Murphy*.

It purported to be the true story of an American woman who claimed to have lived a former life in Ireland. Though book club lists of this period featured the escapist fiction of Taylor Caldwell, Daphne du Maurier, and Frank Yerby, another kind of historical fiction was biblically inspired, as exemplified by the novels of Lloyd C. Douglas. Following up on the success of *The Robe* (1942), he published another best seller in *The Big Fisherman* (1948). Its reception was a sign that many seekers after peace of mind in the here and now were finding their most reliable answer in the various publications interpreting the Christian faith as an aid to meaningful living.[27]

The three biggest religious leaders of the 1950s not only depended on the visual power of television to present their sermons to millions of viewers, they responded to them through highly popular books. Evangelist Billy Graham, who started out on his periodic revival crusades in the late '40s, hit the best-seller list in 1952 with *Peace with God*. The following year Catholic bishop Fulton J. Sheen did the same with *Life is Worth Living*. But the Reverend Norman Vincent Peale surpassed them both with *The Power of Positive Thinking* (1952), probably because it offered more practical psychological advice for confronting the problems of daily living. However, the Bible, that all-time best seller, maintained its leadership in the inspirational-reading category with the appearance in 1952 of the Revised Standard Version. This new Bible may have upset fundamentalists, but it was easier to read than the more poetic King James Version. Thus, in the 1950s the mediated vision was conditioned to a variety of religiously inspired sources through which to escape present-day anxieties. In fact, the solace of religious conviction was strong enough to be equated with patriotic fervor as a powerful force to counter the threat of a godless Communist takeover. Even so, evidence of another kind of alien force sprang up in the late '40s, adding to the uncertain mood that would continue to pervade the ensuing years.

## UFOs, Fantasy Fiction, and New Visions in Science Fiction

Soon after the first sighting of an unidentified flying object (UFO) in 1947 and the popular labeling of it as a "flying saucer," similar reports began to proliferate, and during the

1950s many of the forms of media culture reflected a widespread fascination with the phenomenon. Although most sightings and alleged encounters were either rationally explained or determined to be hoaxes, the possibility of UFOs' existence continued to gain support from a growing cult of "believers." Citing a military coverup to avoid the kind of panic that had occurred during the 1938 radio broadcast of *The War of the Worlds,* numerous books and magazine articles contended that UFOs did exist, backing up their argument with reports of those who claimed they had either witnessed their appearance and/or had had actual contact with their alien occupants. Books, such as the pointedly titled *Flying Saucers are Real* (1950) and *Flying Saucers Have Landed* (1953), were overt attempts to capitalize on the mania. Although the U.S. Air Force's *Report on Unidentified Flying Objects* (1956) did not confirm the existence of UFOs, it did reveal some pertinent facts as to their possibility.

For those who considered the UFO phenomenon as nothing more than a passing fad, its role as a popular source of diversion and escapist entertainment seemed unlimited, as fiction, film, comic books, and merchandise spin-offs abounded.[28] The genre of science fiction, of course, had realized a head start in depicting the kind of subject matter inspired by the UFO craze, particularly in that dealing with alien contacts. In the 1950s, it also discovered a more conducive format than the pulp magazine in which to express itself—the paperback book. By now, not only the paperback but the digest medium and men's adventure magazines had begun to supplant the pulp's escapist mission of transporting its readers to any place on earth and beyond. That a hardback novel could earn even greater returns as a low-priced paperback had been realized by the astronomical reprint sales of best sellers, as noted. Now, publishers like Ace Books and Ballantine recognized that the market for science fiction paperbacks as well as other original novel categories was ripe to exploit.

Two exemplary writers who started out in the pulps and then reinforced their popularity in the paperback market were Ray Bradbury and Robert Bloch. They were not strictly science-fiction writers but fantasists whose work would influence later writers' psychological approach to both the science-fiction and horror/suspense genres. After selling his first story to *Weird Tales* in 1943, Bradbury started out on a long, successful career. Inspired in his youth by the fiction of

Edgar Rice Burroughs and the *Buck Rogers* comic strip, he evolved into a creative composite of the mediated vision's escapist desires, drawing on his childhood dreams to produce compelling fiction structured around the conflict between the nostalgic past and a foreboding future. *The Martian Chronicles* (1950), a collection of thematically unified short stories, was a prime example of Bradbury's unique way of blending these two antithetical elements. Bloch, on the other hand, found urban life a suitable setting to blend fantasy and reality to create the "thriller" type of suspense fiction that became popular in the 1960s. By this time, too, the paperback market was responding in volume to the mediated vision's demand for fiction in the horror/suspense, fantasy, and science-fiction categories.

At a time when UFO "sightings" and the uncertainties generated by the fear of atomic devastation were pervasive, science-fiction writers were attracting a growing readership. While many of the students of *Astounding* editor John Campbell's school, such as Isaac Asimov, A. E. van Vogt, and Robert A. Heinlein, were into a productive period of creativity, a number of other writers were making names for themselves by indoctrinating readers into highly imaginative ways of fantasizing reality, mainly through their uses of futuristic and sociological concepts. These were the visionaries who looked ahead to the era of New Wave SF that would attract a predominantly adult readership and even command academic respect. In *The Space Merchants* (1953) C. M. Kornbluth and Frederik Pohl teamed up to satirize how consumer advertising tactics might control life in the future. The potential roles of telepathy and teleportation informed the intricate plots of two enduring novels by Alfred Bester in the 1950s: *The Demolished Man* and *The Stars My Destination*. Walter Miller Jr.'s multilayered *A Canticle for Leibowitz* (1959) was such a challenge to interpretation it became studied in the classroom. Among the more maturely conceived works of the newer writers was Philip K. Dick's *The Man in the High Castle* (1962), which focuses on the supposition that the Axis had won World War II. In his first novel *The Lovers* (1952), Philip José Farmer, by developing the taboo theme of sexuality Heinlein had explored, opened up an area that he and Theodore Sturgeon would take to new heights in a more sexually tolerant era.[29]

But the most acclaimed SF output during this time was that

of Isaac Asimov, Arthur C. Clarke, and Robert A. Heinlein. *The Foundation Trilogy*, comprised of works the prolific Asimov initiated in the '40s and published as a series of novels in the '50s, heralded the SF novel of ideas, while the visionary insights of *I, Robot* (1950) set forth the laws that govern robotic behavior. On the other hand, the Englishman Clarke brought a humanistic flavor to his philosophically oriented SF world in works like *Childhood's End* (1953) and *The City and the Stars* (1956). Through his prophetic vision, he would proceed in the 1960s to endow his highly imaginative output with some of SF's most daringly speculative concepts about the cosmos. Heinlein, whose fiction ranged from works for a younger audience to those for adults, was arguably the most influential as well as controversial author of this era, who was not averse to didacticism in his writings. His juvenile fiction culminated in 1959 with *Starship Troopers*, whose theme disturbed some due to its glorified picture of the military's dominant role in the future. His most famous novel, *Stranger in a Strange Land* (1961), by anticipating the youth movement of the '60s, became a cult classic. This and others of his works, in promoting the SF genre as philosophical discourse, indoctrinated the mediated vision into the realization that, whether in a positive or negative light, the future could be treated as fantasized history in which reality is transformed into the thinking person's mode of escapist entertainment.[30]

Shortly, the output of both Heinlein and Clarke would alert the moviemakers to SF as a timely source for serious films about the future's potential impact on the human condition as opposed to the highly fantasized drive-in movie fare of the 1950s. That SF had begun to attract a more mature audience was also evidenced by the appearance of Heinlein's stories in *general* magazines and the advent of high-quality publications of digest size, like *Analog*, *Galaxy Science Fiction*, and the *Magazine of Fantasy and Science Fiction*. They supplanted the outdated visions of *Planet Stories*, which ended its long run in 1955 along with other pulps whose stories were in the adventurous mold. That the SF genre had legitimated itself was the startup of reprint anthologies and even genre histories that became popular in the postwar years. Another significant factor was the mushrooming fan base that subscribed to fanzines and attended annual conventions.

Now reflecting a more mature vision was the artwork that appeared in popular publications. Solid testimony to this achievement is disclosed in Vincent Di Fate's *Infinite Worlds: The Fantastic Visions of Science Fiction Art* (1997). Among the most important and revered SF artists he cites is Virgil Finlay, whose prolific cover and interior work charted a new course for the digest and paperback cover artists. In a career in which he illustrated the stories of such SF and fantasy masters as A. Merritt, August Derleth, and H. P. Lovecraft, Finlay displayed a painstaking stipple technique that allowed him to capture surrealistic moods unlike that of any of his contemporaries. In surpassing Margaret Brundage's exotic cover art for *Weird Tales* while shunning the standard scene of a semi-nude girl in the clutches of an alien, he depicted erotically alluring women for symbolic or atmospheric purposes. Another feature of the digest-sized SF magazines of the 1950s–60s was an occasional humorous, even sentimental cover, something rarely seen in earlier pulp artwork. Masters at creating this kind of illustration were Hannes Bok, Edd Cartier, Kelly Freas, and Wallace Wood, who was also a highly regarded comic book artist.

## THE COMIC BOOK TAKES TO FANTASIZED REALISM

While SF was attracting a more mature audience to the print media, one comic book publisher was utilizing SF subject matter to express serious thematic messages, even though they were mainly directed at the medium's traditional younger audience. Helping realize this mission, Wally Wood was among a group of talented artists like Al Feldstein, Harvey Kurtzman, Al Williamson, and Bill Elder who were working for the publications of Entertaining Comics (EC) in the early 1950s. *Weird Science* and *Weird Fantasy*, in particular, exhibited a whole new approach to comic book SF as compared to the space-opera heroics of the earlier Planet Comics. Indeed, the EC stories dealt with such unlikely but timely comic book topics as prejudice, gender concerns, and the nuclear arms race, usually resulting in a surprise or shock closure to make a moral point.

EC's success in the SF genre sparked numerous imitations during the '50s, from those published by new entries into the comic book field like Avon and Ziff-Davis to the output of the DC and Marvel lines. Comic book crossovers of heroic characters from television SF series such as Captain Video and

Tom Corbett offered some competition, due mainly to the popularity of their TV counterparts, paralleling a trend that saw other TV series and movie personalities appear in the comic book format. Conversely, *Space Family Robinson*, a 1962 comic book about the first space-age family, proved popular enough to provide the basis for the highly popular TV series *Lost in Space*. Other SF-oriented series such as *The Twilight Zone* and *Outer Limits* were naturals for the comic book medium, but *Twilight*'s unique approach to fantasizing reality won it longer-lasting appeal as a comic book. That the SF classics of Jules Verne and H. G. Wells were readily adaptable as comic books was exemplified in the twelve works by these authors published in the *Classics Illustrated* series from 1947 to 1961. All these crossovers pointed out the ongoing interdependence of the visual forms of creative expression within the media culture.

The trend toward fantasized realism in the comic book also saw a proliferation of the crime, horror, war, and Western genres. One of the new, more daring was the adult-slanted romance comic book reminiscent of the true confession magazines. Originated in *Young Romance* (1947) by the versatile team of Joe Simon and Jack Kirby, the genre's success quickly spawned multiple imitations. Nevertheless, many observers still had difficulty in perceiving the comic book medium as intended for any audience other than children. Consequently, by the 1950s the realistic renderings of romantic encounters and especially the unbridled violence depicted in the crime and horror comics were arousing the censure of parents, educators, and media editorialists.

Though the horror genre first appeared in the late '40s, it was the EC line's talented artists who took it to new heights (or depths) in the '50s. In spite of the honorable intent of its SF line, the gruesomely illustrated covers and stories in EC's *Vault of Horror*, *Crypt of Terror*, and *Haunt of Fear* series, as well as a similar output by many other publishers, brought the wrath of the critics to a head in 1954 with the publication of Dr. Frederic Wertham's *Seduction of the Innocent*.[31] In it, he singled out the comic book's emphasis on crime, sex, and violence as a major contributing factor to the growing problem of juvenile delinquency. The ensuing Senate subcommittee's public hearings resulted in a report that called for a regulatory comic book code prohibiting any reference that might tend to undermine the morals of the nation's youth. "All scenes of horror, excessive bloodshed, gory or gruesome crimes, depravity, lust, sadism, masochism shall not be permitted"—so stated the Comics Code Authority established in 1954. Its enactment may have pleased the cultural watchdogs, but it either put some publishers out of business or sent the diehards scurrying for alternative avenues to explore.[32]

EC's William Gaines was among the latter group who, after discontinuing his entire line of SF, crime, war, and horror comics, successfully pursued an alternate route. Having published a humorous comic book since 1952 called *Mad*, Gaines countered by turning it into a magazine in 1955 that satirized the media as well as other forms of American culture. (*Mad*'s cultural significance is discussed later in this chapter.) But while EC was in the comic book business, it produced the best written and best drawn publications in the field, to which the inspired adaptations of a number of Ray Bradbury's stories attested.[33] Despite the devastating blow publishers had incurred, those who remained in the business knew that the real market for comic books lay in producing escapist fare in the vein of fantasized realism. Thus they continued to develop ways to skirt the Code's edicts.

In 1953 the three-dimensional comic book, like its movie counterpart, had a brief stab at success but proved to be yet another period fad. Except for such tried-and-true DC characters as Superman, Batman, and Wonder Woman, the war-era superheroes were now virtually extinct. But by the mid 1950s DC editors surmised that the time might be right to resurrect the superhero concept for a new generation of fans. In 1956 it was tested in an updated rendering of the Flash, who had been billed in the 1940s as the fastest man alive. This character's positive reception precipitated the return of such old favorites as the Green Lantern, Hawkman, and the Atom. While the popular Superboy character, whose adventures recounted Superman's early life as a teenager, had first appeared in 1945, DC's introduction of Supergirl in 1959 anticipated a rise in feminine interest and a revitalization of the Superman mythos. The following year also saw an updating of the 1940s' superhero team, the Justice Society of America as the Justice League, which garnered a favorable reponse from young fans.

With the rebirth of the superhero icon, Marvel Comics, DC's longtime rival, having endured its share of economic woes, was now looking to emulate its major competitor's success. And under the leadership of Stan Lee, a longtime comic book creative force, Marvel's approach to portraying the superhero proved to be refreshingly different. It, in fact, downplayed a character's special powers in deference to human weaknesses young readers could identify with. In this vein Marvel introduced the Fantastic Four in 1961 and the following year the Incredible Hulk along with a reprise of the original Sub-Mariner in his villainous role against his 1940s' foe, the Human Torch. Though these characters were favorably received, it was a neurotically defined character called Spider-Man, introduced in 1962, who would become Marvel's most popular superhero. During this time Marvel was also bringing on other new characters like Thor, Iron Man, and Dr. Strange, along with unique team players such as the Avengers and the X-Men—an all-star lineup that soon put it in the black. After its publishing tenures as Timely in the '40s and Atlas in the '50s, the Marvel house name was affirmed for good in the early '60s.

The superhero revival resulted in highly imaginative stories enhanced by a fantasized realism that expanded on the postwar comics' obsession with the perils of atomic holocaust, the threat of alien encounters, and the controversial Korean War.[34] It also posited a nostalgic return to the mediated culture of the past, a mood that would become widespread during the last third of the century. The comic book's involvement in this trend was initiated in the early '60s by older fans' interest in it as both a collectible and an art form. In fact, their enthusiastic response to comic book letter columns reflected a kindred fan base, which in turn inspired the origin of "fanzines." As privately published minimagazines of articles devoted to the comic book's history and profiles of its leading characters, they would become sounding boards for "fandom" activities like those that SF fans had been engaging in since the 1930s. In responding to the fanzine ads offering old comics for sale, the general public could never have imagined the astronomical prices such an ephemeral form would command in the years ahead.[35]

Attesting to the comic book's worth as an art form was the quality artwork that began to appear in the late '50s and early '60s. Artists like Murphy Anderson, Nick Cardy, Steve Ditko, Gil Kane, Jack Kirby, Joe Kubert, and Alex Toth, to name some of the more outstanding, utilized a sense of cinematic perspective and layout that gave the comic book a visual vitality it had rarely known in its formative years. These artists' output not only led to the creation of cult followings and the collection of their original art, it informed the media culture that comic book art as a unique visual form of creative expression had untapped possibilities.[36]

## NEWSPAPER COMICS' TRANSITION TO FANTASIZED REALISM

Although the mediated vision's affection for the newspaper comic strip continued unabated during the postwar years, new trends revealed changing tastes that would inform its future direction. Except for a few features still running since their origins in the 1930s and '40s, the adventure strip was beginning to fade by this time. Of the timely SF strips like *Beyond Mars* (1952) and *Jet Scott* (1953), only *Twin Earths* lasted longer, from 1952 to 1963. Attuned to the film noir era, Alex Raymond returned from the war to begin his superbly drawn private detective strip *Rip Kirby* (1946), while Milton Caniff forsook *Terry and the Pirates* in 1947 to create another of the all-time serial strips in *Steve Canyon*.[37]

In the late 1940s, a photorealistic drawing style like Raymond's was an essential ingredient for a serial strip's success. While King Features signed eminent illustrator Frank Godwin to draw the horse racing strip *Rusty Riley* (1948), readers had never seen a better-drawn Western title than Warren Tufts's *Casey Ruggles* (1949).[38] In this light, Stan Lynde's *Rick O'Shay*, which started out in 1958 as a comic send-up of the Western genre, ultimately developed into a realistic strip, embellished by Lynde's drawing skills in depicting nature and nostalgic scenes of the mediated vision's long-revered West of myth. Television crossovers also inspired some of the better drawn Westerns, as Hopalong Cassidy and Roy Rogers showed up in the comics pages in 1949. But the artwork of José Luis Salinas for *The Cisco Kid* (1951) ranked it among the best artistically rendered strips of all the comics genres.

By 1962, the TV hospital series *Ben Casey* and *Dr. Kildare* were spawning spin-offs in the comics, but the growing popularity of the daily soap-opera serials had the greater influence in inspiring popular comic strip titles in the *Mary Worth* vein, such as *Rex Morgan, M.D.* (1948), *Judge Parker* (1952), *The Heart of Juliet Jones* (1953), and *Apartment 3-G* (1962), all rendered in a realistic illustrative style. The dramatization of other people's real problems that had begun with the radio soap opera of the 1930s had now invaded the province of the newspaper comic strip, thanks to the more immediate visual influence of television.

Real problems of more universal import contributed to the popularity of some strips. In 1946 Ed Dodd inaugurated *Mark Trail*, whose title character was an outdoorsman who advocated the conservation of the natural scene for the mutual benefit of humans and wildlife. This feature's attention to such concerns foreshadowed issues that the mediated vision would be increasingly alerted to. Similarly, *Big Ben Bolt* (1950) was a different kind of boxing strip in that its hero is a man of both cultivated tastes and philanthropic goals. Initially drawn by talented illustrator John Cullen Murphy, the strip's later run portrayed its title character as not only heavyweight champion but a champion of worthy causes, many of which emanated from the social issues of the time.[39]

That the immediate concerns of contemporary life could provide the material for a popular humorous strip was also evidenced in a highly original feature that began to appear in 1948. When Walt Kelly brought his colorful menagerie of swamp creatures from the comic book to the newspaper, *Pogo*'s satirical jabs at the political system and those who were a part of it soon won this strip a national following. In Kelly's vision the fantasy of George Herriman's *Krazy Kat* and the satire of Al Capp's *Li'l Abner*, then beginning its most assertive phase of deriding the American social and political scenes, came together in a way that was ingeniously his own.[40] Kelly, in fact, "had a knack for uniting [his] verbal and visual elements into an interdependent whole, while . . . [introducing] an ever-increasing lineup of real characters dressed in allegorical costume and going in all directions through free association, double entendres, and figures of speech."[41] Even so, readers had little difficulty recognizing the "real characters" Kelly portrayed, reveling in the genius of his wit that revealed them as all too human in their foibles and self-aggrandizing ways. In the eyes of the mediated vision, *Pogo* was a paradoxical blend of escapist fantasy and the inescapable reality of contemporary issues and concerns.

But strips appearing in the comics' traditional humorous vein would ultimately result in the demise of the photorealistic feature. When 1950 saw the inauspicious debut of a comic strip whose sensitivity to the real world is filtered through the anxieties, fears, and wish fulfillments of precocious children and a humanized dog, no one could have realized the cultural impact it would eventually have. Creator Charles Schulz dramatized this unique undertaking in such an underdrawn, yet appealing manner that *Peanuts* would become the most popular newspaper strip ever conceived. The multiple spin-offs into merchandise and other media forms not only attested to the feature's enduring popularity, they made Schulz the wealthiest newspaper cartoonist ever. Structuring it around the loser image of Charlie Brown, whose persona is a child's version of Everyman, Schulz added to his cast of characters over the years, with each one playing a special role in Charlie Brown's vision of everyday life's demands on the individual. Prominent among them are his female antagonist Lucy Van Pelt, who persists as a cynical reminder of his imperfections, and his dog Snoopy, whose fantasies of highly romanticized experiences appear in marked contrast to Charlie Brown's personal conflicts with day-to-day reality. Through this comparison, though, Schulz presents the mediated vision yet another variation of its perennial conflict with the disenchantment of the mundane and the solace to be had in escapist indulgence. But the real reason for the popularity of *Peanuts*, until ill health would force Schulz's retirement in 1999 and end its long run, was its deceptively simple approach to a philosophy of life that takes on spiritual overtones at times. Charles Schulz's all-child world in which its characters engage in an adult-styled language served to remind readers that the concerns and problems dramatized in the strip were also their own.[42]

When Ernie Bushmiller's *Nancy* was into its most popular period in the 1950s, another little girl character that originated as a panel cartoon in the *Saturday Evening Post* and continued in comic book format vied for equal attention as a comic strip beginning in 1950. If Nancy was a crusty, short-tempered individualist, the title character of *Little Lulu* came across as a domineering feminist in her authoritarian manner with the boys in her life. While the tradition of the mischievous boy renewed its appeal in Hank Ketcham's daily panel series and Sunday page titled *Dennis the Menace* (1951), another highly popular panel feature, Bil Keane's *The Family Circus*, started out in 1960 focusing on an average middle-class couple and their children's cute sayings and amusing antics. In this light the family strip conventions of Chic Young's long-running *Blondie* continued to inspire spin-offs—among them *Hi and Lois* (1954), Mort Walker and Dik Browne's insightful look at the suburban lifestyle of the 1950s. The enduring popularity of the family-life genre would see all these still running at century's end.

An updated variation of the family strip appeared in 1946 when the postwar teenage set came to the newspaper comics in the form of popular comic book character Archie. Though the strip's title character and his high school friends were at center stage, while the family and school scenes functioned as main points of conflict, there was hardly a hint of the delinquency problems brewing in the real world of youth culture. In fact, the escapist world of *Archie*'s small-town milieu prefigured the socially antiseptic realm of the '50s' TV sitcom.

As substantially less space on the comics page presented a growing problem for cartoonists to develop their strips, the minimalist drawing style began to predominate in the humor strips, reflecting the social vision of a new school of comic strip artists. A prime example of this trend was Mort Walker's *Beetle Bailey*, whose title character started out as a college man in 1950. But not until he joined the army, where he would remain for the next fifty years, did the strip achieve widespread popularity. In its satirical characterizations of military types, *Beetle Bailey*'s simplistic humor was enhanced by an unembellished drawing style that reinforced its basic theme of the individual versus the mindless authority of a bureaucratic system, an increasingly familiar topic to the mediated vision by this time. Also in a satirical vein was the elementary school setting of the American educational system in Mell Lazarus's *Miss Peach* (1957), a send-up of the teachers, administrators, and students who comprised it. As a young impressionable teacher, Miss Peach, in her naive, dedicated manner, stands in marked contrast to the undisciplined, self-serving behavior of her students. As such, *Miss Peach*'s timely humor derided the public school educational system during a time when the Russians' successful space program was a pointed reminder of America's shortcomings in the classroom.

That the visual gag had become a central focus of the comic strip humor of this era was deftly demonstrated in Johnny Hart's *B.C.* (1958). Though this strip was drawn in the most economical of styles, it offered a wide range of topical matter through the interaction of a varied cast of characters in an anachronistic prehistoric setting. By involving them in sight and verbal gag situations, many of which pertained to the quest for answers to questions of a philosophical or even theological nature, Hart created a virtual human comedy by attending to comic strip art in its purest form.[43]

In the fantasy/whimsy tradition of *Krazy Kat* was the fanciful humor of Jack Kent's short-lived *King Aroo* (1950). Like its predecessor, too, *King Aroo* revealed that comic strip humor was at its best when it created a special world unto itself in which the mediated vision found a daily escapist fix in the fantasizing of real-world issues and concerns. In a similar but surreal vein was Irving Phillips's *The Strange World of Mr. Mum* (1958), a panel feature whose bizarre situations were ahead of their time in conditioning the mediated vision to humor inspired by an offbeat imagination.

To satirize the anxieties that devolved on individuals during this time, Jules Feiffer introduced his topically subversive kind of humor in 1956 under the title *Feiffer*. In a cinematic sequence of sketches he voiced his neurotic urban characters' confessions about their problems in romance, work, and life in general. In fact, his candid views on contemporary life, particularly the failure of its political leadership, came across as the most cynical kind of humor of any cartoonist during this period.[44] In the area of the political cartoon itself, Herbert Block, who signed his name "Herblock," established his reputation for trenchant wit during the postwar years. Beginning in 1945, his work for the *Washington Post* took many noted politicians to task, while his recurrent Mr. Bomb character symbolized the atomic age's concerns of living on the brink. A multiple winner of the Pulitzer Prize, Block and his satirical humor set the visual style and standard for many political cartoonists of the time and those to come.

From some of the most realistically drawn serial features ever created to the sketchily drawn humorous strips and panels that dominated this era, newspaper comics were still proving themselves as a resilient and highly adaptable medium of creative communication. For this reason the mediated vision found the comics' transition to fantasized realism to be among the most appealing sources of media-made entertainment.

## THE MAGAZINE COMPETES WITH THE
## VISUAL DOMINANCE OF TELEVISION

In spite of the inroads television was making on its readership by the 1950s, the mainstream magazine still promoted itself as the media culture's traditional information source for current events as well as a personal guide to the latest popular diversions and the world of entertainment. What the newspaper reported, the mass-circulated magazine dramatized in word and picture, with its primary emphasis, of course, on the photographic layout. To compete with TV's visual range, then, the magazine continued to emphasize subject matter that encompassed both the sensational and the mundane, as long as it had appeal to the mediated vision. Whatever the Russians did to heat up the cold war was big news, of course, as was its successful space orbit of the earth in 1957, which spurred America's lagging technology to prepare for the space age. During this time, too, Fidel Castro's insurgents were looking to establish socialism in Cuba, which would ultimately lead to a whole new spin on American–Cuban relations and future complications involving Russia and the arms race. Looming over all these events was the threat of atomic warfare, which created an ominous mood that pervaded the entire era. To help counter it and sell themselves, popular magazines often showcased whatever they thought might help detract their audiences from a doomsday outlook.

The major picture periodicals, *Life* and *Look*, in focusing on events at home and abroad, covered everything from the latest fashions and fads to the newest technological breakthroughs. In fashion, for example, a popular 1946 topic was the advent of the most revealing woman's swimsuit yet. Designed by who else but a Frenchman, the bikini proved how difficult it was at the time to avoid even a fashion connection with the atomic age, since it was named after a Pacific atoll where nuclear tests had been conducted. Another Frenchman, Christian Dior, promoted a line of women's fashions in 1947 that *Life* dubbed the "New Look." Heralding the revival of high style, it fancied long, flared skirts set off by wasplike waists, fancifully designed hats, pointed-toe shoes, and sophisticated accessories. This glamorous look, made affordable to middle-class women by the development of synthetic fabrics, resulted in a conformist air of fashion that, along with the functional cocktail dress, predominated until the controversial sack dress and loose-fitting chemise appeared in the latter part of the '50s. Though style-conscious men had taken to wearing sport jackets with pastel-colored nylon shirts and the still essential hat, magazine advertising generally promoted conservative male fashions, ranging from the gray flannel suit of the businessman to the buttoned-down shirt/tweed-jacket look of the Ivy League college man. Socially acceptable for young men during warm weather was the casual look affected by wearing Bermuda shorts. College women wore them, too, but were more inclined toward plaid skirts, pastel sweaters, and saddle shoes. Ironically, the late '50s' rapidly developing teenage culture, in its rebellion against any fashion that smacked of conformity, established a conformist code all its own. As the magazines revealed, then, fashion, whether conformist or rebellious, was yet another fantasized way to promote the self.

Readers were also alerted to the latest fads in toys, games, and even such zany social behavior as male college students attempting to see how many of them could fit into a telephone booth or organizing a panty raid on a coed dormitory. Destined for a longer life than most realized was the Frisbee, a miniature flying saucer responsive to the laws of aerodynamics when tossed through the air. While the flying saucer craze generated a variety of toy miniatures, television programs also produced their share of faddish merchandise for children, as the popular series featuring the Hopalong Cassidy and Davy Crockett characters did. A more updated kind of hero inspiring a new round of spin-offs appeared in 1959 when Walt Disney introduced TV's *Man in Space* series. Extolling the image of the astronaut as a new kind of frontier type, this program's wide viewing appeal helped further the space program's cause. In this same year appeared one of the most popular dolls in the history of media culture—Mattel's fashionable Barbie, which would persist over the years as a model of changing styles in dress as well as an icon of social values for adolescent girls.[45]

While the established board games of *Monopoly* and *Scrabble* continued in popularity, newer games maintained the practice of mirroring the dominant interests of the times, to which game makers Milton Bradley, Parker Brothers, Ideal, and Mattel were quick to respond. Cite a popular TV program, for example, and there was a board game named after it, in addition to those inspired by comics' characters and real-life personalities. During these days before the advent of the video game, board games still functioned as escapist distractions for both juveniles and adults—for the former, from the authority of parents; and for the latter, from the uncertainties of a world in which the threat of nuclear war had created a demand for prefab fallout shelters in suburban backyards.[46]

The popular magazines may have paid a great deal of attention to the diversionary preoccupations of the times, but their focus on the numerous inventions and technical advances of the day proved equally fascinating to the mediated vision. In 1947 Edwin Land's miraculous Polaroid camera that could produce a photograph in sixty seconds was unveiled. By 1960 its time span was reduced to fifteen seconds, and by 1963 even color photos could be generated on the spot. This same year saw the appearance of the Kodak Instamatic camera, showing how far George Eastman's prototypal invention had come in some fifty years. With the coming of such marvelous advances, individuals were afforded the most immediate way yet to preserve not only their cherished social-life events but more private escapist moments.

The invention that held the most far-reaching import for the future of American life was the computer, but when the War Department unveiled the mammoth ENIAC in 1946, with its rapid capability for executing highly complex mathematical procedures, few could have foreseen the cultural impact of its later refinements.[47] The coming of the transistor in 1948 was not only a momentous step toward reducing the computer's size, it opened the door to numerous computerized functions, such as the automatically operated elevator, direct long-distance telephone dialing, and the pocket-sized radio, which became an icon of teenage culture. Following the invention of the silicon microchip and implementation of laser devices in 1958 would come desktop computers, transistorized wristwatches, and, by 1963, push-button telephone dialing. On its way was a brave new world of communications technology that would afford the media culture new horizons to explore and the coming generation many challenging opportunities in the new field of computer technology.

*Life*, in reporting on many of these topics in the 1950s, was now in its heyday with respect to circulation and advertising revenue. Veteran staffer Loudon Wainwright has commented on why *Life* maintained its popularity during an era when magazine journalism was encountering its most serious competition from television: "*Life* seemed to see things the way its audience saw them." As the magazine of the mediated vision "in a time of increasing affluence and great change from wartime austerity (and an accompanying need for reaffirmation of traditional stabilizing values), *Life* was playing back to its readers images of their country and of themselves that seemed both authentic and reassuring."[48] Conditioned to this posture, then, readers relished such special issues as the 1946 tenth-anniversary number with its survey of the war years and ten years of social change as well as a hopeful look ahead to the future's promise. The first issue of 1950 focused on the major events and figures of the twentieth century's first fifty years in a thematic feature titled "American Life and Times, 1900–1950." By the time of its twentieth anniversary in 1956, *Life* had broadened the mediated vision's sociocultural horizons with informative treatises such as "The World We Live In," a history of Western civilization, and the social status of American women at midcentury, which ironically foreshadowed the social revolt to come. Such serious subject matter was always balanced with popular features about famous personalities, particularly royalty and movie stars, Broadway hits, epic movies, and notable sports figures. On a darker side were events of international significance like the futile 1956 Hungarian uprising against the Communist regime. No matter the subject, though, it was always humanized through timely pictorial content arranged in eye-engaging layouts.

While the family magazine *Liberty* had already disappeared, 1956 saw the demise of *Collier's*, an event that portended dire straits ahead for *Life*, *Look*, and the *Saturday Evening Post*. Of the three, *Life* would survive longest, owing to an aggressive management that continued to look for novel ways to solidify its image. One of this magazine's most rewarding ventures came in 1959 when it secured the exclusive rights to publish a series on the seven astronauts assigned to the Project Mercury mission. In 1952 *Collier's* had offered a well-received series of articles on space exploration, enhanced by the futuristic illustrations of Chesley Bonestell. But now *Life* was preparing to outdo it with a series on America's momentous attempt to launch men into space. At a time when heroes were few and far between, *Life* promoted the astronaut as a new breed and, as Loudon Wainwright pointed out, "a specific antidote for the national gloom and feelings of inferiority that had bloomed with the Russians' orbiting of Sputnik two years earlier."[49] Thus, *Life* saw this project as a way to renew readers' faith in the American pioneering spirit and also stimulate their lagging interest in the magazine as a longtime leader in pictorial journalism.

The biweekly *Look*, as *Life*'s biggest competitor, strived to maintain a substantial circulation during this era, covering subject matter that ranged from the activities of notable personalities to serious topics of a social or political nature. But the loss of advertising revenue to television would contribute to its end in 1971. This predicament had already sent the *Saturday Evening Post* packing in the late '60s, despite editor Ben Hibbs's move to increase the number of profile pieces about entertainers and famous public figures. Before its demise, the *Post* still cultivated a conservative editorial stance, but in 1961 it had transformed its familiar title logo after the fashion of the eye-appealing design and layout techniques that had been evolving since the end of the war.

Having set new standards for magazine design, *Fortune*, whose abstract covers and interior layout merged image and text, had long provided a model for those magazines daring enough to follow its lead. While photographic composition and montage layouts marked the aesthetic appeal of the fashion publications like *Glamour* and *Vogue*, harmonization of typography and photography characterized the covers and interiors of *Esquire* and *Show*, the magazine of entertainment. Obviously, the cover, as a promotional device, was still the most visually important part of a magazine's makeup.

Until 1963 when Norman Rockwell left for *Look*, the *Post* was still making the most of his appealing cover art. Indeed, his scenes of ordinary people engaged in familiar activities amid the human comedy of American life continued to weave their magic spell on the mediated vision. By this time, too, Rockwell's reputation was secure enough for his classic artwork to reappear in Hallmark greeting cards, calendar series, and advertising for a number of well-known products. To the mediated vision Norman Rockwell was more than just the most popular commercial artist of his time, he was an American institution. However, by the time he went to *Look*, certain social concerns and issues that could no longer be ignored were undermining the sanctity of Rockwell's idyllic world, and his paintings would begin to reflect them, as chapter 2 will reveal.

By the 1950s, that other monument to American idealism, *Reader's Digest*, had become the most successful magazine in publishing history. By its fortieth anniversary in the early '60s the *Digest* was being printed in 13 languages and, with a circulation of 23 million, read in more than 100 countries. Such an achievement had begat even more returns in 1950 with the inauguration of a book club that offered popular novels in condensed form. Although the *Digest*'s single copy price had held at twenty-five cents, it finally began to accept advertising in 1954, presumably to offset rising print costs. Soon, full-color ads on glossy stock were appearing as well as dramatic illustrations for its growing number of true-to-life stories. In an ongoing attempt to focus on the inspirational side of life, *Reader's Digest* continued to respond to the mediated vision's inherent desire to identify with the more positive aspects of an increasingly complex world. Though television never presented a serious threat to the *Digest*'s circulation, another digest-sized magazine would in time surpass it. *TV Guide*, in fact, saw its circulation growth parallel the proliferation of television programming and the establishment of new network-affiliated stations across the country.[50]

With *Time*, the oldest news weekly now a communications institution, the corporation that published both it, *Life*, and *Fortune* introduced a newcomer to its family in 1954 called *Sports Illustrated* (*SI*). A monthly titled *Sport* had been around since 1946 with moderate success, which was why many thought that a weekly devoted solely to reporting sporting activity was pure folly. The skeptics had obviously overlooked the socioeconomic changes that had resulted from the availability of more leisure time and the fact that television's expanding coverage of sports made this era right for such a magazine. The mediated vision, whose traditional outlook on sport was both escapist and nostalgic, readily took to the magazine's colorful layouts of action-slanted photography accompanying reports of the latest games and events and the personalities involved in them as well as an occasional piece on sport's storied past. There were also other unique features about *SI* that drew special attention: its cultural focus on the arts in humanizing the sporting experience (yet another sign of the blending of elite and popular sensitivities); investigative essays of on- and off-field abuses in sport (which would appear more frequently over the years); and even pieces on the need for the conservation of the nation's natural resources. Over the years *SI* would become a revealing mirror of the interrelationship of sport, leisure, and society in American life.

The availability of increased leisure time saw numerous magazines primed to inform readers what to do with it. Traditional male-interest publications like *Popular Science* and *Popular Mechanics* began devoting even more space to hobbies and build-it-yourself projects. A number of magazines promoted individualized activities to help transcend the conformist social patterns of the time, as in such independent leisure pursuits as touring in *Holiday* (1946), playing golf in *Golf World* (1947), implementing the latest electronic developments that enhanced listening to recorded music in *High Fidelity* (1951), and taking to the water in *Boating* (1956). Ironically, these activities would evolve in time into conformist pursuits all their own. That retirees were living longer while pursuing ways to utilize their leisure years was attested to by the kinds of articles appearing in *Modern Maturity* (1958), the magazine of the American Association of Retired Persons (AARP).

However, in 1953 young men began to be informed of a radically different leisure lifestyle by a daring new magazine. *Playboy*, under the fearless direction of its pioneering publisher Hugh Hefner, presented its readers a mixture of escapist fiction, racy cartoons, celebrity interviews, timely articles and erotic photographs of scantily clad females. But the main thrust of Hefner's magazine was to foster his personal campaign against puritanical attitudes toward sex through a philosophy of open sexuality and the pursuit of pleasure as a sophisticated end in itself.[51] Thus *Playboy*'s posture was more socially blatant than that *Esquire* had manifested since the 1930s, and as a result of the newer magazine's surprising success, imitations began flooding the newsstands in the mid 1950s. In contrast to Hefner's high standards of publishing quality authors and enlightening features to emphasize his contention that the death knell for sexual puritanism had sounded, most of his imitators were more inclined to feature risqué subject matter and pictorial spreads of nude women that mainly appealed to prurient tastes.

While long-running magazines such as *Outdoor Life* and

*True* continued to feature topics about males' conventional interests, such as the challenges of the sporting life and adventurous expeditions, fantasized, sexually exploitative periodicals for men began to proliferate in the '60s. As successors to the pulp tradition of sensational, lurid covers that promoted suggestive content, their standard practice was to depict seductive women in prison bondage scenes enduring insidious methods of physical torture inflicted by their demonic captors. In fact, the formulaic covers for such monthlies as *Man's Story*, *Man's Exploits*, and *Man's Epic*, to name only a few, featured such titillating titles as "Lust Slave of the She Wolves," "Lust Orgy of the Wild Nymphos," and "Hitler's Underground Bunker of Lust." Obviously, editors depended a great deal on the suggestive power of the word "lust" to attract a receptive readership.

While these magazines responded to a growing sex-obsessed world that anticipated the real-life sexual excesses of the 1970s, another kind of publication had surfaced in late 1952 that promoted its content as not only true but "Uncensored and Off the Record." In *Confidential*, girlie magazine publisher Robert Harrison went after all the gossip and scandals he could dig up (or fabricate) about public figures and show-business personalities. Clearly, beneath the seemingly placid surface of the 1950s lay a perverse world for which Harrison found a receptive audience, as by 1955 *Confidential*, at twenty-five cents a copy, was outselling all other newsstand publications in the country and spawning dozens of tell-all imitations like *Exposed*, *Inside Story*, and *The Lowdown* (all 1955). However, as the latest to capitalize on the retouched photograph, Harrison saw his efforts crumble under a deluge of lawsuits in the late '50s, prompting him to bequeath his role in this otherwise lucrative business to other daring publishers who deigned to exploit the alleged deviant social behavior of celebrity icons.

Carrying on this tradition became the lot of the tabloid newspaper, and when the *New York Enquirer* changed its name to the *National Enquirer* in 1957, a legend in exploitative tabloid journalism had arrived. Its early years focused on stories about sexual aberrations, human oddities, and gruesome murders visually supplemented by startling headlines and candid photographs. Later, by shifting to the scandalous behavior of the famous and spotlighting features about the occult, supernatural, and pseudoscientific events, the *En-*

*quirer* began to appear at the checkout counters of supermarkets as a highly popular weekly publication.[52] Aimed at a sector of the mediated vision whose interests were far removed from mainstream news stories, the *Enquirer* and its many imitators assumed they were giving their audience what it wanted in a highly entertaining manner, just as the purveyors of tabloid journalism always had.

## REACTIONS TO DECLINING ADVERTISING REVENUE

Though many magazines were hurting from declining advertising revenue during this era, one popular publication with a largely youthful audience seemed to get along perfectly well without it. Following up on the comic book version of *Mad* that spoofed both comic strip and comic book characters, the magazine edition that began appearing in 1955 devoted itself to a mercilessly satirical foray into just about every sector of contemporary society. A favorite target was advertising itself, exemplified in the trenchant drawing styles of Will Elder, Jack Davis, and Mort Drucker that dissected the promotional ploys of many a well-known product. If advertising was the driving force behind a consumer-obsessed society, then *Mad* was itself a cultural force in debunking advertising methods in the eyes of the mediated vision. From its beginnings the magazine's unique covers were attended to by a character who became its trademark mascot—the grinning, droll-faced Alfred E. Neuman. His "What—Me Worry?" posture was, of course, indicative of the kind of zaniness that awaited a customer who purchased the magazine—comic strip takeoffs on television shows, movies, fads, home life, music, politics, the education system, and even classic literature. Hardly any topic was sacred to *Mad* when it came to looking at life from a lighter perspective; and, in large part, readers found *Mad*'s acerbic take on a world seemingly at times on the brink of madness a delightfully appealing panacea.[53]

As far as new markets for advertising were concerned, the plethora of magazines geared to teenage interests that began showing up in the postwar years revealed a growing affluent market to target. Among the earliest publications in this vein was *Hot Rod* (1948), which addressed youthful motorists' fascination with cars. With more money at its disposal, the high school set was reading magazines that also focused on the latest dress styles, fads, and rock music, a fast-growing cultural force in the 1950s. Accordingly, numerous one-shot publications appeared spotlighting the most popular singers, whose styles ranged from the clean-cut manner of Pat Boone to the swivel-hipped gyrations of Elvis Presley. As promotional boons to the radio, movie, and recording industries, other popular singers like Frankie Avalon and Tommy Sands were also featured as teen idols. But by the mid 1950s it was Elvis Presley whose image reigned supreme as both the most influential rock singer and leading heartthrob of teenage girls. Though some publications like *Datebook* still leaned toward the more antiseptic images of Pat Boone and Ricky Nelson, *Cool*, *Dig*, and *Teen Life* made much more over Elvis Presley as a youth icon, clearly a sign of changing tastes in the wind. Popular young movie stars also provided favorite subject matter for these publications, as evidenced by the flood of stories published about James Dean before and after his tragic death in 1955. To advertisers, though, the most important development arising from the proliferation of teen magazines, as well as the movie and TV fan publications, was their role as a highly visible medium for marketing products to a growing affluent audience.[54]

## The Sociocultural Impact of Electronic Media Advertising

While a number of radio's live dramatic series such as *Dragnet* was still attracting listeners in the late 1940s, the advent of magnetic recording tape in 1946 provided editing alternatives for "transcribed" radio programming. But by the 1950s a general shift to television viewing had begun. The upshot of this transition would be the transformation of radio's traditional programming into a narrowcasting format that responded to special interests. As TV adopted the kinds of shows that radio had pioneered, the latter medium started to concentrate on the very things that had characterized its beginnings—music and news. Radio also placed more emphasis on programming it was naturally proficient at: on-site news coverage, call-in talk programs, some of whose popular hosts like Larry King in his pretelevision days would start broadcasting nationwide in the 1970s, and public service reports such as airplane-monitored traffic conditions to motorists, as car radios now comprised a high percentage of the listening audience.

In 1955, the NBC network, whose ninety-minute variety program called *The Big Show* (1950–52) had been a last-ditch effort to attract listeners to this longtime format, adapted to the new demands on both radio programming and advertising by introducing a model weekend show called *Monitor*. In addition to the usual news and music segments, it featured comedy skits, celebrity interviews, and eyewitness reports of special events and breaking news. In contrast to the conventional way of contracting with a sponsor for an entire show, *Monitor*'s time latitude allowed for spot advertising on both a national and local basis. And like television, radio experimented with ways to promote a sponsor's product by convincing listeners they were not only being informed but entertained.

On the other hand, the main aim of privately supported radio was to inform through educational programming while avoiding the commercialization of network radio. Since the frequency modulation (FM) broadcast band was static free, a growing legion of independent FM stations in the 1950s began programming classical music for discerning listeners. These stations' attention to national news reports and cultural topics, as well as technological advances in transmitting the high-fidelity sound of recorded classical music, revealed them as predecessors of the National Public Radio (NPR) network and television's Public Broadcasting System (PBS). Ironically, by the late '60s, in the wake of the rock music revolution and further advances in radio technology, the FM broadcast band would become a haven for "free-form" rock music programming.

Equating product sponsors with the kind of music a growing teenage audience wanted to hear in the 1950s, commercial radio saw a new type of salesman/entertainer emerge —the "disc jockey" or DJ. On his *Make-Believe Ballroom* program in the late 1930s, Martin Block had formulated a style for the appealing personality who popularizes the recordings of well-known singers as well as up-and-coming hopefuls, interspersing the music with fan talk relating to a song and its performer. But in the mid 1950s when the popularity of the music DJ Alan Freed had dubbed rock 'n' roll peaked, Freed's illegal practice of plugging a tune for a fee was uncovered. As the most prominent disc jockey in the record promotion business, Freed became so entangled in the so-called payola racket that, following a federal investigation, he was compelled to leave the industry in 1959. By then, though, black-styled rock music and its spin-offs were fairly well entrenched as a force in American youth culture, a development affirmed by the black-inspired voices of many other popular DJs like Wolfman Jack who, though white, introduced hipster slang to the nation's proliferating independent AM radio stations.[55]

When radio conceded its role as a purveyor of family entertainment to the predominant presence of television, it had realized it could never emulate the visual power that television commanded in the marketing process. Yet, in its own way of promoting products that made airtime possible, radio continued to prosper. Most car owners deemed it an essential accessory and households usually had several on hand, while outdoor people, including street-roving teens, depended on pocket-sized transistor radios to satisfy their music listening habits. Ironically, during the time that watching television was becoming a nationalized habit, listening to the radio had become more of a personalized experience, especially among youth who had made listening to the radio an essential part of their social lives.

Television, in becoming the dominant medium for advertising, realized early on its advantage in presenting entertaining ads whose images moved—in effect, offering a visually immediate way to identify with a product by dramatizing its worth. As early as 1948 Milton Berle's *Texaco Star Theater* featured four gas-station attendants at the ready, singing the praises of their program sponsor's product. That same year Ajax Cleanser introduced its animated Pixies as marketers of an essential household item. By the 1950s viewers were besieged during commercial breaks with the likes of the Old Gold dancing cigarette pack; the antics of Sharpie, the Gillette razor company's animated parrot; "Speedy" Alka-Seltzer, whose name promised quick relief for upset stomachs; and the majestic gait of Budweiser beer's Clydesdale horses. Overall, though, real-life personalities would persist as the most effective TV salespersons, especially those celebrated faces the mediated vision immediately recognized.[56]

Just as magazines and radio had, television considered women, as longtime consumers of home products, cosmetics, and fashions, to be natural targets for its pitches. With the kitchen now the center of the household, TV came on with its updated images of appliance saleslady Betty Furness and General Mills's cooking expert Betty Crocker to inform "the Keeper of the suburban dream" (as *Time* labeled the era's housewife) about both appliances that took the drudgery out of kitchen chores and food products the whole family would go for. While women informing women about what they needed to know to benefit the quality of home life made good sense, television also began using women to promote major products of broader appeal like automobiles, ostensibly because of their key role in selecting a family car. Thus, viewers were presented the engaging manner of singer Dinah Shore extolling the merits of the popular Chevrolet and Julia Meade's more sophisticated approach to selling the upscale Lincoln. In fact, the glamorous promotion of these products revealed the automakers as TV's biggest sponsors at the time. Of course, men hardly objected to such come-ons when their inveterate love affair with the automobile was being enhanced by the sight of an attractive female showcasing a new model's virtues.

The male role in TV advertising adhered to the traditional masculine image that the other media forms had established. Baseball players Mickey Mantle and Stan Musial were esteemed enough to sports-minded youth of the 1950s to promote Wheaties cereal as the "Breakfast of Champions." Even the spreading acknowledgment of smoking as detrimental to one's health failed to deter TV ads' portrayal of smoking as not only a masculine rite but a socially significant custom for both men and women, particularly at a time when the suburban cocktail party had become a weekend ritual. Although the advent of filter-tipped cigarettes were advertised as a deterrent to the effects of nicotine, the promotion of filter-tipped Marlboros continued to make the most of smoking as a macho experience by centering its ads around a ruggedly handsome cowboy known as the Marlboro Man. The marketing success of Marlboro marked the beginning of a flood of filter-tip brands, each with its own distinctive approach to smoking as a pleasurable experience. In equating commercialism with escapist diversions, television realized, of course, that the most receptive programming in which to promote male-oriented products like cigarettes and beer was sporting events. The in-between innings of a baseball game, for example, proved a naturally receptive time for this sort of thing. But as the camera became more adjusted to the tracking of a football game, its numerous time-outs also adapted to timely commercial spots.

In the 1950s, when popular children's programs like *The Mickey Mouse Club* began reaching a wide audience, advertisers uncovered this demographic as ripe for marketing purposes. In addition to publicizing the merchandise spin-offs that these shows inspired, the promotion of new games and toys found a natural outlet in children's programming, particularly in the cereal-sponsored Saturday morning cartoon shows whose fantasized characters not only helped sell their sponsors' products but sensitized their youthful audience to its own escapist version of the mediated vision.[57]

The sociocultural impact of TV commercials stemmed from their visual power to entertain while promoting those things of the good life that enhanced or improved self-image. In turning the mediated vision in upon the self, the ads for automobiles, for example, stood out as minidramas in which a new car was presented as a highly desirable status symbol and, since the 1920s, integral to the mediated vision's ongoing dream of getting ahead in life. As the social image of the automobile loomed ever larger in the eyes of the nation's increasingly affluent youth, TV advertisers envisioned yet another receptive audience to target.

By the early 1960s, then, when television viewing had become a nightly ritual among household members, the most immediately accessible way yet had arrived for the mediated vision to realize its escapist dreams through TV's equation of advertising and entertainment. Vance Packard may have exposed the subliminal advertising techniques of the Madison Avenue hucksters in *The Hidden Persuaders* (1957), but the mediated vision's positive reception of television entertainment also revealed its tolerance for TV advertising, which it grudgingly realized was what made such programming possible in the first place. Nevertheless, to maintain its command, the TV commercial would have to explore ever more unique ways to be entertaining in the intent of selling a product to its highly critical audience.

## THE NEW CONSUMERISM: DEFYING DEBT TO BUY ON CREDIT

While expensive items like cars were often purchased on time-payment plans, credit card buying was also on the rise by the late 1950s, particularly at retail outlets. Concurrent with the arrival of suburban shopping centers, local TV advertising began to herald the coveted things that these meccas of consumerism stocked, serving mainly to attract housewives and the young set who would soon become their most supportive customers. In contributing to a growing cashless society, new credit-card holders justified their purchases as self-deserving, a sign of the growing desire to attain both immediate gratification and the enhancement of self-esteem. As TV commercials continued to implore a consumer society to buy whatever it desired whenever it wanted, credit-card/installment-plan buying, despite the debt and interest charges incurred, soon established itself as the most convenient way to avoid self-denial and turn a deferred future into the immediate present.[58]

## THE ESCAPIST PURSUITS OF YOUTH AS A MASS-MEDIATED FORCE

In the youth-oriented culture that America was becoming by the 1960s, teens were making a significant impact on adult tastes, whether adults realized it or not. In 1963 the Pepsi-Cola Company launched a TV advertising campaign to help expand its soft-drink market by identifying teenagers as the "Pepsi Generation." To glamorize the good times that Pepsi wanted young viewers to associate its product with, the California beach scene's bikini-clad girls and sun-bronzed surfers that the Beach Boys' echo chamber–mixed songs celebrated were the stars of its commercials. These ads' attention to a new subculture was a sign of youth's arrival as a separate entity within an evolving fragmented social scene that would characterize the rest of the century.

During the early postwar years euphoric young married couples were obviously not too concerned about birth control, as a prolific rise in the national birth rate occurred. In fact, between the years 1946 and 1954 over 75 million babies were born. Popularly referred to as baby boomers, those born in the last half of the '40s would become the first wave of the counterculture youth movement that exploded in the 1960s. Other than being raised in more affluent times, the most significant factor that set this generation's upbringing apart was its subjection to the liberal tenets of a best-selling book titled

*The Common Sense Book of Baby and Child Care* (1946).
Written by pediatrician Benjamin Spock, this work advocated
a permissive posture toward nurturing children, which later
resulted in some social critics blaming Dr. Spock's liberal
methods as a contributing factor to the juvenile delinquency
problems that became so prevalent in the 1950s–60s.

In marked contrast, most children who had grown up in the
1930s–40s were subjected to old-fashioned disciplinary methods of child rearing. Generally, such austerity seemed to have
paid off, as by 1955 there were over 2.5 million youths en-
rolled in the nation's institutions of higher learning, many of
whom were the first of their families to attend college. Their
conformist ways and conservative views showed few signs of
the kind of radical behavior that would erupt on campuses in
another ten years. Indeed, this security-minded generation
was seemingly oblivious to any problems beyond itself and
clearly uncommitted to the sociopolitical stances that had
motivated the radical students of the 1930s. Because of their
reluctance to identify with "causes," students of the 1950s
were dubbed the "Silent Generation."

Ironically, college-age women of this time were cultivating
an independent air that anticipated their more proactive social role in the years ahead. In 1962, *Cosmopolitan* editor
Helen Gurley Brown published *Sex and the Single Girl* in
which she argued that marriage should be delayed if a young
woman wanted to enjoy a liberated sex life and realize her potential in both the workplace and the social scene. The following year Gael Greene's *Sex and the College Girl* revealed that
many coeds had been experimenting with premarital sex for
some time, thus substantiating the findings of the Kinsey Report. These were brave new commentaries on the role of the
New Woman in the '60s. But the most shocking examples of
female emancipation were soon to come in the feminist movement.

Generally, fashion was still conservative. The well-dressed
modish look of movie stars Grace Kelly (who forsook Hollywood in 1956 for a real-life role in European royalty), Elizabeth Taylor, and Audrey Hepburn set the style in the 1950s
for many young women, just as the Ivy League look did for
young men. But by the mid '50s the signs of a self-promo-
tional, antifashion manner was starting to show up in the
dress of America's youth. An early influence was the leather
and denim attire of Marlon Brando's motorcycle gang in *The*

*Wild One* (1953) that some daring teenagers began to emulate. Such rebellious dress was more indicative of an attitude
than a style due to its implied indifference to fashion's status
quo. Shortly, its nonconformist posture assumed a more collective identity in the laid-back style (jeans or khaki pants,
open-necked shirt, and sandals) of the bearded social rebels
known as the "Beat Generation," after the kind of "beatific"
characters depicted in Jack Kerouac's novel *On the Road*
(1957). Coming as it did when society's conformist behavior
was in question, the book was an instant best seller. Its antiestablishment views were complemented by the works of other
"beatniks," as they were popularly labeled—in particular,
those of poets Gregory Corso and Allen Ginsberg, whose
counterculture poem *Howl* (1956) gained the rare status of a
best seller. By refuting the materialistic values of the time,
the Beats pursued a lifestyle that fostered personal freedom
and a spontaneous sense of individualism. Thus, in the search
for self-realization through mystic spiritual experience, the
Beat movement sought to intensify this end through sex,
drugs, alcohol, and jazz. As the jazz musicians did with their
music, the Beats felt their lives could be improvised to transcend the prison of societal commitment. To them, then, black
hipster's cult language as well as the individualistic styles of
progressive jazz characterized a lifestyle that was both
purely spontaneous and self-expressive.

Following the breakup of the big bands in the late '40s,
many of their former members began to appear in small jazz
ensembles that showcased their improvisational skills. While
the Gerry Mulligan and Dave Brubeck groups were prominent in popularizing postmodern jazz sounds, such established black musicians as trumpeters Dizzy Gillespie and
Miles Davis, saxophonist Charlie Parker, and string bass
player Charles Mingus contributed to the highly improvisational style known as bebop or the "cool" sound that had such
an emotional impact on the Beats. In the 1950s, piano jazz
stylings ranged from the complex manner of Thelonious
Monk and Bud Powell to the poetically popular renderings of
Erroll Garner. In the meantime, both Count Basie and Duke
Ellington managed to keep their unique big band sounds
alive, and when Ellington played at the first Newport Jazz
Festival in 1954, his vibrant orchestral interpretations of the
progressive jazz sound made a lasting impression on media
culture's music-oriented sector.

While the Beats were making their presence known in the late '50s, Greenwich Village nightspots began focusing on another kind of music that emanated from America's grass roots. The folk song tradition that Woody Guthrie had nurtured in the 1930s was revived in the late '40s by Pete Seeger when he introduced a folk-singing group called the Weavers. Their output stimulated sporadic interest in this predominantly acoustic-instrument genre. But by the 1950s and early '60s it had evolved into the folk music craze that a popular group called the Kingston Trio helped commercialize along with other recording groups like the Brothers Four and the Highwaymen. Its popularity culminated in 1963 in a TV series called *Hootenanny*, a weekly nostalgic tour of the nation's folk-music past. Then in that same year, singers Joan Baez and Bob Dylan appeared at the annual Newport Folk Festival where they injected a timely note of protest into their performances. Though Baez was a devotee of the traditional folk ballad, she was not averse to singing songs derivative of the time's sociopolitical problems. And with Dylan surprisingly turning from his customary acoustic renditions to the electronic for the first time, folk rock as a proper vehicle for sociopolitical protest suddenly found a receptive audience among the growing youth counterculture.

While folk and the avant-garde sounds of progressive jazz had more appeal to college-age youths, teenagers were about to discover a new kind of electronically styled music with which they would cultivate a strong identity. A visionary named Les Paul, who since the 1940s had experimented with the amplified sound and design of the solid-bodied electric guitar, put his own version of such an instrument on the market in 1952. While Paul and his singer wife Mary Ford recorded some of the time's most popular hits through a unique overdubbing and multitracking system, his technology would ironically inspire a generation to create a raucous kind of music that echoed its own restlessness and sense of alienation.[59] The mood was reflected in the movie roles of Marlon Brando and James Dean—Brando in his sexual bravado and Dean as a misunderstood loner. The upshot was a new kind of visually styled music in which youth could indulge its new sense of social identity, either through attending a live concert or listening to the music that radio DJs played in the new 45-rpm format showing up in record shops and on soda-shop jukeboxes.

## THE IMPACT OF NEW TECHNOLOGY ON RECORDED MUSIC

The heightened attention to the development of essential technology in World War II led to numerous breakthroughs that would have an impact on mass media entertainment, particularly in the area of recorded music. The late '40s saw the introduction, as noted, of magnetic tape recording, stereophonic sound, and the vinyl microgroove record, thus setting the stage by the 1950s for the marketing of high-fidelity records whose slower speeds superseded the conventional 78-rpm recording. Now one long-playing (LP) record of 33$\frac{1}{3}$ rpm could accommodate a lengthy classical composition, while record albums offered Broadway musical scores and film sound tracks as well as romantic mood music featuring the richly amplified orchestral sounds of Percy Faith, Jackie Gleason, and Les Baxter. These more expensive recordings were naturally directed at older listeners' nostalgic affinities.

## THE SOCIAL FRAGMENTATION OF POPULAR MUSIC GENRES

During the late 1940s and early '50s, prior to the advent of youth's rock music obsession, most popular genres of recorded music produced for adult audiences were competing with themselves for ascendancy on the popularity charts and subsequent success in the marketplace. While *Billboard* magazine charted the top hits in its categories of the popular ballad, mood music, folk/country, novelty, and a new label for race music—rhythm and blues (R&B), radio stations began touting what they called the Top Forty recordings, of which a growing number were popular R&B releases. Although the honky-tonk sound of country music was not yet high on the standard pop charts, singers like Hank Williams, Ernest Tubb, and Kitty Wells were helping build a growing popularity that had begun in the war years. Something about the country singer's stoic posture toward life's problems, especially those pertaining to romance, was catching on with listeners other than those of the rural sector, for hearing plaintive songs about personal problems somehow made them easier to bear. But the mellow voice of Eddie Arnold foreshadowed a more sophisticated approach to this kind of music.

To a more mainstream audience the most popular singers

were the male vocalists who had started out on their own after the demise of the big bands. In this vein were Tony Bennett, Perry Como, Dean Martin, and Frank Sinatra. In fact, Sinatra's popularity had grown to the point that he avoided recording singles for the more profitable thematic LP albums. Popular, too, in the early '50s were female vocalists Jo Stafford, Dinah Shore, Rosemary Clooney, and Patti Page, all of whose recordings appeared regularly on radio and jukebox menus throughout the nation. From R&B and country to traditional ballads, then, the media culture was infiltrated by a plethora of escapist musical styles at this time. But all this was about to change.

To capitalize on the technological advances in sound reproduction, small-group bands began to experiment by merging the amplified sound of the solid-bodied guitar and the human voice to create pulsating aural effects. This process and its offshoots would have significant import in promoting and marketing a rock band's style. Indeed, by focusing on both its aural and visual aspects, the recording of later rock music, along with its dynamically designed packaging, would become a major industry in responding to youth's escapist inclinations. Although by the mid 1950s established recording companies like RCA Victor and Columbia were promoting their LP recordings and new stereophonic players for the mass market, they were also preparing to tap the youth market in a big way.

As a visually expressive musical form, rock 'n' roll had a natural appeal to youth from its beginnings. In 1954 a little known band called Bill Haley and His Comets recorded a number whose simple lyrics derived from its dance-motivated title of "Shake, Rattle, and Roll." The tune's most impressive feature was a rhythmic drumbeat that accentuated its lyrics, a winning combination that resulted in sales of over two million copies. And when Haley's "Rock Around the Clock" was used as the theme for the 1955 film *Blackboard Jungle*, as noted, rock music began to take off, prompting a seemingly endless run of recordings by bands that seemed to pop up overnight along with a deluge of rock-themed B movies. As action-oriented music that inspired an erotically physical style of dancing, the term "rock 'n' roll" seemed an apt description of its visual appeal to teenagers seeking ways to express their newfound sexual urges. Soon, just about any rock singer and/or band with access to the new recording technology were producing instant hits, as names like Chuck Berry, Fats Domino, Lloyd Price, and Little Richard became commonplace in the conversation of young fans. Ignoring the dominance of New York as a recording center, independent, modest-sized record companies sprang up in unlikely places, particularly in the Southeast where Memphis, Nashville, and New Orleans had become hotbeds of the black R&B style and its blending of traditional blues and gospel music. Recording in the 45-rpm speed that jukeboxes accommodated, upstart companies such as Sun in Memphis and Chess in Chicago produced records that dared to compete with industry giants RCA Victor, Columbia, Decca, and Capitol. Their success put the larger companies on alert for any performer who consistently appeared in the Top Forty ratings of independent radio stations.

That R&B recording artists were black was hardly a deterrent to white youths who appreciated their more emotive style as opposed to the formulaic pop songs that white singers like Perry Como, Tony Bennett, and Jo Stafford recorded. Even white vocal groups like the Four Aces and the Crew Cuts had difficulty keeping pace with the popularity of black combos such as the Coasters, whose songs about teen life hit home with young audiences. Also the Platters' special way with ballads like "Only You" and "My Prayer" were slow-dance favorites of teens. Black music stylists ranged from Little Anthony and the Imperials' rhythmic cadences of "doo-wop" to the more gospel-rooted mode of "soul" that Ray Charles and James Brown expanded on in the 1960s. By this time, too, R&B had developed into the more sophisticated urbanized sounds of Motown Records, which featured the lush voice of Marvin Gaye and such top-rated vocal groups as the Four Tops and the Supremes. Over the course of its development, R&B conditioned the mediated vision to a subtle acceptance of its sounds, most auspiciously at first by youths who saw it as offering a sense of escape from the restrictions of school and home life. By the mid 1960s R&B was beginning to curry favor with white adults, although many parents were still wary of adverse social effects its uninhibited expression might have on their offspring.

With many of the Southern AM frequencies in the 1950s specializing in either rock music, country, or R&B, the interdependence of radio and the recording industry was affirmed. The exposure to rock also resulted in a number of white country musicians merging their own styles in a hybrid form that disc jockeys referred to as "rockabilly." In fact, Buddy Holley, Jerry Lee Lewis, and Carl Perkins would become big names in its performance and recording, but destined to become the biggest of them all was an unknown named Elvis Presley. Having listened to radio music as diverse in style as bluegrass, rock, and R&B, Presley, in his early recordings, was inspired to combine the elements of country, rock, and black-styled music to forge his own version of rockabilly. As the answer to Sun Records' search for a white singer who could adapt his style to the popular R&B recordings that young audiences were listening and dancing to, Presley became the first white American singer to achieve widespread popularity through the rockabilly recordings he made for Sun.

With a singing style that generated a hypnotic social impact on youthful behavior, Elvis Presley inherited his visual sense of stage presence from black performers' flair for flamboyant showmanship that emphasized not only the way music should be heard but how it should look in performance. Music in motion, then, was Presley's modus operandi, and its feel for the times had a natural appeal to a visually charged TV generation. As a history of African American music style has observed: "It was not only Elvis's appropriation of black music that attracted teen audiences but his libidinous approximation of black stage antics, which extended even to his choice of clothing."[60] Girls may have been emotionally moved by his performances, but male teens responded by emulating Elvis's dress as well as his longer hair style and sideburns. The look was soon affected even by older males, whose dress also became more stylishly flamboyant. Rock music, it seemed, had dictated a new kind of youthful lifestyle, when appearance itself would become a badge of cult membership.

In rock music, then, black and white cultures came together in the Elvis image, which received its first widespread exposure on Ed Sullivan's popular television show in 1956. This highly publicized event, along with a later recording contract with RCA Victor, revealed that in the eyes of millions of teenagers the reputation of Elvis Presley as a bona fide rock star was now firmly established. But not until he was drafted by the army in 1958 and military public relations transformed his controversial image into that of a clean-cut

American boy, did he win the favor of the many parents and clergy who had condemned his music.

However, by the time of his discharge a new wave of rock singers were in vogue, serving to undermine Elvis's image as a teenage singing idol, though he furthered his career as the most popular singer in film. Ironically, in the end his turning to old standards and sentimental ballads would make Elvis a concert favorite with older Las Vegas audiences. The high point of his movie career had been the film he made in 1957 for MGM, *Jailhouse Rock*, which not only made Elvis Presley an international star, it clearly demonstrated that in rock music a performer's style was more important than the music. All the mediocre films he made over his career reflected this fact, showing how much a factor the mediated vision was in helping an American musical idol continue to exert a popular fantasy image.

TEEN CULTURE'S SOCIOLOGICAL IMPORT FOR THE FUTURE

By the end of this era in 1963, teenagers had cultivated their own unique escapist culture centering around high school social life that was romanticized in movies and teen magazines. If youth culture was characterized by alienation from the mainstream, then the theme of estranged youth was never so poignantly dramatized as it was in J. D. Salinger's 1951 novel, *The Catcher in the Rye*. Its teen protagonist Holden Caulfield rejects the patterned behavior of his parents, teachers, and all the others he labels as "phonies" to take off on his own in hopes of finding out what real life is all about. In the 1950s there were many self-proclaimed Holden Caulfields around, both male and female, which, of course, was a major reason for the book's widespread popularity.

In identifying with Holden, then, youthful rebels found solace in the rock ballads that, in their dealing with the social realities of being young, were directed at their main interests, particularly those songs about the problems and pleasures of young love. Permissive parents, in allowing their offspring a freer lifestyle, appeared to be renewing their own lost youth through their sons and daughters, many envisioning them involved in an innocent world of school activities and drive-in restaurants where they spent their money on hamburgers, Cokes, and the sanitized jukebox tunes of Ricky Nelson, Fabian, and Bobby Rydell. These were some of the featured singers that host Dick Clark was showcasing on his afternoon TV dance program *American Bandstand* in the late '50s. But Clark also recognized that teens' favorite songs were also being sung by black performers featured on his show, and that white teens' color blindness concerning musical taste was helping bridge the racial gap—a longtime social problem whose serious implications for the nation at large was about to erupt in full force.[61]

High school couples listening to such music while spooning over a hamburger and Coke at the local drive-in seemed harmless enough, but what could happen later, either in a car at the drive-in theater or lovers' lane, transcended the realm of the Andy Hardy/Henry Aldrich films to result in one of the most serious problems facing teenagers at this time—an unwanted pregnancy. Since most parents were reluctant to discuss sexual matters with their offspring, instructional manuals appeared that dealt with the "do's and don'ts" of teen dating. But many girls were attracted to the popular romance comic books whose illustrated stories in the vein of the "true romance" magazine dwelled on the problems encountered in romantic relationships. That ignorance about sex among teens was widespread was revealed in the investigative reports that mass-circulated magazines published on the sexual behavior of American youth. In 1949 the *Ladies Home Journal* had posed the big question, "Where Do Teen-Agers Get Their Sex Education?" The answer, of course, was from each other. The division between youthful folly and parental authority could precipitate another, more deviant way for teenagers to express their sense of alienation—indulgence in criminal behavior that the justice system labeled "juvenile delinquency."

In 1955 Benjamin Fine attempted to analyze the reasons for a growing lack of respect for authority among American youth. Fearful for the nation's future if remedial measures were not taken to stem the rising tide of young offenders, he predicted that by 1960, "[i]f the rate of juvenile delinquency continues to mount at the rate experienced during the last five years, the number of boys and girls going through the juvenile courts will skyrocket."[62] Which, of course, is precisely what happened. But youth's growing lack of respect for authority was starting to express itself through other, more insidious ways that by the mid 1960s would explode in the sociopolitical rebellion of college-age youth.

## MEDIA CULTURE'S ROLE IN THE DEMOCRATIZATION OF LEISURE

By the late 1950s the media's depiction of an increasingly affluent society was sensitizing the mediated vision to a whole new outlook on the import of play in everyday life, viewing it as an integral adjunct to one's lifestyle. The posture of youth whose attempt to make life in the present more agreeable by living it as intensely as possible was catching on with adults as well. Working males committed to keeping up with the monthly routine of making mortgage and car payments found themselves anticipating the ritual respite of two-day weekends and paid holidays when, in addition to coordinating the backyard cookout, they were free to do whatever they liked. Many of their leisure activities were creative in nature, involving projects that gave the hobby-kit people plenty of business, while the more practically minded turned to carpentry and gardening. For the less industrious the high-fidelity phonograph or the latest book-club selection beckoned. For the sporting set there were opportunities for boating, fishing, golfing, and hunting in its season. The trend away from mass-oriented amusements to more individualized activities was undoubtedly in reaction to the conformist social patterns of the time. At any rate, this kind of avocational involvement among "The Leisured Masses," as a national magazine labeled most Americans in 1953, inspired the pertinent observation that "Leisure has been democratized," an acknowledgment that the middle class was now acquiring membership in the heretofore exclusive leisure class.[63]

The New Leisure had even helped transform the ingrained American concept of work for work's sake by creating what John Kenneth Galbraith called a "New Class" of workers who were looking for jobs that were appealing and satisfying—the kind of job in which salary was not so much a factor as an "[e]xemption from manual toll; escape from boredom and confining and severe routine; the chance to spend one's life in a clean and physically comfortable surroundings; and some opportunity for applying one's thoughts to the day's work."[64] With advances in technology, automation, and computer systems opening up opportunities in hundreds of different trades and professions, the job future for this New Class looked especially bright.

The suburban housewife now found her tasks preparing meals, doing the laundry, and cleaning the household much less demanding and time-consuming, thanks to the array of cooking aids and electrical appliances now available. She still maintained a tight schedule divided between her household duties, shopping, and attending to her children's organized after-school pursuits. Her main leisure activities involved meeting with her peers in social gatherings for coffee, gossip, and/or playing cards. At home she could watch the "soaps" that had now made the full transition from radio to television or read book-club novels and subscription magazines while listening to records on the stereo player. There was also the Saturday night cocktail party for which she planned its outlay of food and drink. As an informal escapist ritual, it provided an ongoing source of gossip, especially if any inebriated guests crossed the line of social respectability. Occasionally, husband and wife might take in a heralded first-run movie, a venture requiring the services of a babysitter to mind the children. Going to the movies was a leisure activity that soon faded once their offspring reached the socially independent years. Besides, by the late '50s it was common knowledge that many of the choice films would soon be appearing on TV.

By this time, too, the family togetherness that characterized what *Life* magazine called "The Good Life" was being put to a real test when the husband's vacation time rolled around and the family car was tuned up for a trip to some planned destination like Disneyland. While the more venturous were flying to Europe for two-week tours, many seemed content to spend their time at the beach or a mountain retreat. An early sign of things to come occurred in 1946 when mobster Bugsy Siegel opened up his Flamingo Hotel in Las Vegas. By the 1960s it had become the model showplace for an area that would blossom into an escapist playground for adults, featuring shows starring well-known entertainers, legalized gambling, and other activities proscribed by society. As descendants of the old lawless West, places like Vegas and Reno introduced the mediated vision to a fantasized world that offered an intensely self-indulgent way to appreciate the present by escaping from it.

As the most popular family destination, the new theme park of Disneyland, which had opened in Anaheim, California, in

1955, was heir to the metropolitan amusement park that had evolved throughout the century. On a grander scale, Disneyland offered visitors an idealized world of exotic and adventurous attractions where they could escape present-day reality by returning "to the places of the heart, to a happy past, to memories and dreams of a perfect childhood."[65] Upon leaving their suburban lifestyle outside the gate, then, family members were ushered into an escapist realm where they surrendered themselves to a pervasively nostalgic milieu featuring such venues as Fantasyland and Frontierland that were offset by the idealized future that Tomorrowland's scientific wonders heralded. Overall, though, the park's insistent devotion to the past not only sought to recreate a way of life that was no more but, ironically, had never been. In its grandiose formulation of a purely escapist domain, Disneyland, as a fantasized retreat from the maddening pace of postmodern car culture, stood as an indictment of the workaday urban world.[66]

Leisure as a spectator activity also took on mass appeal during this era through attractions that ranged from watching team sports to gambling at the race tracks. Not only were more fans attending organized sporting events, they were also viewing them on the ever-expanding medium of television, which, as discussed earlier, was in the process of making the province of sport its eminent domain. With the individualized leisure sports of bowling, fishing, hunting, tennis, and golf on the rise, television capitalized on the opportunity for increased advertising revenue by devoting more weekend program time to them. At first the elitist nature of golf confined it to a limited viewing audience, but the success of young golfers Arnold Palmer and Jack Nicklaus helped attract a more avid middle-class following to their sport. Along with the game's democratization and a commensurate rise in advertising revenue, even the technical problems of televising it would soon be resolved. But it was boxing and the team sports of baseball, football, and basketball that saw the greatest growth in spectator appeal during this time, to which their increased TV coverage attested.

## SPORTS AS BOTH A BUSINESS AND AN ENTERTAINMENT MEDIUM

With many well-known professional athletes returning after the war, the year 1946 had sports fans thinking that things would be just as they had been before. Joe Louis and Billy Conn met again in their long-awaited rematch, but this time Louis won a decisive victory to retain his heavyweight title, which he held until his retirement in 1949. It was this fight's renewal of the race issue that presaged developments that would radically change the face of American sports. Because professional football was primarily northern-based at the time, the Cleveland Browns' signing of a black fullback named Marion Motley in 1946 did not have the national impact that the Brooklyn Dodgers' signing of a black baseball player did in 1947. Yet when Jackie Robinson began playing major-league baseball in the face of racist taunts from both players and fans, the racial divide in the country's most conservative team sport was finally breached, paving the way for a multitude of black players to come, and not only in baseball. In 1950 only three blacks were playing professional basketball, but by 1959 Bill Russell was helping the Boston Celtics win the first of eight straight championships. Slowly, but inevitably, the white sector of the general public was taking on the more egalitarian and tolerant outlook of the mediated vision, a perspective that would never again see American sport as it once was. Especially with winning as the prime motivating factor in the business side of organized sports.

During these years of dramatic change, baseball continued to be dominated by the New York Yankee team, which, from 1947 to 1962, won ten World Series championships to entrench itself as a franchise of unequaled success. Then, when the failing franchise of the Boston Braves moved to the emerging market area of Milwaukee in 1953, it was justified as a necessary business move. But a sign of more dire things to come, as far as disregarding fans' devotion to a team was concerned, occurred when the longtime Brooklyn Dodgers franchise departed Ebbets Field for Los Angeles in 1957, a move that substantiated baseball's status as more a business than a game and a sign of professional sports' inevitable national expansion.

Despite the power that owners maintained to move their teams, baseball's popularity continued. But it would soon find its long reign overtaken by the intensely emotional, violent game of professional football, whose growing popularity was attributable in large part to television. Assuring the sport as a natural for the TV screen was the thrilling championship game between the Baltimore Colts and the New York Giants in 1958. Also by the '60s the Green Bay Packers were demonstrating the worth of the free substitution rule in their success with a formidable lineup of strategic specialists, an omen of football's tactical future. The game must have had a premonition of its continued success when the Professional Football Hall of Fame was opened in 1963, fittingly in a city where one of the original teams had played—Canton, Ohio.[67]

A key reason that the game of football was becoming so visually appealing to television viewers was due to certain technical strategies that Roone Arledge, a programming genius of the American Broadcasting Company (ABC), helped originate. Realizing that boxing, TV's most popular sport since the late '40s, was fading in interest by the late '50s, Arledge sensed that viewers were ready for a change in sports programming, particularly in the way team sports were telecast. By interpreting contemporary sporting experience as primarily a form of show business, he transformed both college and pro football into an intense viewing experience through technological innovations introduced in the 1960s: strategically positioned cameras for long shots as well as those hand-held for close-up views, split-screen projection, pertinent graphics, and instant replay of a game's videotaped highpoints. The upshot of this expanded approach to televising a football game was that viewers were afforded a more intensely personal relationship with it as opposed to that communally experienced at the stadium.

Thus, by focusing on sport as dramatic spectacle in which crowd color and its ambient sounds are synchronized, Arledge helped establish a visual technology that turned sporting events into grandiose entertainment venues. In the *Wide World of Sports* series, begun in 1961, he demonstrated that even events not usually considered in the traditional category of sports had widespread entertainment value, as, for example, the demolition derby's unrestrained car-wrecking competition. Accordingly, as ABC's sports programming ratings soared, advertising revenue rolled in. But Arledge's greatest innovative achievements were yet to come, most auspiciously in 1970's inauguration of pro football aired in prime time on Monday nights and in the dynamic showmanship he brought to televising the Olympic Games.

From the first Games after the war in 1948, the Olympics continued to expand, adding more events and attracting more participants as well as larger audiences on-site and soon through satellite TV. In Melbourne in 1956 nationalist interests again resurfaced when the government-subsidized Russians, eager to promote the merits of their socialist system, outshone the usually victorious Americans. In this politically divisive era, the media's attention to the Olympics as a repository of records and statistics that showcased nationalistic achievement would continue as it had since the Berlin Games in 1936.

## Women's Changing Role in Sport

From the 1950s into the '60s, among the most notable Olympic achievements were those recorded by women, indicative of their steady progress since the early part of the century.[68] At Rome in 1960, for example, black American sprinter Wilma Rudolph won three gold medals, paving the way for the success of both black and white women athletes. Because of women's surprising success in athletics, some wondered if their achievements might be attributable to genetic imbalance since their winning performances appeared more male-like than female. Although such a sexist view generated a degree of controversy, the growing participation of women athletes in such a world-stage event as the Olympics prompted increased media emphasis on the personal profiles of minority athletes to reveal organized sports as a window of individual opportunity. Nevertheless, the sexist posture toward women athletes would persist as a reflection of prevailing attitudes in the larger society.

By the 1950s, cheerleading, whose physical demands made it an all-male activity in the early years of the century, had evolved into a football game fixture in which a bevy of well-endowed young women in eye-catching attire urged their team on to victory through the coordination of cheers and gymnastic displays. In comparison to women performing as athletes, this role was considered a more socially acceptable feminine activity—from high school through college to the level of professional sports. In the 1960s, when television transformed professional football into a form of mass entertainment, the camera often highlighted the sideline gyrations of a team's cheerleaders, until critics complained that their revealing costumes were more a promotion of sex than a team. To many the Cowgirls of the Dallas Cowboy organization typified such exploitation of the cheerleader's role in the sports scene. They, in fact, were thought to epitomize the "essence of pro cheerleading: glamour, sex appeal, celebrity, and merchandising success."[69] This is why the female cheerleader was now considered an integral part of sport's commercialized pageantry, and why the mediated vision relished the whole package of the game and its attendant trappings as yet another escapist experience that televised sport provided to captivate and entertain its audience.

### FROM TRIUMPH TO TRAGEDY: THE DREAM TURNS TO NIGHTMARE

In assessing the ten-year period from 1947 to 1957, *U.S. News & World Report* called it "a time of change and accomplishment unmatched in the history of America, or of any other nation." The article went on to discuss the implications of a higher standard of living that had made possible the New Leisure lifestyle and the physical comforts afforded by advances in science and technology. Not only were Americans more prosperous than ever before, it contended, they were more secure, healthier, and enjoying longer lives. Accordingly, they were raising larger families, while engaging in the individualized activities that more leisure time afforded. The report also pointed out that economic prospects for the college graduate looked good as technology continued to create new jobs in such promising areas as plastics, electronics, communications, and aviation, and to meet the demand more youths were attaining a higher educational level. As production achieved record highs in both industry and farming, a continuous flow of essential products and an abundant supply of food were offered for mass consumption. The report even painted a positive picture of the strategic defense mechanisms that science/technology had produced to defend against possible attack in the ongoing cold war: the H-bomb, jet fighters and bombers, guided missiles, and the "world's first atomic-powered submarine, the *Nautilus*." The piece then concluded that "the decade just ending has been a real age of miracles . . . that promises even greater miracles in the decade that now lies ahead."[70] The "miracles" would keep coming, of course, but by the mid 1960s they would be overshadowed by unexpected developments that threatened the sociocultural stability of the nation by fomenting a new set of uncertainties.

In retrospect, the era of 1947–1957—and the ensuing six years through 1963—evolved from collective feelings of relief and optimism at the close of World War II through periods of doubt and questioning created by a series of ominous developments: the fear of a Communist conspiracy, the Korean conflict, the politics of brinksmanship that the threat of the bomb engendered, the sociopolitical direction of the Cuban insurrection, the burgeoning civil rights movement spearheaded by Southern blacks, and finally that dark day in Dallas in 1963 when President John F. Kennedy was struck down by an assassin's bullet. In looking back from that point, it would appear that the glowing outlook of the *U.S. News* report had blinded it to numerous social issues that underlay the surface of the bright picture it painted. For one, women were finding it increasingly necessary to seek employment to help supplement their husbands' salaries and ease the pressure of making the mortgage payments on their split-level homes in the suburbs as well as their cars and other items purchased on credit. This instant-gratification brand of consumerism was generating an air of uneasiness, a feeling that the luxuries and creature comforts that suburban living demanded did not necessarily guarantee happiness or even a successful marriage, to which a rising divorce rate and its impact on the children of broken homes soon attested. With women away at work, too, many homes found latchkey children left to their own devices after school. Thus, unaccustomed pressures on both parents resulted in a rise in the consumption of two prohibitive forms of escape—alcohol and drugs, especially tension-easing tranquilizers. Indeed, prescription drugs would become increasingly popular as a cheaper alternative to psychoanalysis.

The article also seemed oblivious to American know-how falling behind the momentous Russian space achievement of 1957 (later surpassed in 1961 when a cosmonaut became the first man to orbit the earth). Even though America's Explorer VI satellite had astonished the world with the first views of Earth from space in 1959, the United States would not feel absolved of the Russian space achievements until astronaut John Glenn completed his orbiting mission of Earth in 1962. To the mediated vision the heroic image of the astronaut would grow in stature, but Glenn's feat proved to be the country's last major space triumph of this era. It would prove a significant step leading to John Kennedy's mission to put a man on the moon in the 1960s.

In succeeding the aging Dwight Eisenhower and his conservative administration in 1960, John F. Kennedy, as the country's youngest president at forty-three, brought the refreshing aura of youth to Washington politics. It was also reflected in the programs he introduced, in particular the Peace Corps, which sent idealistic young volunteers to aid Third World countries, and his faith in the future, as epitomized in his support of exploring the "New Frontier" of space. In the eyes of the mediated vision the Kennedy style also displayed a personally positive approach to confronting the mounting problems of the present—one of relaxed self-confidence tempered with wit and vitality. Following the tragedy in Dallas, then, the nation could only speculate about the promising future Kennedy had optimistically forecast—even more of a reason now for the mediated vision to retreat into the escapist modes that the purveyors of media-made culture continued to create for it.

## SIGNS OF AN EVOLVING POSTMODERNIST MILIEU

As noted, toward the end of this era in the early '60s, the subject matter of popular fiction and the movies as well as the ubiquitous medium of television strived to cultivate unique ways to make sense of an increasingly complex world by fantasizing it. By this time, too, certain artists were challenging the complex subjectivist visions of abstract art by creating an impersonal arts realm that owed much of its inspiration to everyday artifacts and the omnipresence of mass advertising. Thus originated the movement that cultural observers dubbed pop art and whose attraction to the commodity icons of consumerism and media culture was ironically expressed through the traditional elitist forms of painting and sculpture. In 1963 this interrelationship gave rise to the first major pop art exhibit at New York's Guggenheim Museum, which featured the controversial works of Andy Warhol, Robert Rauschenberg, and Jasper Johns. In particular, Rauschenberg's "combine" projects that incorporated the throwaway items of a consumer society reflected these artists' fascination with the pervasive but temporal, impermanent nature of commercialism. The pop art movement, then, was one of the first significant indicators that American media culture had transitioned from the modern era into the postmodern. In fact, the period from the late '60s into the 1970s, which saw a breakdown of the rigid distinctions between elitist taste and commercial art, precipitated a new consciousness in the arts, a phenomenon whose sociocultural import is examined in more detail in chapter 2.

The final years covered in this present chapter also saw the ongoing democratization of American society result in a variety of opposing creative perspectives that signified another postmodern characteristic—the subcultural segmentation into special interest sectors. For example, the hobby mania of the 1950s, as a reflection of the desire to perform as an individual in a time of mass conformity, saw hobbyists deriving therapeutic release from avocations as far apart in kind as woodworking, gardening, and watercolor/oil painting.

Despite its reputation as an elitist endeavor, the role of creating art as a "Sunday painter" became highly popular, especially after celebrated figures like Dwight Eisenhower and Winston Churchill praised painting as a pleasurable, relaxing activity. With the "leisured masses" welcoming the creation of "art" as an escapist avocation, then, the notion that anybody could become an artist was enhanced by the advent of a consumer product in the 1950s that induced even the least talented to take up painting. But art purists, reacting to the thousands of paint-by-number sets purchased by a multitude of would-be artists, naturally decried a system in which to complete a picture one had only to color in predesigned spaces.[71] Nevertheless, the paint-by-number "artist" seemed doggedly determined to emulate the representational manner of Norman Rockwell's idyllic vision or the primitive style of a Grandma Moses rural scene. In formulaically painting familiar subjects and scenes, then, these self-appointed artists stood in marked contrast to the time's critically favored abstract painters whose spontaneous methods, many felt, were overly contrived and even bogus in effect. But, as noted above, a new vision of the role of art in postmodern society had begun to appear. Ironically, it would elevate the treatment of the American scene's familiar subject matter to a level of high critical regard.

As antithetical postures abounded in other creative realms as well, they too found a place in the media culture. Rising playwright Edward Albee, for example, contributed his ironic, complex vision to the theater of the absurd in his early plays, *The Zoo Story* (1959) and *The American Dream* (1961), works that challenged long-enshrined societal values. While the more comprehensible works of Arthur Miller and Tennessee Williams's plays were intended to disturb as much as entertain theatergoers, Neil Simon's romantic comedy, *Barefoot in the Park* (1963), proved a welcome antidote to their dark moods and the vicious tirades of Albee's married couple in *Who's Afraid of Virginia Woolf?* (1962). In musicals, subject matter ranged from the unlikely street-gang warfare of Stephen Sondheim and Leonard Bernstein's *West Side Story* (1957) to Alan Jay Lerner and Frederick Loewe's *Camelot* (1960), whose mythical setting in the court of King Arthur was likened to the idealistic aura of the Kennedy administration, at least until late 1963 when it was understandably compelled to close down.

While movies of the late 1940s and early '50s offered audiences both the dark world of film noir and the fantasized appeal of MGM's colorful musicals, the last years of this era were showing films as disparate in intent as the Academy Award–winning *Tom Jones*, based on the bawdy eighteenth-century novel of the same title, and *Lilies of the Field*, whose theme extolled the efficacy of religious faith (both 1963). In 1963, too, movie audiences' reception of the black humor of Stanley Kubrick's cold war satire, *Dr. Strangelove, or How I Learned to Stop Worrying and Love the Bomb*, revealed how much sociocultural attitudes toward the atomic age had changed since the publication of John Hersey's best-selling *Hiroshima* (1946), his poignant account of the terrible devastation wrought by the atomic bomb in Japan in 1945. Although the movie version of Vladimir Nabokov's *Lolita* was not as sexually explicit as the author's 1955 novel, its story of a pubescent girl's affair with an older man also revealed just how far the movies had come by 1962 in treating such taboo subject matter.

During this time, too, popular music found itself splitting into two main camps comprised of those who still relished the traditional romantic ballad and those who welcomed the new electronic rock sounds. Though folk music had made a big splash in the early '60s, even its songs could seem as far apart in intent as the fairy-tale spirit of Peter, Paul, and Mary's "Puff the Magic Dragon" and Bob Dylan's protest-charged

"The Times They Are a-Changin'" and still find avid listeners, especially among the young.

While fiction in a purely escapist vein attracted a large following for the increasingly popular James Bond spy thrillers,
mainstream fiction like Joseph Heller's *Catch-22* (1961) and
its satire of mindless bureaucracy in a World War II military
setting led many to acclaim it the most representative novel
of this time. Evidence of prime-time television acceding to
elitist tastes were Ingrid Bergman's appearance in the title
role of a 1963 production of Henrik Ibsen's *Hedda Gabler* and
Julie Harris's in George Bernard Shaw's *Pygmalion* the same
year. Throughout this era, too, the timely sociopolitical satire
of comic strips *Li'l Abner* and *Pogo* continued to amuse their
followers, as did the traditional family humor and warm-
hearted situations of longtime favorites *Blondie* and *Gasoline
Alley*. Although the varying perspectives of fiction, television,
and the comic strip were indicative of the media culture's ongoing deference to special interests, their inherent intent,
whether topically realistic or appealingly fantasized, was to
provide timely entertainment in an era of growing doubt and
uncertainty.

Ignoring the larger problems of the time, the 1962 Seattle
World's Fair was already looking ahead to the good life of the
twenty-first century that technology would supposedly foster.
But earlier in 1959 one of the more polarized as well as prophetic events took place when Vice President Richard Nixon
showed up at the U.S. Exhibition in Moscow. His ideological
debate with Russian premier Nikita Khrushchev over the materialistic merits of the American way of life, as symbolized
by the kitchen appliances on display, put the Russian leader
on the defensive as to socialism's lack of production variety
in contrast to capitalism's wide consumer choices. In effect,
then, these world leaders' standoff looked ahead some thirty
years hence to a final resolution of whose social system would
prove the more meaningful in serving its people.

But to what extent had American media culture's ongoing
democratization process impacted social change since the
late 1940s? During this era, two of its chief critics, Clement
Greenberg and Dwight MacDonald, argued that the dominance of what the former labeled "kitsch" and the latter
"Masscult" was inevitable in a democracy tempered by the
forces of capitalism and technology.[72] Gilbert Seldes echoed
their basic criticism of popular or media culture's failure to

challenge its audience intellectually when he commented in 1950 "that the popular arts not only convey a flat and limited picture of life, they actually encourage people to limit the range of their emotions and interests."[73] Less than twenty years later, though, the assessments of these three would be subject to question in that the popular arts, or the media culture, due to revolutionary advances in communications technology, were not just providing escape for the American people, they were affording them a wider, more open range of choices through which to obtain a panoramic "picture of life" and thereby experience "emotions and interests" previously denied them.

Seldes, as a promoter of what he called the public arts, contended that the people themselves needed to take a more proactive role in determining how these forms could better serve them in a time of great change. For, as he had written, the "persistence of change reflects the one emotion all Americans hold in common, that the future is theirs to create. It is a confession that the present is not perfect and an assertion that nothing in the present can prevent us from changing for the better."[74] Ironically, though, by 1963 and the end of this era, the imperfections of the present had begun to undermine the promise of the future, anticipating the nation's internally divisive years ahead when the mediated vision would look more longingly to the nostalgic consolation of a fantasized past rather than the uncertainties of an ambivalent future.

# 2

## 1964–1979—Adjusting to Postmodern Social Challenges

Definitions seem to vary with every citation, yet the use of [postmodernism] to describe recent developments in the arts (and in other forms of social life from urban planning to theology) suggests a widespread belief that a coherent change in sensibility marks our era and distinguishes it from the "modernism" that came before.
—Christopher Reed, "Postmodernism and the Art of Identity"

The postmodern is a cinematic age; it knows itself through the reflections that flow from the camera's eye.
—Norman K. Denzin, *Images of Postmodern Society: Social Theory and Contemporary Cinema*

SOCIOLOGICALLY, THESE WERE YEARS WHEN SUCH GROWING PROB-lems as air and water pollution, the potential exhaustion of the country's natural resources, and worldwide overpopulation were kept at the forefront through an ongoing round of polemical books, TV/print–media reports, and protest movements. But it was the spontaneous demonstrations and angry confrontations over the war in Vietnam, as well as mounting support for the civil rights movement, that commanded center stage in the 1960s. These issues, as well as a sharp rise in violent crime, resulted in a growing social divisiveness that, ironically, the media culture's venues of film and television would begin to draw on to formulate an escapist milieu of fantasized reality.

Prior to and after the passage of the Civil Rights Act in 1964, the nation was galvanized, if not polarized, by the violence imposed on those blacks and whites alike who participated in organized demonstrations to challenge the South's voter registration policies and imposed segregation of commercial and public facilities as well as its educational institu-

106

tions. But television news coverage revealed racism as a pervasive national problem, manifested in not only the 1963 confrontations between police and protesters in Birmingham but the 1965 riots in Los Angeles and later the northern cities of Chicago, Cleveland, and Detroit.

Undoubtedly, the times were right for a civil rights revolution, as in addition to blacks, other minorities seized the opportunity to champion their causes.[1] The older population, now living longer, had grown large enough for the more militant to reinforce their rights through a movement called the Gray Panthers that focused primarily on health care and social security benefits. During this era, too, the homosexual sector, which was surprisingly larger than most people had thought, grew more proactive in its efforts to transcend discriminatory practices that had kept it literally underground in a homophobic society. American Indians, the least visible element of all, also began to organize in the early '70s to demand their long-abused rights as citizens.

These years also saw progress in the women's movement, whose forceful leadership kept its concerns at the forefront of political agendas.[2] The suburban housewife, now duly informed by the feminist-oriented articles she read, began to question her homemaker role as the key to a full and happy life. Like Betty Friedan, the author of the controversial best seller, *The Feminine Mystique* (1963), many of these women had attained a higher educational level than their mothers, which in itself was motivation enough to question their lot. With birth control research giving rise to the Enovid contraceptive pill in the 1960s, another kind of revolt was in the making, one that would culminate in the most radical expression of social independence yet for women—the sexual revolution of the 1960s–70s.

While the U.S. population had grown to 205 million by 1970, some argued that continued growth of the world's population was posing threats to the future of life on the planet, especially in Third World countries where birth control was virtually unheard of and an insufficient food supply persisted. This was clearly the case posited by Paul Ehrlich in *The Population Bomb* (1968), which warned that famine would soon contribute to the death of millions of people. A threat to both human and marine life was also being fomented by American industry's longtime practice of depositing its wastes in the nation's waterways. In addition, the devastation of such natural resources as the woodlands through unregulated timber cutting and strip mining was upsetting the ecosystem, resulting in the near extinction of certain species of wildlife.[3] Even though legislation was enacted to protect air, water, and other resources, occasional accidents such as oil spills and nuclear power plant leakages continued to be cited. And though some remedial progress would be made by the late '70s, the earlier Earth Day celebration (1970) in its intent of alerting the nation to ongoing environmental concerns was punctuated by comic strip character Pogo's timely comment as to the real source of the problem: "We have met the enemy and he is us."

In 1973, that most revered instrument of personal mobility—the automobile, though now deemed a major contributor to air pollution—was slowed down by an unexpected problem. The nation's chief source of petroleum, the Near Eastern organization of oil-producing countries (OPEC), curtailed its flow of exportation, which not only resulted in a serious shortage of gasoline, it drove the price of a gallon of gas up higher than it had ever been before. This situation, along with growing unemployment and a spiraling inflationary rate turned the 1970s into the nation's most economically depressed time since the 1930s.

Paradoxically, though, the tumultuous years of 1964–79 represent an era when the mediated vision saw this barrage of mounting problems inspire the predominant subject matter for the major entertainment forms of fiction, movies, and television. In other words, the real world's proliferating social/political problems, environmental concerns, and the cold war threat of atomic warfare were considered ready-made sources from which the purveyors of media culture could mine new versions of fantasized reality. And with the advent of a more liberal posture toward censorship, the upshot was that practically any realm of formerly taboo subject matter would become fair game for transgressively explicit, even culturally iconoclastic, portrayal.

## Youth Power's Impact on Fashion and the Social Scene

In the media spotlight since the 1950s, American youth culture of the '60s was still cultivating its own versions of escapist experience that would have widespread influence on the mainstream culture's growing affinity toward absorbing and emulating youthful lifestyles. But despite the media's fixation on youth's caprices, it would take some time for conservative adults to adjust to their extremes of dress as a way to promote self-identity.

Although the well-dressed image of First Lady Jackie Kennedy served as a mainstream fashion model in the early '60s, women's styles had begun to reflect counterculture trends through the casually informal manner of ready-to-wear street attire. Leading the way was London designer Mary Quant who introduced the tunic dress's short hemline that British model Twiggy helped popularize. But for many women, the ultimate emancipated look in fashion's attempt to express one's "real self" appeared in the mid '60s in Quant's controversial miniskirt with its wanton display of the legs, culminating later in an even shorter look. By the 1970s daring young women were taking to tight-fitting hot pants made of body-adaptive synthetic material in a variety of colors. The style's pronounced leggy appearance was erotically enhanced by the new seamless pantyhose and high-ride platform shoes or boots. During this time, too, pantsuits for women became socially acceptable, a reversion to the androgynous look of some 1940s' movie starlets, as the media pointed out.

The mod style of London's Carnaby Street also made an impact on American men's dress. As the conservative nature of men's fashions gave way to a liberalizing trend, shirts showed up in a wide range of startling colors and psychedelic designs. While this more ornate look expressed itself in an assortment of styles, dress jackets appeared made of such materials as suede and the more masculine-styled leather and denim. However, the new polyester leisure suit's attempt to convert formal wear into a more casual style was short-lived. Though the wide, colorfully designed tie now prevailed, the hat as an accessory had become less essential to the well-dressed male. And with longer hair in vogue after the moptop grooming of the Beatles rock group, more attention was paid to the style-cut cultivated in a coiffed, blow-dry manner. Like women's fashion, men's was purposely intended to call attention to the liberated self.[4] And those desirous of realizing such an end usually succeeded, if only for brief spans, as fads in dress appeared and just as soon disappeared. Ironically, style as an inversion of social convention was about to become the fashion. As reported by the media, it reflected both the time's evolving social fragmentation and the state of media culture itself.

By the late '60s, the era of deregulated fashion had developed into an unrestrained obsession for self-expression among the young, as seemingly the more outrageous one's attire, the more acceptable it was to one's peers. The most visible performers in this fashion circus were the dropouts from society known popularly as hippies.[5] Through a "do-your-own-thing" approach to dress, they fabricated their own anti-style of tie-dyed jeans, T-shirts emblazoned with a timely slogan ("Make Love, Not War"), thrift-store discards, granny dresses, peasant work caps or bandannas, and sandals—or preferably no footwear at all.

Because of the bizarre clash and mix of anachronistic clothes that many hippies wore in a long-haired, unisex display of their antiestablishment posture, most outsiders concluded that these social rebels were products of hallucinogenic drugs, which, of course, many of them were. Extolling an antiwar message of peace and love during this time of global and societal conflict (hence the flowers worn as symbolic gestures), these latest spin-offs of the American Bohemian tradition rejected the conformist family lifestyle of their parents by either living as "families" of their own creation in rural communes or "making it" in the drug-energized urban scene of their mecca—the Haight-Ashbury area of San Francisco. Here in the late '60s the so-called flower power movement "turned on" in a social explosion of drug-inspired hard rock music, sexual freedom, and drug experimentation. In 1969 the movement revealed how nationalized it had become when some 400,000 "flower children" showed up at a farm near Woodstock, New York, to hear their rock music idols in concert, an event that identified them as "Woodstock Nation." Dubbed a "happening" in the time's parlance, the rock concert spectacle, with its open invitation to self-expression through drugs and sex, was both the aural and visual symbol of youth culture's social defiance.

But as a youth-engineered purposeful rejection of society's demands, the hippie rebellion was derided by the mainstream because its hedonistic lifestyle scorned the worth of long-enshrined American values. Yet, before the hippies' dream of an idealized world deteriorated, as so many utopian visions had before them, their way of life made a significant impact on media culture. As key players in the sexual revolution, they helped promote the notion that "clothing and other forms of body decoration [such as flowers, tattoos, beads, beards, and long hairstyles] were never designed to conceal . . . but were primarily intended to render the body more sexually attractive."[6]

Thus, the hippies' emphasis on nudity as a natural state was in line with the time's cultivation of more liberal beach fashions, as by now the conservative women's swimsuit styles of the 1950s gave way to a general acceptance of the previously shunned bikini. This set the stage for the most radical developments in women's swimsuit design yet: Rudi Gernreich's sensational but short-lived topless suit in 1964, the Cole company's Scandal suits, which used elastic fishnet to tantalizing effect, and the String styles of the 1970s, whose open display of the erogenous zones was thought to be the ultimate in swimsuit design.[7] As far as the rebellious posture of youth itself was concerned, though, nudity reached its zenith in the early '70s in the "streaking" phenomenon, as zealous college students bared all to run through public places, seemingly for both shock effect and the sheer thrill of doing it.

During a time of growing emphasis on the visual stimulus of fashion, an occasional show of nostalgia for the past surfaced, as revealed in a revival of 1920s' styles inspired by the 1974 movie version of F. Scott Fitzgerald's *The Great Gatsby*. Even styles from the more recent past were fostered by the 1950s' teen-life milieu in films like *American Graffiti* (1973) and *Grease* (1978), based on the long-running Broadway musical. Another 1950s influence emanated from the popular 1970s TV series *Happy Days*, inspired by the box-office success of *American Graffiti*. But within the show's nostalgic context, a sign of changing times appeared in the carefree lifestyle of a biker character whose black leather jacket became a coveted icon among male teenagers. Regardless of the never-ending parade of sartorial variations, no matter how unique, the meaning of fashion itself remained the same as it always had in the eyes of the mediated vision—a tangible way for both young and old to realize a sense of personal identity amid any pressing concerns and to feel good about themselves in the process.

### YOUTH'S ROLE IN THE DIVISIVE POLITICS OF A CONTROVERSIAL WAR

A major contributor to the youth rebellion was the societal unrest that had been building since the early 1960s. The Viet-

nam quandary that President Lyndon Johnson helped esca-
late in 1964 brought things to a head, especially when on-site
TV reportage began to focus on the horrors of combat that
young American soldiers were enduring. The upshot helped
splinter the nation into two main antagonistic factions—those
who wanted to accelerate the fighting to attain victory and
those who demanded an immediate withdrawal on the
grounds that the conflict was morally wrong. The most vocif-
erous of the latter position were college males subject to the
draft, whose plight helped reinforce folk singer Joan Baez's
protest songs at the University of California's Berkeley campus in 1964. Captured by the ubiquitous TV camera, similar,
often violent protests were staged at other schools around the
nation, even at some of the most academically traditional of
the eastern schools.

After the conservative tenure of Johnson's Republican successor Richard Nixon prematurely ended with his resignation
in 1974, due to his role in the media-obsessed Watergate scandal, South Vietnam soon fell to the Communists. To the mediated vision the nation's role in a seemingly pointless war in
distant Southeast Asia, even though its justification was ostensibly to contain the spread of Communism, had been a
drawn-out, fearsome nightmare from which it would be slow
to awaken.


### ELECTRONIC SOUNDS: EXPLOITING THE OUTER LIMITS OF POPULAR MUSIC

In the manic kind of atmosphere that this era generated,
the mediated vision was acculturated into a variety of escapist venues. Youth's version of this end found its most spontaneous release in a type of electronic music whose raucous
ambience would reverberate throughout the rest of the century. While rock 'n' roll, the musical sound of the '50s, lapsed
into a dormant state, New Wave jazz, rhythm and blues (R&
B), and country music continued to attract followings. During
the early '60s, acoustic-styled folk music had found a center
of identity in Greenwich Village's Folk City, where the voices
of social protest foreshadowed hard rock's uninhibited antiestablishment posture. Soon, in fact, rock music's culturally
defiant lyrics and screaming guitars would become dominant
factors in reflecting and reinforcing youth's ongoing rebel-

lious attitude. A major figure in this development was Bob Dylan, who came out of the folk music scene in 1965 to fashion the self-referential singing persona of the rock artist.[8] This was the beginning of his "electric" guitar era in which he introduced his drug-influenced, personally expressive mood recordings to the counterculture. Both Dylan's persona and unique songwriting ability would stimulate an innovative approach to studio-created rock music and the later output of a talented group from abroad whose fresh musical style was initially intended to be seen as much as heard.[9]

Growing up in England, the foursome who became the Beatles readily acknowledged the American influence that Elvis Presley, Chuck Berry, Little Richard, Buddy Holley, and country singer Carl Perkins had on their early music. After merging the sounds of their icons into a distinctive style of their own, it evolved from the big hit period of their first American tour, highlighted by an appearance on the *Ed Sullivan Show* in 1964, to the classic studio-recording era in London. This was when the Beatles, in replicating the culturally defiant posture of Bob Dylan, produced their groundbreaking, best-selling albums that relied on daring instrumental sounds and varying recording speeds for their aural effects— *Rubber Soul* (1965), *Revolver* (1966), *Sgt. Pepper's Lonely Hearts Club Band* (1967), and *Abbey Road* (1969).[10]

Thus, the thing that assured the reputation of the Beatles as highly experimental innovators was the evolving maturation of their music—from the simplistic romantic ditties that appealed to a teen audience to the later drug-stimulated, technically manipulated works, whose ingenious effects exhibited a persistent progression toward complexity. The Beatles' influence was strong enough to direct hard rock music toward a future of varied stylistic interpretations, as seen in the wave of other innovative British groups that appeared, each striving to be more audacious than the others in both fashion and musical style. All of them, in fact, from David Bowie's space-age theatrics and the Rolling Stones' defiantly hard-core performance image to the psychedelic effects of liquid-light displays at Pink Floyd concerts, conspired to transform the rock concert into an emotionally intense, media-made event. Even after the Beatles' breakup in 1970, the legacy of their recording innovations and showmanship would endure the rest of the century.

As the Beatles' British successors did, then, so their Ameri-

can counterparts capitalized on the fruits of recording experimentation and, in their performances, the promotional
gimmickry of long hair and antifashion or flamboyant dress.
From the drug and/or alcohol-influenced performances of un-
conventionally named groups such as Jefferson Airplane and
the Grateful Dead to those featuring Jimi Hendrix's guitar
wizardry and Janis Joplin's shrieking voice, shock impact
was an essential component, inviting extremes of outrageous
dress and behavior among not only performers but those attending a concert. Thus, both performers and hallucinogenic
technical effects combined to turn the rock concert into a
spectacle of hypnotic visual appeal to rebellious youths. Cap-
tivated by what they saw and heard, they sought to expand on
their concert experiences by listening to their favorite performers on album recordings and radio stations that by the
late '60s were narrowcasting hard rock to a ready-made audience.[11]

## POPULAR MUSIC'S CULTURAL AND TECHNICAL ACHIEVEMENTS

In the 1970s, rock music affirmed itself as an accepted component of media culture, heard not just in recordings and on
radio but in the sound tracks of film, TV programming, and
commercials. Helping cultivate this new cultural image was
the performing and recording career of Bruce Springsteen
who, in developing a positive rapport with the media, reaffirmed a relationship that had dissipated since the heyday of
the Beatles. His populist approach to rock music, obviously
inspired by his blue-collar New Jersey origins, was marked
by a sense of honest revelation that centered on the problematic side of the American experience. In 1975 his best-selling
*Born to Run* album demonstrated that the real-world issues
of folk music's protest tradition were readily adaptable to the
more experimental focus of rock.

Such topically inspired music recalled the lyrical posture
of folk/rock icon Bob Dylan, whose intensely personal vocal
style of the late '60s was enhanced by the overdubbing and
multitracking of studio recording. On the other hand, a singing team with the unlikely name of Simon and Garfunkel updated the acoustic conventions of folk music with their
popular songs of satirical comment about contemporary life.
In contrast to the output of the hard rock scene was that of

vocalists/composers James Taylor and Carole King, who produced unique versions of the romantic ballad in their best-selling albums. Other directions in the burgeoning recording business appeared in Motown's R&B stylings of black group performers like the Supremes and the Temptations and the soul singers Marvin Gaye and Aretha Franklin. Gaye's songs, which ranged from romance to social comment, pioneered the function of tape manipulation in augmenting the vocal sounds of soul music. By influencing many white singers to emulate their voice stylings, black performers, whose output was now widely accepted in mainstream media culture, made an indelible mark on the development of popular music.

Anticipating fortunes to be made, the recording corporations moved to capitalize on the new technology that promised even more fabulous breakthroughs. As André Millard notes, the popular music business now had "the same goals of artificiality and illusion that had made Hollywood the vanguard of recorded sound."[12] In the recording vanguard of this windfall period, of course, were the Beatles, who, in London's Abbey Road studio, charged their drug-fueled recording of the *Sgt. Pepper's Lonely Hearts Club Band* album with so many unique sound effects that a live concert could never hope to replicate them. Similarly affective were the soaring voices and echo-chamber effects of the Beach Boys' recordings that featured the catchy songs of the group's leader, Brian Wilson. His talent culminated in *Pet Sounds* (1966), an album that revealed Wilson's experimental side as having matured since the highly popular surfing songs. Likewise, recording producer Phil Spector demonstrated the expansive possibilities of his "wall of sound" dimension that merged the vocal and the instrumental in the recordings of the Ronettes and the Righteous Brothers, among others. Such technical innovations were made possible by Robert Moog's revolutionary work with the sound synthesizer and related breakthroughs in the computer field from the 1960s to the '70s.[13]

By this time, then, the musical sector of the media culture was highly aware of the technological marvels that made listening to recorded music, whether popular or classical, a more intensely personal, even visual-like aural experience. Such marvels of technology, from the 1950s' reel-to-reel magnetic tape in cartridge format to the compact cassette in 1964, not only heightened the stereophonic sound of the home player, its minimal size afforded more storage space. It also provided further opportunity for listening on the automobile's built-in player unit. Now, both the means for home recording and the advent of the portable stereo player offered listeners an even more personalized way to enhance their musical pleasure. Ironically, the portable player and its 120-decibel sound peak, which many dubbed the "boom box," often saw its turned-on owner an unwelcome intruder into the relative quiet of a neighborhood. Though the technology for producing rock music had helped it acquire a more mature reputation, its subversive approach to reflecting youthful self-expression fomented a culturally divisive reaction from conservative music devotees as to what good music should be and sound like. Consequently, rock music would persist as a postmodern barometer of social fragmentation.[14]

## SELF-INDULGENCE AS ESCAPIST EXPERIENCE: THE SEXUAL REVOLUTION

By the 1970s, the stage was set for a widespread obsessive search for a more self-gratifying lifestyle across the generations, resulting in multiple ways to pursue this end. Disenchanted with the political process as the solution to the pervasive problems that plagued the time, many seekers after self-fulfillment began placing more stock in a personally expressive kind of experience. Its main purpose was to intensify the development and realization of self, either physically, mentally, or sexually. On a physical plain, opportunities for maintaining fitness ranged from organized exercise regimens like aerobics and bodybuilding at the local health spa to jogging and controlling one's weight through a strict diet of health foods. To pursue mental health, a variety of experimental programs came into being, from transactional analysis sessions designed to improve interpersonal relations to the radical nude encounter groups of California's Esalen Institute. Spiritually, some looked to find solace and inner peace in the Hindu discipline of transcendental meditation or the more endemic experience of Christian fundamentalism, which was now being promoted by a growing number of evangelical television programs. But the more daringly venturous were seeking self-fulfillment through open sexual relationships during an increasingly permissive time for such activity.

The social centers for unattached males and females during the late '70s were the singles bar and the sexually charged aura of the discotheque. In 1960 singer Chubby Checker had introduced a highly popular dance craze called the Twist that allowed couples to create their own movements in responding to rock rhythms. It was the prototype of the improvisational dance styles that by 1977 set the stage for the disco scene when thousands of nightspots with names derivative of Los Angeles's Whisky-Au-GoGo and New York's Peppermint Lounge sprang up across the land. Here, amid the changing colors of strobe lights and sexy go-go girls setting the beat in their elevated cages, couples gyrated to the Hustle or any other popular dance beat a disc jockey might feature on a two-turntable record setup that kept the music continuous. Creating a musical fantasy world by merging image and sound, the disco found its most publicized combination of glamour and glitz in New York's Studio 54 where celebrities showed up in droves to "make the scene," in the time's parlance. The white leisure suit transformation of John Travolta's blue-collar character in the frenzied dance sequences of the 1977 film *Saturday Night Fever* revealed the disco as an escapist retreat where dancers, no matter their status on the social scale, could participate in an intensely self-expressive experience—yet another sign of the media culture's democratizing power to bring socially disparate sectors together.

With sex a natural player in such social gatherings, its role became more blatantly open than ever before. While the arbiters of public mores were still debating the problem of pornography and what constituted obscenity, the sexual revolution came into full flower, seeming to substantiate the radical hippie notion that sex should be free for the asking. Even after the Supreme Court determined that pornography and its related concerns were matters best monitored and adjudged by community standards, ingenious methods for skirting problematic issues were devised. Much to the chagrin of local officials who tried to suppress the practice of nude sunbathing, this longtime outdoor activity grew more inviting to those so inclined in the more liberal climate of the time. Even in the unlikely heartland of America at a place in Indiana aptly named Naked City, nudist practices were commercialized to the extent that an annual contest to name Mister and Miss Nude America was celebrated.

Couples enjoying each other's company not only in the nude

but sexually was the purpose of California's Sandstone Ranch near Los Angeles that emerged in 1969. To its upscale members the concept of liberated sex represented the Sandstone founder's intent to create a socially open milieu where women are sexually emancipated, thus eliminating the male's need for a double standard. Other California experiments in free love sprang up in the 1970s, among them the Morehouse commune near San Francisco, which subscribed to the naive notion that societal and individual problems could be readily resolved by involvement in uninhibited sexual experiences. After the manner of the hippie communes, variations on the concept of liberated sex also welcomed the use of drugs as an enhancement to such revels. Although most of these radical social experiments carried the seeds of their own demise, some would survive to become oases of escapism in the more conservative time of the 1980s. Their flaunting of society's conventional attitudes toward human sexuality seemed to reflect the media culture's now overt tolerance of such behavior, particularly as it was being depicted in fiction and film.

Among married couples the ultimate unconventional sexual activity materialized in the practice of "swinging." Subscribing to an open marriage concept, these emboldened sexual adventurers engaged in husband/wife swapping by responding to the ads in the multiple swinger publications that existed at the time. Inevitably, the movement evolved into the establishment of clubs for the express purpose of introducing like-minded couples to each other. Thus what had started out as a more clandestine experience wound up in the late '70s in the orgiastic atmosphere of Plato's Retreat in New York, a swing-club rendezvous where members could indulge themselves in just about any sexual fantasy imaginable, depending on the inclinations of one's partner(s).[15]

For those less disposed to the indiscriminate nature of group sex, varied opportunities for sexual involvement of a more private order presented themselves. A rising divorce rate among older couples led to the desire to rekindle the ardor of youth by striking up impromptu acquaintances in singles bars and discotheques. Fashion, of course, played a major part in stimulating the attraction between the sexes. Women, in particular, took advantage of the new freedom to display their charms in the latest styles—from hot pants and tight-fitting designer jeans to the follow-up intimacies afforded by seductive lingerie from the mail-order house of

Frederick's of Hollywood. Helping promote the adventurous side of sex was publisher Hugh Hefner's Playboy Philosophy of liberated sex, which was not only promoted by his magazine but glamorized in the lush setting of his Chicago Playboy Mansion and Clubs that expanded into an international chain in the '60s. Anticipating the full flowering of the sexual revolution in the '70s, Hefner practiced what he preached by forging his own personal image of the sexual sybarite.[16]

Even for the more conservative types attracted to self-induced sexual outlets, a flood of accessories were now available from urban adult stores. In addition, the ads in sexually themed magazines and mail-order catalogs promoted a variety of sex toys designed to enhance any desire or whim a male or female customer might entertain. For the orally squeamish partner there was even a market for body candy and deodorants. Clearly, something for everyone's "taste" had become the guiding motto of the recreational sex business. During this time, then, when the acceptance of sex as a recreational pursuit superseded most attempts to be discreet or coy, many sexual fantasies were carried out in the private sanctuary of bedrooms with mirrored ceilings reflecting couples performing their own theatrical version of lovemaking on satin sheets or the popular water bed.

It would seem, then, that in this time of promiscuity when sexually liberated women were freely participating in transient sex, prostitution would have lost its perennial allure. Paradoxically, though, the solicitation by those who engaged in the oldest profession was rampant—from high-priced call girls to erotically dressed streetwalkers whose main competition came from the "massage" parlors that were springing up all over. In the 1970s the glamorous side of prostitution was exploited when a New York madam named Xaviera Hollander attained celebrity status with her best-selling book *The Happy Hooker* (1972), an explicit revelation of her life in the sex-for-pay business. Not surprisingly, efforts were afoot in California to legalize prostitution, but it was Nevada that became the first state to sanction this business with the opening of the Mustang Bridge Ranch near Reno. Ironically, the real-life prostitute now appeared to be transcending her negative image in fiction and film by becoming something of a fantasized sex object—from the glamorous call girl who entertained the lonely out-of-town businessman for an entire evening to the independent hooker who could turn a dozen tricks in that same time.

Because of the more open atmosphere accorded it, the consequences of indiscriminate sex could create dire problems for those ignorant of ways and means to prevent pregnancy and disease. To counter the possibility of pregnancy, the intrauterine device known as the IUD and the more effective Enovid pill were in widespread use by the mid '60s, prompting a decline in male condom use. When a pregnancy did occur (a situation on the rise among teenagers whose naïveté and unpreparedness found them highly susceptible), the opportunity for an abortion was legalized following the Supreme Court decision of 1973. But due to those who held strict religious convictions, this decision precipitated angry debates and violent reactions that would plague the nation for the rest of the century. Sexually transmitted diseases were also a serious problem that escalated during this time. But since most such afflictions were treatable, their threat would pale in comparison to the spread of the deadly AIDS virus that could destroy one's immune system.[17] Consequently, by the 1980s and the transition to a more conservative social climate, the nation would see a pronounced decline in the practice of promiscuous, unprotected sex.

Due to the increase in sexual problems and personal concerns stemming from ignorance of the facts, the time was right for the advent of the media-popularized sex authority who doled out advice in magazine columns, books, and even on radio/TV talk shows. A leading voice was Dr. Ruth Westheimer, whose brave commentary on *Sexually Speaking* covered topics and discussions ranging from the problems of sexual dysfunction and their resolution to the use of aphrodisiacs to enliven the sex act.

At a time when the drug culture had even invaded the household with new prescriptive drugs like Valium (approved for use in 1963) to help calm the nerves of overwrought housewives and career men stressed out by their professional lives, the illegal drugs of the hippie scene—marijuana and LSD (the abbreviated form of its scientific name)—were often resorted to for their powers to enhance and prolong sexual activity. Thus, during this era, either privately acceptable or socially illegal ways were inducing both men and women to engage in an intense search for the ultimate orgasmic experience as the great escape.

## THE MOVIES CAPITALIZE ON THEIR NEW CREATIVE FREEDOM

In this time of liberal creative expression, Hollywood started promoting the sensational elements of graphic sexuality, violence, and social deviance as box-office attractions. Big changes in distribution and marketing strategies played a key role in this process as Hollywood's major studios were being absorbed by giant corporations whose powerful interests embraced many areas other than the media. To help ensure corporate moneymaking objectives as well as filmmakers' creative goals, Jack Valenti, the new head of the Motion Picture Producers Association (MPPA), conceived a plan to counter the deteriorating Production Code and sanction quality films whose realistic scenes of violence and sexual content were integral to plot development. The result was a rating system instituted in 1968 that categorized films by degree of problematic content and segregated audiences by age. Now, general audiences would be admitted to films rated G and mature audiences to those rated M, later modified as PG, or parental guidance, for admitting youths. While R meant that youths under sixteen would not be admitted unless accompanied by a parent or guardian, X was intended to deny admittance to anyone under sixteen. The new code's overall social impact on going to the movies was that the mediated vision now took on a fragmented perspective that reflected both generational alienation and the rapidly changing mores of the time.

Ironically, the more liberal milieu that the movie people had long looked forward to was also playing into the hands of opportunistic independent filmmakers who were turning out a flood of X-rated films on shoestring budgets that attracted former as well as new adult patrons to the theaters. Among the first to profit from the X-rated tag was producer/director Russ Meyer's *Vixen* (1968), which centered on the nymphomaniacal behavior of its title character. As an independent production, it was successful enough for 20th Century–Fox to contract with Meyer for a mainstream X-rated film called *Beyond the Valley of the Dolls* (1970). Though panned by the critics, its box-office success mirrored the liberated attitude of a sex-obsessed time through what Meyer described as the depiction of "unbridled sex, the kind of sex people fantasize about."[18]

However, Meyer's somewhat comical scenes of simulated

copulation would pale in comparison to the erotic high points of two 1972 hard-core independent productions that, while banned in most communities, were among the big money-makers of the year. In a field where performers were mostly unknowns, *Deep Throat*, by promoting the special fallatio talent of one Linda Lovelace, made her into a porn star, while *The Devil in Miss Jones* did the same for Georgina Spelvin. Just as the star system had promoted the traditional Hollywood film, so porn stars helped build the pornographic movie industry in the 1970s. Thus, viewers flocked to grind-house theaters to see former Ivory Soap–ad model Marilyn Chambers perform in the orgiastic revels of *Behind the Green Door* (1972) or the fantastic demands on the women who dared take on the well-endowed John C. Holmes, the male answer to the porn-film superstar.

Because of its run-ins with community standards and court-ordered closings, *Deep Throat* received so much media publicity that many upright citizens found out-of-the-way movie houses where they could see what all the excitement was about. In appealing to the tastes of jaded viewers who thought they had seen everything, hard-core sex movies kept producing ever more sensational variations on their over-worked themes, including gay/lesbian features and those that equated sex with extreme violence, so that by the mid-1970s the industry stood at the peak of its success. What awaited it for even greater returns was accessibility to private home viewing by means of the TV videocassette, which in the 1980s would become a staple of adult video stores and bring about an end to the "Adults Only" theater.

## Variations on the Themes of Sex and Violence in the Movies

Urged on by the inroads television had made on it and the threat of competition from the porn movie influx, Hollywood began to invest in its newfound creative freedom by producing both blockbuster movies of general appeal as well as those that incorporated the most graphic elements of violence and sex yet seen in mainstream films. Although the tradition of the musical was reprised in the '60s in three highly acclaimed films—*Mary Poppins*, *My Fair Lady* (both 1964), and *The Sound of Music* (1965), the last half of the decade saw a

Hollywood split between its traditional role of producing up-beat movies for general audiences and those capitalizing on the new license to feature sex and violence that would define the publicity for many an upcoming movie. The year 1967, for example, introduced moviegoers to a barrage of offbeat subject matter they were unaccustomed to seeing: a mother's seduction of her daughter's boyfriend in *The Graduate*, racial violence in *In the Heat of the Night*, and the problems of an interracial romance in *Guess Who's Coming to Dinner?* While the bank-robbing sprees depicted in *Bonnie and Clyde* fomented a pornography of film violence, the following years saw satanic worship as the focus of *Rosemary's Baby* (1968), the drug culture centered on in *Easy Rider*, the lure of wife swapping in *Bob & Carol & Ted & Alice*, and male prostitution in *Midnight Cowboy* (all 1969). The latter film was the first X-rated film to win best picture honors, which in itself was indicative of a growing critical acceptance of Hollywood's daring new filmmaking role.

An influential factor in the new realism was the appearance of a new wave of independently minded film directors in the 1970s, many of them products of university film schools and young enough to have grown up under the visual impact of both movies and television. Such auteurs as Peter Bogdanovitch, Francis Ford Coppola, George Lucas, Martin Scorsese, and Steven Spielberg would become as famous as their stars for the movies they made. Of course, numerous established directors were still around, making groundbreaking films, as Mike Nichols did in *Carnal Knowledge* (1971), Robert Altman in *M\*A\*S\*H* (1970) and *Nashville* (1975), and William Friedkin in *The French Connection* (1971) and *The Exorcist* (1973). Their films not only tackled topics and themes alien to the conventional movie screen, they drew on language and situations that would have outraged censors of Production Code days. For example, *The Exorcist*'s gruesome scenes depicting the effects of satanic possession on a young girl far exceeded the limits of good taste in setting the tone for many such films to follow.

In relishing the cinematic freedom of the new realism, the younger directors turned out movies founded on the daring verve of the youthful eye. In Bogdanovitch's *The Last Picture Show* (1971), the 1950s' setting of a small Texas town and its troubled youth reveals that the past is nowhere near as nostalgic as viewers might like, especially in this film's use of black-and-white photography to depict its bleak, joyless milieu. The exact opposite in mood and atmosphere, but no less effective in capturing the spirit of a time and place, was Lucas's *American Graffiti* (1973). Its teenage character types of the 1950s and early '60s inspired numerous spin-offs in film and TV, as noted, revealing the postmodern penchant for reviving the nostalgic past as real experience.

For that sector of the mediated vision that delighted in being scared out of its wits in the horror film tradition, Spielberg's *Jaws* was the surprise blockbuster hit of 1975. Its story of a giant shark terrorizing a peaceful beach resort showed that, in effect, no setting was immune, no matter how serene or familiar, from the movies' new approach to horror as gripping suspense. This film also revealed Spielberg's growing fascination with fantasized reality. Thus the escapist appeal of the horrific or disastrous event became big box office in the '70s, as revealed in such mainstream hits as *The Poseidon Adventure* (1972) and *The Towering Inferno* (1974), earning producer Irwin Allen the apt title of "Master of Disaster."

During the 1960s the B-type horror film had begun to exploit the new latitude to center on gory violence as escapist entertainment. Leading the way was England's Hammer studio, which revived the Universal monsters introduced in the 1930s—Dracula, Frankenstein, and the Mummy. Indeed, its color productions made any bloody scene appear even more graphic. During this time, too, Roger Corman was still exploring the limits of violence and sex as essential ingredients of the horror film in a prolific outpouring of movies he either directed, produced, or distributed. His ongoing attraction to elaborating on the tales of Edgar Allan Poe showed up in *Tomb of Ligeia* and *The Masque of the Red Death* (both 1964), while Poe disciple H. P. Lovecraft inspired *The Dunwich Horror* (1969). From the late '60s into the '70s the Corman touch was also evident in both his crime and science-fiction films that took advantage of the open license to depict extreme aberrant behavior. In this vein George Romero's low-budget independent production, *Night of the Living Dead* (1968), set a graphic standard for suspenseful horror in old-fashioned black and white by portraying an army of corpses leaving their graves to eat the flesh of the living. In paving the way for plumbing new depths of horror, this film as well as those of Corman foreshadowed the unredeemable "slasher" movies for which *The Texas Chainsaw Massacre* (1974) was the model. Based on a real-life murderous rampage, it earned over 30 million dollars, inspiring two sequels as well as other slasher films like the *Halloween* series that began in 1978. Although they appealed mainly to youthful audiences, mature viewers had to wonder whether these films were a reflection of society's ills or a contributor to rising crime rates. Social critics were also wondering to what lengths the purveyors of escapist horror would go to create the ultimate visual experience of violence for violence's sake.

That realistic violence had become an essential ingredient of mainstream movies was vividly attested to by the brutal knifing Jack Nicholson's nose endures in Roman Polanski's *Chinatown* (1974), whose 1930s setting was filmed in the mold of a gritty private-eye pulp story. But for visually graphic violence the epic Western was now in the running for top honors. And in this category no mainstream Western ever exceeded the explosive punch generated by director Sam Peckinpah's *The Wild Bunch* (1969), a tale about a group of mercenary outlaws shooting up the Mexican border scene during the country's revolution, only to be done in themselves in a veritable bloodbath of gunfire. With criminal violence on the rise in the 1960s and '70s, the bloody, slow-motion shots of this film and the vengeful tribal violence of Francis Ford Coppola's Oscar-winning *The Godfather* (1972) seemed to mirror the malaise of the larger society. Ironically contrasting the close personal ties of the conventional Italian American family with the brutal code demands of the dominant Mafia family, this film was successful enough to produce a sequel in 1974 that, in also winning best picture honors, was as violent, if not more so, as the prequel. Attesting to their popularity and Hollywood's growing obsession for producing money-making sequels, a third film would appear in 1990. By the 1970s, then, film violence had become a proven staple for selling a movie, as it would be throughout the rest of the century.

## THE MOVIES' GRAPHIC LOOK AT SOCIETAL ABERRATIONS, WAR, AND SOCIAL PROBLEMS

Thus, the realistic portrayal of the dark underside of the American Dream and its repercussions became Hollywood's way of making a telling comment about the postmodern condition. Accordingly, *Nashville* (1975) drew on the popularity of country music, whose celebrated performers were now a powerful force in the media culture, revealing them as self-centered representatives of a national malaise. Clearly, the ironic intent of director Robert Altman was to show "just how bountiful and destructive American popular culture is, and how the world of appearances and hype often beguiles and rules Americans."[19] Similarly, Sidney Lumet's *Network* (1976), in its uncompromising indictment of the television industry's rampant commercialism, suggested that its seductive programming was becoming the ultimate reality to the mediated vision. Allan Pakula's *All the President's Men* (1976) revealed that misdeeds in high places were no longer immune from exposure by centering around the determined efforts of two Washington newspapermen to uncover the Nixon administration's Watergate shenanigans. In its expressionistic film noir vision, Martin Scorsese's *Taxi Driver* (1976) dared to look deeper than any of the time's films into the sordid underside of the postmodern scene by focusing on the crime and social deviancy of urban nightlife through the eyes of a violently obsessed cab driver character played by Robert De Niro.

In the 1970s, Hollywood had also begun to draw on the politically divisive implications of the Vietnam conflict as a microcosm of the nation's internal problems. Although the patriotic fervor of World War II was personified in George C. Scott's Academy Award portrayal of the brilliant but eccentric General George Patton in *Patton* (1970), the last truly patriotic war movie in the traditional Hollywood manner was *The Green Berets* (1968) in which John Wayne played a dedicated combat leader in war-torn Vietnam. (While *The Dirty Dozen*, released in 1967, had a World War II setting, its cast of criminal soldiers made it more a paean to violence than patriotism.) But the damning reviews of *The Green Berets* reflected the degree to which the country's attitudes toward war had changed since 1949 when films with World War II settings like *Sands of Iwo Jima* and *Battleground* could still stir an audience's patriotic emotions. In the late '70s two war films revelatory of the polar attitudes of the 1960s appeared. Ironically, Michael Cimino's *The Deer Hunter* (1978), in its emphasis on the working-class values of three small-town army volunteers, implied that fighting in Vietnam was a patriotic duty. Yet certain episodes, particularly that in which the trio, as prisoners of war, are coerced by their Vietcong captors into playing Russian roulette, grippingly reminded viewers of the war's seeming pointlessness. Because of Francis Ford Coppola's growing reputation as a director, his *Apocalypse Now* (1979) was anticipated as the definitive film about America's abortive involvement in the Vietnam War. But the film's plot lapses into metaphorical ambiguity when the transformation of its story into allegorical myth becomes a part of Coppola's method in presenting his vision of war as senseless nightmare.

In numerous mainstream movies of the 1970s, other "wars" of timely social implications were also being waged. Jane Fonda, who was versatile enough to have performed in the title role of the science-fiction spoof *Barbarella* (1968) and as a prostitute in *Klute* (1971), made a film about the dangers of the nuclear power industry in *The China Syndrome* (1979). She was also controversial enough in real life to alienate herself from the American right wing by taking sides with the Communists in the Vietnam imbroglio. But some critics saw her Oscar-winning role as the outspoken call girl in *Klute* as the feminist expression of the 1970s' version of the New Woman, a posture that would define a number of such films about real-world issues during this time. The suddenly single woman's search for a new identity was the theme of *Alice Doesn't Live Here Anymore* (1974) and *An Unmarried Woman* (1978). While the former film dealt with the trials of a widowed wife, the latter explored the ramifications of a common predicament of the time—what life was like after a husband leaves his wife for a new start. Fortunately, films like these succeeded in bringing a fresh approach to situations that were previously tinged with a soap-opera flavor. The reverse situation of a husband whose wife has left him was developed in the highly acclaimed *Kramer vs. Kramer* (1979), which won five Academy Awards, including best picture. This film was notable for its focus on another common problem of the era—the psychological impact of separated parents on young children's emotions. By this time the mediated vision's idealistic conception of the traditional nuclear family that the movies of the 1930s and '40s had portrayed was relegated to the realm of nostalgic recall. Nevertheless, many of these later films, in keeping with the mediated vision's escapist inclinations, strived to depict positive resolutions to what appeared to be hopeless situations.

During this era the African American experience saw few

positive depictions of it in the vein of *The Learning Tree* (1969) and *Sounder* (1972). Ironically, *The Great White Hope* (1970), adapted from Howard Sackler's play based on the controversial boxing career of Jack Johnson, focused on the rampant racism of the century's early years at a time when the civil rights movement was helping sensitize moviemakers to the need for a more central role for blacks. The short-lived "blaxploitation" films of the early 1970s took it upon themselves to depict the black man as either a violent enforcer in the private-eye mode of *Shaft* or a vengeance-bent vigilante-type at war with the white establishment in *Sweet Sweetback's Baadasssss Song* (both 1971). Such films may have been highly popular with black audiences, but they did little to advance the cause of better understanding between the races. Even though the films of Sidney Poitier, ex-football player Jim Brown, and comedian Richard Pryor attracted the white crossover movie audience, these actors' mass appeal lay in their identities as entertainment personalities rather than as crusaders for a cause. Undoubtedly, the serious film portrayal of the problematic side of the black experience was generally considered too publicly controversial for Hollywood to tackle at this time.[20]

As though to counter the feeling of helplessness engendered by the time's rampant violence and societal disorder, a new wave of movies appeared in the 1970s that signaled a return to conservative values. Nevertheless, they sought to fight fire with fire through violent-bent antiheroes who exacted justice by taking the law into their own hands. The image of the solitary avenger of crimes against the individual and society was embodied in the self-motivated figures of Clint Eastwood in *Dirty Harry* (1971) and Charles Bronson in *Death Wish* (1974) as well as these films' sequels. Foreshadowing this kind of film were the violent Westerns Eastwood made for director Sergio Leone in Europe in the 1960s, most typically the first in the series, *A Fistful of Dollars* (1964). (In the '70s Eastwood himself would embark on a successful directorial career.) The revival of ideological values, even at the price of vengeful violence, helped rejuvenate a perplexed mediated vision, which by this time had been inundated by a glut of movies with sensationalized content intended to sell themselves.

Controversial subject matter of a socially disturbing nature was hardly a problem to the underground filmmakers whose private visions inspired avant-garde films on whatever topic or theme they felt so inclined to interpret. Since the war years an experimental, noncommercial movement known as the New American Cinema had been under way. Its anti-Hollywood influence was evident in the early exhibitionist, nonnarrative films of pop artist Andy Warhol, such as *The Chelsea Girls* (1966). Even in his first commercial film *Trash* (1970), Warhol focused mainly on socially transgressive subject matter that appealed more to a cult following than traditional moviegoers. And though this film, with Paul Morrissey as director, utilized conventional Hollywood filmmaking narrative techniques, its shocking content was disturbing to most moviegoers. Indeed, the morally degenerate characters of *Trash* and *Andy Warhol's Bad* (1971), despite the latter's overall comical tone, represent, in their violent reactions, drug addictions, sexual deviancy, vulgar language, and prurient obsessions, the dregs of postmodern society. Yet in portraying them as products of the moral decay and failure of interpersonal relations in the larger urban society, these films stand as ironic comments on it. While the filmmaking freedom of the time was exploited by Warhol, it was taken to more outrageous excesses by director John Waters in his revolting, tasteless *Pink Flamingos* (1973). Such freedom of expression foreshadowed David Lynch's perverse, enigmatic visions in the surrealistic *Eraserhead* (1978) and the voyeuristic obsessions of his *Blue Velvet* (1986), which depicted the degenerating mores of small-town America.

## The Movies' Realistic Approach to Nostalgia as Escapism

In a postmodern atmosphere of growing social problems and moral issues, then, it appeared that filmmakers were cashing in on the aberrations of a world gone morally bankrupt. But there were those who countered this milieu by responding to the mediated vision's nostalgic affinities, returning it to what now appeared to be a more stable past. However, such films seemingly reacted to the notion that "nostalgia has much less to do with the past than the present; it is present anxieties, concerns, and existential discontinuities that evoke and amplify it."[21] In this light, the socially fragmented 1970s certainly contributed its fair share to fostering a pervasive desire to escape the problems of the present.

A number of nostalgically flavored movies of the time were, in fact, direct throwbacks to the past: *Summer of '42* (1971), which depicted a young boy's coming of age in the war years; the previously mentioned *Sounder* (1972), whose story depicted the tribulations of a black sharecropper's family in the 1930s South; *The Way We Were* (1973), a love story starting out in the divisive political milieu of the 1930s; *Rocky* (1976), an updating of the B-movie boxing films of the 1930s. This film's inspirational emphasis on the worth of the work ethic not only helped it capture best picture honors, it resulted in a long-lasting series in the mode of the 1930s programmers structured around a popular central character; and *The Sting* (1973), set in the '20s but whose musical sound track featuring the ragtime compositions of Scott Joplin echoed the spirit of an earlier time.

With continuing technical improvements in the quality of theatrical sound, the new composers of sound track music were highly sensitive to its power to suggest what a particular time and place both sounded and looked like. In this respect, Elmer Bernstein, Jerry Goldsmith, Lalo Schifrin, and John Williams, to name some of the time's more preeminent composers, were kept busy producing film scores that conjured up not only psychological moods but a sense of time and place.[22] Sound track recordings, whose album covers reprised a film's ambience by replicating the poster art that promoted it, ultimately achieved a nostalgic mystique of their own, as, for example, the best-selling album of *Saturday Night Fever* would in returning listeners to the disco-dancing mania of the '70s.

During this time, the movie musical also showed a natural feel for recreating the past. *The Boy Friend* (1971) was based on a 1920s send-up of the musical show. The 1930s setting of *Cabaret* (1972) was prewar Berlin, Germany, while the movie version of Broadway's *Grease* (1978) transported viewers back to the high school days of the 1950s. The past, of course, was a natural source for the musical biopic. *Funny Girl* (1968) focused on the early career of singer-comedienne Fanny Brice, and *Lady Sings the Blues* (1972) depicted the legendary singing career of Billie Holiday. By the late '70s even recently deceased rock singers were being canonized by the movies, as, for example, the tragic careers of Buddy Holley in a 1978 film and Janis Joplin in *The Rose* (1979). Films were also made of Broadway musicals inspired by classic and popular literary sources. *Oliver!* (1968) drew on Charles Dickens's *Oliver Twist* and won best picture. *Hello, Dolly!* (1969) was based on Thornton Wilder's *The Matchmaker*, and *Fiddler on the Roof* (1971) found its source in a play based on the stories of Russian Jewish family life by Sholem Aleichem. In 1974 Hollywood fittingly drew on its own nostalgic repository for musical material when the feature film *That's Entertainment* appeared as a memorable compilation of clips from all the notable MGM musicals that had been made since the advent of sound. Its popularity warranted a sequel in 1976 with added scenes from comedies and dramatic productions.

The movies' longtime attraction to romantic sentiment ran the gamut from the tragic young romance situation of *Love Story* (1970) to Neil Simon's comic takeoff on urban romance in *The Goodbye Girl* (1977) and Woody Allen's semiautobiographical approach to it in *Annie Hall*, winning him Oscars for 1977's best film, best original screenplay, and best director. As Allen's biggest success to date, it relied on numerous filming devices to enhance the film's character development. Indeed, daring experimentation would become a hallmark of Allen's many ensuing films.[23]

Ironically, this time of creative freedom also saw the nostalgic appeal of traditional movie genres satirized through off-color humor, as Mel Brooks's *Blazing Saddles* and *Young Frankenstein* (both 1974) did to the Western and the horror film respectively, and *Animal House* (1978), to the college life film. The mysterious power of certain films to achieve nostalgic cult status, as many had by this time, was typified in fans' ongoing allegiance to *The Rocky Horror Picture Show* (1975). Based on a British rock opera, it was a hybrid musical send-up of the horror, science-fiction, and teen-rock genres. Astonishingly, this movie's cult following grew to the extent that a national ritual of audience participation began to express itself at regularly scheduled midnight showings.[24] Although such an appreciative response seemed to echo the communal spirit of the 1930s' moviegoing experience, spontaneous individual reactions to particular scenes by members of the cult audience obviously reflected an enduring familiarity with the film's offbeat plot.

## THE ROLE OF SPECIAL EFFECTS IN FILM FANTASY

In 1977 two mainstream films that charged the science-fiction genre with a fantasized realism not only garnered critical acclaim but won over both young and older audiences in the process. Steven Spielberg's *Close Encounters of the Third Kind* and George Lucas's myth-inspired *Star Wars*, through their use of the latest advances in special effects, or what would soon be termed computer-generated imagery (CGI), also achieved blockbuster status among the decade's top-earning films. Of course, special effects had been an integral part of filmmaking from the beginning, but the SF film, in particular, was highly dependent on such technical enhancement in its attempt to transcend the limitations of the immediate physical world and project its subject matter as credible reality. A significant breakthrough occurred in 1966 when the producers of *Fantastic Voyage* utilized the latest film technology to create a vivid sense of reality in a bizarre plot that sent a miniaturized team on a special mission into the inner world of the human body. *Close Encounters* and *Star Wars* were even more revolutionary in their uses of special effects to transform fantasy into reality. In fact, the most recent advances in the developing technology of computerized visual effects were evident in the former film's spectacular final episode that centers on contact with a gigantic alien spaceship, whose human cargo resolves a mystery from the past, and in *Star Wars*' realistic portrayal of spaceship battles that far surpassed the obviously staged scenes of the 1930s' *Flash Gordon* serials. Both films were nostalgic reminders of the mediated vision's sense of the past: *Close Encounters* in its debt to the UFO mania of the 1950s and *Star Wars* in its revival of the pulp magazine, comic book, and movie-serial SF conventions that featured spaceships and robots.[25]

CGI breakthroughs would be a major reason for the movies' growing attention to the SF genre as a serious creative form of blockbuster appeal, especially after the reception of two 1968 films: *2001: A Space Odyssey*, which took viewers on a visionary journey into the far reaches of space, and *Planet of the Apes*, whose unique plot dealt with a future world dominated by a simian race. Its box-office success would spawn a long series of sequels. Two other prime examples of the movies' effective use of advances in computerized technology also reflected the 1970s' postmodernist affinities for nostalgia and fantasy: the remake of the original 1933 production of *King Kong* (1976) and the first in a series of films about comic book superhero Superman in 1978. Even though the later *King Kong* fell short of matching the mythic qualities of the original, its superior special effects were evident in the more realistic movements of the giant ape in comparison to the jerky stop-action cinematography of the original. Prior to *Superman the Movie*, Hollywood had always resorted to a camp manner in bringing a comic book hero to the screen, a method that appealed mostly to a juvenile audience. However, this production, in its overall impact, was recognized as a unique achievement in presenting a fantasy character as a real person. And because of its controlled use of visual effects, particularly in the Superman character's flying sequences, this film won an Academy Award. As a box-office success, too, a sequel was naturally in the offing.

Through the realistic enhancement of special effects, the movies now had the power to transform the most fantasized subject matter into an utterly convincing, immediately realized sense of reality. Accordingly, the years ahead would see the revival of the past's fantasized icons become big business, as not only the movies but the print media, radio, recording industry, television, and other forms of the media culture continued to mine America's nostalgic heritage in response to the mediated vision's identification with the past as a way of breaking down the boundaries between it and the present.[26]

### ANIMATION RESPONDS TO THE CHALLENGE OF NEW FRONTIERS

As the animation studios were now opting for TV programming or feature-length cartoons, the traditional cartoon short, whose complementary use of sound and color had made it an integral part of movie programming since the 1930s, had practically disappeared from it by the late '60s. However, when the team of David DePatie and Friz Freleng created an anthropomorphic character who performed to Henry Mancini's music for the title credits of the feature film *The Pink Panther* (1963), its reception was popular enough to appear in a series of cartoon shorts, the first of which won an Oscar in 1964. But even as an exception to the demise of theatrical cartoon characters, the Pink Panther soon lost its novelty, informing the animation people that their real future lay either in TV production or a field previously considered too financially risky by most animation studios—the feature-length cartoon.

In 1968 an animated feature that billed itself as both a visual and an aural experience was the unlikely titled *Yellow Submarine*. Appearing during the peak of the Beatles' rock music and movie popularity, it featured them as cartoon characters in a slight plot structured around their music and a hypnotic array of psychedelic imagery inspired by the rock music scene's poster art style. The film's visual impact was such that it motivated commercial artists to incorporate the psychedelic approach in their advertising tactics.

Taking a cue from the mainstream feature films of the time, animator Ralph Bakshi drew on the new freedom of creative expression to produce the first X-rated feature cartoon—*Fritz the Cat* (1972). Though Bakshi had acquired the rights to artist Robert Crumb's popular underground comix character, Crumb was less than pleased with the results and even sued to have his name removed from the credits. But after such notoriety proved a windfall for Bakshi's daring venture, he produced *Heavy Traffic* (1973), whose characterizations were drawn from the lower depths of the urban drug scene. It too was a financial success, but due in part to those who still contended that, like the comic book, the animated cartoon should be directed primarily at children, Bakshi's reputation soon fell into decline. His major contribution to the art of animation was the realization that an audience for the maturely conceived feature-length cartoon existed, despite any criticism to the contrary.[27]

That Walt Disney's *Fantasia* had been ahead of its time in 1940 was substantiated when its rerelease in 1968 was promoted as "the ultimate visual experience" to audiences now sensitized to the cinematic nuances of the postmodern era.[28] Moreover, by the 1960s–70s the Disney organization had become committed to the production of feature-length cartoons. Although a brief period of indirection followed the death of Walt Disney in 1966 and the release of his last feature, an appealing version of Kipling's *The Jungle Book* (1967), the Disney magic of *The Aristocats* (1970), *Robin Hood* (1973), and *The Rescuers* (1977) boded well for the future of film animation, especially with the ongoing advances in computerized technology that presaged an era of more productive, rapid output. As though anticipating such a time, Disney himself had reminded his staff as early as 1940: "How very fortunate we are as artists to have a medium whose potential limits are still far off in the future; a medium of entertainment where, theoretically at least, the only limit is the imagination of the artists."[29] Indeed, the combination of undaunted imagination and new technology would enable Disney animators to provide the mediated vision an ongoing output of wondrously fantasized viewing experiences in the years ahead.

## The Movies' Ascendancy in American Culture

Echoing the nostalgic wave of the 1970s was a widespread fascination with Hollywood's storied past, as expressed in an endless run of books about the studios themselves, the directors, the genres, and celebrated stars' careers. With in-depth academic studies about film starting to appear regularly, colleges and universities began to incorporate courses of cinema study into their curricula.[30] Soon, the advent of cable TV would find niche channels not only airing many of Hollywood's classic movies but offering prime-time specials about the influential role of film, as well as that of its directors and performers, in American media culture. The respectability that television accorded the movies was yet another postmodern sign of a mass medium attending to a popular subject area in a way that high culture subject matter used to be attended to. Although such critical attention would continue throughout the rest of the century, television's intent of offering old feature films would serve mainly as an escapist viewing experience that offset the growing attention to reality-based programming, the latest trend in TV's natural inclination toward portraying a sense of the immediate.

## Television Establishes Its Central Role in Media Culture

By the mid 1960s, television viewing had entrenched itself as an integral part of family life, extending from the daytime children's programs to adult prime-time fare that had morphed into a deluge of escapist series programs inspired by the time's popular diversions. The fantasized realism of the James Bond spy thriller, for example, resulted in *The Man from U.N.C.L.E.* (1964–68), as well as a satirical spoof of the espionage genre in a popular sitcom called *Get Smart!* (1965–70). But the cold war spy drama that made a bigger impact on viewers was *Mission: Impossible*, a fantasized thriller whose suspenseful plots attracted a large following during its run from 1966 to 1973. The year 1966 also introduced Gene Roddenberry's well-crafted science-fiction series *Star Trek*, though its original three-year run hardly revealed any signs of the cult phenomenon it would become in later syndication. The hit fantasy series in 1966 was a camp version of comic book hero Batman and his young sidekick Robin. Scheduled twice weekly, *Batman* enjoyed prime-time popularity through utilizing the comic book's standard visual devices and the appearance of numerous name actors given free reign to ham it up in their roles as comic book villains.

However, the soap opera's vicarious take on real-life problems came to prime-time TV in 1964 when the socially devious characters from the small-town exposé novel *Peyton Place* materialized in a series that grew popular enough to appear thrice weekly. By this time, too, the daytime TV soap opera had transitioned into the compelling installments of *The Secret Storm*, *As the World Turns*, and *All My Children*. In its intent of depicting life as a daily round of confronting both personal and interpersonal problems, the soap genre was now captivating its mostly female viewers through an increasing emphasis on formally taboo topics and situations treated more candidly than radio ever had. Thus, subject matter that ranged from sexual problems and drug addiction to abortion and alcoholism, as rendered by programs like *Days of Our Lives* and *The Young and the Restless*, were current enough for many viewers to perceive these series' memorable characters as real-life people whose trials and problems were common to the postmodern scene as well as their own lives.

At the time, children were kept fairly well insulated from such issues and concerns by daytime programming that ranged from the instructive fantasy of *Captain Kangaroo*, whose long run lasted from 1955 to 1982, to the minimalist animation of the Saturday morning cartoon shows featuring anthropomorphic animals and comic book superheroes. Ironically, the cartoon shows' fantasized violence drew criticism from some quarters and even a concerted movement to suppress it. Since the late '60s the Public Broadcasting System

(PBS) had been striving to counteract TV's commercialized offerings in quality programs like *Mister Rogers' Neighborhood* (1966) and *Sesame Street* (1969). That an entertainment mode was integral to these shows' educational mission, though, was exhibited in the former's low-keyed manner of genial host Fred Rogers offering his simple object lessons about nurturing good social relationships and the latter's even more entertaining approach, as typified in the humorous roles of Jim Henson's Muppet characters.

At night, other than what their parents allowed them to watch, children's viewing was mainly limited to early evening series like *Flipper* (1964), which centered on a dolphin as a lovable Lassie-type character. Programs that first appeared during this era, whose appeal was to child and adult alike, were Walt Disney's *Wonderful World of Color*, the annual presentations of MGM's classic 1939 movie *The Wizard of Oz*, and the animated versions of Charles Schulz's *A Charlie Brown Christmas* and Dr. Seuss's *How the Grinch Stole Christmas*. Overall, the time's programming for children, like that for adults, was characterized by an overabundance of escapist fantasy, which, social critics charged, was acculturating both youths and adults into a mass-mediated, fantasized perception of life and their expectations of it. Such an outlook was clearly evident in the proliferating situation comedies of the 1960s.

As the most popular fantasized genre during this time, the sitcom structured around the nuclear family or social group resulted in some unique variations. To satirize the goings-on in the contemporary home, *The Munsters* and *The Addams Family* (both 1964–66) derived their caricatures of family types from, respectively, the classic horror films and the black humor of Charles Addams's popular panel cartoon characters. While *Gilligan's Island* (1964–66) centered on the comical social adjustment of a motley group of shipwrecked misfits, *Green Acres* (1965–71) reversed the premise of *The Beverly Hillbillies* (1962–71) by casting Eddie Albert and Eva Gabor as big-city sophisticates confronting the unfathomable ways of rural life in managing a farm. Clearly, escapist fantasy was the prime factor in this kind of programming, conditioning viewers to avoid the real problems of the turbulent '60s and identify with the minor problems that its characters encountered as well as anticipate their familiar routines in overcoming them.[31]

Although the time's sitcom featured a wide range of characterizations, the one feature that remained constant was the predictability of its plot, which provided viewers escapist comfort in the knowledge that no problem was too big it couldn't be resolved by the end of a half-hour program. Reminiscent of the seemingly pleasant times that inspired them, many of these programs would resurface in later years as nostalgic reruns. However, some programs' attention to real-life issues and concerns, such as a single foster parent's social adjustments in *Family Affair* (1966–71), foreshadowed the reality-based sitcom of the 1970s.

Even though the real world of criminal activity was the source for law enforcement drama, its attempt to solve a case by show's end provided viewers a compelling brand of escapism through realistic characterizations and up-to-date police methodology. Late '60s series like *Ironside*, *Judd for the Defense*, and *Hawaii Five-O* prefigured the even more realistic programming of this genre in the '70s. The appearance of *Marcus Welby, M.D.* in 1969 also foreshadowed the real-world realism of the hospital drama. The fact that its star, longtime movie actor Robert Young, had graduated from the 1950s' sentimental family sitcom *Father Knows Best* to the more demanding role of a general practitioner attested to television's ongoing shift to more realistic programming. Basking in the popularity of *Gunsmoke* and *Bonanza* were such adult Western series as *Wagon Train*, *Rawhide*, and *The Virginian*, whose outdoor realism was now enhanced by the mobile film unit. But before the TV Western began to fade, it also experimented with the time's fantasy obsessions in *The Wild, Wild West* (1965–69), a popular series whose lead characters were exposed to the anachronistic gadgetry utilized by their outlaw adversaries.

## THE RISE OF THE CELEBRITY PERSONALITY AND SATIRICAL COMEDY

Television's receptivity to certain personalities from various fields of entertainment was revealed in the variety show format. While singer/actor Dean Martin's laid-back, personable manner won him a prime-time slot in 1965, comedienne Carol Burnett was awarded her own show in 1967. In it, she and her talented cohorts carried on the 1950s' satirical skits tradition of *Your Show of Shows* that had featured the hilarious team of Sid Caesar and Imogene Coca. Both Doris Day and Dinah Shore, who were well established in records and the movies, also enjoyed popularity on their own TV shows, especially Shore, who was a longtime fixture in both daytime and prime-time programming. Since the kind of informality she evinced was the hallmark of the variety show host, the personality who fit into this mode usually endured, as did Perry Como, Andy Williams, and Bob Hope. They adapted easily to the demands of TV because their humanized approach made viewers feel they were welcome guests on their shows. Conversely, many of the big stars of popular music and the movies discovered their personas were more suited to periodic television specials, as were, for example, Frank Sinatra, Judy Garland, and Jerry Lewis.

In 1967, an omen of things to come was *The Smothers Brothers Comedy Hour* with their stars' edgy blend of folk music and topical satire, but which by later standards would seem quite tame. Even though the show's flouting of mainstream values found a receptive younger audience, its practice of satirizing serious subject matter as entertaining fare made the network bosses nervous enough to cancel it in 1969. Two other shows unlike anything before them in their format of catering to topical humor was an American version of the British *That Was the Week That Was* (1964–65), whose main intent was to poke fun at anything of a politically newsworthy note; and *Rowan & Martin's Laugh-In* (1968–73), a highly popular weekly comedy show whose fast pace incorporated a barrage of one-liners and satirical skits staged by both its cast and celebrity guests in one-shot appearances. The following year saw a rural version appear in *Hee Haw* that attested to the widespread appeal even barnyard humor could generate in this unique format. In fact, both these shows' fast-cut production technique was a portent of TV's future programming style.

## CULTIVATING BROADER CULTURAL HORIZONS FOR THE MEDIATED VISION

During the '60s the dramatic production featuring name actors renewed its allure as a television attraction in such vehicles as the 1955 Broadway hit *Inherit the Wind* (1964), starring Fredric March; Arthur Miller's *Death of a Salesman*, in which Lee J. Cobb reprised his Broadway role; and Tennessee Williams's *The Glass Menagerie*, starring Shirley Booth (both 1966). In 1967, George C. Scott was featured in Miller's *The Crucible*, while 1968 saw George Segal appear in John Steinbeck's *Of Mice and Men*. PBS also furthered its cultural role when it aired the well-received BBC serialization of John Galsworthy's *The Forsyte Saga* in 1969–70. Along with advancing technology, the television tradition of staging both popular and classic drama would continue to find a receptive audience.

That television was offering the mediated vision opportunities to relate to subject matter and events traditionally reserved for elitist tastes was realized in programming like the guided tour of Paris's renowned Louvre art museum in 1964 and a Carnegie Hall concert by pianist Vladimir Horowitz in 1968. The personality of author Mark Twain was brought to life in Hal Holbrook's impersonation of the legendary humorist in *Mark Twain Tonight* (1967). As a reprise of Holbrook's stage version, it came across as ideally suited to television's natural way of humanizing celebrity. The documentary form's appeal to more serious viewers revealed television's natural propensity for visual immediacy through such telecasts as the twentieth anniversary in 1964 of the D-day landing at Normandy with key player General Dwight D. Eisenhower on-site; the life of Michelangelo (1965); the legacy of a nation's culture in *The Italians* (1967); a study of the native African people in the same year; a closeup look at the German nation under Adolf Hitler in *The Rise and Fall of the Third Reich* (1968); and a highly popular series on exploring marine life titled *The Undersea World of Jacques Cousteau* that began in 1968.

The documentary may not have been the most escapist kind of commercial programming for prime-time viewing, but the TV medium, in asserting its natural affinity for making such productions entertaining, achieved many of its finest moments in this format. Notable examples appeared in the output of producer David Wolper whose documented "specials" were aired in prime-time slots. In fact, Wolper's versatility was such that he also produced movies for TV, fictional series, and historically based miniseries derived from timely subject matter, a genre he inaugurated in 1977 with his twelve-hour adaptation of Alex Haley's nonfiction novel

*Roots*, whose sociocultural import is discussed below.[32] But as far as attention to contemporary problems and issues was concerned, the latest trend was toward the compelling "news magazine" format of CBS's *60 Minutes* (1968). Looking to attract a larger share of the TV audience, PBS assumed an even bigger role in programming educational fare of a cultural, humanistic nature. Both the docudrama of commercial TV and PBS's educational programming would play significant roles in offering the mediated vision informative, entertaining opportunities to broaden its cultural horizons.

Live televised entertainment also maintained its visual dominance in the media culture through an ever-expanding range of programming. In 1964, after viewers saw Ed Sullivan's show introduce the touring British rock group the Beatles, American popular music would never be the same. The event's influence was such that sales of Beatle recordings zoomed to the top of the charts. Though at the time no one could have foreseen the kind of cultural impact this group would ultimately achieve, an early sign was the many American rock bands that patterned themselves after their British counterpart, including one intentionally organized to appear in a TV sitcom called *The Monkees* (1966–68). In functioning as a bridge between the counterculture and the mainstream, several of this band's songs even became number one hits.

TELEVISION'S NATURAL ATTRACTION TO
REALITY-BASED PROGRAMMING

From its start, television's informal manner was highly receptive to the guest interview show, as evidenced in the early 1950s by the programs of singer Kate Smith and film star Faye Emerson. By 1966, the more topically derived approach of host Mike Douglas's syndicated daytime talk show would become the model for many future programs. Among the most influential was Phil Donahue's that started out in 1967 centering on significant issues of the times. Merv Griffin, another talk-show pioneer, was awarded a late-night slot in 1969, but when NBC's Johnny Carson, stationed opposite Griffin's CBS program, proved too formidable a competitor, it was canceled in 1971. Basically, the guest interview show at this time functioned as an entertaining exchange between host and guest that, in its main purpose of humanizing celebrity personalities, made them appear more accessible to the mediated vision. However, as postmodern society continued to diverge into subcultural sectors in the 1970s, viewers would become increasingly subjected to guests of socially marginal reputations and even subject matter of a salacious nature.

During the last half of the 1960s, national news coverage was focusing on what many viewers considered a senseless, morally demeaning conflict in Vietnam, especially when they found themselves witnessing the real-world horrors of war in the confines of their own living rooms. It was a viewing experience that sharply contrasted with the generally escapist programming TV had conditioned them to. Closer to home, the medium was also depicting the aftermath of race riots and the student unrest on college campuses, as well as the repercussions of the tragic assassinations of two charismatic political leaders in 1968, the graphic details of which were presented to incredulous home viewers. By now, the on-site newsmen who covered such events, as well as the network anchormen who managed the nightly news desks, had become familiar faces of national import to viewers. But their candid reportage did little to resolve the volatile issues that were now dividing the country.

For years the networks' morning news shows had been waging a war of their own to gain top ratings, and with their evening counterparts having expanded their programs to thirty minutes, the competition grew even more intense. Anchormen Chet Huntley and David Brinkley (NBC), Walter Cronkite (CBS), and Harry Reasoner (who would join ABC in 1970) modified their primary roles of keeping their viewers informed by interpreting the news as a form of entertainment, motivating each network to add soft news features that enhanced this end.

From a progressive perspective, advances in technology were providing viewers a wider scope on world events. The launches of the Telstar (1962) and Early Bird (1965) satellites not only expanded worldwide communications, they presaged the televised viewing of remote live events of international significance such as the Tokyo Olympics in 1968 that turned the entertaining spectacle of sport into a worldwide accessed happening. During this time, though, nothing surpassed the momentous televised event of watching men walk on the moon after the Apollo 11 landing in 1969. Though the lunar orbit of the Apollo 8 mission in the previous year had transmitted a beautifully clear view of Earth, this latest achievement captured by satellite was a tremendous technological triumph for the United States. It not only fulfilled President John Kennedy's goal of putting a man on the moon by the end of the decade, it expanded upon the longtime dream that heretofore had only been dramatized in the science-fiction realm of media culture. It also provided the mediated vision yet another take on the ever-widening horizons that technological advances continued to create for it.

## THE REAL WORLD'S INFLUENCE ON FICTIONAL PROGRAMMING

By now, the violence and social disruption that television news was depicting as facts of real life were also infiltrating the kinds of fictional programming appearing in prime-time slots. Because these shows, in turn, were seen as potentially harmful influences on the morals of youth and the larger society, such programming was becoming a growing issue of concern, criticized in the manner that media culture had so often been in the past. But as political and societal problems continued to mount during the last half of the 1960s, so their effect on human relationships continued to inspire the content of prime-time dramatic series into the 1970s.

From its start, television, as primarily a home-based medium, had been striving to meet the interests of all age groups across the spectrum of the mediated vision, from its daytime offerings for children to the prime-time and late-night programming reserved for an older, more mature audience. Now, at the beginning of the '70s, dramatic series of social relevance revealed a prime-time trend toward attracting youthful viewers by casting young players in serious, demanding roles. The very titles of certain new shows reflected their intended audiences as, for example, *The Young Interns*, *The Young Lawyers*, and *The Mod Squad*. Other youth-oriented programs like *The Rookies* (1972–76) complemented the growing predominance of law-enforcement series whose violent content also appealed to younger, more impressionable viewers.

Seemingly inspired by an era of rampant urban crime when law and order needed championing was an abundance of older protagonists starring in popular police dramas that appeared throughout the 1970s: *McCloud*, *Cannon*, *Barnaby Jones*, and *Kojak*. While each show had its own special approach to tracking down criminals, the one thing they all had in common that attracted viewers across the board was the offbeat personalities of the title characters and manner in which they operated. Not only did they display the essential heroic qualities their roles commanded but distinct personal idiosyncracies and habits that humanized them in the eyes of their loyal fans.[33]

Thus, TV's realistic manner of delineating character and situation helped turn the business of fighting crime into a highly entertaining viewing experience for both young and older viewers. By 1975, when nearly thirty cop shows vied for attention, the overemphasis on violent content gave rise to the familiar hue and cry that the genre was exceeding the standards of societal propriety. This latest attack prompted TV critic Edith Efron to counter "that the success of the cops-and-robbers shows, like that of all the good-vs-evil shows on the air, is exclusively a function of the *continuing heroes*," pointing out that they were the modern-day heirs of drama's ancient "good-vs-evil" thematic convention.[34] In Efron's eyes the heroic actions of the crime drama's protagonists transcended its violent content, conditioning the mediated vision to accept dramatized violence as a justified expression of law enforcement's dedicated mission. Program sponsors certainly approved, as high audience ratings assured increased product sales. But with big cities being wired for public-access cable television by the late 1970s, uncensored programming of a sexually oriented nature was about to create much more controversy than that stemming from televised violence.

## Nostalgia's Influence on Fantasy-Oriented Programming

No less realistic but more naturally fantasized in intent than the law enforcement series were the melodramatic productions categorized as either adventure or fantasy genres. In 1974 *The Six Million Dollar Man* appeared, a series about a bionically structured character whose comic book inspiration resulted in a whole new adventure trend. In 1976 a female version was demonstrating her unique powers as *The Bionic*

*Woman*, paralleled by a string of comic book superheroic characters like *Wonder Woman* in two series (1975 and '77), *The Amazing Spider-Man*, and *The Incredible Hulk* (both 1978). The movies also inspired such fantasized but short-lived TV science-fiction series as *The Invisible Man* (1975), *Logan's Run* (1977), *Battleship Galactica* (1978), and *Buck Rogers in the 25th Century* (1979). TV even updated the long-running juvenile fiction series of the Stratemeyer publishing syndicate as *The Hardy Boys/Nancy Drew Mysteries* (1977–79). Though this program triggered fond reading memories among older viewers, it failed to meet their dramatic expectations in this updated format. Still, in the ensuing years shows responding to the mediated vision's fascination with fantasized reality would continue to pop up each TV season.

Some new shows revealed that even the problems of real life could be fantasized, given the appropriate setting, as in the romantic affairs initiated and dying romances revived within the cruise-ship milieu of *The Love Boat* (1977–87). As a one-hour sitcom, its revolutionary format incorporated simultaneous story lines to attract the viewing interests of different age groups. In the process the show's popularity and TV's promotional power provided a tremendous boost to the cruise-line business. Similarly, the multiplots of *Fantasy Island* (1978–84) were structured around situations that helped spark new romances or rekindle the ardor of relationships on the wane, as each episode opened with the arrival of its principals at an isolated tropical island setting where their host and his cohort devised ingenious solutions to their guest's personal problems.

Television, like the movies, not only resurrected the media culture's iconic characters from the past but created new subject matter that mirrored the mediated vision's nostalgic love affair with the past. Although *The Waltons*, which lasted from 1972 to 1981, took viewers back to the bleak Depression years of the 1930s, it did so in a highly inspirational manner. Indeed, its rural setting and emphasis on the worth of family values in confronting the problems of the time were warmly appealing to the mediated vision's conservative outlook. Another long-lasting popular series in this vein was *Little House on the Prairie*, which started out on a ten-year run in 1974. As the inspirational source for this program, Laura Ingalls Wilder's books about the hard life of the American frontier responded to the mediated vision's affinity for the past as a nobler time, despite the myriad problems one had to endure.

## SITUATION COMEDY DISCOVERS A NEW SOCIAL REALISM

Although the sitcom maintained its status as the most popular escapist television genre, it was showing signs of a growing real-world awareness. While the long-running success of *Happy Days* (1974–84) emanated from its nostalgic treatment of 1950s youth culture, what really assured its popularity was the introduction of the reality-derived Arthur Fonzarelli character, familiarly referred to by his peers as "The Fonz." As a dropout from conventional society, his counterculture lifestyle, though toned down for the show's young audience, contrasted with its family-values orientation, intimating the social change that was coming over middle-class America. That the family unit was adapting to a more youthful lifestyle was underscored by *The Partridge Family* (1970–74) in its title characters' peregrinations as a rock music group. But a highly controversial show that first appeared in 1971 would transform the conventional family setting of the sitcom into a startling new viewing experience, one that would make the reality of everyday life as entertaining as the most fantasized experience.

Norman Lear, the creator of *All in the Family*, took advantage of the widening breach between the conservative and liberal postures of the 1970s to introduce such taboo issues into this revolutionary sitcom as bigotry, sexism, homosexuality, racism, and intimate marriage problems as well as a variety of other topics heretofore considered unsuitable for a family series. Slow to catch on at first, *All in the Family* soon became one of television's most watched shows. If many viewers failed to see themselves in the bigoted Archie Bunker (Carroll O'Connor), the show's central figure, they could surely envision in him the image of others they knew. Overall reaction to the show ranged from praise that it was a lot like life to criticism that it was too much like life. But David Marc and Robert J. Thompson contended that the series' ultimate success was due to its creator's uncompromising vision: "By consistently embedding authorial advocacy into plot and characterization on [serious] issues . . . Lear helped dispel the belief that situation comedy was an intrinsically superficial form that could only support its own status quo."[35]

The popularity of *All in the Family*, which lasted until 1983, was such that it spawned spin-offs of certain featured players in their own series. Archie Bunker's dim-witted but well-meaning wife Edith (Jean Stapleton) occasionally entertained her cousin Maude Findlay (Bea Arthur), whose liberal feminist views incited such a hilariously frustrated reaction from the ultraconservative Archie that fan response to her character warranted a sitcom of her own. As a result, *Maude* (1972–78) was another big hit that displayed Lear's flair for creating offbeat realistic roles. Although Maude enjoyed a more upscale status in society than the Bunkers, her life was more complicated as she endured such problems as divorce, abortion, and her latest husband's alcoholism. Even the character of Maude's outspoken black maid (Esther Rolle) proved popular enough for her to star in *Good Times* (1974–79), TV's first black family sitcom. Though set in an inner-city housing project, it mainly ignored social issues for the humorous focus of the conventional TV family from a black point of view.

Still another offshoot of *All in the Family* dealt with the social climbing ways of Archie Bunker's black neighbors who ultimately moved to a well-to-do Manhattan address in *The Jeffersons* (1975–85). Throughout the life of this long-running series, successful businessman George Jefferson (Sherman Hemsley), as a black version of Archie Bunker, is afforded the opportunity to express his prejudicial opinions about life in a predominantly white man's world. Ironically, this character's outspoken posture was a salient reason for the show's success, as well as another reason Norman Lear was considered a major acculturating force in tempering white viewers' acclimation to black characterization on television.[36] Offbeat humor was also the basis for Lear's *Sanford and Son* (1972–77), starring longtime black nightclub comedian Redd Foxx. This show was unique in targeting not only whites but ethnic types for Foxx's put-down barbs of which he was a master.

In *One Day at a Time* (1975–84), Lear transitioned back to the white world, only this time to focus on the real problems of a divorced, single workingwoman's challenges in raising two teenaged daughters. In confronting her situation with tact and humor, this show's lead character became a role model for many women facing similar difficulties, which undoubtedly accounted for its wide appeal. An earlier popular sitcom, *The Mary Tyler Moore Show* (1970–77) created by James L. Brooks, also centered on a woman character as a kind of role model in its well-crafted plots about the ups and downs of a young, single career woman. As Mary Richards, the series' lead character, Moore, having made a name for herself in *The Dick Van Dyke Show*, was provided ample opportunity to hold her own as a high-spirited female in the male-dominated workplace of television journalism. As another seminal "family" source of characters for spin-off programming, one of the more appealing was *Rhoda* (1974–78), which focused on Mary's girlfriend (Valerie Harper) who returns to her native New York City to become a career woman. Also produced by Brooks, it was daring for its day in allowing for a divorce soon after Rhoda's marriage. By the time *The Mary Tyler Moore Show* signed off, having captured a record number of Emmys, even Mary's boss Lou Grant, played irascibly but likably by Ed Asner, had gone through a divorce himself and wound up in a sitcom of his own. *Lou Grant* (1977–82) returned its title character to the world of newspaper journalism at a time when television was making significant inroads on its waning fortunes but with no less a feel for the day's timely issues that the sitcom now related to.

Even a Korean War setting was no deterrent to *M*A*S*H* (1972–83) in demonstrating that well-acted performances inspired by well-written scripts could treat serious topical as well as taboo issues about human relations in a meaningful way. Derived from the 1970 film about an army surgical unit assigned to treat soldiers wounded in combat, the comical interactions of this series' colorful characters arise from their insecure situation, which, in turn, functions as a satirical comment on the seemingly pointless war they had somehow become a part of. A major contributor to the show's irreverent humor was the sexual innuendos delivered by chief surgeon "Hawkeye" Pierce (Alan Alda) who carries on an endless round of flirtations with the unit's nurses. Drawing on sardonic humor as well as offbeat subject matter to make an antiwar comment had never before been done so effectively as it was in this long-running series that won fourteen Emmys.

Similarly, *Barney Miller* (1975–82) was another sitcom that plumbed humor from the most unlikely and frequently absurd situations to make a telling point. As the police captain of a New York City precinct, Barney Miller confronts a weekly parade of society's disturbed and undesirable types brought in by his investigating officers to be charged for various misdemeanors. Yet the human side of each case keeps surfacing in light of Barney's ethnically diverse lieutenants' reactions to their culprits' concerns and interactions among themselves. In the process the lawmen come across as something of a family unit in their disagreements and commiserations. As a sitcom that took both a humorous and empathetic posture toward the petty crimes of the lawbreakers who came within its purview, *Barney Miller* generated wide appeal to the broad range of economic classes who viewed it. As such, it was an exemplary show in appealing to the diverse TV audience that now comprised the spectrum of the mediated vision.

### THE LEGACY OF THE '70s SITCOM AND INTIMATIONS OF ITS FUTURE

In focusing on the differences of opinions among members of a family or a group, the new TV sitcom of the 1970s, with its dominant perspective on the relentless flow of life's unexpected situations, demonstrated that the family unit, or social group, possessed the innate power to deal with the most trying problem. In effect, the sitcom's humorous take on the serious side of life during a time of discontinuity with the past ironically suggested the mediated vision's natural yearning for a revival of the old-time values inherent in strong family relationships. Or as Jeff Greenfield has concluded about the paradoxical nature of this time's sitcom: "It's almost as if television . . . is trying to put back into the American home those qualities that are no longer there."[37]

Accordingly, a high percentage of television's young adult audience of the time could directly identify with the loss of family values, especially those who were products of divorced parents and broken homes. For many, too, having grown up watching the changing face of society through television, the medium, despite its natural attraction as an escapist venue, had conditioned them to a more realistic take on the world. In fact, TV's growing attention to real issues that youth now encountered was a sign of things to come, as intimated in *Three's Company*, a 1977 sitcom that lasted into the '80s. While its farcical plots centered on the then daring situation of two single women and their male boarder (John Ritter) who, by posing as a gay type with no sexual interest in women, is socially accepted as a live-in. Also shocking for its time was the threesome's suggestive banter that helped turn the show into a big hit among youthful viewers, particularly young women who had begun to flaunt their sexually liberated identities. Thus, the changing tastes and values of young adults, as mirrored in the behavior of television sitcom characters at this time, revealed them to be more interested in resolving their own personal needs and desires than standing up for any special causes. In the 1980s this self-focused identity would take on an even more liberal posture.

## THE MOVIES AND TELEVISION DISCOVER COMMON GROUND

The golden age of television drama may have long faded by the 1970s and with it, playwrights like Paddy Chayefsky and Reginald Rose, but Rod Serling, as one of its prolific creative forces, was still being recognized for his unique approach to writing TV drama. In 1970, an offshoot of his pioneering anthology series *The Twilight Zone*, which had ended in 1964, appeared. Although *Night Gallery* was based on similar thematic material, its format of incorporating three separate stories into a single show failed to project the same dramatic impact as its predecessor and soon floundered. To the mediated vision, Serling would be mainly remembered for the unusual endings to his *Twilight Zone* stories, which were among the most imaginative examples of fantasized realism ever to appear on TV.[38] Yet the message each show sought to convey revealed Serling's vision as grounded in real-world issues. After his untimely death in 1975, an endless round of syndicated reruns would serve as a fitting memorial to his sensitizing not only TV drama but movies to the real world as a source for sensational subject matter.

Of course, old B movies of the escapist type had been shown on late-night television since its early years, but by the mid 1960s more A movies were being featured in prime time. And in 1966, after the high viewer ratings of *The Bridge on the River Kwai*, the blockbuster movie of 1957, the networks began earnestly negotiating for other major Hollywood productions. By 1976, when the long-awaited television appearance of *Gone with the Wind* finally came about as a two-part presentation, the movies had become a prime-time fixture.

Earlier in 1969, as a sign of things to come, ABC anticipated the miniseries trend of the 1970s by promoting movies made specially for TV as *The Movie of the Week*. Now, studios that had been filming TV sitcoms and dramatic series saw a whole new field open up in the making of one-shot and multipart dramatic productions as well as the longer miniseries. More attuned to the times were the one-shots, promoted for their mature treatment of controversial subject matter. *That Certain Summer* (1972), for example, dealt with homosexuality, while *Helter Skelter* (1976) documented the Charles Manson cult's murderous rampage. Undoubtedly the most controversial drama to appear during this time was the two-part *Flesh and Blood* (1979) that centered on an incestuous relationship between a mother and her son. But not only the sensationalized subject, now the length of the miniseries had become a factor in keeping viewers, as, for example, the ten-hour-long *Wheels* (1978), based on Arthur Hailey's best-selling novel about the downside of the automotive industry.

Until the appearance of *Roots* (1977), though, TV producers were unsure about the kind of influence the miniseries format would have on the viewing habits of their audience. There had been *Rich Man, Poor Man* (1976), a three-part version of the Irwin Shaw novel, but *Roots* was scheduled to run over eight consecutive evenings. There was also a question about how its subject matter would be accepted. With the brutal slave trade's role in supplying the early agrarian South its essential labor needs as a background, author Alex Haley's book had traced the history of his family from its African origins through bondage in slavery to its freedom following the Civil War.

However, any concerns the ABC network had about the series' reception were negated when *Roots*'s overwhelming success not only assured the acceptance of the miniseries format, it revealed television's power to cut across ethnic, class, and cultural lines to get at the truth about how certain long-standing race problems had originated and persisted. Also, the viewing intimacy of a household setting apparently proved a more accommodative theater in which to show such sensitive material. As the most watched production in television history, then, *Roots* inspired a successful sequel in 1979 that carried its characters' story into the next generation. From a sociological perspective, the *Roots* phenomenon had ironically worked to bring together disparate viewpoints on a controversial subject area through a medium devoted primarily to the entertainment interests of American media culture. What the print medium had been doing in intermingling fact and fiction, television had now made even more meaningful to viewers through its power to dramatize historical experience in a visually immediate manner.

## Signs of Television's Future Directions

Truly, the 1970s was a groundbreaking, experimental time for the television industry, an era, in fact, that set a course for the years ahead. Not only did the miniseries prove that it could effectively command viewer interest, the ninety-minute format had now become an accommodative mode for prime-time dramatic productions. To achieve a more intimate sense of audience identification, some sitcom series scrapped the edited enhancement of sound track laughter to film in front of a live audience. Older sitcoms, recouping their worth as residuals, were syndicated as either daytime or late-night reruns. And that durable staple of daytime TV, the quiz/game show, which inaugurated the long-running appeal of shows like *Jeopardy* (1964), *Hollywood Squares* (1966), and *Wheel of Fortune* (1975) during this time, extended its popularity to viewers other than women as syndicated programs that began to fill early evening time slots in the '70s.

As censorship became largely a voluntary matter, the major legacy of the '70s to prime-time programming was a bolder, often defiant approach to controversial subject matter. Bringing the decade to a fitting, if comically outrageous, close was ABC's *Soap* (1977–82), a sitcom that mercilessly satirized the daytime soap opera by exposing viewers to the most shocking matter imaginable at the time (for example, impotence, incest, transsexualism, satanism, etc.). But the show never took itself as seriously as the conservative forces that wanted it boycotted, only to see its ratings rise as a result of their efforts. Even in its comical fashion, *Soap* was evocative of the real-world moral corruption that characterized the plot of a highly popular prime-time program starting up in the late '70s. *Dallas* (1978–91) was a dramatic series structured around a wealthy oil baron's family whose plethora of interpersonal problems revealed self-aggrandizement as a major player. Ironically, the more socially conservative

1980s would see this situation show up in other dramatic series of similar bent.

Other developments also revealed the '70s as a momentous era for television's future. That the black entertainer's identity on TV had evolved into much more than an ancillary role was demonstrated by comedian Flip Wilson's high ratings as the first black to host his own comedy-variety show in the early years of the decade. But this genre, as a leftover from the golden age of TV, was doomed. In fact, by 1979, the cancellation of the long popular *Carol Burnett Show* marked the demise of the comedy-variety show as a TV tradition. Bold new approaches to the genre's comedy element would be explored in the stand-up routines and takeoff sketches featured in a 1975 show called *Saturday Night Live*, which introduced late-night audiences to the zany antics and satirical spoofs engineered by its colorful lineup of countercultural performers.[39] To contend with the weeknight popularity of Johnny Carson on NBC's *Tonight Show*, the other networks kept trying to come up with acceptable competitors, but had little success in emulating Carson's engaging and occasionally risqué style, of which devoted fans had made a nightly viewing ritual.

Weekends continued to be a propitious time for scheduling programs directed at children and sports-obsessed males. To counter a growing backlash arising from the public's realization that cereals were more confectionary than nutritious, the Saturday morning cartoon shows sought to indoctrinate their youthful viewers into a highly commercialized world in which breakfast foods and toy/game products were promoted by animated hucksters who became as popular to children as the characters in the shows they sponsored.[40] Males interested in hunting and fishing as well as the traditional team sports in their seasons were bombarded by regularly scheduled events on both Saturday and Sunday. And in 1970 ABC capitalized on professional football's popularity by presenting games in Monday night prime time. Because of the large amount of revenue to be made, both college and professional sports readily adjusted to TV's demands for scheduling the times of games, especially during prime time when even the traditional daytime game of baseball began appearing.

By the mid 1970s, network news coverage, in its standardized morning and evening time slots, was interpreting the significant news event through reporters' personal interaction with those involved in the event. As a result, the TV reporters and commentators, from those in the field to those who anchored the network news programs, had taken on celebrity status. Such was the case with Walter Cronkite, considered by the political polls to be "the most trusted man in America," and Barbara Walters, who became the first woman network coanchor and later a candid interviewer of celebrities in prime-time appearances. TV news programs also started to supplant the traditional entertainment functions of newspapers and magazines by incorporating features into their format that dealt with such topics as evolving lifestyles, consumerism, and, of course, celebrity interviews. That problematic subject matter categorized as "news" could be made entertaining was demonstrated by CBS's *60 Minutes*, which started out on its long run in 1968 as a prime-time news magazine show.[41] Its investigative reporters developed a forthright journalistic style that made them stars in their own right, as their weekly appearances were highly anticipated by devoted viewers.

Concerning PBS programming, supposedly addressed to more discerning levels of taste, *TV Guide* published an article in 1971 that identified "the affluent, the college-bred and, quite often, the politically liberal" as the major audience of public television.[42] Nevertheless, throughout the decade certain signs pointed to PBS's program fare taking on a more democratic air. Certainly, many parents approved of their children watching a show called *The Electric Company* (1971) that taught reading skills through visual enhancements. In the early 1970s British cultural imports continued to show up, such as the *Civilisation* series, in which Kenneth Clark's scholarly commentary enlightened viewers. But, as noted, the mainstream networks were also presenting programming in a high-culture vein. NBC's *Hallmark Hall of Fame* maintained its role begun in the 1950s with productions of such dramatic classics as *Macbeth* and *Cyrano de Bergerac* in addition to popular musical entries like *Kiss Me, Kate* and *The Fantasticks*. The networks' growing attention to the docudrama also broadened the cultural horizons of the mediated vision in spite of the genre's tendency to alter historical fact. After all, the TV producers reasoned, what they were turning out was not so much education as entertainment for their viewers. Underlying any variations in programming, then, was the subtle notion that the pervasive force of television was creating a democratized synthesis of mass and genteel tastes, as evidenced by the rating responses to prime-time theatrical and cultural programming.

That the autonomous worlds of the movies, theater, and television had overcome their earlier fear of intermedia competition was attested to by the fact that each entity now hosted its own annual awards televison show. Complementing the movies' Academy Awards were the theater's Tony Awards, and television's Emmy Awards that were also highly anticipated events. Though they continued to function independently, these forms' interdependence was reflected in the large number of works that crossed over into each medium of creative expression for reinterpretation. But as to which had the greater capability to respond to a mass audience, television obviously had the advantage, as throughout the 1970s it introduced the various program innovations that would solidify its position as a prominent sociocultural entity. During this time, then, television's network programming, from the purely fantasized to the more reality-based format, had become a powerful force in influencing the mediated vision's perception of life in a postmodern society. By the end of the 1970s, with cable TV on the verge of becoming a nationwide reality and most households wired for access to the televised realm of media culture, reality-based programming was beginning to morph into a new hybrid form of visual escapism. The extent of its sociocultural impact is examined in chapter 3.

## TELEVISION'S NEGATIVE IMPACT ON THE MEDIATED VISION

Even though television had evolved into the most powerful democratizing cultural force in American history, it had also become something of a visual addiction to many viewers, especially the young. Subsequently, numerous studies were beginning to assess TV's adverse effects on children from too much watching, especially its controversial content. Adults, like their children, were also retreating into the narcotic release that TV programming provided. For youth and adults alike, then, the problem that television viewing presented, social critics charged, was that instead of contributing to a more enriched living experience, it was turning many viewers into isolated, inner-directed escapists from the realities of an increasingly complex world. In effect, it was a visual experience that presaged the computerized world of virtual reality, whose inroads would begin to be felt in the 1980s.

## THEATER: A FRAGMENTED MIRROR OF POSTMODERN CHANGE

Playing a dominant part in both the creative inspiration and economic fortunes of the theater were the subversive sociopolitical events of this era that revealed the country as a society of diverse sociocultural identities. Nevertheless, drama maintained its traditional commitment to entertaining audiences even while alerting them to the social and moral problems of the times. Though Tennessee Williams's career began to fade after the success of *The Night of the Iguana* (1961) and its 1964 film version, Arthur Miller strived to add to his reputation with works like *After the Fall* (1964) and *The Price* (1968). These plays' attention to one of Miller's dominant themes—the meaning of individual responsibility in an increasingly disintegrated society, as intimated by the tensions between members of a family or social group—had special significance during this time. And in 1971 *The Price* found a receptive audience as a television vehicle starring George C. Scott—yet another production that affirmed TV's role as an effective cultural medium for dramatic theater. Earlier, Miller himself had tried his hand at writing for the mass media with his screenplay of *The Misfits* (1961), in which his ex-wife Marilyn Monroe was a featured player. From this era to century's end, the prolific Miller would continue to explore the interpersonal failings of individuals subjected to the alienating tendencies of the postmodern condition.

To many, the most influential playwright of this era was Edward Albee. Even had he never written another play, he would have found a lasting place in the annals of American drama with *Who's Afraid of Virginia Woolf?* (1962), discussed earlier. Once again the close relationship between the movies and theater was demonstrated in 1966 with the highly successful film version of the play. Although his reputation declined after the Pulitzer-winning *A Delicate Balance* (1966; film, 1975), he would later regain it by creating highly experimental plays like *Seascape* (1975), which echoed his off-Broadway roots and for which he won a second Pulitzer.

If the failure of interpersonal communication was a major

theme of Albee, it was also integral to the output of the most successful playwright of this era. Neil Simon, whose forte was not serious drama but the comedy of human relations (or non-relations, as some might term it), parlayed his background as a television comedy writer into a long string of hit plays. Beginning in 1961 with *Come Blow Your Horn*, he continued to turn out audience-pleasing productions like *Barefoot in the Park* (1963), *The Odd Couple* (1965), *Plaza Suite* (1968), *The Sunshine Boys* (1972), and even the books for the musicals *Promises, Promises* (1968) and *They're Playing Our Song* (1978). Since many of his works acquired additional popularity as movies, the versatile Simon also tried his hand at screenwriting, resulting in one of his better efforts in *The Goodbye Girl* (1977) despite its penchant for TV sitcom gags. As a master of verbal sparring, Simon placed his characters in situations that foment the antic attempts of each one to gain the upper hand over the other. But in the process they reveal themselves as undeniably human. Simon's unerring instinct for creating plays out of subject matter familiar to the middle-class theatergoer made him the most popular as well as successful playwright in the history of American dramatic comedy. Because of his humanized approach to creating fantasized realism, which found an extended audience in film, Neil Simon was the most popular playwright of American media culture during this time.

However, out of the subversive milieu of the '60s came certain polemically oriented dramatists who were motivated to utilize theater as a platform to protest the time's political vagaries and social injustices. Naturally, the political system was a prime target, as the hawkish administration of Lyndon Johnson felt the satirical sting of Barbara Garson's *MacBird!* (1967) in its none too subtle parallel with the royal machinations of Shakespeare's *Macbeth*. Concerning race problems, the most influential black dramatist was LeRoi Jones, whose rejection of the American value system and culturally separatist stance moved him to adopt the Muslim name Amiri Baraka. His plays, especially the critically acclaimed *Dutchman* (1964), not only served as an embittered statement against the ingrained racism of American society, they inspired other black dramatists to take an agitprop posture in their works. The most notable literary figure to contribute to the movement was novelist/essayist James Baldwin, whose play, *Blues for Mr. Charlie* (1964), drew on the background of the civil rights movement in the South to forge a poignant perspective on the evils of racism, anticipating the plays of August Wilson in the '80s. Howard Sackler, author of *The Great White Hope* (1967), charged his award-winning play with contemporary relevance by basing its protagonist's conflict on the racism that socially defiant black boxer Jack Johnson encountered in the century's early years. After moving to Broadway in 1968, Sackler's commercially successful play also became a hit as a film, starring its lead, James Earl Jones. As yet another of Broadway's offerings promoted as sensational theater fare, this play not only entertained audiences, it reminded them that in a very real sense all was not right in postmodern America.

Though plays with gay themes were now appearing in off-off-Broadway venues, it was not until 1968 that *The Boys in the Band* became the first production about gays to appear on Broadway. In it, author Mart Crowley candidly focused on the lifestyle that male homosexuals daringly pursued in a homophobic society, a subject just then coming out of the shadows. By breaking the comical stereotype of the gay character familiar to entertainment media, Crowley's play portrayed gays as fully realized individuals whose sexual preference was the main difference between them and heterosexuals. Gay theater would develop an even stronger, more sensitive social voice in the AIDS era, culminating in the early '90s in Tony Kushner's Pulitzer-winning two-part production, *Angels in America*. Drawing on elements of myth and fantasy, it explored problems inherent in the American experience that emanated from the AIDS epidemic of the 1980s.

Paralleling these developments was the inception of a feminist theater that would start to flower in the '70s with the advent of numerous regional theaters that served as creative havens for women playwrights. Initially hampered by its lack of talented playwrights, the movement had begun to define itself in the '60s in the output of Adrienne Kennedy and Megan Terry and, by the '70s, in mainstream dramatists like Marsha Norman, Beth Henley, and Wendy Wasserstein. Characterizations varied from the hardened criminal background of Norman's self-divided protagonist looking to forge a new life for herself in *Getting Out* (1978) to the comedic treatment of Henley's and Wasserstein's characters. Prime examples appear in the former's Southern gothic setting of *Crimes of the Heart* (1978) and in the latter's portrayals of college graduates whose frustrated personal goals spark the dramatic conflict of *Uncommon Women and Others* (1977). All these playwrights' women are presented as strivers either searching for a personal identity heretofore denied them by society's sexist demands or looking for a way to transcend the personal insecurities that the circumstances of life have dealt them. During the latter years of the century, Wasserstein would continue to focus on the evolving feminist sensibility as a comedic mirror of not just women's concerns but men's across the postmodern spectrum. Thus, like the socially oriented playwrights of the 1930s, agitprop dramatists of the 1960s–70s, by focusing on the problematic social issues of their times, were motivated to create works that were not only socially relevant but compellingly entertaining.

### Variations in Experimental, Regional, and Musical Theater

Off-Broadway theater, which had originated during 1959–61, initially shunned the commercialism of Broadway by offering alternative or experimental drama performed in the Greenwich Village environs of the Caffé Cino and the La MaMa Experimental Theatre Club. Ironically, by the 1970s, many of the increasingly competitive off- and off-off-Broadway productions had entered the theatrical mainstream as critically and commercially successful enterprises in their own right.

Of course, rebellion and experimentation had characterized the American theater since the 1920s, but in the more liberal atmosphere of the 1960s when censorship restrictions were considerably more relaxed, playwrights and the directors of alternative theatrical groups took full advantage of their new freedom, even exploiting nudity as an antiestablishment statement. But most problems arose when sexual relations were either simulated or actually staged, as they were in *Che!* (1969), an all-nude countercultural production that was closed down on opening night. Nevertheless, Kenneth Tynan's sex revue *Oh! Calcutta!* of the same year managed to dodge the law and enjoy a long run, attracting curious patrons from all walks.

Compared to such daringly innovative off-Broadway production companies as the Circle in the Square and Joseph

Papp's Public Theater, the Open Theatre was the most avant-garde in attempting to subvert traditional theater. Despite these companies' radical stance, though, they afforded many young hopefuls valuable training in developing their talent and skills for acting and playwright careers, not only in theater but television and the movies. Thus, the creative ferment of both the off- and off-off-Broadway scenes in the 1960s and '70s provided career starts for many young actors and rising playwrights whose works were staged there. Among the more notable were Sam Shepard, Lanford Wilson, and David Rabe, whose plays mirrored the time's milieu of social disintegration and interpersonal disconnection.

Although Shepard drew themes from America's heritage of the Western myth and such popular areas of media culture as rock music and movie conventions, his prolific output in the '60s embodied an absurdist view of contemporary life projected in a maze of symbols that mystified audiences. But by the late '70s his dark vision transitioned toward a more comprehensible portrayal of his main theme: the failure of family relationships, as depicted in *Curse of the Starving Class* (1977) and *Buried Child*, the 1979 Pulitzer Prize winner. While the metaphorical implications of the former play's title refers to a family's moral and spiritual disintegration, the latter's challenged audiences to find meaning in a not-so-nostalgic rural setting where a family's reunion is haunted by past sin that suggests the rootlessness of their present lives.

Lanford Wilson, on the other hand, was more direct in creating drama structured around a world of societal misfits searching for some semblance of meaning to their defeated lives. But since the early success of *Balm in Gilead* (1965), which revealed his skill at delineating urban riffraff characterizations, Wilson softened his naturalistic outlook through the comical perspective of *Hot l Baltimore* (1973). In the setting of a rundown urban hotel in which the goings and comings of its transient, low-life residents connote the vagaries of a morally bankrupt postmodern society, Wilson ironically shows how his characters' humorous interaction helps them construct a sense of community as a buffer to their situations. The play was somewhat unique for its time in that it was popular enough to cross over into television as an appealing sitcom.

To David Rabe, the Vietnam War was his objective correlative for dramatizing postmodern social disorientation. In a series of plays in the '70s—*The Basic Training of Pavlo Hummel* (1971), *Sticks and Bones* (1972), and *Streamers* (1976)—Rabe depicts his ill-fated characters' involvement in a meaningless war to suggest the schizophrenic consequences that the war has had on both the American consciousness and conscience. Rabe would expand on this theme and its grim ramifications in his script for the film, *Casualties of War* (1989).

Also in the 1970s, David Mamet came out of Chicago as a new dramatic voice exploring the failure of interpersonal communication and the problems of alienation in postmodern life. The versatile Mamet, who would also make a name for himself as a novelist and television/Hollywood scriptwriter, first attracted attention with his plays, *Sexual Perversity in Chicago* (1974) and *American Buffalo* (1975). Their male-dominated world is comprised of deviously motivated schemers who reflect the loss of communal identity through their scatological language and self-aggrandizing behavior. Exceptionally prolific, Mamet would delve deeper into this theme in the '80s and '90s to achieve greater distinction as a keen observer of the self-indulgent lifestyle in postmodern America.

In the '70s, off-Broadway's alternative concept spread to other hinterland locales around the nation, stimulating the growth of regional theater and the inauguration of a communal interest in theater. In such a creative ferment, inspired efforts thrived, and during the next twenty-five years not a few quality productions made it to the brighter commercialized lights of Broadway. These were plays that ranged from the epical to those that examined the social and political issues of the American experience. Initially, as the productivity of the regional theater system continued to proliferate, theatergoers were offered a wide range of opportunities to access theatrical output. Statistics of the time reveal that by "the end of the 1970s, sixty professional regional theaters were presenting 642 productions of 490 plays in 115 playhouses in fifty-eight cities."[43] The democratization of the theatergoing experience was also complemented by the spread of college/university-based theaters supported by their drama departments. Some even housed their own acting companies whose productions drew high critical praise. By the late '70s, then, Broadway could no longer claim itself as the center of American drama, as many of its productions as well as playwrights had emanated from the burgeoning realm of both alternative and regional theater.

Though musical theater in a traditional vein like *Hello, Dolly!* (1964) and *Mame* (1966) was still enjoying long runs in the 1960s, the plot-oriented influence of Rodgers and Hammerstein had begun to fade, as evidenced by the more thematic or concept emphasis of other long-running productions like *Fiddler on the Roof* (1964), *Man of La Mancha* (1965), and *Cabaret* (1966). In 1967, the controversial *Hair*, billed as the "American Tribal Love-Rock Musical," influenced a number of ensuing rock musicals by mythologizing its conceptual Age of Aquarius. The next year innovative director Tom O'Horgan brought this Public Theater production to Broadway in a dazzling extravaganza of rock music and dance. Derived from youth's drug-influenced counterculture stance in the '60s, *Hair*'s choreographic effects, along with the shock impact of a scene in which the cast appears totally nude, reinforced its theme of universal peace and communal love that the rock music generation ostensibly professed. Similarly, in 1971, O'Horgan staged Andrew Lloyd Webber's *Jesus Christ Superstar* as a biblically inspired production that strived to create a more intimate relationship between performers and audience, a main goal of experimental theater at the time.

Although Michael Bennett's *A Chorus Line* (1975) recalled the backstage movie musicals of the 1930s, it was both the epitome of the concept musical and a production hailed as the decade's "finest musical" and the "archetypal Broadway musical."[44] In deference to a plot, it sought to focus on the integral role of dance in a musical production as performers audition for a place in its choreographed sequences. This kind of musical theater, by integrating the key components of music and dance, had now become a "musical" in both its purest form and truest sense, thus reinforcing the role of the director as choreographer. Of course, the composer-lyricist in the musical concept mode also played a major part, of which the time's most productive was Stephen Sondheim who, with director Harold Prince, produced such well-received shows as *Company* (1970) and *A Little Night Music* (1973).

Many of this era's musical productions generated a nostalgic aura, seemingly in escapist reaction to the time's tumultuous milieu. *No, No, Nanette* (1971) revived the 1920s' original show that had made tap dancing the rage. *Grease* (1972) was inspired by the youth spirit of 1950s rock 'n' roll, and the all-black performers of *The Wiz* (1975) forged a rock version of

*The Wizard of Oz.* While *Bubbling Brown Sugar* (1976) echoed the Harlem lifestyle of the 1920s and the black musical revues of that time, *Ain't Misbehavin'* (1978) was a loving tribute to Fats Waller's unique piano stylings.

## THE THEATRICAL LEGACY OF THE 1960s–70s

Like other entertainment forms attempting to attract audiences in an increasingly competitive time, the theater was compelled to relate to a wider diversity of subject matter, particularly as the media culture began to reflect the special interests of the socially diverse groups that now comprised it. The highly stylized artwork for the posters designed to promote theatrical productions served as visual reminders of this trend. Prominently placed in New York subway stations and airports where thousands of commuters and travelers viewed them daily, the visually appealing theatrical poster publicized the sensitive subject matter of such plays as *Equus* (1974) and *The Elephant Man* (1978), as well as that inspired by the comic strips of media culture like *Peanuts* in *You're a Good Man, Charlie Brown* (1967) and *Little Orphan Annie* as *Annie* (1977). Some posters even evoked the nostalgic aura of past artistic tastes in the art nouveau style for the musicals *Godspell* and *Follies* (both 1971) and the art deco manner for *Sugar Babies* (1979). In addition, the distinctive stylings of such artists as Edward Gorey and Maurice Sendak helped make the Broadway poster an art form unto itself.

The theater's freedom of social expression, afforded both in language and in manners during this period, extended its irreverent influence to other theatrical forms of entertainment and social behavior. The solo theater of nightclub standup comedy provided performers the self-appointed prerogative to say whatever they wanted, as long as their routines generated laughs. The off-color words fearlessly voiced by stand-up pioneer Lenny Bruce at the risk of arrest, the racially derived humor of black comics Redd Foxx, Dick Gregory, and Richard Pryor, and the self-confessional monologues of Bob Newhart and Woody Allen would lead to the "subversive," reality-based humor of the 1980s and '90s. Preparing the way, television introduced the media culture to a wide assortment of comics whose styles ranged from the social satire of Mort Sahl, George Carlin, Jonathan Winters, Bill Cosby, and Phyllis Diller to the Jewish put-down brand of humor practiced by Myron Cohen, Alan King, Jackie Mason, Henny Youngman, and Don Rickles. Anticipating the censorship freedom of cable TV, stand-up comedy ironically offered audiences a unique way to escape by laughing at the real-life personal foibles and tensions from which this kind of humor was derived.[45]

The sexual freedom that triggered the nudity phenomenon of the late 1960s' musical theater soon found itself replicated in the appearance of topless waitresses in bars, nightclubs, and even restaurants. In the wake of disco dancing's popularity, numerous topless clubs across the country offered the erotic sight of seminude go-go girls dancing in elevated cages as strobe lights highlighted their gyrations. Concurrently, the male obsession with oversized female breasts resulted in such variant types of overt display as topless girl bands, wet T-shirt contests, and even wrestling matches in which contestants competed in a variety of substances, from mud to Jell-O. Challenging the limits of the law in cities like New York and Los Angeles were peep shows featuring the erotic gyrations of nude women and even staged sex acts that offered the ultimate in voyeuristic entertainment.

But as jaded attitudes evolved during this era, live variations on sexual themes either faded away or adapted themselves to the fads of the times. By 1979, equal time for women to savor their sexual freedom was answered by a Hollywood nightclub called Chippendales where a cast of male strippers catered exclusively to a female audience. Undoubtedly, the most popular form to survive the era was the so-called "gentlemen's club" where in one night a favorite female exotic dancer could make more in tips than her ancestral sister in burlesque made in a week's salary. As it had since the penny arcade peep shows of the 1890s, covert sexuality would continue to find more overt ways to express itself to that sector of the media culture that had become accustomed to the concept of fantasized sex as theater.[46]

## ONGOING SPECIALIZATION TRENDS IN PRINT MEDIA

That the media culture now reflected a nation of spreading subcultures in the 1970s was attested to by the multitude of new mass-distributed magazines directed toward special interest audiences. In the early part of the decade, two publications appeared that were timely harbingers of these type magazines' future. In responding to the feminist movement's militant stand, editor Gloria Steinem's *Ms.* found a receptive audience of women in 1972 who now saw themselves performing more significant societal roles than just that of housewives or sex objects.[47] Two years later, the Time corporation introduced a democratized pictorial weekly called *People*. Displayed at supermarket checkout counters along with the usual array of tabloids, *People* dealt mainly with the mediated vision's perennial fascination with celebrity culture. Through articles and photographs focusing on the fortunes and misfortunes of both the well-known and heretofore unknown, it proved to be a highly profitable venture. Thus, the success of both *Ms.* and *People* reinforced the notion that publications dealing with (1) special causes and (2) subject matter of current appeal had a relatively good chance of making it in the risky business of magazine publishing.

Of course, the special interest magazine was hardly new to the mediated vision, as typified by older periodicals that had continued to publish since their inception—from the venerable *National Geographic* to the irreverent *Playboy*. Even though these publications also carried articles of general interest, they succeeded mainly because of their editorial postures that appealed to a select readership, and therein lay the challenge to the success of any new special interest publication. In offering targeted readers what they wanted, specialty magazines provided them the opportunity to assume a personal identity in a growing bureaucratized society that seemed bent on denying one this end. Accordingly, by the end of the 1970s the specialty magazines mirrored the nation's subcultural diversity as comprised largely of those who, in pursuing their own interests, looked to cultivate a stronger sense of self, hopefully to avoid postmodern uncertainties. Now the diverse sectors of the media culture saw the publishing industry quick to respond to such subject matter as celebrity gossip, travel, sports, hobbies/handicrafts, sexual fitness, and even a pervasive nostalgia for the memorabilia of an idealized past.

## MAGAZINES' FASCINATION WITH NOSTALGIA

That a nostalgic mood pervaded the 1970s was yet another sign of the postmodern escapist posture emanating from the need to transcend the discontents of the present. According to a 1971 *Time* essay that posited reasons for the era's nostalgic obsessions, the mediated vision, in selecting only what it liked about the past, helped explain nostalgia's natural function in reviving it, either by fantasizing or mythologizing its appeal.[48] In this light, the nostalgic mood of the '70s was strong enough to inspire the revival of *Life* in a special-issue series, beginning with its appearance in 1978 as a downsized monthly. Both the defunct *Liberty* and the *Saturday Evening Post* (the latter had succumbed in 1969) were resurrected in 1971 with reprints of articles and features that had appeared in their heyday. *Liberty* replicated the artwork of its old covers in this latest venture, while the *Post* drew on its repository of Leyendecker and Rockwell covers for internal reproduction. Nostalgia even inspired these publications to reprint old-time ads in their vintage look, thus reminding the mediated vision of a quality item's longevity in the consumer scene. The comment of a reader in its letters column (Summer 1971), thanking the editor for reviving the *Post* as "part of a world that too many of us thought no longer existed," revealed the nostalgic side of the mediated vision as very much alive.

The obsessive quest to rejuvenate the past was also apparent in numerous short-lived publications of lower circulation. *Nostalgia Illustrated*, for example, featured a potpourri of articles and photographs about old movies and their stars, sports heroes of the past, collectible toys/games, memorable events, and reprints of old-time comic strips, all of which the magazine billed as "The Pleasures of the Past." That these nostalgic "pleasures" had approached the level of myth was exemplified by the growth of fan cults as well as the proliferation of one-shot publications and fanzines that attended to their special interests.

With the related trend toward collecting memorabilia also in full swing by the 1970s, the antique and collectible journals would promote this activity as a strong cultural force the rest of the century. Then, too, the media's ongoing attention to the spell of the past in a multitude of topical books and television specials offered the mediated vision another alternative for temporary release from current realities as well as a buffer to future concerns, looming ever more complex and threatening. Since the late 1950s, even the historically oriented *American Heritage* journal, recognizing the importance of social history in explaining the past's relevance to the present, had published numerous nostalgically inspired essays.[49] Thus, by fostering a return to what was once familiar terrain, nostalgia became a democratizing force in blurring the mass and elitist perspectives of the mediated vision.

## SEX AS A POPULAR MAGAZINE TOPIC

Although other specialty magazines of this era attended in part to nostalgic subject matter, their overall emphasis was on more immediate ways to escape the concerns of the present. Toward this end *Playboy* became a valid social indicator, rising to a peak monthly circulation in 1972 of seven million copies. While its sophisticated approach to sex was meant to appeal to the reader who shunned conventional male sporting activities for the urbane life of a "swinging" bachelor, a large segment of this subculture longed for a magazine with an earthier perspective on erotic subject matter. By the late '60s the trend toward more graphic expression in the print media escalated with the advent of *Penthouse*, which publisher Bob Guccione had started in England on a shoestring budget. As noted earlier, *Playboy*'s success spawned dozens of men's magazines that had been appearing since the 1950s—all offering a bountiful pictorial parade of undressed women in provocative poses. But *Penthouse*, in a 1970 issue, dared to display the first mass-circulated magazine photograph of a model's pubic hair area, instigating a competitive war between *Playboy* and *Penthouse* of full-frontal nude foldouts. But the publication that made a fetish of raunchiness in magazine erotica appeared in 1974 with the first issue of *Hustler*. Its tastelessness would involve renegade publisher Larry Flynt in a controversial round of bouts with both his competitors and state/community laws on obscenity. Even so, those who looked for escape in print-media sex were well rewarded during this exploratory time of the erotic magazines' attention to sexual explicitness.[50]

Attention to women's sexual interests found a prominent outlet when editor Helen Gurley Brown transformed the once-staid women's journal *Cosmopolitan* into both an authoritative source of sexual know-how for the single career woman and a highly prosperous publication. To embellish its new equal-time editorial stance, a 1973 issue published a centerfold featuring film star Burt Reynolds in the nude. The following year saw the first issue of *Playgirl*, a monthly that included a centerfold featuring what it termed "the male nude of the month," usually another media-made celebrity. By this time, then, Theodore Dreiser's Carrie Meeber, whose daring behavior for her time was portrayed in his 1900 novel, had evolved into an independent professional woman who knew her men and what she wanted from them—at least, according to *Cosmopolitan* and *Playgirl*. Yet, in her own way, Carrie had achieved the same end. Though women's unconventional social behavior had become more acceptable by the 1970s, their inherent ways in dealing with men were still in place.

## THE PRINT MEDIA CONFRONTS THE REALITIES OF CHANGING TIMES

A growing audience with special age-group interests at the time was comprised of citizens over fifty-five, as attested to by the burgeoning circulation of *Modern Maturity*, the magazine published by the American Association of Retired Persons (AARP). Living longer and enjoying better health than their forebears, these people were also better educated and blessed with more money and leisure time to expend.[51] Imbued with the values of an earlier day, they were also the largest social group that continued to read newspapers during a time when their readership was in sharp decline.

To cope with television advertising's visual advantage in reaching out to a large audience, both magazines and newspapers employed a variety of means. Mass-circulated publications like *Time* began to produce regional and demographic editions—multiple runs of the same issue that carried articles and advertising directed at different geographic areas and subcultural groups of the media culture. This method of circulation may have targeted smaller audiences, but it afforded a cheaper ad rate for regionally based clients while opening up a larger overall revenue share for a magazine. The influence of television's visual look also played a prominent role in not only an ad's layout but a magazine's overall appearance. Another short-lived but timely influence on its makeup emanated from the underground press of the late '60s, whose bold experimentation with psychedelic effects in typography and pictorial content derived from the youth counterculture's obsession with drugs and rock music.[52]

With more people relying on television for hard news coverage, the urban/regional newspaper began devoting more space to the sensational story and an abundance of entertaining features as well as human-interest subject matter. To report them, papers introduced a more captivating writing style than what the formulaic manner of print journalism had traditionally held to. In fact, by the late 1960s, when many urban evening dailies were either folding or losing readers due to both the dominance of television and mounting publishing costs, many reporters were prompted to formulate a more entertaining, personalized approach. Its origins could be traced to 1962 when young reporter Tom Wolfe joined the staff of the *New York Herald Tribune*, and, as Richard Kluger observes, implemented "a new kind of journalism, one that said that how people lived their lives was as important and meaningful to report on as the official news dispensed by governments and institutions."[53] The upshot of Wolfe's efforts was a visual kind of literary journalism that adapted the techniques of fiction to reporting real-life subject matter. By promoting his intensely personal style in magazine essays and several books, Wolfe was recognized as the father of New Journalism. Its influence also showed up in the works of writers as diverse as Truman Capote and Norman Mailer, who created what became known as the nonfiction novel, discussed later.

The alternative newspapers of the late '60s underground press, in their relentless questioning of the Establishment, were also amenable to a subjective reporting style in protesting or advocating solutions to sociopolitical issues. Publications like New York's *Village Voice*, the *Los Angeles Free Press*, and the campus-based *Berkeley Barb* were among some five hundred in existence by 1969.[54] Theirs was a perspective that would be carried on by the tabloid *Rolling Stone*, whose original role of evaluating the countercultural role of rock music ultimately evolved into a magazine covering the whole spectrum of media culture.

While mainstream papers were greatly indebted to the New Journalism, more conventional reportage was often resorted to, as the *Washington Post*'s series of stories did in exposing the Watergate break-in scandal during 1972–74. Its doggedly investigative methods in the old muckraking style by two of its reporters led to the resignation of President Richard

Nixon, informing the mediated vision that even the honored status of the presidency was not immune to transcending the limits of the law for political gain. Accordingly, the freedom of the press to report such illegal activity not only helped reinforce the general notion that many politicians were deceptive but revealed the powerful sociopolitical role that the media were playing in the postmodern era.

With the popularity of scandal magazines like *Confidential* fading by the mid 1960s, tabloids such as *Inside News, Midnight*, and the long-running *National Enquirer* gained ascendancy. Emboldened by a new sense of expressive freedom in the '60s, they kept publishing their usual graphic stories about sexual aberrations, physical deformities, gruesome accidents, and gory murders, supplemented by tasteless pictorial content. With a multitude of tabloids competing for sales by this time, such candid coverage was evidently paying off. But the *Enquirer*, after experiencing a falloff in sales by the late '60s, began to tone down its reportage to focus on more topical subject matter like UFO phenomena, medical and health-related findings, human interest stories, and astrological predictions. But its major area of interest remained celebrity happenings, both the good and the bad. Upgrading its makeup with color photographs to complement as well as enhance the punch of its bold headlines, the *Enquirer* approached a weekly circulation of over six million by the late '70s. Apparently, too, it considered the coverage of celebrity problems worth the risk of a lawsuit, as that sector of the mediated vision conditioned to expect such subject matter never seemed to tire of it. In directly responding to what its readers wanted to read about, then, the *Enquirer* became the leader of the tabloid pack.

## NEWSPAPER COMICS ADAPT TO SOCIAL COMMENTARY

Many urban dailies, despite their varied efforts to build circulation, continued to struggle financially. A management maneuver that aided survival was chain ownership, and by 1978 over half of the country's daily newspapers were corporately owned. To help maintain circulation, publishers grew increasingly dependent on an abundance of syndicated daily features whose entertainment appeal addressed special interests. From the lifestyle section to the sports pages, from the columns of nationally known social/political commentators to Ann Landers's personal advice and, of course, that old mainstay, the comics, newspapers relied extensively on entertaining content to market themselves.

Though appearing in ever smaller format, the comic strip was still holding on to its traditional place in a newspaper's makeup. A prime example of the gag strip's ongoing trend toward minimalist artwork appeared in 1964 in Johnny Hart and Brant Parker's daily feature titled *The Wizard of Id*, a zany anachronistic takeoff on the Middle Ages' ruling hierarchy. While the overall layout of soap-opera strips like Alex Kotzky's photorealistic *Apartment 3-G* was hurt by minimalism, they continued to attract a following in the 1970s, undoubtedly due to the popularity of the TV genre. But a number of long-running adventure strips folded. Among them was *Terry and the Pirates*, which had been carried on by artist George Wunder from 1947 to 1973. Even Milton Caniff, the esteemed creator of *Terry*, was enduring a drastic decline in syndication subscriptions of *Steve Canyon* during the 1970s. By downplaying the element of pure escapism, the realistic strips with a military slant like Wunder's and Caniff's suffered a reader backlash in the wake of the Vietnam conflict's unpopularity.[55] Also seemingly out of place in the liberal milieu of the '70s was *Li'l Abner*, which Al Capp had transformed into a personal platform for his now conservative views on society and politics. During this socially divisive time, Capp's satirical voice had begun to ring hollow, and he was compelled to end his once celebrated strip in 1977. Other serialized features with long runs that closed down in the decade were *Smilin' Jack*, *Mickey Finn*, and *Abbie an' Slats*. Even a number of longtime humorous strips were axed. Clearly outdated, these features had run their course, while new strips were tailoring themselves to concepts that responded to the ever-changing social attitudes of the mediated vision.

Thus, in this more open-minded time, a surprising but refreshing kind of humor derived from the sensitive subject of race showed up in the work of two black cartoonists—Ted Shearer's *Quincy* (1970) and Morrie Turner's *Wee Pals* (1974). By placing their juvenile characters in urban settings, ethnic diversity was the natural source of their amusing but insightful situations. As another sign of changing times, the adventure strip *Dateline: Danger* (1968), paired black and white lead characters after the manner of TV's *I Spy* (1965), which had cast comedian Bill Cosby as the partner of main character Robert Culp. In 1970, a female black came on the scene in the title role of *Friday Foster*, a serial strip with soap-opera overtones. Clearly, the comics' syndication credo of something for everybody had grown even more democratized by the late 1960s. In 1966 even the Vietnam War inspired the right-wing views of *Tales of the Green Beret*, based on the army's Special Forces guerilla operations. But, as the demise of *Steve Canyon* demonstrated, this strip's focus on an unpopular conflict doomed it to a short life.

Ironically, after the death of its creator in 1968, one classic serial strip found new life in 1970 when the nostalgic mood of the time inspired a popular reprint volume of Harold Gray's *Little Orphan Annie*, covering its heart years of 1935–45.[56] Then, in 1974, reruns of the strip that had appeared in the 1930s began to show up in syndication. The popularity of the 1977 Broadway musical *Annie*, which would ultimately appear as a movie in 1982, even inspired the start of an updated version of the comic strip in 1979. The upshot of the multimedia impact of the *Annie* revival was a mass proliferation of licensed merchandise spin-offs.[57] In fact, the *Annie* phenomenon was an omen of both comic strip adaptations to come in the movies and the comic strip nostalgia that found substance in numerous reprint books during this time. Even historical surveys and studies of the comics as a cultural force had started to appear in abundance. These were books that not only appealed to the nostalgic inclinations of the mediated vision but also reflected a growing scholarly interest in this indigenous American art form.[58]

Other than nostalgia, an effective antidote to the problems of the 1970s was humor, and a new array of humorous comics responded during this time. Among the most popular in the anachronistic manner begun by Johnny Hart's *B.C.* was Dik Browne's *Hagar the Horrible* (1973), a spoof of the Viking age drawn in the minimalist style that by now had become a standard of comics with a daily punch line. In 1978, the familiar image of the indolent household cat provided a windfall for Jim Davis, the creator of *Garfield*, as the amazing popularity of his title character was parlayed into multiple merchandise spin-offs. Other favorites of the time were Jeff McNelly's *Shoe*, whose newspaper editor and reporter characters satirized types familiar to its Pulitzer Prize–winning editorial cartoonist; *Momma*, Mel Lazarus's send-up of the self-centered family matriarch; and *Tank McNamara*, a strip about a bumbling sports reporter whose comical take on the sports establishment fittingly appeared in many papers' sports sections. Starting out in 1970, *Doonesbury*, the creation of Yale graduate Gary Trudeau, went on to win a Pulitzer Prize in 1975. Appropriately, its trenchant satire of the political scene relegated it to the editorial page of many newspapers. This strip's attention to real-world issues and concerns epitomized the times' trend toward utilizing a traditional escapist form to focus on the real world as a source of topical humor.

That the humor of the 1970s' comic strip was more topically sensitive than that of its predecessors was characterized by the output of two socially perceptive women cartoonists. In *Cathy*, which began in 1976, Cathy Guisewite seemingly relied on her own autobiographical experiences of daily life to use in her title character's life that hit home in a comical, yet truthful way. Then, in the last year of the decade, Canadian Lynn Johnston started a family strip that gave a fresh twist to just about every interpersonal incident that might occur among the members of a well-off middle-class family. In the process, *For Better or Worse* generated a subdued kind of humor derived from its creator's real-life influences, alerting comics fans to the realization that amid the unexpected situations arising out of daily routine the serious side of family life was not too far removed from the humorous. Through their more humanized perspectives on the domestic activities of daily life, women cartoonists, from Edwina Dumm to Lynn Johnston, had provided their readers with a bounty of entertaining insights into the give-and-take of the human comedy, thus paving the way for other talents to come.[59]

In spite of the newspapers' ongoing, relentless search for a winning comic strip formula to regale their readership, more new entries failed than made it in this highly competitive field in which success had always hinged on the capricious nature of the mediated vision. In response to faddish trends, even the adventure genre still managed to surface from time to time. For example, the popularity of the movie *Star Wars* resulted in the appearance of a number of features with science-fiction themes. In fact, both *Star Wars* and TV's *Star Trek* were transcribed into the comic strip format. Also, the resurgence of the comic book superhero saw Marvel Comics' most popular characters appearing in the newspaper comics section. Of these, the most enduring was *The Amazing Spider-Man*, which started out in 1977. A major reason for the strip's appeal to fans during this unsettled time was creator Stan Lee's humanized focus on the title character's personal hang-ups, as discussed below.

## THE COMIC BOOK SUPERHERO: FROM CAMP HUMOR TO A NEW HEROIC CONCEPTION

In the face of mounting costs, the comic book publishing industry still carried on its endless search for the heroic superstar or fantasy genre that would generate the biggest sales returns. Throughout this era and beyond, megapublishers Marvel and DC were in rugged competition to dominate production among the thinning ranks of those who still hung on in this highly competitive field. But the uncertainty resulting from the rapidly changing tastes of comic book fans drove the industry in a variety of new directions. While the superhero revival continued unabated, much of it was charged by the nostalgic interest in golden age characters that older fans' privately printed fanzines had generated. Accordingly, Marvel brought back three of its popular heroes of the 1940s—the Human Torch, Sub-Mariner, and Captain America—to enchant another generation of readers.

In 1966, the unexpected popularity of television's camp version of the Batman and Robin characters proved a big boon to DC's fortunes, as sales of comics featuring them soared amid the "Batmania" that swept the country. The upshot was big profits from licensed products, not to mention the rights to a 1966 *Batman* movie, a camp replication of the TV series. A Saturday morning cartoon TV series structured around superhero characters also contributed to the merchandise bonanza, culminating in the 1973 Hanna-Barbera *Super Friends* program that brought DC's leading characters together.

Although a short-lived 1966 Broadway musical comedy, *It's a Bird, It's a Plane, It's Superman*, saw the central character's flying ability naturally limited by the restrictions of the stage, film's technological advances in special effects now made it more receptive to depicting the unique powers of costumed comic book characters. The result was a more serious, heroic approach, as in TV's interpretation of DC's Wonder

Woman in two weekly TV series in the 1970s. But it was *Superman the Movie* (1978), the first straight treatment of the superhero as a mythical icon, whose box-office success resulted in two more blockbuster films that appealed to both youth and adult audiences. The first film's startling special effects that enhanced the unique abilities of the Superman character helped pave the way for high-quality productions of other comic strip and comic book characters, most notably, Batman.

Again, the era's pervasive nostalgic mood was a major force behind the revival of old-time comic book heroes, prompting DC to resurrect other legendary characters like Plastic Man in 1966 and, in 1973, the most popular superhero of the 1940s, Fawcett's Captain Marvel, whose publishing rights were now defunct. By 1974, DC was even offering oversized reprints of original comic books as *Famous First Editions*. At a dollar a copy they provided young readers a look at how Superman, Batman, and other heroes had appeared in their early days as well as older readers a chance to revitalize childhood memories.

An earlier indication of adult fans' nostalgic fascination with the comic books of their youth was Jules Feiffer's personal reminiscences of the classic comic book icons in *The Great Comic Book Heroes* (1965), which also featured their original stories. A more serious approach to the comic book's heroic era was James Steranko's two-volume bountifully illustrated *History of Comics* (1970–72). A talented comic book artist himself, Steranko emphasized the cultural connection between pulp magazine heroes and the superheroes of the comic book's so-called golden age (1938–45). Accordingly, the 1960s' paperback revival of earlier pulp characters like Tarzan, the Shadow, and Doc Savage precipitated their resurrection in comic book format during the '70s. Also the publication of *All in Color for a Dime*, a 1970 hardback collection of nostalgic essays about the early comic books that had first appeared in fanzines, stimulated widespread interest.[60] As though it were a godsend to the industry, comic book publishers, in their revival of old-time readers' favorite characters from the past, rode the wave of nostalgic fever from the '70s on, looking to indoctrinate new generations of fans into the comic book version of the mediated vision's escapist desires.

Another noteworthy trend had originated in 1964 with the appearance of the Warren Publishing Company's black-and-white comic book *Creepy*, which featured horror stories in the 1950s' EC vein. Because this publication appeared in the adult magazine format, it circumvented the Comics Code restrictions against such fare, and its immediate success inspired a companion publication titled *Eerie*. Upon the revision of the Comics Code in 1971, graphic realism in comic book stories was revived in full force. As the relaxation of restrictions now allowed the fantasized depiction of monsters, werewolves, and vampires involved in various kinds of mayhem, other publishers' versions of the horror genre began flooding the market.[61]

In the early 1970s, Marvel's sword-and-sorcery comic books, inspired by the vintage pulp heroes Conan the Barbarian and Kull the Conqueror, helped reinforce fantasized realism as the ingredient most readers were looking for, prompting a host of imitations. With violence back in style, then, Marvel came up with a black-and-white magazine, *Savage Sword of Conan* (1974), directed primarily at an older audience, revealing the comic book format as responsive to infinite variations of fantasized realism. In addition to its ongoing line of superheroes, Marvel's ceaseless experimentations in the mainstream format brought back the earlier X-Men team as the *New X-Men* (1975) for a highly successful run. The following year a daring venture into social satire showed up in *Howard the Duck*. Its title character was fashioned in the vein of the comics' funny animals, but its counterculture behavior projected the flavor of the then defunct underground comics. Earlier, Marvel had even produced its own version of the underground posture in the short-lived *Comix Book* (1974). Thus, in gradually reverting to their pre–Comics Code status, the new comic books now made Dr. Fredric Wertham's crusading efforts to suppress crime/horror comics seem all in vain. In setting the visual standards for what it desired as entertainment, the mediated vision had come through once again.

Contributing to the comic book's more liberal approach to its subject matter was the Code's modification of the ruling against stories that cited drug use. Reacting to the peer pressure of urban street life that was leading youths into drug addiction, DC and Marvel produced the first of their comic books of social relevance in 1971. In them the Green Lantern/Green Arrow and Spider-Man stories conveyed an explicit message to young readers about the harmful effects of drugs.

Now, the harsh reality of current social issues had invaded the fantasy world of comic books for the first time, attempting to demonstrate that stories dealing with delinquent behavior and other problematic concerns like environmental abuse, women's rights, and racial prejudice could educate readers as well as entertain them.

Concomitantly, a 1971 *Time* essay noted that "with responsibility has come respectability. One of the newest things about the new comics is that they are being taken seriously as an art form by critics and as an authentic cultural expression by sociologists." To substantiate this observation, the piece also noted the spate of "learned histories" the comic book had inspired, its appearance in art exhibits and inclusion in college courses, and even the popular reception of comics artists as speakers on college campuses.[62] Here, then, was yet another postmodern sign that challenged the concept of high culture's strictly elitist role.

Some new characters of the '70s echoed a positive response to minority concerns of the time, as, for example, Marvel's introduction of the feminist heroine Red Sonja and the black heroes, Luke Cage and Black Panther. At DC both fantasized reality and nostalgia undoubtedly played a hand in the decision to discard the camp image of Batman and return to its original concept of a dark, avenging knight, thus providing the prototype for the upcoming blockbuster movie. It would appear, then, that while the ongoing experimentations of the comic book industry were looking to secure big profits during the economically depressed 1970s, they were also looking fondly back to earlier successes, hopefully to capitalize on their revivals for lucrative returns.

*Factors in Creating a Mature Comic Book Audience*

Instrumental in the evolution of a more mature vision in creating adult-oriented comics were the underground cartoonists of the late 1960s. Everything the Comics Code stood for, their output intentionally violated—in particular, the rules governing the portrayal of sex, violence, drug use, and traditional American values. The very titles of publications like *Big Ass*, *Young Lust*, and *Bizarre Sex* were pointed reminders that these "comix" (a term that signified their X-rated content) represented the counterculture posture of the youthful cartoonists who drew them. The work of such social rebels as Robert Crumb, Gilbert Shelton, S. Clay Wilson, Jay Lynch, and Trina Robbins was circulated through outlets known as head shops, where drug-related paraphernalia were available. Influenced by EC Comics and the parody-inspired magazine humor of *Mad*, these artists displayed a cultural defiance that would infiltrate the daring temper of overground independent comics publishing.

During its heyday the center of comix publishing was San Francisco, the mecca of the counterculture revolution, where publishing houses with names like Rip-Off Press, Last Gasp, and Krupp Comic Works (later Kitchen Sink Press) produced titles such as those cited above and, of course, *Zap*, whose 1967 appearance made it the prototype of the underground comix book. It also featured Robert Crumb's initial foray into the comix field, and as its guru, his ensuing work featured himself as a confessional voice for a long line of fearlessly de-picted characterizations satirized as products of postmodern life. Of these, the most celebrated was an anthropomorphic character named Fritz the Cat, especially after his 1972 ap-pearance in the first X-rated feature cartoon that bore his name. Outrageously pornographic, Crumb's antiestablish-ment posture took on the entire American social scene as the target of his merciless satire. As this male-dominated field was decidedly sexist in the way it portrayed women, the fe-male reaction began to express itself in comix publications produced by women artists. Nothing, certainly not the eternal war between the sexes, escaped the venomous vision of the devil-may-care underground cartoonists during this era.[63] Accordingly, the counterculture's trademark disrespect for authority grew even more ubiquitous through its psychedelic portrayal on posters, T-shirts, and the covers of rock music albums as well as in the satirical magazine *National Lam-poon*.[64]

By this time, older fans who had urged the comic book in-dustry to draw on its heritage were strong in numbers and or-ganizational strength. To bring them together for social and commercial purposes, the prototype of the annual comics convention was inaugurated in New York in 1965. At these events old comics were bought, traded, and sold, while deal-ers made business contacts, and fans heard comic book pro-fessionals emote on their past triumphs and discuss the latest trends. Helping to solidify fan unity were the privately pub-lished fanzines and adzines like *Alter Ego* and *The Buyer's*

*Guide for Comic Fandom*. This latter publication not only carried ads for old comics and related material, it kept fans informed through editorials and updated reports about the latest developments in the comic book industry. *The Buyer's Guide* also capitalized on the nostalgia rage by publishing reprints of vintage comic strips and golden age comic books. While the prices for reprints were reasonable enough, those for original comics were rapidly escalating as collectors kept driving up the value of rare comic books to astronomical levels. By the end of the '70s, for example, some were asking as much as $15,000 for a mint copy of *Action Comics* No. 1 (1938), which featured the first appearance of Superman. To respond to the growing interest in the value of comic books, a private collector began issuing an annual update in 1970 called *The Comic Book Price Guide*, which, in grading books by condition, presented collectors and dealers a pricing standard for their wares. Ironically, the inflated prices that ensued would attract knowledgeable speculators as well as investors who originally knew little or nothing about the comic book subculture.[65]

Another soon-to-be high-priced collectible was the original comic book artwork produced by influential artists like Jack Kirby, whose seminal work dated from the late 1930s. Still practicing as a journeyman artist, he contributed new characterizations as well as his unique vision of complex mythological realms to the comic book cosmology, warranting the title "King of the Comics." His younger, highly talented peers, such as Neal Adams, John Buscema, Steve Ditko, Gil Kane, Joe Kubert, John Romita, and Berni Wrightson, brought a new, more mature look to the genre through the brilliant stylings of their own personalized visions, which were much more cinematic and realistically illustrative than the unskilled work of the early comic book.[66] Highly experimental and innovative in responding to the trends of the time, not a few of these artists branched off from mainstream comics to become independent creative forces who addressed new, more mature audiences.

With the underground comix phenomenon fading by the 1970s and the advent of the direct-sales method of distributing the output of independent publishers through nationwide comics shops, the traditional houses of Marvel and DC began to realize the sales potential of this innovative marketing concept. But despite their intent to attract a more mature level of readership, comic books were still subjected to criticism by the cultural guardians. Of course, controversial subject matter in the comic book format—from the sexually obsessed eight-page underground booklets of the 1930s to the crime/horror publications of the 1950s—was hardly a new issue. Problems always arose when publishers strayed from the general understanding that comic books were intended for children. Now, with more freedom to create, artists and their publishers looked to change this perception, turning out a new wave of books not only for youth but the adult market. In 1973 Kitchen Sink Press, which had focused on keeping the underground tradition alive, revived Will Eisner's Sunday newspaper supplement feature *The Spirit* in a more maturely conceived light. Then in 1978 it began publishing *The Spirit Magazine*, after securing the rights from Warren, its former publisher. The success of this venture would provide the impetus for Kitchen Sink, in the wake of the ongoing nostalgia craze, to reprint a series of classic newspaper comic strips in the 1980s.[67]

In 1977 another inducement to a more mature sense of creative freedom appeared as *Heavy Metal*, which, after its French counterpart, took a more sophisticated and explicit approach to sexual themes, as indicated by its subtitle, "The Adult Illustrated Fantasy Magazine." Enhanced by realistic artwork, maturely conceived plots, and the new license to create, the so-called comic book was indeed becoming a misnomer, as by the late 1970s the appearance of titles that carried complex stories over a series of issues prefigured what would be termed the graphic novel, a format that transformed the dramatic impact of fictional narrative into pictorial form.

### The Roots of the Graphic Novel

In 1978, Will Eisner, whose long career had championed the comic book medium as a literary form, published *A Contract with God*, a partly autobiographical account of life in a New York tenement neighborhood in the 1930s. It was a highly influential work in presenting reality-based subject matter in the graphic novel format. Also in 1978, Art Spiegelman began serializing *Maus*, which was based on his father's experiences in the Nazi Holocaust. It would become the first graphic novel awarded a Pulitzer Prize. That real-life subject matter could be readily adapted to the traditional fantasy form of the comic book was also exemplified in Jack Jackson's bold attempt to rectify the gross distortions of Indian history in *Comanche Moon* (1978), as well as Harvey Pekar's autobiographical accounts of life's unexpected events that break up everyday routine in his annual editions of *American Splendor*, starting out in 1976. Thus, by this time, one could concur with comics scholar Robert C. Harvey that "comic books [were not] exclusively children's literature anymore," for the real world had now invaded the sanctity of their traditional fantasy world.[68]

Helping promote the superheroes' continuing popularity as cultural icons were realistic television series featuring such characters as Marvel's Amazing Spider-Man and the Incredible Hulk. The fact that they were interpreted in a serious light, in contrast to the earlier camp version of Batman, betokened a growing respect for the comic book medium. Also by this time, Stan Lee, the corporate head of the Marvel Comics empire, had furthered the comic book's cause by speaking on college campuses and even before a full house of fans at a Carnegie Hall "Marvelous Evening." Recognizing both the comic book and television's role in responding to the escapist wishes of the mediated vision, Lee was quoted in a 1978 interview: "I think the television industry has finally gotten wise to something we at Marvel Comics have known for years, and that is that people love realistic fantasy."[69] The phrase "realistic fantasy," which intimated a pastiche of the real and the fantasized, was an apt one in the postmodernist sense, for it not only applied to the comic book subculture but all the expressive forms that comprised the media culture at this time.

### TELEVISION ADVERTISING'S RESPONSE TO A DIVERSIFIED AUDIENCE

While the ubiquity of consumer advertising was evidenced by its ongoing proliferation in newspapers and magazines as well as through outdoor signage, brand-name packaging, and mailouts, television had become the predominant advertising medium during this era. Accordingly, *TV Guide* pointed out in 1977 that since 1967 the number of network commercials had increased by well over 65 percent.[70] Ignoring youth's rebellion against the materialism of American life during the late '60s, commercial TV targeted not only the mainstream audience but the young as major consumers. To enhance this age crossover process, product spokespersons, whom audiences identified with as individuals like themselves, appeared more often.

During this time, too, women, who had always played a key role in consumer advertising, were being increasingly fantasized as sex symbols to promote such male-directed products as automobiles, personal appearance aids, tobacco/alcohol items, and even electronic equipment. The message of such come-ons clearly implied that males' attraction to women could be enhanced simply by relating to these products. To enthrall the male ego, then, TV ads featured a bevy of sexy models, typified by the Nordic blonde who cajoled men to use Noxzema shaving cream with the sultry command to "Take it off, take it *all* off!" Other models were better known, or soon would be—Joey Heatherton in her suggestive commercials for Certa mattresses, Susan Anton for Muriel cigars, and Suzanne Sommers for Ace Hardware. Even actress Farrah Fawcett-Majors's sexy blow-dry hairstyle could catch the male eye in her commercials for a woman's hair conditioner. Although some ads were portraying the independent working-woman in a self-realized feminist light, as did Virginia Slims cigarettes' contention that "You've come a long way, baby," the fantasizing of women as sex objects in mass-media advertising would evolve in an even more daring fashion. And due to television's blatantly visual manner, it hardly needed to resort to the print-ad tactics of subliminal messages that psychologist Wilson Bryan Key identified in his book *Media Sexploitation* (1976).[71] As the fantasy aspects of television advertising became more prevalent, from the musical jingle to the staged minidrama, viewers began to perceive this kind of salesmanship as a form of entertainment designed to address special interests.

That the male image could also sell women's products was amusingly demonstrated in 1974 in the ads featuring football star Joe Namath wearing Beautymist panty hose, which, as the commercial boasted, could make "any legs look like a million dollars." As a rule, male celebrities took on advertising roles that befitted their achievements in business, athletics, and entertainment. Thus the pitches of corporate chairman Lee Iacocca for Chrysler, Olympic decathlon champion Bruce Jenner for Wheaties, and aging singer/movie actor

Bing Crosby for Minute Maid orange juice were highly effective in promoting their products to certain classes and age groups. But beer drinkers were more readily attracted to the earthy commercials inspired by the comaraderie of working-class men imbibing their favorite brew at "Miller Time" or pursuing the Schlitz ads' reminder that it was not too late "to grab for all the gusto you can get." To hype its low-calorie Lite Beer at a time when watching one's weight had become of national concern, Miller outdid all the other breweries with its popular commercials that brought high-profile personalities and ex-athletes together in comic situations that entertained as they promoted.

Among the most popular TV commercials were those that featured readily identifiable fantasy characterizations. Since the 1950s Leo Burnett's ad agency had been creating commercial images of high entertainment appeal to the mediated vision—among them, animated characters like Tony the Tiger, who made Kellogg's Frosted Flakes a favorite breakfast food of children; the Jolly Green Giant and the Pillsbury Doughboy, who became familiar grocery store icons to American housewives; and the real-life image of Morris the cat, whose finicky manner not only sold a lot of Nine Lives catfood but endeared him to cat lovers all over the country.

Ironically, around the time that smoking was declared a health hazard, Burnett introduced the Marlboro Man to help undermine the effeminate notion of smoking filter-tipped cigarettes. In establishing the masculine identity of a rugged cowboy as salesman, after the mediated vision's perennially fantasized conception of the Western myth, both Burnett's agency and the makers of Marlboro prospered by turning it into the world's leading brand. Long after the 1971 banning of tobacco advertising on TV, the image of the Marlboro Man was still being perpetuated in ubiquitous print and billboard replications.

In a consumer society where the pervasive imagery of competitive advertising relentlessly bombarded the public eye, the unparalleled success of Leo Burnett's stable of commercial icons can be attributed to his agency's understanding that the advertising process must be entertaining enough to overcome consumers' natural aversion to the hard-sell pitch. Although Burnett was a champion of the catchy commercial slogan in media advertising, of which many were introduced by his agency, he realized that the appealing character image was an even more powerful agent in selling a product, particularly in a culture that was rapidly becoming more visual than verbal.[72] In effect, the eponymous images created by the Burnett agency were featured actors whose entertaining pitches in TV's commercialized scenarios had great appeal to viewers' escapist inclinations.

The power of television's visually persuasive techniques was of such import it not only influenced the layout styles of print media but the promotion of political campaigns, as viewers' votes were either won or lost through the kind of image a candidate projected. On occasion, though, the deceptive side of product advertising surfaced, as when consumer advocate Ralph Nader's book, *Unsafe at Any Speed: The Designed-In Dangers of the American Automobile* (1965), attacked the auto industry's promotional tactics in general and General Motors in particular for the marketing of the Chevrolet Corvair, a car that had obvious safety defects. Though advertising had a long public service role in alerting the public to worthy causes and issues of concern, here was the case of an industry giant violating the trust of the people by using the mass media to promote a suspect product for commercial gain. The upshot of Nader's efforts was the Corvair's removal from the market and the eventual inclusion of safety equipment as standard features in automobiles. His work also marked a triumph for truth in advertising as well as the start-up of a consumer-protection movement and increased public awareness of the need for governmental reform of regulations controlling public health, industrial pollution, and highway safety. Once again, the reality of contemporary life had invaded the escapist sanctity of the mediated vision, but certainly for good reason. Nevertheless, its long love affair with the automobile would continue as it always had.

Although television's adoption of the shorter thirty-second commercial in the 1970s marked the start of a new advertising era, the cost of its airtime, particularly for those programs with the highest ratings, would continue to rise. But with the entrenchment of the television medium as the most dominant source of mass entertainment, corporate sponsors would deem the expense of TV advertising as essential and necessary in the intensely competitive consumer society of the late twentieth century. Though the TV commercial was an ephemeral form, it, like all mass-media advertising, continued to mirror the changing sociocultural outlook of the mediated vision. In this light, a perceptive analysis of TV commercials' social significance contends that "they reflect an idealized but remarkably cogent view of a society whose video-addicted citizens have come to accept commercials as fixtures of their daily lives."[73] While recording the evolving tastes of children and adults alike, the TV commercial, as a spontaneous form of media culture, affirmed its mission of beguiling the fragmented sectors of this culture with romanticized fantasies of wish fulfillment.

## THE LITERARY SCENE: BRIDGING ELITIST AND POPULAR TASTES

Literary critic Morris Dickstein has pointed out that by the late 1960s the American cultural scene was attending to the plays of Shakespeare and classical music as well as the Beat poetry of Allen Ginsberg and rock music, while recognizing film as the visual counterpart of literary expression. Thus, he concludes that during this time "the line between high culture and popular culture gave way . . . and on some fronts was erased entirely."[74] Accordingly, the culturally reflective forms of traditional and experimental fiction were now plumbing the pervasive terrain and imagery of media culture for metaphors and symbols that reinforced their authors' views on the dominance of a media-made ethos as well as the growing technological complexity and social fragmentation of postmodern life.

In the best-seller category, such novels of Hollywood film potential as Arthur Hailey's *Hotel* (1965), *Wheels* (1971), and *The Moneychangers* (1975) focused respectively on the theme of self-aggrandizement in the corporate power structure of the nation's hotel, automobile manufacturing, and banking operations. Though the mediated vision had always considered the affluent lifestyle as a viable sign of success and self-fulfillment, these works' focus on the downside of affluence, as revealed in the morally bankrupt lives of their characters, echoed a dominant motif of this era's popular fiction—the gratification of self through both material and sensual means. In this more liberal time, then, best-selling novelists were motivated to sensationalize the most intimate experiences of the individual beset by the problems of postmodern life. Such a purpose generally resulted in explicit descriptions of the excesses of self-indulgence, in particular those related to wanton sexual behavior. Typically, in the blockbuster novels of Harold Robbins, such as *The Adventurers* (1966) and *The Pirate* (1974), sex is not only an essential component of their plots, it functions as a complement to the exotic, self-centered lifestyle of their characters.

Even in mainstream fiction the overt examination of sexual adventure became a significant factor, as boldly delineated in the extramarital goings-on in the middle-class, small-town community of John Updike's *Couples* (1968). It was an updating of a literary tradition that had been evolving since the socially iconoclastic fiction of Sherwood Anderson and Sinclair Lewis. As Grace Metalious's *Peyton Place* had demonstrated over a decade before, a more liberal understanding now persisted that an author's realistic attention to sensational elements such as sex had a great deal to do with a book's marketing success and its appeal as a film version. Elizabeth Long has commented on the promotional role of sex in the popular fiction of this time as taking on the function of a "commodity." Through its social context, the novelist could reveal "the fragmentation and alienation of the wider social order on an intimate level."[75] Ironically, subject matter that had long been suppressed as pornography had now become generally acceptable by the mediated vision, as long as it was presented and promoted in the proper context of both traditional and best-selling fiction dealing with real-life issues.

That the postmodern milieu increasingly subjected the individual to dominant social, bureaucratic, and even violent forces over which he or she had little control was pointed out in mainstream novels like John Updike's *Rabbit Redux* (1971), whose 1960s setting reveals rapid social change as a formidable antagonist for its central character; Joseph Heller's *Something Happened* (1974), whose protagonist feels trapped in a meaningless relationship with his family and those he deals with in the corporate structure; and James Dickey's *Deliverance* (1970), in which a weekend canoe trip turns into a nightmare of perversion and brutality for its key figures, the central focus of the novel's gripping 1972 movie version.

On a more popular level, the element of senseless violence also helped make a best seller but a mediocre film of Judith Rossner's *Looking for Mr. Goodbar* (1975). Its young heroine is propelled by her low self-esteem into an obsessive need for casual sex with complete strangers, leading to a tragic end. Similarly, the violently suspenseful nature of horror fiction, which had become highly popular since the late '60s, revealed both the individual and the community as prone to victimization. Two shocking novels—Ira Levin's *Rosemary's Baby* (1967) and William P. Blatty's *The Exorcist* (1971)—dwelled on the power of evil as a satanic presence that could both alienate and possess. From its start in the 1970s, the best-selling neogothic fiction of Stephen King—*Carrie, Salem's Lot,* and *The Shining*—had a postmodern slant that focused on both the individual and his/her milieu's subjection to alienating forces of a dark, horrific nature.[76] The film versions of these novels elevated the horror genre from its traditional B-movie status to big box-office popularity that would last the rest of the century.

In drawing on events from the historical past in an era generally afflicted by historical amnesia, much postmodern writing merged fact with fiction to project what the social, cultural, and/or political atmosphere of an era might have been like. E. L. Doctorow's *Ragtime* (1975), for example, centered on the melting-pot urban problems of American life at the beginning of the twentieth century, much of which the 1981 film version missed out on. Paralleling the advent of the nonfiction novel, William Styron's controversial *The Confessions of Nat Turner* (1967) centered on a historical figure from the rural Virginia past to recount his instrumental role in a slave rebellion and revaluate the roots of American racism. More recent historical developments of a malevolent nature, such as the horrific firebombing of Dresden, Germany, by allied planes in World War II, informed Kurt Vonnegut's surreal *Slaughterhouse-Five* (1969). Similarly, the amoral fallout of war directed the plot of Robert Stone's *Dog Soldiers* (1974) when a Vietnam veteran becomes involved in drug trafficking. The unique perspectives of these and many other novels toward their subject matter could only be considered as escapist entertainment through their imaginative power to transport the reader to another realm of experience.

Moreover, in *Slaughterhouse-Five*, Vonnegut's manner of crossing the time line between past and present by transitioning to a science-fiction milieu implies that a fine line exists between fantasy and reality and that the significance of much that happens in the real world can be more poignantly realized through a fantasized mode. This bold postmodern venture contributed to a growing critical respect for the science-fiction genre during this era when insightful writers like Philip K. Dick and Joanna Russ developed a literary vision of their own toward contemporary issues of social, political, and philosophical import. By adapting SF's conventional fanta-sized approach to serious subject matter, the implications of its issues could be presented in a more dramatically effective mode than that of conventional fiction. Thus, Vonnegut's oblique references to the horrors of the Dresden firebombing help reinforce his stand on the pointlessness of war.

Like Vonnegut, such writers as John Barth, Donald Bar-thelme, John Hawkes, and Thomas Pynchon implemented revolutionary techniques that ignored the conventional nar-rative and characterization methods of mainstream fiction. In fact, the experimental avant-garde writer sought to restruc-ture the novel in a playfully expansive mode more suited to dealing with the complexities and absurdities of a media-driven, image-addicted postmodern society in which con-flicting powers vie for ascendancy. While widely reviewed if not widely read, this kind of esoteric metafiction proved so mystifying to interpret that its primary audience became the professors and their students in the college classroom. From the 1940s–50s' dominance of the New Criticism in the acad-emy to the methodologies of deconstruction and poststructur-alism that academic critics employed in the century's latter years, literary criticism became the recognized province of scholars instead of journalists. In the classroom, then, litera-ture professors, many of whom had analyzed the avant-garde authors' output in scholarly articles and books, lectured their students on these works' significance for a postmodern age.[77] However, this radically different kind of fiction, by positing literary puzzles to decipher within a web of myriad stylistic and structural devices, remained a generally marginalized reading experience. Nevertheless, Pynchon's densely com-plex *Gravity's Rainbow* (1973) was introduced to a wider pub-lic as a Book of the Month Club selection.

But as far as reaching a wider audience through the movies was concerned, most fiction in the experimental mode was considered too self-reflexive for filmic interpretation, though Barth's earlier, more conventional novel *The End of the Road* (1958) appeared as a movie in 1970, and Vonnegut's *Slaugh-terhouse-Five*, in 1972. Both films received mixed reviews. While highly revered by literary critics, the esoteric vision of experimental fiction naturally found rough going in reaching a public largely attuned to the cultural inroads that an image-dominated mass media had made on American culture.

More reader receptive in its attention to the sociocultural and political vagaries of postmodern times was the new hybrid form of writing referred to as the nonfiction novel. Utilizing fictive techniques to produce factual reportage about contemporary life, it had emanated from the kind of reportorial writing called the New Journalism, as noted earlier. By the late '60s, Tom Wolfe, its self-styled progenitor, had established himself as the master of a prose style that could make a newspaper/magazine interview or investigative report read like an excerpt from a novel, to which his best-selling collection of essays, *The Kandy-Kolored Tangerine-Flake Streamline Baby* (1965), attested. In the format of the nonfiction novel itself, both Truman Capote in *In Cold Blood* (1966) and Norman Mailer in *The Armies of the Night* (1968) brought the novelist's skills to the narration of events involving real-life people and events. While Capote reconstructed the aftermath to a heinous crime committed by two mass murderers, Mailer focused on the 1967 march on the Pentagon in protest of the Vietnam War, going so far as to project himself as a character in this and other works in a journalistic vein. Both Capote's *In Cold Blood* and Mailer's *The Executioner's Song* (1979), his probing examination of a psychopathic killer's career, responded to the postmodern fascination with senseless violence as played up by the mass media, becoming best sellers in the process. In drawing subject matter from the media, as well as seeing some of their works made into movies, both authors became media-made icons themselves.

Although the postwar years saw reputable Jewish American novelists assimilating the mainstream values of American culture, the vision of life their works projected still retained something of the Yiddish flair for dramatizing the trials of individual experience as challenges to one's moral sense. This sensibility ranged from the picaresque encounters of Saul Bellow's protagonist in *The Adventures of Augie March* (1953) to the search for answers to the big questions about life in later novels like *Herzog* (1964) and *Humboldt's Gift* (1975) and Bernard Malamud's theme of redemptive suffering in *The Assistant* (1957) and *The Fixer* (1966). A younger writer who compromised his Jewishness with the dominant social values of American culture was Philip Roth.

His hybrid vision provided the settings for a spate of novels during this era, most sensationally in *Portnoy's Complaint* (1969), whose sexual explicitness incited a great deal of criticism from the conservative Jewish sector. But as films, both it and Malamud's *The Fixer* failed to live up to their literary significance.

Pursuant to the examples of Richard Wright and Chester Himes, the social outsider posture of black novelists, especially that of James Baldwin, decried the continuing injustices of a racist society. Paradoxically, while blockbuster novelist James Michener anticipated the patriotic fervor of the nation's bicentennial in his best-selling *Centennial* (1974), Alex Haley's version of the nonfiction novel, *Roots: The Saga of an American Family* (1976), revealed another, darker take on the American past. Its intent was to sensitize readers to a new understanding of the African American heritage, as the television production also did, discussed earlier. Then, too, respecting the extensive research that Haley had to undertake, the book was something of a literary triumph in itself.

Presaging a religious awakening in the ongoing search for self-identity in the '70s (the years Tom Wolfe labeled the "Me Decade") was Richard Bach's surprising best seller, *Jonathan Livingston Seagull* (1970), which attempted to revitalize the American people's fading sense of spiritual values. In relying on the instructive wisdom of the animal fable, its plot depicts the flying exploits of a lone seagull whose main aim in life is to soar above his fellows. Thus, the tale's basically simple message implies that to achieve a higher purpose in life, one must realize the worth of resisting the way of the crowd through strong personal convictions. This slight book's popularity was such that it appeared as a film in 1973, yet another example of Hollywood's intrinsic goal of capitalizing on whatever has wide appeal to a certain time.

Another surprise best seller, as well as a highly popular film, was *Love Story* (1970), Erich Segal's sentimental approach to interpreting young love as one of life's most intensely cherished but fleeting relationships. In resurrecting the melodrama of fiction's tragic romance story, it responded to the mediated vision's inherent longing for a more meaningful relationship between the sexes during a time when the sexual revolution had seemingly demeaned it. Thus, the popular fiction of this era, as particularized in the best-selling novel, substantiated its longtime appeal. And much of the reason for its popularity can be attributed to the media and the power of diversified marketing.

## NEW MARKETING DIRECTIONS IN BOOK PUBLISHING

Readers' reception of both fiction and nonfiction, whether in the increasingly expensive hardback or cheaper paperback format, had disproved the admonition that television would kill off the reading habit. If anything, it and the other media persisted as supportive allies in keeping the media culture informed of a newly published novel's worth, whether in the controversial, edifying, or escapist mode. As a result, the ongoing democratization of the nation's reading habits was strongly enhanced by the burgeoning popularity of the paperback book. Another factor was the appearance of book clubs that catered to specialized interests, even one that promoted the latest quality paperback publications.

In the 1970s, paperback publishing houses established themselves as disseminators of book culture on a scale never before realized, reaching audiences as culturally diverse as the academic and the general public, as well as those more attuned to special subcultural interests. Although the hardback maintained its role as the traditional way to introduce a major work or potential best seller to the public, the paperback's potential for reaching a mass market was considerably greater. By this time, in fact, its marketing outlets of drugstores, supermarkets, airports, and bus stations had been supplemented by the spread of chain bookstores in shopping malls across the nation. Exhibited in eye-catching display stands, paperback best sellers of the '70s like *Papillon, Jaws, The Thorn Birds, Semi-Tough*, and *Shogun* practically sold themselves, especially through their tie-ins with movie or TV productions.

The more tolerant attitude toward controversial subject matter helped, too, resulting in highly publicized movie versions. By the late '60s, fiction that focused on a surfeit of violence and sex qualified as coveted blockbuster film property. As though to capitalize on the success of Vladimir Nabokov's *Lolita* (1955; film, 1961), coauthors Terry Southern and Mason Hoffenberg's *Candy*, which depicted a sexually precocious girl's adventures, was initially published in France, but appeared in paperback in the United States as early as 1964, resulting in a 1968 film version featuring megastars Marlon Brando and Richard Burton.

In 1966, the same year as the Supreme Court's liberal ruling on the obscenity issue, Jacqueline Susann published *Valley of the Dolls*, which was rushed into film in 1967 along with a tie-in paperback edition. Although its sensationalized sexual content attracted many moviegoers and readers, both the movie and the book were critical failures. Nevertheless, the time's open mood toward sex propelled Susann and others on to greater paperback and film riches. A more critically favored writer than Jacqueline Susann was Erica Jong, whose fearless feminist stance and graphic language in *Fear of Flying* (1973) helped parlay her uninhibited feelings about the sexual autonomy of women into a hardback/paperback best seller. Clearly, women candidly writing about heretofore socially taboo subject matter was an added incentive for higher sales. While the guardians of morality occasionally complained, sex-oriented fiction, from the most explicit hard core to the most critically praised, entered mainstream publishing in the 1970s with a flourish, apparently to stay.

Accordingly, profit-motivated houses stayed abreast of the times by publishing fiction that capitalized on highly sensational content, as Bantam did with *Valley of the Dolls*, *Jaws*, and *The Exorcist*; and New American Library (NAL), with the horror novels of Stephen King. Dell, which had enjoyed bountiful profits from its paperback reprint of *Peyton Place* in the 1950s, achieved further success with the sensationalized novels of Joseph Wambaugh, Sidney Sheldon, and Danielle Steel. While Fawcett went for the blockbuster works of popular authors like Mario Puzo and James Michener, paperback pioneer Pocket Books, which maintained a backlist of best sellers, began to publish the contemporary fiction of Harold Robbins and Herman Wouk in the late '70s.

But the leading paperback publishers bolstered their reputations through their publication of the most notable writers of the twentieth century. Both Bantam and NAL, in fact, maintained a list that was a veritable who's who of American novelists. While Ernest Hemingway, John Steinbeck, Robert Penn Warren, Philip Roth, and Carson McCullers all appeared under the Bantam logo, NAL kept alive the works of such renowned writers as William Faulkner, Truman Capote, James Baldwin, Flannery O'Connor, Sinclair Lewis, and J. D.

Salinger. Its Signet line also afforded readers the opportunity to read the classic fiction of early American authors. From the high school classroom to the college level, students were introduced to influential authors through these cheaper paperback editions, thus providing another democratizing force that helped broaden the intellectual horizons of the mediated vision.

Responding to another growing audience, Ballantine capitalized on its fascination with fantasy literature, epitomized in the late '60s by the popularity of J. R. R. Tolkien's *The Hobbit*. This house also leaned heavily toward the science-fiction category. But both it and the fantasy genres were more prominently attended to by Ace Books, which reprinted the popular titles of the Edgar Rice Burroughs canon and the sword-and-scorcery tales of Robert E. Howard as well as the works of newer SF authors like Frank Herbert and Ursula Le Guin. In fact, Ace, Gold Medal Books, and Ballantine were starting to publish paperback science-fiction originals, a practice that would see the industry turning to other genres as first-run novels in paperback. Along with Fawcett, Ace Books also helped popularize the gothic romance as early as the 1960s, a category that by the '70s had evolved into the sexually oriented romances of Avon and Harlequin Books that had wide appeal to female readers.

Throughout this era, the strategies for marketing fiction and nonfiction in both hardback and paperback format developed in the wake of successful publishing houses' acquisitions by large corporations, many of whom were in the mass-media business themselves. Their blockbuster deals with authors and concurrent tie-ins with movies and TV productions placed a pronounced emphasis on appropriate cover design and illustration to promote and sell a book, especially as a paperback. Most cover layouts, in fact, duplicated the newspaper/magazine/billboard artwork that publicized a book's movie or TV version—imagery already familiar to the eye of a potential customer. In the '70s, commercial gimmickry also began to play a conspicuous role in enhancing sales, as display racks exhibited books whose covers were adorned with embossed effects, die cuts, and foil as well as a variety of superimposed typographic styles. Even so, the cover art for such popular genre fiction as detective/mystery, Western, romance, suspense/horror, and science fiction still depended on the familiar situations and clichés that had always appealed to the mediated vision. For example, in the fantasized realism of the covers that James Bama did for Bantam's revival of the 1930s' pulp hero Doc Savage as well as that Frank Frazetta created for Ace's series of Burroughs's novels, one could still detect the influence of the pulp cover artists of an earlier time. Though realistic interpretation was essential to the eye appeal of a paperback cover in order to attract a potential reader, such art purposefully avoided visualizing the world as it actually is, attempting instead "to create a world that is *just real enough*."[78] It was an effect that naturally responded to the mediated vision's growing infatuation with the escapist experience as an ideal blend of reality and fantasy.

### THE ONGOING APPEAL OF NONFICTION

A major player in keeping readers informed of the time's sociocultural upheaval and ferment was the nonfiction book that explored big questions and topical subject matter. Indeed, it found a receptive audience in both hardback and paperback editions, as the best-seller lists revealed. The pervasive social problems of postmodern times resulted in numerous publications that underscored the mediated vision's imminent fear of a future that seemed to anticipate more a milieu of uncertainty than certitude. The book that did more than any other to advance this notion was Alvin Toffler's *Future Shock* (1970) in which the author analyzes the social effects of rapid change on postmodern life. According to Toffler, technological developments in the emerging superindustrial sector were having an overwhelming sociological as well as psychological impact on family and community life, consumerism, subcultural lifestyles, and the larger sphere of human relationships. By the end of the decade, Christopher Lasch's *The Culture of Narcissism: American Life in an Age of Diminishing Expectations* (1979) saw the problem of human relationships as resulting from the increased emphasis on the pursuit of self-gratification in a society in which devotion to leisure time's escapist diversions had become a dominant obsession.

Also the problems of racism and sexism that had been exacerbated in the '60s spawned a group of crusaders who expressed their causes in intensely polemic ways, as did revolutionary Eldridge Cleaver's virulent attack on America's ingrained racist posture in *Soul on Ice* (1968) and Kate

Millett's fearless feminist stand in *Sexual Politics* (1970) that identified the social oppression of women as a result of society's patriarchal sexual dominance. In fact, it was during this era of unprecedented sexual freedom that the feminist struggle for sociopolitical equality began to gather force. Helping pour more oil on the fire was the adversarial stance of Norman Mailer, particularly in the antifeminist views he espoused in *The Prisoner of Sex* (1971). Major targets of Mailer's reaction to the female antagonism toward male sexual supremacy were the authors of controversial books that dwelled on the clitoral orgasm as essential to a woman's sexual pleasure. Toward this end Germaine Greer's best-selling *The Female Eunuch* (1971) daringly proposed that women assume a more aggressive sexual role. Later, Shere Hite's survey of 3,000 respondents in *The Hite Report: A Nationwide Study on Female Sexuality* (1976) concluded that since a high percentage of women were not experiencing satisfactory sex, they needed to "define their own sexuality" by playing a more active role in the sex act.[79]

Although *The Double Helix* (1968) detailed the major breakthrough of two British scientists' 1953 discovery of the body's complex DNA structure and its genetic code implications, the time's most popular books about the human physical condition were those on sex, especially the instructional manuals offering sexual advice. In 1970 appeared the provocatively titled *Everything You Always Wanted to Know About Sex (but Were Afraid to Ask)*. And in spite of the fact that many of the answers Dr. David Reuben offered in reply to the book's offbeat questions were suspect and soon dated, it was an instantaneous best seller. The most popular how-to-do-it manual in the vein of the *Kama Sutra*'s ancient guide to sexual techniques, which had resurfaced in 1964, was Alex Comfort's *The Joy of Sex* (1972). With its explicit all-encompassing illustrations of a couple engaged in a variety of sexual positions, one would have thought a sequel to be redundant. Nevertheless, it soon appeared in the aptly titled *More Joy of Sex*. In the book publishing world, sex as fantasized, escapist experience had become big business. In fact, the period from the late 1960s to the mid 1970s was the golden age of the sexual advice book, as a stream of supposedly helpful titles appeared, of which many were directed at women—from *The Total Woman*'s biblically inspired message, that within the bonds of marriage all sexual acts are sacred, to *The Sensuous*

*Woman*, which dwelled in part on the techniques of oral sex. Clearly, the print medium was a big factor in making any topic related to sexuality socially acceptable.

And if one happened to be more intellectually inclined to know more about theories of sexual behavior, a veritable library of books awaited perusal. From a popularizing perspective, Desmond Morris's *The Naked Ape* (1967) traced the how and why of contemporary sex practices to humanity's primordial ancestors. Following up on the no longer shocking Kinsey reports were the clinical studies produced by the team of William H. Masters and Virginia E. Johnson: *Human Sexual Response* (1966) and *Human Sexual Inadequacy* (1970). Though published in a more sexually liberated time, these works' forthright analyses of their authors' findings about human sexual behavior still incited controversy, especially the first book's attention to the significance of the clitoral orgasm and the second to the pervasiveness of sexual dysfunction in America.

Truly, in the wake of the so-called sexual revolution the deluge of books about sex-related topics were representative of a social mood never before or since equaled. As though to sum up the sexual vagaries of the 1970s, Gay Talese's long-awaited book, *Thy Neighbor's Wife*, appeared in 1980, his investigative report on the sexual revolution and the major players involved in it.[80] However, by this time the mediated vision, literally inundated by the voluminous literature on sex, had grown jaded about the subject. In the aftermath of these promiscuous times, in fact, engaging in sex would become less a fantasized adventure than a highly risky undertaking. Indeed, without the proper precautions, there was the possibility that indulgence in unprotected sex could lead to death, as those unfortunates who contracted a new, mysterious social disease, acronymically called AIDS, would discover.

Two 1974 best sellers looked beyond the time's self-serving prescriptions for improving sexual experience to present unconventional ways for leading a fuller life. In *Zen and the Art of Motorcycle Maintenance*, Robert Pirsig intimated that servicing the products of Western technology could inculcate in one the self-discipline of Eastern philosophy, and Annie Dillard's *Pilgrim at Tinker Creek* revealed how a Thoreauvian reverence for the wonders of the natural world could bring about a sense of inner peace. In another positive vein was

Tom Wolfe's best seller *The Right Stuff* (1979), which examined the progress of the space program. In acclaiming the astronaut as the latest American hero, Wolfe viewed the venture into the new frontier of space as a renewal of the American pioneering spirit as embodied in the astronaut's character.[81] These books revealed that the traditional values of the American way were still alive and well, differing only in the manner in which their authors related them to the sociocultural changes and challenges of the postmodern era.

Popular books in the conventional self-help and informational modes found social change a welcome inspiration in their longtime role of advising readers how to resolve personal problems, overcome larger concerns that might hinder advancement in the workplace, and improve their physical well-being. While Erich Berne's *The Games People Play* (1964) alerted readers to the gamesmanship roles many perform to control interpersonal relationships, *The Peter Principle* (1969), named after one of the book's coauthors, warned that corporations had created a work environment in which personnel rose no higher than the level of their own incompetence. A growing health consciousness and the popularity of jogging as an aid to physical fitness made Jim Fixx's *The Complete Book of Running* (1978) into a best seller. As the aerobic exercise mission caught on, a flood of related books on improving one's physical condition would appear throughout the rest of the century.

By the mid-1960s, in the wake of President Kennedy's assassination, reflective and investigative books began to appear, dealing respectively with his shortened administration and the facts surrounding his tragic death. Among the most read were Arthur Schlesinger Jr.'s *The Thousand Days: John Kennedy in the White House* (1965) and William Manchester's *The Death of a President* (1966). Soon, a nostalgic haze began to surround the Kennedy years, reminiscent of a hallowed time approaching the realm of myth. In the '70s, by contrast, the Nixon administration's nefarious dealings in the Watergate affair prompted the investigative work of two *Washington Post* reporters, culminating in their best-selling exposé, *All the President's Men* (1975). Made into a well-received film in 1976, it represented only the beginning of an era when the formerly suppressed subject of misdeeds within the jurisdiction of the nation's highest office would be treated by the media as entertaining melodrama.

In 1971, the *New York Times* set a journalistic precedent by defying Department of Defense authorities to publish *The Pentagon Papers*, which exposed the political machinations behind America's involvement in the Vietnam War. The attention to momentous topics of timely interest had already prompted the paperback industry to gear up for the production of what it called the "instant" book. Here, Bantam set the pace by demonstrating its remarkable capability for marketing a book dealing with an event of significant import within days of its happening. Although this marvelous development in communications helped make the American people the best informed in the world, it also served to sensitize the mediated vision to sociopolitical problems that underscored the uncertainties of life in the postmodern age.

## POLITICAL AND SOCIAL ISSUES AS FORCES IN POSTMODERN POETRY

Although poetry did not command the cultural authority it had during the first half of the century, unique voices began to be heard in its second half that sensitized their audience to the sociopolitical concerns and cultural interests of feminist, gay/lesbian, and ethnic groups. After the example of Allen Ginsberg's *Howl* (1956) and its intensely personal critique of American culture, other poets were similarly motivated to draw on their private experiences as a pretext for a public posture. Exemplary of this trend were the literary careers of Adrienne Rich and Robert Bly, whose collections of poetry and prose reached wider audiences than the avant-garde poets had. By the '90s, in fact, their challenges to the political process or championing of special causes would turn them into media personalities.[82]

## COMMERCIALISM AND TECHNOLOGY AS CREATIVE FORCES IN POP ART

In reacting to the tenets of modernism, the pop art movement, which many critics saw as something of a passing fad, became instead a strong cultural force by the late 1960s. Influential figures of the movement who had emerged during the decade—in particular, Andy Warhol, Roy Lichtenstein,

James Rosenquist, Mel Ramos, and Claes Oldenburg—continued to produce work into the '70s that was largely inspired by the familiar images spawned by the media culture of movies, comics, and consumerism as well as the commonality of the postmodern American scene. Attuned to the ubiquitous presence of such imagery, these artists' output paradoxically helped enshrine the visually oriented products of media culture rather than trivialize them. And in spite of pop art's initial penchant for controversy, its general acceptance in so short a time was without precedent in the history of art. Accordingly, the proliferation of museums (twenty opened in 1968 while many others were under construction) whose orientation was toward the new and nostalgic, helped cultivate the public's surprisingly open reception of this kind of art as another form of visual entertainment.[83] The upshot of this phenomenon was a more democratized arts milieu in which the blending of the genteel and the popular culminated in a new consciousness in the arts that would last the rest of the century.

After a number of exhibitions in the early '60s marked the arrival of the pop art movement, particularly the 1963 exhibition at New York's Guggenheim Museum, by the mid '60s pop's most recognized practitioner and public figure, the daringly irrepressible Andy Warhol, had become as much a celebrated personality as the movie stars whose images he replicated in his work. Integral to Warhol's ironic vision was his reliance on innovative technical procedures that worked to his advantage in creating art that smacked of the commercialized, technological culture that had inspired it. Thus, the photomechanical method of silk-screen printing was instrumental in replicating one of the most pervasive of everyday consumer objects in *210 Coca-Cola Bottles* (1962), suggestive of Warhol's understanding that assembly-line reproduction was integral to life in a consumer society. He also utilized the photoscreen method to evoke his feel for the movies' pervasive impact on the mediated vision by reproducing the familiar faces of such popular movie stars as Warren Beatty and Natalie Wood. But it was the smiling multiple likenesses of Marilyn Monroe in Warhol's *Marilyn Diptych* (1962) that became one of his most recognized works. In 1967 he captured the media's fixation with this same iconic image through his *Marilyn* portfolio of screen-prints, whose repetitive portraits varied only in their ten shades of color.

In a society inundated by both consumer imagery and the icons of the media culture, Warhol exhibited a special flair for singling out its most socially revelatory motifs. As Michele Bogart observes, Warhol's art offered a solution to the problem "stemming from the disjunction between the romantic fine arts ideal and the demands of a culture dominated by commercial mass media."[84] With the imagery of commercialism, the mass media, and everyday life as his subject, then, Warhol helped depersonalize the subjectivity of traditional art.

The nation's obsession with celebrity culture was also influential in sensitizing Warhol to not only the transience of fame but the ever-looming finality of death, a tabloidlike milieu he had infused in his 1963 *Death and Disaster* series as well as the photographic mode of *Big Electric Chair* (1967). Marco Livingstone has commented that Warhol "was particularly astute in realizing that our overexposure to images in the public domain, whether of famous faces or horrific events, gradually divests them of any apparent emotion and at the same time gives them their iconic power by engraving them in our memory through the force of repetition."[85] Thus, Warhol's output, in its affinity for encapsulating media-made images and events in the traditional modes of painting and photography, had the overall effect of blurring, if not undermining, the longtime hierarchical division between the elite and mass cultures.

Beginning in 1964, other familiar icons of consumer culture inspired Warhol to replicate as "sculpture" the corporate world's mass-produced cartons that packaged such readily recognized products as Heinz tomato ketchup, Del Monte canned fruit, and Brillo soap pads. Little wonder, then, that he called his studio The Factory, for like the big corporations that produced goods for the mass market, he sought to generate works for both the art market and the museums. That Warhol was unabashedly commercial in his artistic endeavors lay in his contention that a work of art was as much a salable commodity as a piece of furniture. With respect to both the marketing power of art and the American society's monetary obsession, then, Warhol's outlook could hardly have been more symbolically expressed than in his *192 One-Dollar Bills* (1962).

*Other Developments in Pop Art's Homage to Media Culture*

On a grander scale than Warhol, sculptor Claes Oldenburg turned to the mass-produced items of fast-food chains and consumer goods to create larger-than-life, often grotesque reproductions and environments, which sufficed as graphic reminders of their omnipresence in contemporary life. Roy Lichtenstein, in drawing on the comics art realm that Warhol and Mel Ramos had also delved into, created a series of works, which directly emulated as well as absorbed the elements of comic book panel art. In large-scaled replications of single panels from the romance and war genre comic books, Lichtenstein created melodramatic works that, ironically, became major museum attractions.[86] By drawing on an ephemeral form that attempts to generalize emotions according to its readers' expectations, he was apparently demonstrating how the pop manner can make use of a mundane form of media culture to objectify the creative act in contrast to the abstract expressionists' subjective intent of showcasing the artist's inner vision.

Even so, from the late 1960s into the '70s, pop art's expressive output in the areas of minimalism and photorealism, as well as in the forms of collage, assemblage, and the environmental "happening," attempted to correlate the polarities of both abstract and representational techniques into intense, collective visions of a commercialized, technocratic world. While James Rosenquist's photorealistic paintings presented immense panoramic collages of contemporary import, Edward Ruscha focused on the familiar sights and scenes of American road culture, and Tom Wesselmann continued to turn out his series of exhibitionist nudes that epitomized the time's fascination with sex. Some pop artists were influenced by the underground comix of the counterculture, while the hippies' attraction to hallucinogenic drugs found its own artistic expression in the psychedelic posters of Peter Max, a style that was commercialized in print advertising, on rock music record jackets, and in fashions. Aided by airbrush techniques, certain artists employed a precisionist manner in reinterpreting commonplace sights of the American scene, charging them with a stylized appearance that transcended their instantly familiar real-world state. Thus, from an overall perspective, pop art and its varied expressive forms ignored the traditional distinction between high and low culture to formulate a mediated vision of contemporary life as a merging of the dominant forces of commercialism and technology. Regardless of the culture critics' opinions of such an output, either as outlandish sham or social commentary, pop art would continue to reflect the culturally fragmented fallout of a materialistic, urbanized way of life.

## TECHNOLOGY AS A CREATIVE FORCE IN ART AND MUSIC

The artist who had the strongest impact on the relationship between art and technology was Robert Rauschenburg. As a visionary who, along with Jasper Johns, had played a hand in the early development of pop art, he devised a theory based on his personal conviction that the gulf separating art and life was the artist's province. To him, then, the creation of art could be inspired by any material source and expressed through any available medium. To illustrate his unique aesthetic sensibility, he incorporated a wide variety of throw-away articles—what most viewers would consider junk—into his "combine" works or assemblages. To showcase them, he sought out unconventional locations, such as vacated warehouses, as opposed to the common practice of exhibiting in public museums.

In 1966, as further evidence of his radical views, Rauschenberg headed up a project that brought artists and engineers together in a theatrical happening called *Nine Evenings: Theatre and Engineering*. Its underlying purpose was to sensitize the art world to an understanding that the time had now come for technicians and artists to work together in the creative process. Along with Rauschenberg, engineer Billy Kluver and avant-garde music composer John Cage were instrumental in staging this production, which some saw as the beginning of an exciting new age of innovative creativity in the arts. The upshot of their efforts was the establishment of Experiments in Art and Technology (EAT), whose acronym became well known through its exhibits in the United States and abroad. Although EAT was disbanded in 1975, its emphasis on the creation of art through the cooperation of artists and technicians lived on in the output of those who learned to adapt the forms of videotape, computers, and laser light to the purposes of artistic creation, especially in the area of musical composition.

As John Cage's indeterminately styled music had prefigured, the creation of electronic music in the postmodern era was greatly enhanced by proliferating advances in sound technology since the 1950s. By the 1960s major breakthroughs followed in the wake of the magnetic tape recorder and the Moog synthesizer that could process a wide range and variety of natural as well as artificial sounds into unique arrangements. The challenge to transcend the limitations of performed instrumental and vocal sounds was met by another pioneer of electronic music, Germany's Karlheinz Stockhausen, who was also influenced by the visionary theories of Cage.[87] In the 1960s and '70s, he not only produced exploratory works that placed him in the avant-garde of electronic music, he experimented with the effects of multidirectional sounds in his compositions. Ultimately, his work, due to its atmospheric intimations of the vastness of space, would add a visual dimension to the sound tracks of both science-fiction and documentary films about outer space. But to Stockhausen, electronic music had much more to offer than just its inherent power to fantasize; that in its role as "a means to a new awareness," he contended, it "will transform people, we will become like [it], more open, cosmically oriented."[88] By the close of the '70s, then, this ongoing partnership of creativity and technology promised a whole new range of listening as well as viewing experiences for the mediated vision.

### SCIENCE'S ROLE IN TRANSFORMING FANTASY INTO REALITY

Respecting the wondrous developments in science and technology, a science-fiction air of fantasy seemed to characterize these years. As astrophysicists began to attend to the outer space phenomena of quasars and pulsars to uncover clues to the secrets of the universe, discoveries and ventures pointed to space as the next great frontier awaiting exploration. In 1964 the unmanned Ranger 7 had photographed the moon's crater-pocked surface, while in 1965 Mariner 4 sent back the first close-up views of a barren Martian landscape, which naturally ran counter to the expectations of science-fiction fans conditioned by popular writers' fanciful visions of the storied planet's alien races and fantastic life-forms. Satellite technology allowed for more prophetic monitoring of weather conditions as well as the facilitation of worldwide communications, a key factor in the advent of Marshall McLuhan's "global village." Ongoing progress in aeronautical engineering resulted in the gigantic Boeing 727 passenger plane in 1964 and supersonic air travel in 1969 in the form of the British/French-developed Concorde aircraft, which could transport its passengers across the Atlantic in around four hours. In that same year the era's most momentous achievement occurred when the Apollo 11 mission succeeded in landing on the moon and beamed back television pictures of astronauts Buzz Aldrin and Neil Armstrong cavorting in the dust of the desolate lunar surface. Astonishingly, in less than a hundred years the mediated vision had been indoctrinated into a revolutionary new way of viewing not only the world but the cosmos.

These years also saw a number of marvelous advancements in the field of medical science that would impact the way the mediated vision viewed the life process. By 1978, the assisted creation of life itself was realized through the process of in vitro fertilization and the birth of the first test-tube baby. But the most revolutionary scientific development of this era resulted from genetic engineering experimentations with DNA cell structure. In heralding science's capability to control hereditary genes, the potential to alter life's basic components was another development right out of science fiction. It resulted in the first cloning of an animal in 2000, an achievement many saw as a warning of dire consequences for tampering with the laws of nature.

## THE NEW YORK WORLD'S FAIR, 1964–65:
### TECHNOLOGY AS ENTERTAINMENT

The prelude to these years of scientific and technological wonders was manifested in another World's Fair hosted by New York City in 1964–65. During the twenty-five years that had lapsed since the 1939–40 fair, many of its predictions of "Building the World of Tomorrow" had been realized. Although the symbol of the new fair's Unisphere proclaimed a universal theme of "Peace through Understanding," one of its subthemes—"Man's Achievements in an Expanding Universe"—was closer to describing what the fair was really all about: the promise and boundless potential that science and technology afforded in improving the lot of humankind. The Seattle World's Fair of 1962, known as the Century 21 Exposition, had also envisioned the good life that science and technology promised for the future. But by 1974, Spokane's Expo '74 focused on the environmental issues and social concerns that so-called "progress" had fomented. Thus, New York's 1964–65 fair, in paying homage to the time's most outstanding achievements in science and technology, stood as the last to promote progress in the optimistic vein that the prototypal Chicago Exposition had done some seventy-five years earlier.

Accordingly, the nation's growing fascination with exploring the new frontier of space was a priority item, as the popularity of the fair's exhibits in NASA's and the Defense Department's Space Park clearly demonstrated. A number of the major corporations' pavilions also offered displays related to space technology and exploration. Some utilized multimedia technology that allowed visitors to experience such simulated space journeys as Cinerama's "To the Moon and Beyond," Ford's "Into the Space Age," and General Motors' space ride in its updated "Futurama" exhibit. All these attractions helped proclaim the notion that the symbolic gesture of the "The Rocket Thrower" sculpture adjacent to the Unisphere was more representative of reality than fantasy.

That the computer was establishing a place for itself in the corporate scene was exemplified in exhibits throughout the fair announcing the arrival of the information age. Accordingly, those who visited the IBM pavilion became involved in venues designed to show how beneficial the computer could be as a tool, especially in its mission of providing instant information about a multitude of topics. IBM's most popular attraction was the "Information Machine," a giant theater into which 500 visitors were moved hydraulically up into its confines to view a multimedia film comparing the function of the computer to that of the human brain. The Bell System pavilion, which offered a riding tour of communications history, also introduced amazing new inventions such as the Picturephone and the touch-tone phone. Thus, in accordance with the fair's major theme, the advances in electronic communications would supposedly bring people closer together in a world of ongoing marvels.

The mysterious power of electricity, which had been a central focus of the Chicago fair in 1893, was overshadowed in 1964 by the wonders predicted through the source of nuclear power, a main theme of General Electric's Carousel of Progress. Here, the Walt Disney Corporation, which had played a major role in its development as well as the exhibits of Ford and Pepsi-Cola, introduced its Audio-Animatronic models. Through them visitors viewed the benefits of electronic power in the American home from the past to the present, lulled all the while by the theme song, "There's a Great Big Beautiful Tomorrow." Then, ignoring any reference to the downside of atomic energy, a multimedia film demonstrated how it would become a chief player in the good life it promised for the nation's future.

Similarly, plastics and related synthetic polymers and their roles in the production of marvelous consumer goods were showcased at the fair as major contributors to a futuristic lifestyle. The DuPont pavilion, in fact, dramatized the history of chemistry and its impact on progress through a musical production called "The Wonderful World of Chemistry." In equating show business with technology, the DuPont exhibit's emphasis on the high quality of life that chemical technology would provide the consumer not only made a complex subject entertaining, it pointed out the postmodern manner of blending the polarities of technology and popular culture.

In glossing over the historical past to illuminate the concept of progress and an idealized vision of the future, the 1964 New York Fair, like the visionary conception of the 1893 Chicago Exposition, avoided the day's pressing social, economic, and environmental issues that would soon erupt in periodic outbursts of societal unrest. As a commercialized showplace in search of the identity its themes extolled, the fair's various and sundry exhibits were designed to nurture the optimistic outlook of the mediated vision by creating an escapist, fantasized realm that promised an even better life than many were enjoying in the prosperous present.

## THE NEW YORK FAIR'S VERSION OF ART AS ENTERTAINMENT

The postmodernist arts milieu was also reflected in the contemporary painting and sculpture displayed in the Pavilion of Fine Arts and the pop art work affixed to the exterior of the New York State Pavilion. However, Andy Warhol's serigraphy on canvas titled *Thirteen Most Wanted Men* was considered too controversial and ordered removed from the building's facade. Undoubtedly the mug shots of criminals on the run were not only too realistic for the fair's fantasized setting but suggestive of a growing concern in the outside world. Though the output of the pop artists who exhibited at the fair became trendy conversation pieces among fairgoers, it was a work of sculpture in the classical mode that stole the show.

That elitist art could still impress fairgoers was clearly demonstrated by the reception of Michelangelo's *Pieta*, whose theatrical setting in the Vatican pavilion was enhanced by piped-in mood music while visitors viewed its glorified grandeur from a moving platform. The portrayal of art as theater was yet another sign of the postmodernist tendency to popularize traditional art, a trend that even the most conservative museums would relate to. When the fair's venerable planner Robert Moses remarked that the stars of his showplace were Michelangelo and Walt Disney, this telling observation pointed out the postmodern sensibility that deigned to bring elitist and popular tastes together. In 1989 an analyst of the 1964 fair's cultural legacy noted: "The exploitation of the pop style—combining high and low art—to sell a product or a vision was a brilliant move that was already embraced by both artists and corporations and one that has proliferated to this day."[89]

## PLANTING THE SEEDS FOR WALT DISNEY WORLD

From the wide variety of mass-produced souvenirs and knickknacks to the miniature replication of the Vatican pavilion's *Pieta* that were marketed to fairgoers, the fair commemorated itself as a spectacle of pastiche that would have a significant impact on the postmodern development of the theme park. Indeed, Walt Disney's highly imaginative contributions to some of the fair's most popular exhibits were portents of a new venturous spirit that would characterize both the new theme parks and his own.

In addition to the projects Disney produced for GE and Ford, the around-the-world boat ride and its theme of "It's a Small World," created for the UNICEF/Pepsi-Cola pavilion, was among the most appealing attractions to fairgoers. Derived from Disney's improved Audio-Animatronics system in which the mechanical movements of doll-like children were synchronized with music and sound effects to represent the nations of the world, the boat journey conveyed the idyllic concept of all people living in peace and harmony. To many, though, the most inspiring as well as impressive exhibit of this kind was the state of Illinois's "Great Moments with Mr. Lincoln." Viewers were enthralled by the lifelike appearance of the sixteenth president voicing excerpts from his speeches and letters. While such exhibits were replicated at California's Disneyland, technological developments on a more major scale would culminate in the opening of a second theme park in Florida and add a new dimension to the vacationing experience.[90]

## WALT DISNEY WORLD: MARKETING A NEW PACKAGED LEISURE IMAGE

When it opened in 1971, Walt Disney World's mission was to establish more of a multipurpose escapist image than the California park offered. In fact, it was conceived not so much as an amusement park as it was a resort unto itself, providing access to on-site hotels as well as a diversity of recreational and sporting activities. As such, Disney World introduced vacationers, particularly families, to the concept of packaged leisure—a one-stop escapist retreat insulated from the cares and concerns of the outside world. Counter to the meandering layout and chaotic architectural design of the traditional amusement park, the Magic Kingdom phase of the park's construction (the most obvious parallel to Disneyland), was designed to involve the visitor in an immediate harmonious aura of pure escapism. Indeed, the park's overall escapist tone was set at its very entrance where the nostalgic air generated by Main Street, U.S.A. stood as Disney's personal homage to the small-town atmosphere of a bygone era. Its sanitized appearance also lent itself to his natural feel for fantasizing reality in the manner that the mediated vision desired.[91] Thus, the park's re-creation of dreamworld experience was encapsulated in such venues as Adventureland, with its emphasis on the lure of exotic locales; Frontierland's devotion to fostering the look and feel of the old West; and Fantasyland, which featured the major characters of the Disney cartoon canon. To visitors, all of these components came across in a highly beguiling fashion due mainly to their eye-appealing decor, landscaping, and horticulture, which the Disney World support staff meticulously maintained.

Of them all, though, Tomorrowland proved to be the most problematic and paradoxical in that the nature of its futuristic programming demanded continuous updating. By the mid 1970s two of its most fabulous attractions had opened—the Space Mountain ride and the Carousel of Progress, an updated version of the project Disney had created for the GE pavilion at the New York fair. Also the latest technical virtuosity in Audio-Animatronics developments greatly enhanced the historical flavor of Liberty Square and the Hall of Presidents. Thus, at Disney World both the idyllic future and nostalgic past met in an enchanted realm that attempted to enshrine both the nation's heritage and its future promise. And the swelling ranks of visitors reveled in what they saw, for it provided a welcome retreat from the problems that were becoming increasingly common in the unpredictable times of the 1970s.

Even though Tomorrowland would present a perpetual challenge to the imagination and ingenuity of the Disney creative staff, who were appropriately dubbed "Imagineers," no undertaking seemed too big or challenging for them to carry through to fruition. Comprised in the main of artists, engineers, architects, audiovisual experts, and computer programmers, the Disney Imagineering staff would realize even greater accomplishments during the 1980s and '90s through a plethora of exciting new attractions.[92] In addition to the Magic Kingdom's featured attractions, the concept of a planned city—the Experimental Prototype Community of Tomorrow (EPCOT) Center—was to be the most imaginative monument yet to the Disney vision. Projecting an idyllic outlook intended to showcase the urban community as it should be, its utopian, escapist conception held a natural appeal to the mediated vision. And from the '70s on, the plans for EPCOT Center were always a major focus, even though its construction would vary significantly from the original plan to become more a venue for corporate achievements. Disney himself recognized the transient nature of his dream project when he predicted that it would "always be introducing and demonstrating and testing new materials and new systems." And because of this mission would "always be a showcase to the world for the ingenuity and imagination of American free enterprise."[93] As such, then, the EPCOT concept was intended to function in a continuous state of becoming through the process of testing and meeting ever-new challenges, thus transcending the static utopian vision that Chicago's White City had symbolized.

Even the shock of Walt Disney's death in 1966 after a period of failing health did not deter the energies of those dedicated to fulfilling his magnanimous dream of shaping the world as the mediated vision wanted it to be. Accordingly, the years up to the 1980s saw the completion of the Magic Kingdom phase, the continued expansion of the resort areas, and the introduction of new ideas and concepts that looked beyond EPCOT Center to even more intriguing developments. Many would stand as monuments to the seemingly boundless creative imagination of the Disney Imagineers. But by the 1990s one of the most timely of these ventures would involve organized sports, featuring a golf resort and a diversified sports complex—a sign that such activity had become as much a part of the entertainment venue of Disney World as it had in the larger sphere of things.

### Sports: A Composite of Escapist Retreat and Real-World Problems

In 1976 Robert Lipsyte's *SportsWorld: An American Dreamland* contended that overplay by the mass media, management's unbridled commercial interests, and the emphasis on winning had resulted in a "grotesque distortion of sports." His metaphor for this predicament—"SportsWorld"—symbolized a system that was perpetuating "a pattern that is basically antisports, that denies the joy of healthy play and competition to the society as a whole."[94] By the 1970s, then, competitive sport, as Lipsyte saw it, was functioning primarily as commercialized spectacle catering to the escapist wishes of the mediated vision.

Naturally, the development of televised sports as a form of mass entertainment provided a receptive conduit to promote and sell commercial products, a process that generated additional wealth for those in position to direct the system toward their own self-aggrandizing ends. Marxist critic Paul Hoch had decried this development as a power move that not only cheated fans but also athletes in *Rip Off the Big Game: The*

*Exploitation of Sports by the Power Elite* (1972). Moreover, culture analyst Christopher Lasch had also analyzed how American sport was functioning not so much as an edifying experience for the masses as a form of show business.[95] While writers like James Michener in *Sports in America* and Michael Novak in *The Joy of Sports* (both 1976) offered cases for the redemptive powers of both participant and spectator sports, athletes themselves had helped reinforce the postures of both Hoch and Lipsyte in a flood of self-confessional books. Among them were Jim Bouton's *Ball Four* (1970), which revealed the self-centered behavior of major-league baseball players as less than honorable on the field and off; Dave Meggyesy's *Out of Their League* (1971), which observed that a large number of professional football players were dependent on drugs; and Gary Shaw's indictment of college football coaches out to win at any cost in *Meat on the Hoof: The Hidden World of Texas Football* (1973).

Although the muckraking and self-confessional sports books would keep appearing over the rest of the century, the mediated vision's inherent love affair with sports generally ignored such criticism to maintain a long-standing escapist relationship with them. Accordingly, as both college and professional sports, along with the personalities they celebrated, grew more visible as a source of diversion from the mid 1960s through the '70s, they drew more spectators than ever before. A major factor in this development, as Lipsyte averred, was the attention accorded sports by the mass media. Television revenues had played a major role in the success of the new American Football League and its eventual incorporation in 1970 as one of two conferences compromising the older National Football League (NFL). Thus the format was set for what would become the most highly promoted and anticipated sports event in the nation's history—the Super Bowl, in which the NFL's two conference champions would play for the world championship of professional football. With the spread of more professional teams across the country, in football as well as baseball and basketball, nationwide interest in a team's fortunes was not only intensified, franchise owners enjoyed the largess of both gate receipts and lucrative television contracts. In the '70s, the networks justified periodic increases in advertising rates on the basis of a team's popularity and the size of the marketing area in which its games were televised. This practice would lead to even bigger TV contracts for all the professional leagues as well as larger salaries for the players, especially when free agency came into being.

## KEY FACTORS IN THE TRANSFORMATION OF POSTMODERN SPORTS

Pro football's acclimation to television through its bureaucratic coaching style and innate propensity for violence turned it into the most visually entertaining and watched team sport of the postmodern era. The combination of television and professional football also helped college football build on its popularity, especially after its style of play began to look more like the professional game. Evolving into a training ground for the professional teams, college football became a game in which specialization played a major part in recruiting a player, whose only role might be kicking field goals. Indeed, the outcome of many games now turned on whether a team could capitalize on the conversion of field-goal opportunities.

In responding to on-site spectator interest, another sign of things to come was the opening in 1965 of Houston's Astrodome, the first covered, multipurpose entertainment facility where fans could watch a sports event in air-controlled comfort in spite of outside weather conditions. When New Orleans followed suit with its Superdome, a pattern was set for other franchise cities to emulate. Eager to attract a football or baseball franchise, city officials gave in to the building of these spectacular edifices at taxpayers' expense rather than that of a team owner's. Such outright disregard of civic priorities offered more evidence of Paul Hoch's "Power Elite" membership exercising its self-aggrandizing privileges. Likewise, the power of baseball owners to exploit ways to generate more revenue was evident in 1969 when they had the two major leagues each split into divisions whose seasonal winners vied in a play-off series to determine who played in the World Series.

Increasingly looked upon as entertainers, professional athletes were now becoming an integral part of celebrity culture, whose images were promoted by the media for as long as their careers lasted. Increasingly, though, the most frequently exploited side of an athlete was their off-field misbehavior, centering mostly on their drug and women problems as well as other highly sensationalized matters. The long-accepted belief that participation in sports was a character-building experience never seemed to have rubbed off on many athletes of this era, as the tell-all books about their self-centered lives revealed. Despite the positive societal contributions of many role-model athletes, the aberrant behavior of their peers dominated the time's tabloid-oriented news, which reported a growing number involved in criminal activity ranging from spouse abuse to drug trafficking.

Despite professional sport's inherent problems, fans continued to support their favorite teams. Even after a thirteen-day baseball players' strike over free agency at the beginning of the 1972 season, many returned to the games. Helping attract them was Hank Aaron's pursuit of Babe Ruth's career home-run record of 714, which he broke in 1974, winding up his career in 1976 with a total of 755. Lou Brock, another black player, broke Ty Cobb's legendary stolen base record of 892 in 1977. Such achievements not only substantiated the acceptance of the black male athlete, his role as a talented achiever would add a whole new dimension to the media's coverage of spectator sports.

Not until the late 1960s did blacks begin to be more readily accepted in professional sports, and some were even making a name for themselves in intercollegiate sports at Southern schools. The fact that eight recipients of the Heisman Trophy during the years 1965–79 were black running backs reflected a growing acknowledgment that as far as speed was concerned, black athletes were far superior to whites.[96] Because of the large influx of black players during this time, college basketball's style of play changed dramatically with respect to quickness, jumping ability, and showmanship. Contributing to the growing popularity of professional basketball in this era was the Boston Celtics, who with Bill Russell as their coach (the first black coach of a professional team) won their eighth straight NBA championship in 1966. They captured two more in 1968 and '69 and two in the 1970s. By the middle of the 1970s blacks comprised over half the players in the NBA, and their dominance added a great deal to the entertainment aura of the sport.

Reflecting its ongoing democratization, tennis even found a black male representative in Arthur Ashe, who won the U.S. Open in 1968, the Australian in 1970, and the Wimbledon championship in 1975. As a role model, the modest Ashe stood out in marked contrast to the boxer Cassius Clay who served notice to the media that the day of the athlete as self-promoter had arrived. Indeed, as Muhammad Ali, his adopted Islamic name, he weathered the storm of controversy surrounding his refusal to be drafted into the army in 1967 on religious grounds and went on to become the first boxer in history to win the heavyweight title three times. In the process he also became one of the world's most recognized figures, as the media celebrated his exploits both in the ring and out.

Another controversial sports figure of the time was both a supporter of Muhammad Ali and a media analyst who professed to "tell it like it is." In 1970 Howard Cosell teamed up with two ex-NFL players to do the color commentary for ABC-TV's *Monday Night Football*, the start-up of the network's gamble to promote pro football as a prime-time event. It would prove its worth by becoming a long-running seasonal viewing ritual for football fans. While Cosell's acerbic comments were couched in overwrought language that did little to endear him to viewers, partner Don Meredith offset his lofty posture through an earthy-type humor that fans relished. In this new format, sport enhanced its image in the eyes of the mediated vision much as it always had—a temporary refuge from everyday concerns. It also helped bring fans together from different race/socioeconomic sectors in a common bond, an accomplishment no other social institution could boast of. Even so, the sociopolitical realities of the time were revealing sport as a microcosm of the larger world's problems.

Nowhere was this realization more evident than in the Olympics of this era. In the 1968 Olympics in Mexico City, for example, the clenched-fist salute of two black American sprinters on the victory stand as a symbolic protest against racial discrimination back home did not set too well with Olympic officials, not to mention many spectators. As the Japanese had done at Tokyo in 1964, so the Germans staged the 1972 Summer Olympics at Munich as a monument to their new demilitarized and highly prosperous nation. Even as the most widely televised Olympics yet, viewers were hardly prepared for the shock of Palestinian terrorists venting their rage at Israeli statehood by killing a Jewish athlete and seizing ten teammates, including their coaches, as hostages. Unfortunately, an abortive rescue attempt resulted in their deaths as well. When the Munich Games, as well organized and resplendently staged as they were, came to their tragic close, the mediated vision now realized that even the sacred refuge of the Olympic Games was no longer immune to the ills of the wider world.

A different real-world problem the Munich Games uncovered was the mounting expense incurred in hosting the Olympics. The realities of mismanaged finances also impinged on the Montreal Summer Olympics of 1976 after its construction and operational costs resulted in a deficit of over a billion dollars. To counter such a problem in the future, Olympic officials would look increasingly to the commercial support of television, ironically resulting in further denigration of the Olympic ideals by transforming the event into a grandiose entertaining spectacle.

By now, too, the traditional mission of the Olympics to promote international accord among competing nations, through which their athletes could pursue personal dreams and spectators could see them realized, had degenerated into a milieu of overzealous nationalism. As far as American competitive success was concerned, the nation's athletes had not been faring as well overall as they had in the past. Of course, there were the outstanding individual achievements in swimming, the expected victories in track's sprint events, gold medal winners Bill Toomey (1968) and Bruce Jenner (1976) in the decathlon, and the success of many skilled women athletes. But in 1972 the men's basketball team was defeated for the first time, ironically enough by the Russians, on disputed calls at the end of the game. While American prowess in gymnastics had never really been established, the Soviet Union and its satellite countries took the opportunity to surge to the forefront with a superb cast of women athletes intended to extol the worth of the socialist system, which had the added effect of heightening cold war tensions. Much of the success of Russian and Eastern bloc competitors was attributable to a state-supported training system, while U.S. athletes had to endure a dearth of funding support and the harsh restrictions of an amateur system. Despite the protestations of the American Amateur Union (AAU), the trend toward the professionalization of the nation's amateur sports was very much in the air by the end of the 1970s.

In 1972 federal legislation was passed that mandated schools and colleges to provide female students the same opportunities to participate in athletics as males had. Although women athletes were already making their mark in Olympic events, this law, known as Title IX, would have a significant impact on women's future role in sports. In particular, it opened up team games like basketball, which many had deemed too strenuous for women to play. By 1976, in fact, it had become an Olympic sport. During this era, too, the winning ways of tennis players Billie Jean King and Chris Evert, along with golfer Kathy Whitworth, attracted a great deal of media attention. Indeed, as role models these superstars of women's sports blazed a trail for young women aspiring to compete in the traditional male sanctuary of sport. In 1973, Billy Jean King proved that a woman could compete successfully against a man in the much ballyhooed "Battle of the Sexes" tennis match with Bobby Riggs, winning in straight sets before a nationally televised audience.

This event was a prime example of what sports, in large part, was rapidly becoming: commercialized melodrama in which athletes performed as celebrated personalities. Other TV shows like *Superstars* presented popular athletes competing with each other in staged marathon events. Though fans may have viewed these shows as escapist entertainment, critics labeled them "trash sports." Even longtime golf tournaments like the Bob Hope Desert Classic got into the celebrity act by inviting popular entertainers and other notables to play as amateur competitors. But the epitome of the sporting event as circus appeared in the late '70s' televised exploits of daredevil Evel Knievel engaging in his seemingly impossible motorcycle jumps.[97] In the spirit of such spectacular events, an overload of media publicity about them and their idolized participants was generated. By this time, in fact, television had begun utilizing its special power to humanize the sports experience through an intimate look into the lives of participating athletes, depicting them as not only celebrity types but ordinary beings who had problems like anyone else. Thus, due to the media's ongoing flair for exploitation, athletes' "private lives, contract battles, social and political views became as much grist for the gossip mills as had the lives of Hollywood stars a generation earlier."[98]

## THE GROWING INTEREST IN LEISURE ACTIVITIES AND INDIVIDUALIZED SPORTS

By the time of the gala celebration of the nation's two-hundredth birthday in 1976, Americans were participating in a variety of self-enhancing leisure activities. They not only had the time, they had the money to invest in such pursuits. Travel agents were being besieged by clients who, instead of booking the conventional European guided tour, opted for the escapist opportunities for romance and the good life afforded by a seven-day Caribbean cruise. The onboard provision to gamble was an added attraction, as during this time gambling had become highly appealing to those who could afford it (and even those unfortunates who could not). In 1964 the New Hampshire Sweepstakes had signaled the coming of a state lottery system, which by 1971 evolved into New Jersey's statewide cheap-ticket lottery with a periodic payoff. It was a pattern that revenue-hungry states would implement and manage throughout the remaining years of the century. In 1977, another sign of things to come was Atlantic City's gambling casinos, which functioned as an eastern version of Las Vegas. As a form of escapism derived from the hope of cashing in on a big win, casino gambling was the utmost fantasy trip, until the reality of losing too much, and too often did, for those bettors who paid a big price for attempting to escape the real world through gambling.

During the '70s, golf and tennis became increasingly popular as televised sports, due mainly to growing participation interest. Centering on the superb play of Arnold Palmer and Jack Nicklaus, who by 1975 had won his fifth Master's, golf continued to build its appealing image through a bountiful increase in the construction of golf courses across the nation. Despite the game's psychological challenge to best one's self, it offered an open opportunity to escape everyday reality in a fantasized habitat of natural beauty. As a result, thousands of middle-class men, taking advantage of the availability of more leisure time, elected to try and "best" themselves, both for the fun of playing and fitness' sake.

Although on-site and televised spectator sports dominated this era (one could even gamble on them in Las Vegas), the abundant availability of leisure time invited many to participate in individualized athletic activities. Such opportunities seemed to counter Robert Lipsyte's charge that citizens had been denied "the joy of healthy play." While writer James Michener advocated change to rid organized sport of its abuses, he also championed the important role of sports participation in citizen's lives. Michener, in fact, contended that sports were a kind of last frontier, fully deserving of our protection in order to keep them free from those influences that tended to divert their essential mission of "enlarging the human adventure."[99] In addition to golf and tennis, plentiful evidence of the popularity of handball, bowling, softball, and youth sports not only revealed the notion of participating in sports for the sheer fun of it, but the spread of the fitness movement at this time and a sport-for-all philosophy that would pervade the remaining years of the twentieth century. Although such activities were intended to offer participants a self-fulfilling alternative to the overly organized side of athletics and their intent of winning mainly for the sake of winning, postmodern sport would see itself become even more fraught with problems in the years ahead. Such an ominous development would even devolve on the lowest entry level, organized youth sports, and mirror the moral malaise of the higher echelons of organized sports and even the society at large.

Hollywood would resort to its traditional method in selling *The Best Years of Our Lives* as a romance. But for those that saw the film, it struck a different note—the struggle of the military to renew their civilian lives in the postwar years (RKO, 1946). Author's collection.

Communism, both imagined and real, became a powerful force to deal with in the 1950s, as dramatized in *I Married a Communist* (RKO, 1950). Author's collection.

In the *Blackboard Jungle* juvenile delinquency was another social ill that graphically displayed itself in high school teacher Glenn Ford's class's gross misbehavior. Ironically, this movie stumbled onto rock 'n' roll music as a theme by highlighting Bill Haley and the Comets' "Rock Around the Clock" (MGM, 1955). Author's collection.

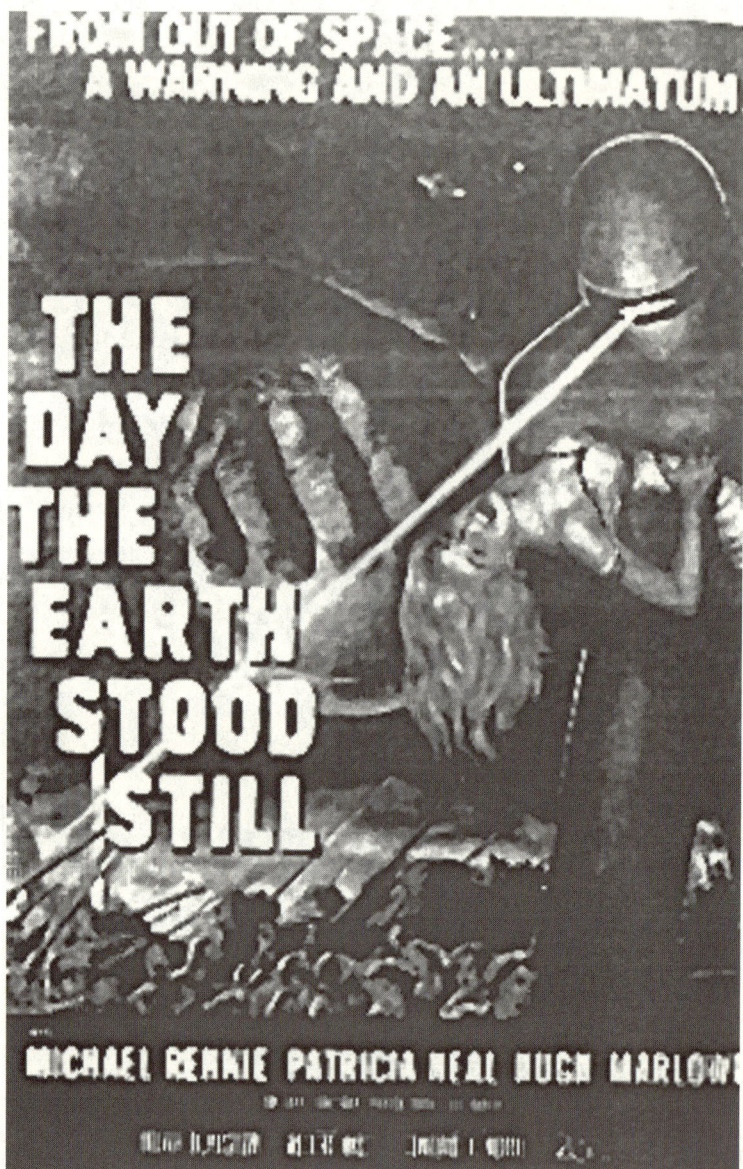

The threat of Communism and Unidentified Flying Objects (UFOs) clearly were the inspiration for *The Day the Earth Stood Still* (1951, 20th Century–Fox). It was the first science-fiction film that moviemaker and audience took seriously. Author's collection.

*The Moon is Blue* was banned in certain areas due to its use of sexually suggestive language (Allied Artists, 1953). Author's collection.

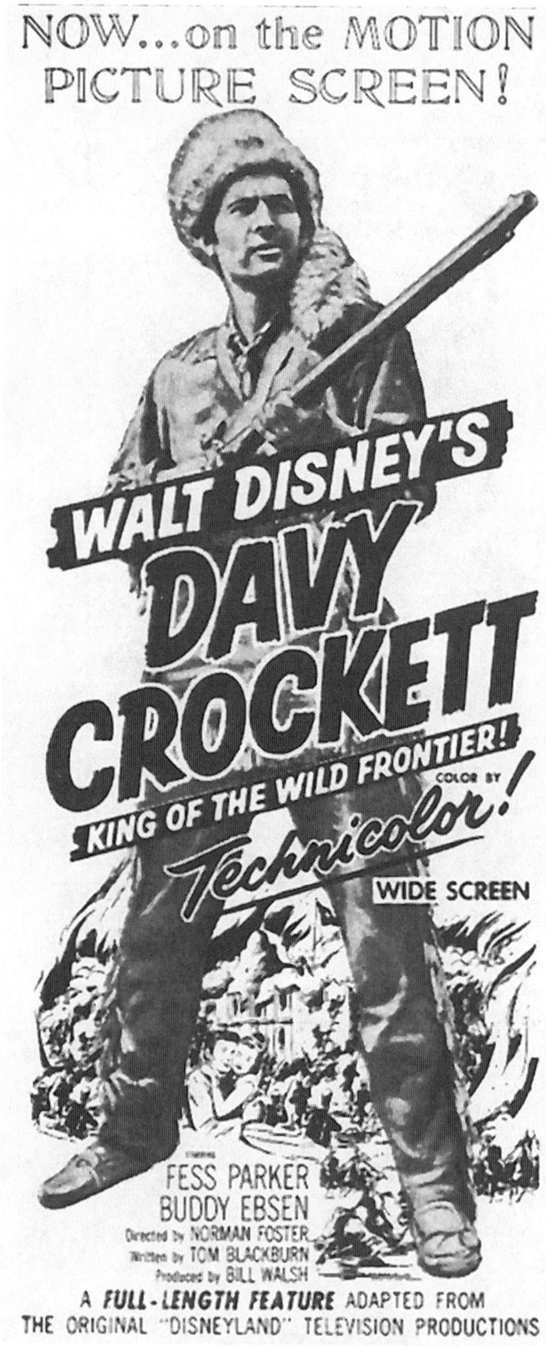
NOW...on the MOTION PICTURE SCREEN!
WALT DISNEY'S
DAVY CROCKETT
KING OF THE WILD FRONTIER!
COLOR BY
Technicolor!
WIDE SCREEN
FESS PARKER
BUDDY EBSEN
Directed by NORMAN FOSTER
Written by TOM BLACKBURN
Produced by BILL WALSH
A FULL-LENGTH FEATURE ADAPTED FROM THE ORIGINAL "DISNEYLAND" TELEVISION PRODUCTIONS

**Television Invades Hollywood:** Walt Disney's popular TV feature *Davy Crockett* made it to the big screen in 1955 (Walt Disney Productions). *Marty* was first written for television by Paddy Chayefsky, then was made as a movie in 1955 with the production qualities of the small screen intact (United Artists). Author's collection.

Old Hollywood vs. New Hollywood: *Sunset Boulevard*'s Gloria Swanson, as an aging actress of the silent era, takes in young Hollywood scriptwriter William Holden as a lover. She intends to revive her screen career but there are tragic results (Paramount, 1950). Author's collection.

Stanley Kubrick's *Dr. Strangelove* (Columbia, 1963) was a suspense comedy about the unfunniest subject imaginable: a crackpot American Air Force general launches a nuclear attack on Russia that reaches the no call-back point. Audiences were compelled to laugh at a threat carried out that dominated the last half of the twentieth century. Ad from author's collection.

THE MOST ASTOUNDING MOTION PICTURE SINCE MOTION PICTURES BEGAN! WARNER BROS.' AMAZING FULL-LENGTH FEATURE IN NATURAL VISION

# 3 DIMENSION

Beauty and terr
meet in your sea
...as every thrill o
its sensation story
comes off the
screen right at you!

The half-man half-monster who stalked a panic-swept city for th
show-world beauties he craved for his Chamber of Horrors!

## "HOUSE OF WAX"

WarnerColor

This is the FIRST feature picture in 3-dimension produced by a major studio!
Showings throughout the U.S., Canada and Great Britain begin THIS MONTH!

VINCENT PRICE · FRANK LOVEJOY · PHYLLIS KIRK · CAROLYN JONES · PAUL P?C

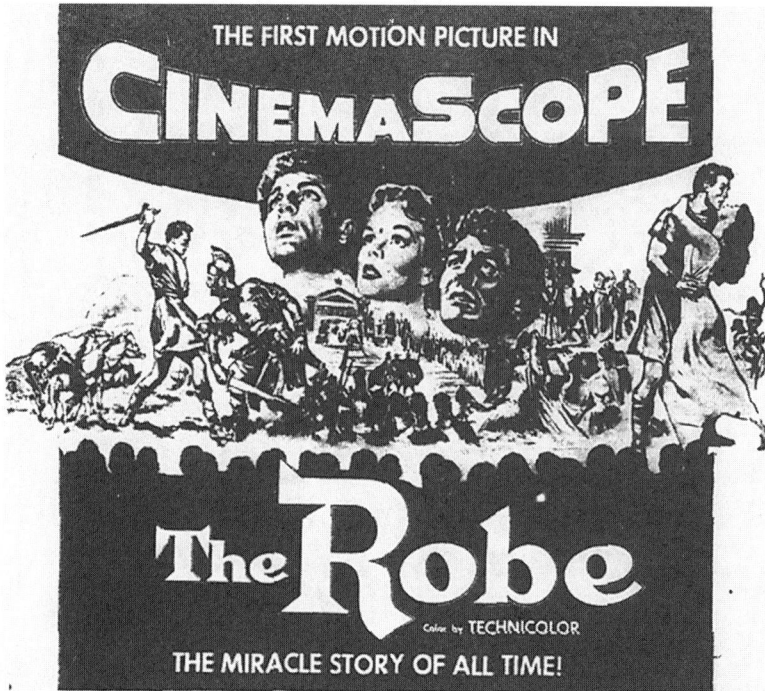

THE FIRST MOTION PICTURE IN

CINEMASCOPE

The Robe

Color by TECHNICOLOR

THE MIRACLE STORY OF ALL TIME!

20th Century-Fox presents the New Dimensional Photographic Marvel!
The Modern Miracle You See Without Glasses!

Technological Advances to Lure Movie Fans Back to Theaters: Third Dimension's *House of Wax* (Warners, 1953). But 3-D films' novelty failed to catch on, surpassed by CinemaScope, as introduced in *The Robe* (20th Century–Fox, 1953) with wide-screen projection enhanced by stereophonic sound. Both ads from author's collection.

The film version of Edward Albee's play *Who's Afraid of Virginia Woolf?* (Warners, 1966) proved itself as exhausting a dramatic experience as the Broadway play. Author's collection.

The first real X-rated film was *Midnight Cowboy* (United Artists, 1969). It was an Academy Award winner as best picture of the year. Ad from author's collection.

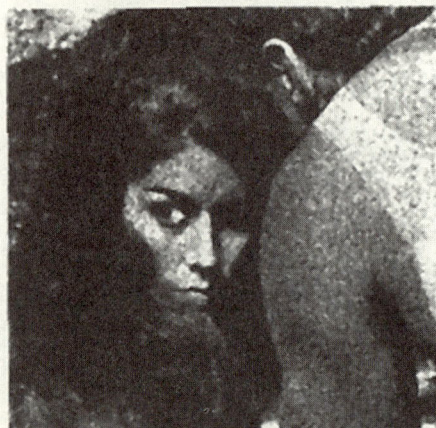

Independent film director Russ Meyer gave movie audiences his X-rated version of a nymphomaniac's wild ventures in *Vixen* (Meyer, 1968). It prompted 20th Century–Fox to contract with Meyer for *Beyond the Valley of the Dolls* (1970), its first X-rated film. Critics panned it for its scenes of simulated sex. Ad from author's collection.

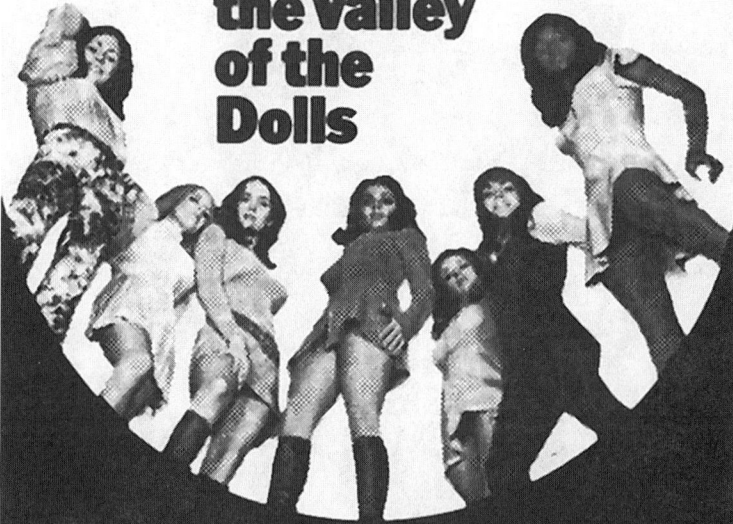

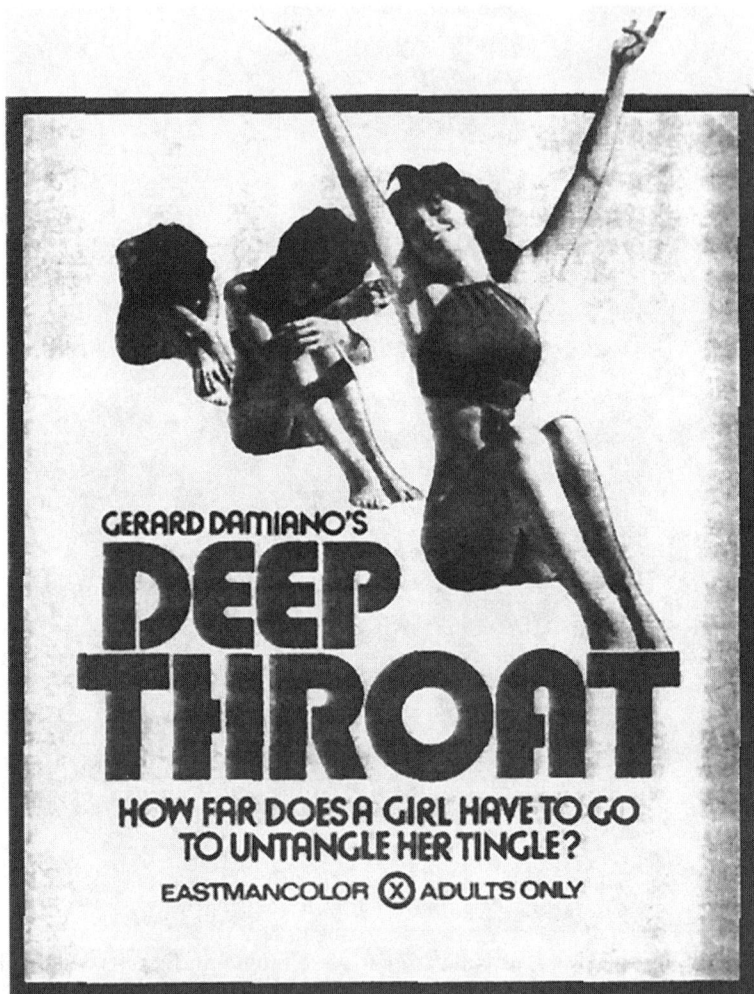

In 1972 appeared the infamous *Deep Throat*, made so by the fellatio talent of one Linda Lovelace. Produced and directed by Gerard Damiano, who grew rich by scheduling the film at out-of-the-way locations so "upright" citizens could see what all the excitement was about. Ad from author's collection.

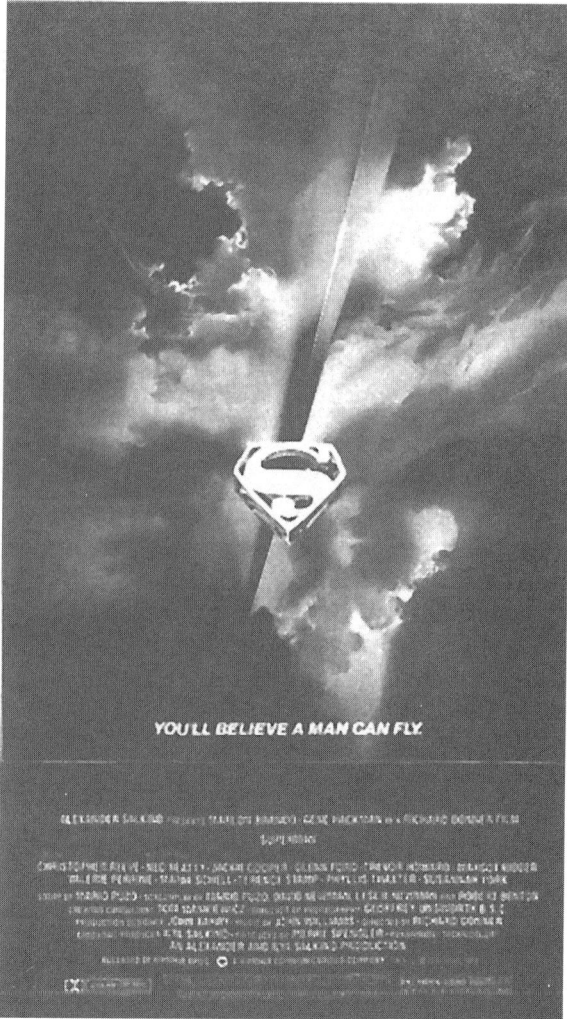

The first *Superman* blockbuster movie appeared in 1978. The ad caption "You'll Believe a Man Can Fly" helped the film win an Academy Award for its convincing flying episodes. Ad from author's collection.

By the '90s, movies were appearing with black-featured characters. This was because of Denzel Washington's acting skills in the title role and Spike Lee's directing ability in *Malcolm X* (Warners, 1992). Photo from author's collection.

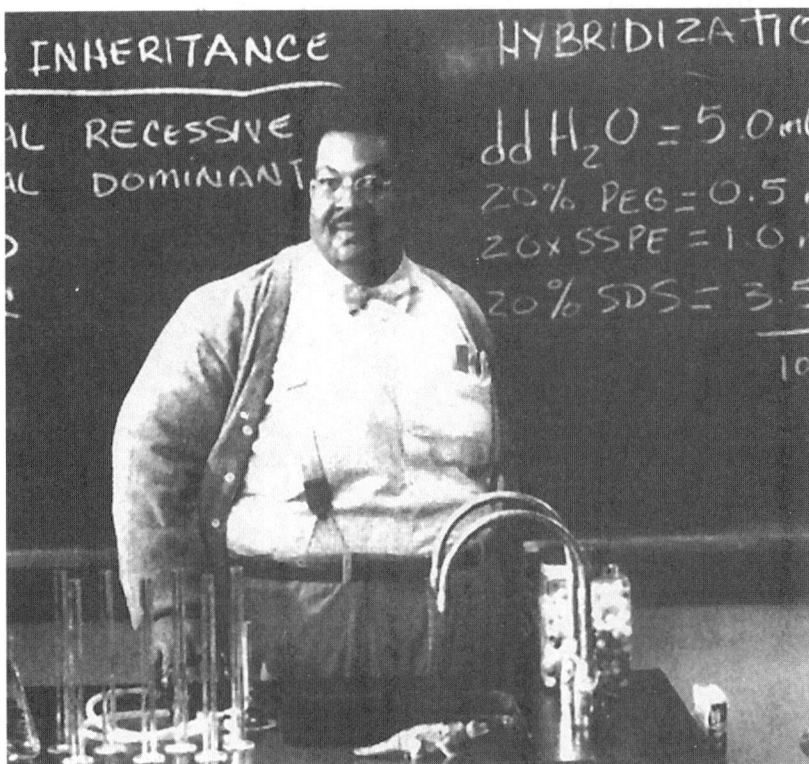

By the year 1996 the remaking of Jerry Lewis's *The Nutty Professor* (1963) with Eddie Murphy in the title role, the movies were utilizing advanced special effects. That's really Eddie Murphy as Professor Sherman Klump, a brilliant scientist who is working to resolve the problem of obesity (Universal). Photo from author's collection. In 2000, computer-enhanced imagery proved how effective it could be when a sequel appeared: *Nutty Professor II: The Klumps* (Universal). Eddie Murphy impeccably played all the parts of the Klump family by himself.

**Three Ever-Popular Television Programs that Survived as Reruns:**
1. *All in the Family* was the most realistic family comedy that appeared thus far in the early '70s. In this photo only Lionel Jefferson seems to have something to laugh about, much to Archie Bunker's chagrin. Lionel was the son of the social-climbing Jeffersons who lived next door. As a working-class bigot, the Jeffersons proved the bane of Archie's existence. But *All in the Family* proved so profitable to CBS that it ran from 1971 to 1991. Photo from author's collection.

2. As seen through the youthful eyes of Arthur "the Fonz" Fonzarelli (Henry Winkler) and Richie Cunningham (Ron Howard, destined for future fame as a director of big films) *Happy Days* seemed aptly titled, enjoying a ten-year run from 1974 to 1984 for ABC. Photo from author's collection.

3. In the shared Miami home of *The Golden Girls* (NBC, 1985–93) we saw some hilarious comedy enacted for which the show was awarded ten Emmy Awards. Of the four residents, here are two old TV professionals—Betty White and Bea Arthur. Photo from author's collection.

# 3

# 1980–2000—Fantasizing Reality as a Refuge from Real-World Uncertainties

[W]e are a nation of would-be actors. No other culture has ever been so drenched in make-believe. Children spend more time watching television than going to school, and most of what they watch is fiction . . . Actors are national celebrities, and show business is widely recognized as a metaphor for the conduct of life.

—Thomas M. Disch, *The Dreams Our
Stuff Is Made of: How Science
Fiction Conquered the World*

The Internet is as persistent as it is potent, an indelible and uncontainable presence in the culture. In fact, the Internet isn't separate from the culture at all; it is the culture. All the trash, flotsam and spillage of our society gets its moment there, where the tiniest obsession has its spot on the shelf, right next to Bach and charity and sunsets.

—Daniel Okrent, *Time*, 10 May 1999

DURING THE TWENTIETH CENTURY'S FINAL TWO DECADES, THE theatrical style of media-made culture infiltrated practically every sector of American society. It was a sociocultural phenomenon pervasive enough to characterize the administrations of three presidents who wielded worldwide influence. In fact, former movie star Ronald Reagan seemed a throwback to a 1930s Frank Capra hero, not only for his acting know-how but his small-town origin's loyalty to old-time values and traditions. Such a storied background, coupled with his personable manner of communicating his policies, projected an optimistic aura during the transition period following the frustrating domestic and foreign relations problems of Jimmy Carter's term in office. Though the major achievements of Reagan's Republican tenure were not realized until his second term, he was off to as positive a start as he could possibly have hoped for with the release of the Americans whom Iran had held hostage during the last phase of Carter's office. Later, Reagan's tough dealings with the Russians kept him in high esteem, ushering in a new sense of nationalism and leading to the decline of Communist expansion and warmer relations with the Soviets. As Franklin Roosevelt's folksy geniality had charmed radio listeners a half-century earlier, Ronald Reagan's positive television image, reinforced by his understanding of the "affinity between politics and acting," in Neal Gabler's words, helped distract viewers from such pressing issues as crime and the problems of the indigent.[1] Although Reagan's attention to military buildup and disdain for government-supported welfare in favor of privatism were praised by many, certain covert operations that came to light during his administration were widely condemned. Yet despite the ignominy of the Iran-Contra affair, he left office as one of the nation's most popular presidents. He had even managed to survive an assassin's bullet with the true grit of a movie hero.

George Bush, his successor, also tended to avoid domestic problems by paying more attention to a strong foreign policy. Although he was born into wealth, Bush displayed all the hallmarks of the American success story—a Yale athlete, decorated World War II navy bomber pilot, and a profitable venturer into the Texas oil business. The highlight of his term in office was the decision to counter Iraqi leader Saddam Hussein's invasion of oil-rich Kuwait in 1991, thus making himself a leading player in this brief war. Coded as Operation Desert Storm, it was extensively covered by television, in particular by the Cable News Network (CNN), a twenty-four-hour satellite news outlet that had begun airing in 1980.

While not exactly escapist fare, war as a form of reality-based entertainment was yet another venue that advancing technology made available to television viewers. As a media event of worldwide import, too, the Persian Gulf War introduced fascinated viewers to a new kind of technological warfare, highlighted by the precision targeting tactics of the "smart bomb" along with the devastation wrought by cruise missiles, all with the visual impact of a Hollywood spectacular. Culminating in a resounding American victory, the Gulf War offered a degree of national redemption after the disastrous campaign in Vietnam. But Bush had difficulty resolving the ever-mounting debit problems of the economy during his tenure, and by 1992 the voters were looking to new leadership through the appealing overtures of the Democratic party platform.

Throughout the 1980s, the problems of the poor and the homeless, the concerns of minorities, the persistent crime rate, especially among the young, and environmental issues were largely ignored by the Republicans. As usual, their underlying philosophy appeared to be predicated on the belief that the inherently corrective manner of the American way would set things right.

With the problems of society and the economy continuing to mount, then, the stage was set for William Jefferson Clinton, a Democratic dark horse from Arkansas, to arrive on the presidential scene and promote his policies of reform and moderation in all things—except in his personal life. In fact, the dark side of his otherwise popular two-term presidency contained the sensational elements of a television melodrama: the rumors about him as a marijuana-smoking draft dodger during the Vietnam conflict, the shady Arkansas real estate deal that dogged him throughout his administration, and his persistent denials of sexual indiscretions that turned out to be true, culminating in his tabloid-saturated affair with a White House intern. Pursuant to the charge of lying under oath about his trysts with her, Clinton had to endure the humiliation of an impeachment trial. Incredibly, he maintained his popular profile among the people, which seemingly reflected the more tolerant posture of the mediated vision at this time.[2] As far as carrying out the goals of his office was concerned, though, Clinton could point to such accomplishments as a balanced budget, reduced unemployment, and a working policy of social welfare reform.

The most momentous sociopolitical development of these years, as far as the West was concerned, was the breakup of the Soviet Union and its adaptation to a modified form of market-driven capitalism. Emblematic of this transition was the unlikely appearance of a popular McDonald's hamburger outlet in Moscow. Fittingly, by the close of Reagan's tenure in 1989, the most symbolic event that spelled an end to Russian domination in eastern Europe was the tearing down of the Berlin wall after its twenty-eight-year existence.

## DEVELOPING PROBLEMS OF INTERNATIONAL IMPORT

Prior to Russia's capitulation, the United States had maintained its international vigilance by turning its attention to various trouble spots that had erupted during the Reagan administration—Beirut, Grenada, the Middle East, and even the drug traffic emanating out of Panama. Until the NATO alliance's bombing of Serbian targets in and around Belgrade in 1999, then, the most concentrated military force was organized to counter the Iraqis in Kuwait. Due mainly to the threat of nuclear weaponry, much had been done to forestall all-out war in the world. But acts of terrorism and other troubling developments near the close of a war-ravaged century portended the potential for a conflict of cataclysmic consequences, as the Islamic countries maintained their militant posture toward the West. Concurrently, Communist China, which now had access to the atomic bomb, continued its military buildup. By the late '90s the possibility of sporadic conflict, if not outright war, was still in the air, affording the mediated vision all the more reason to look to the diversions of media culture for escapist release.

Other growing concerns of international import that the media focused on during these years resulted from ecological imbalances in the environment and its devastation by natural disasters. The decrease in the ozone stratospheric layer that shielded life and vegetation from ultraviolet radiation was revealed as the result of products with chemicals containing chlorofluorocarbons released into the air. Thus, an international debate arose over the problem of global warming, or what was referred to as the greenhouse effect. Another contributing factor was the destruction of the world's tropical rain forests, leading to an imbalance of carbon dioxide in the atmosphere. Oil spills were another continuing problem, most disastrously in 1989 when an Exxon tanker's spillage of eleven million gallons in Alaskan waters had a devastating impact on the area's wildlife. In addition to these concerns, the natural disasters created by tornadoes, floods, snowstorms, hurricanes, earthquakes, and even volcanic eruptions were common occurrences, or so they seemed, as those who subscribed to cable news programming such as CNN's were informed about them as soon as they happened. Television, through its power to convey a sense of the immediate, had now sensitized the mediated vision to the catastrophic event as commonplace—from the natural disaster to passenger plane crashes, terrorist acts, and, most frequently, violent crime.

## Ongoing Social Problems in the Domestic Scene

While international terrorism was rampant during the last two decades of the century, domestic crime, ranging from serial-killer rampages to racist-motivated murders, not to mention the various categories of interpersonal abuse, was also prominent. And, of course, television persisted as a spontaneous conduit for reporting these events and their consequences. Even TV's fictional programs were capitalizing on the sensationalism of real-life crime by dramatizing it. Although the overall crime rate was reported to be in decline by the '90s, an alarming increase in criminal activity among youth occurred during this time. Other than drug use, which remained a persistent problem, many attributed these acts to the violent content featured in television shows, movies, and video games as well as ready access to prohibitive information, such as the making of bombs that appeared on the unregulated Internet system. In addition, the easy acquisition of various kinds of firearms induced impressionable, antisocial youths to undertake the self-appointed mission of inflicting random violence on their classmates during the school day.

The American people may have been the best informed in the world during these years, but many were wondering about the kind of contagious effects the overexposure to violence in the media was having on the nation, especially its young. Did such programming merely reflect the problem? Or was it an inspiration for more violence? Although these questions would be endlessly debated, one thing was certain— never before had the mediated vision been exposed to as much media-transmitted violence as it was during the last twenty years of the twentieth century.

## Cable Television's Impact on Programming Venues

The 1980s not only saw the advent of around-the-clock news service on cable TV but a fourth national broadcast network in Rupert Murdoch's Fox system, which was an offshoot of his acquisition of the 20th Century–Fox film corporation in 1985. As an Australian who had started out in the newspaper business, Murdoch displayed an aggressive enterprising nature in creating his international media empire that included American newspapers and magazines, among which were the circulation-leading *TV Guide*, numerous foreign publications, and even publishing houses. A postmodern version of William Randolph Hearst, Murdoch was described as "the driving force behind the most far-reaching communications empire in existence."[3] Indeed, his holdings made the pioneering satellite efforts of American television mogul Ted Turner pale by comparison at the time. But both Murdoch and Turner's enterprises were finely tuned to the escapist desires of the media culture's growing segmented sectors, as attested to by Fox's orientation toward programming for youth and black audiences and Turner's attention to the nostalgic inclinations of older viewers by acquiring vintage movies and short subjects of the defunct Hollywood studio system, particularly the entire film library of MGM for his Turner Classic Movies cable channel.

During this era, cable television, because of its specialized programming aimed at niche audiences, became the dominant force in transforming both the face of TV programming and the mediated vision's reaction to it. Thus, cable was instrumental in undermining the media power of the long-established broadcast networks. As early as 1976, a sign of things to come was the appearance of the first satellite cable channel (Turner's WTBS) and Home Box Office (HBO) with its subscription service for recently released movies. By the end of the 1980s, over 60 percent of American homes were subscribing to cable TV, while many of them were utilizing videocassette recorders (VCRs) to tape the commercial-free movies that HBO made available around the clock, as well as to record any other cable or broadcast entries, even in absentia. In the 1990s, numerous new cable networks were catering to special interests, as a multifaceted lineup of channels became available by subscription in most areas of the country. Not only were twenty-four-hour news services vying for viewers but also channels that specialized in sports, cartoons, home shopping, weather, music, history, TV reruns, as well as old movies, governmental proceedings, talk shows to which viewers could call in their questions or opinions— and so on. Also, through the promotion of pay-per-view scheduling, subscribers could access both new movies and live sporting events, not to mention the sexually explicit programming available through public cable in larger cities.[4] Thus, cable television had, in an amazingly short time, broadened the mediated vision's range of choices among entertainment and cultural sources. Indeed, its seemingly unlimited potential promised even more specialized viewing venues in the future.

## REALITY-BASED TELEVISION AS ESCAPIST ENTERTAINMENT

However, cable TV's expanded services foreshadowed an increasingly permissive posture toward programming content. While the technology was now in place for immediate "live coverage" of so-called breaking news, often of the most shocking nature, viewers of broadcast TV were also being subjected to highly violent content in reality-based series of the late 1980s that focused on factual stories about the deviant acts of criminals. This category's most popular programs, like *Unsolved Mysteries* and *America's Most Wanted*, reenacted actual crimes supposedly in the way they had occurred, both to entertain as dramatic "news" and perhaps aid in the capture of a fugitive still on the loose. Ironically, in drawing viewers into their versions of mediated reality, these shows were naturally disposed to blurring the line between fact and fiction.

Although a later show called *Cops* derived its appeal from the live-action coverage of police investigating on-site cases, it also presented its graphic take on reality "in an entertaining way that [drew] upon traditions of crime fiction and tabloid journalism."[5] The technology that resulted in the portable or handheld video camera was the reason for this series' sense of spontaneity and thus the viewer's immediate feeling of "being there." Sensitized by extensive news coverage of the innumerable crimes that occurred in postmodern society, from routine bank robberies to the inexplicable actions of serial killers, most viewers of crime reality programs experienced the catharsis of traditional drama when they saw criminals brought to justice and societal order restored, at least temporarily. Aware, too, that they themselves could be victimized, viewers developed a sense of preparedness through watching such programs. And despite these shows' tendency to function as entertainment, their pervasive theme of real-life justice ultimately triumphant had great appeal to the conservative sector of the media culture.

As to its TV origins, crime reality programming dated back to the dramatic police series *Dragnet* (1951–59), whose realism was enhanced by star Jack Webb's curt dialogue and the production practice of filming at outdoor locations. The show was widely imitated, as its gritty narrative tradition was carried on from the 1960s to the '70s by such programs as *The FBI* and *Police Story*, which, like *Dragnet*, purportedly based their stories on actual cases. Though the central figures of these shows hardly seemed to have a life away from their law enforcement duties, the appearance of *Hill Street Blues* (1981–87) introduced viewers to the realization that those who enforced the law also had real personal problems. To dramatize this end, the series was structured around strong characterizations and multiple plotlines that extended over more than one show. Its technique attracted a more select following and established a kind of soap-opera style for other series to emulate. Other reasons for the show's durability were its groundbreaking use of daring language, edgy references to sexual relationships, and a film noir focus on the dark realities of urban life.

Thus *Hill Street Blues* stood in marked contrast to the glamorized private detective role of mistake-prone Tom Selleck in the 1980s' *Magnum, P.I.*, whose posh Hawaiian settings lent it a highly fantasized aura. Although *Miami Vice*, another popular detective series (1984–89), revealed a graphically realistic side by centering on two narcotics cops and their encounters with drug lord violence, its rock music sound track and special attention to the sexy women of the South Beach scene as well as the fashionable designer attire of its principals merged in a postmodern pastiche of glitzy glamour and shocking violence.

By the 1990s, as a more liberal attitude infiltrated the realism of broadcast television, attributable mainly to the competition of cable TV, a concerted choice viewing trend in police/court series like *NYPD Blue*, *L.A. Law*, *The Practice*, and *Law and Order: Special Victims Unit* (whose "victims" had fallen prey to sex crimes) resulted in increasing amounts of violent and sexual content as well as offensive language. Consequently, these shows' degree of realism was such that impressionable viewers could be induced into believing that what they were watching was, in the mode of reality programming, real life as opposed to a dramatization. Because of TV's visual power to project a more focused sense of reality seemingly more real than the diffused experiences of everyday life, viewers were now exposed to intensified violence in the guise of fantasized entertainment.[6]

That those who gravitated toward the wrong side of the law commanded an ongoing fascination for the mediated vision was grimly but entertainingly portrayed in the award-winning HBO series, *The Sopranos*, which originated in 1999. Ignoring the conventional limitations on vulgar language, violence, sex, and nudity, its stories were structured around a family head whose sinister involvement with mobster types reveals both their aberrant and human sides. That even the most disturbing realities of postmodern life could take on an entertaining aura was apparently the reason for the mediated vision's attraction to such an intensely realistic but humanly realized dramatic production as *The Sopranos*, whose success anticipated a long run.

Reality programming that merged information with entertainment, or what is known in the business as "infotainment," often made it difficult for the viewer to distinguish between the two. As tabloid journalism now leaned heavily toward sensationalizing fact, so reality TV exploited the appeal of celebrity culture in the upscale *Entertainment Tonight*, mostly leaving the scandals, social indiscretions, and sex crimes to tabloid news programs like *Inside Edition*, *Hard Copy*, and *A Current Affair*. The latter show, which was syndicated nationally in 1986, was Rupert Murdoch's initial foray into tabloid TV and proved both a hit and the Murdoch empire's unerring instinct for targeting viewers' escapist tendencies. Undoubtedly the same kind of audience that savored the print tabloids also relished the exposé kind of TV fare. But by 1997 so many tabloid newsmagazine shows had appeared, the wonder was how much more sensationalism and sleaziness could still be foisted off on viewers. Nevertheless, the competition for ratings resulted in special programs of the most low-down, sensational kinds as, for example, "Cheating Spouses Caught on Tape" and "World's Scariest Police Chases." Gross social behavior and nerve-numbing violence appeared to be the trademarks of these so-called "shockumentaries," a sign of the numerous reality-inspired programs to come that would involve nonactors in real-life situations.

Among the earliest programs of this sort was Music TV's *The Real World* (1992), a show that focused on the daily living habits of a group of young people, thus setting a model for later reality-based programming pitched to a demographic sector. By 2000, the rage for voyeuristic TV had even prompted traditionally conservative CBS to schedule a similar show called *Big Brother* and the more popular *Survivor*. In it a group of castaways was subjected to the hardships of being marooned on a desert island, with a million dollars as a reward for the most self-reliant survivor. In its revelation of viewers' attraction to staged reality as entertainment, the show's high ratings assured more of the same.

### REAL-WORLD ISSUES IN SOAP-OPERA AND DRAMATIC SERIES PROGRAMMING

In the meantime, the daytime soaps, in depicting the impulsive follies and social vagaries of its characters, continued to offer an earthy look at their problems through candid dialogue and depiction of their aberrant behavior. As a result, popular series like *The Young and the Restless*, *All My Children*, and *General Hospital* attracted their mostly women viewers, from homebound housewives taking a break from domestic routine to college girls avoiding the academic realities of the classroom to follow the latest escapades of a favorite show's characters. Also attesting to the soaps' popularity was the publicity accorded their leading actors in print media such as *TV Guide* and the tabloids.[7] In the '80s, *General Hospital*'s reality-derived focus on the medical profession found prime-time counterparts in hospital dramatic series like *Trapper John, M.D.* and *St. Elsewhere*. With a pervasive sense of life's uncertainties at their center, death itself was a natural player in hospital drama. By the 1990s the life/death conflict of TV's hospital setting took on an even more immediately compelling ambience in such shows as *Chicago Hope* and the emergency-room tension of the long-running *ER*, both of which capitalized on the doctor as a heroic type in postmodern culture.

As a more elite spin-off of the soap's reality-styled programming, the prime-time serial, structured around the self-aggrandizing lifestyles of its main characters, came into vogue in the '80s. CBS's *Dallas* (1978–91), in the manner of an updated Western in its theme and setting, had established the dramatic pattern for the format in the late '70s, through a cast of characters whose roles revolved around the conniving behavior of a fascinating villain. Attendant to *Dallas*'s surprising international success, other popular clones soon appeared, in particular *Dynasty* (1981–89) and *Falcon Crest* (1981–90), whose principals carried out their devious affairs and self-serving misdeeds in glamorous contemporary settings. Despite these shows' inherent posture that the rich are not necessarily the happiest of people, they acclimated viewers to a world of fantasized reality programmed as escapist entertainment. That even an ordinary small-town setting in this genre could generate special appeal, if the situation were intriguing enough, was proven by the surrealistic *Twin Peaks*, to attract an elitist cult following.

Although the status of the prime-time serial was in decline by the late '80s, in 1992 the Fox network, in its mission to target the escapist fantasies of a youth audience, patterned *Melrose Place* after this social group's increasingly self-indulgent lifestyle. Even more daring in sexual content than its models, the show enjoyed an astonishing seven-year run before bowing out in 1999. In that same year, NBC joined the youth movement by canceling its thirty-five-year-old daytime soap *Another World* to introduce *Passions*, a throwback to the Peyton Place exposé by centering on a small seaside town in Maine called Harmony. Its ironic name belied the offbeat activity that went on in it, especially among its young residents.

## The Situation Comedy's Concession to Subversive Subject Matter

Helping situation comedy hold its own in a period of decline by the 1980s were the social aberrations of postmodern life that continued to invade its content, as if such ingredients were necessary to keep attracting audiences. In contrast to the calculated disciplinary tactics that Bill Cosby practiced in his long-running show (1984–92), other family sitcoms revealed the consequences of parental laxity and frustrations involved in raising children. Fox's *Married . . . With Children*'s ten-year run from 1987 to 1997 owed its longevity to uninhibited satirizing of the dysfunctional family, a common enough social condition since the 1960s. Because the show's tasteless jokes about sex and bodily functions revealed how daringly outré the genre had become by this time, David Marc noted that this series stopped "short of convincing satire" by functioning as "more a burlesque of situation comedy than a sitcom."[8] Surprisingly, though, it was an animated cartoon series in the family sitcom genre that presented the most acerbically satirical jabs at the American way of life in the 1990s.

*The Simpsons*, which started out in 1989 on its long run, operated in outrageous but witty counterpoint to all the cultural values that the conventional 1950s family sitcom had stood for. It, in fact, assumed a wide-ranging subversive posture that poked fun at everything in the contemporary scene, from suburban life and popular culture to political excess. In the freewheeling manner of an animated world, the show's characterizations, particularly those of fourth-grader Bart and his moronic dad Homer, interact with the show's other representative figures to present hilarious but incisive takes on postmodern society's problems—rebellious children, mismanaged schools, dysfunctional parents, problems in the workplace, and misguided public officials, to name only a few. Ironically, the fantasy form that Walt Disney had pioneered as an escape from reality was now transforming reality itself into escapist entertainment.

Cashing in on *The Simpsons'* surprising success, animated series for adult audiences began to inundate prime-time scheduling, especially on Fox. One in particular, *King of the Hill*, beginning in 1997, transposed the concerns of suburban living to a Texas setting with a cast of neighborhood characters whose strained relationships and redneck idiosyncrasies contributed a great deal to the show's Southern-styled humor.[9]

That both *The Simpsons* and *King of the Hill* were prime-time hits revealed the Fox network's fearless approach to the kind of fantasized reality programming it subjected the mediated vision to in the waning years of the twentieth century. Indeed, with a varied lineup of hip sitcom series since its inception, Fox, in broadening its programming base to capture a diversity of viewers across the generational and ethnic divides, had become a serious competitor of the established networks. In fact, by the late '80s, Fox's influence had become a powerful force to reckon with in television programming.

However, ABC, CBS, and NBC promptly countered with

edgy sitcoms of their own that also drew large, faithful follow-ings. This was particularly true of shows structured around strongly defined female characters. ABC's *Roseanne* (1988–97), whose title characterization of a harried working-class mother was its central focus, gained much of its humorous punch from Roseanne Barr's experience as a risqué stand-up comic. Thus, in her sitcom role, the sarcastic remarks she proffered were reminiscent of the vulgar tone of her night-club act, enabling her to establish an earthy image of the sit-com mother. Although some older viewers were put off by her crude counterculture interpretation of the conventional sit-com mom, others found the caustic verbal sparring between Roseanne and her blue-collar husband (John Goodman), as well as the acerbic put-downs of their children, a refreshing feature that contributed to the longtime popularity of this se-ries. Thus, the show's offbeat attention to its characters' prob-lems through their comical but honest interaction was the real reason for *Roseanne*'s success, as a similar orientation was to other viewer-receptive but controversial sitcoms.

CBS's version of the opinionated female was *Murphy Brown* (1988–98), whose title character (Candice Bergen) was a TV news reporter with liberal views that were tellingly reflected in her personal life, most shockingly when she has a baby out of wedlock. Though such an unlikely event upset morally con-servative viewers, it was accepted by many as a reflection of the times, since couples were now openly experimenting with living together rather than marrying. Other subversive topics alien to the earlier sitcom, such as Murphy's bout with breast cancer, kept the show on a long run. ABC's *Grace Under Fire* (1993–98) focused on the plight of a divorced woman who has to support her children through blue-collar work. True to her times, though, the title character, aptly played by Brett But-ler, exhibited a sharp-tongued off-color wit that not only rein-forced her self-sufficient ways, it turned this show into a sitcom hit.

The four single females featured in CBS's *Designing Women* (1986–93) were Southern working girls who shared the same apartment suite but whose differing personalities humorously showcased their take on life in the big city of At-lanta. As many problems of single sitcom women of this time revolved around sex, this situation found its most explicit revelations by the late '90s in HBO's well-received series, *Sex and the City*, and its focus on the amorous activities of professional young women in New York's singles scene. Another series, which dared to structure this premise around a group of retired single women, was NBC's surprise hit, *The Golden Girls* (1985–93). Going against type, these women were undeterred by age in their common goal to enjoy their latter years. In fact, the show's four principals exuded a comically volatile chemistry through their candid reaction to subject matter and situations normally considered inappropriate for an older age group. That this demographic category found a ready-made audience should not have been too surprising, as by this time the country's so-called senior citizens comprised a sizable sector of the population, who were leading healthier lifestyles that translated into longer lives.

As it had been since the time of Theodore Dreiser's *Sister Carrie*, controversial subject matter seemed to lend itself naturally to themes about the problems and concerns of women. In 1997 a highly promoted episode of *Ellen* had the title character "coming out" to declare herself a lesbian in both her TV role and real life. The show resulted in a widespread debate over both the propriety of such subject matter for television and the fact that the show's star, Ellen DeGeneres, used it to declare her real-life sexual preference. Since a 1971 episode of *All in the Family*, homosexual characters had been occasionally appearing in television series, conditioning the mediated vision to the reality and acceptance of such socially marginalized characterizations. A 1994 *Roseanne* episode was structured around a "lesbian kiss" planted on the show's title character in her daring venture to a gay hangout. By 1998, the gay character of *Will & Grace*, who shared an apartment with a straight woman, was a popular fit, though in 2000 the usually masculine-defined John Goodman appeared miscast in the role of a gay father in the short-lived sitcom *Normal, Ohio*. Nevertheless, by this time homosexuality as either a topic or in characterization did not pose as much of a controversial issue as it once had.

As the problem of alcoholism was considered more appropriate in a dramatic context, drinking had been treated in the sitcom, if at all, in a naturally humorous light. However, the freewheeling comic approach of NBC's *Cheers* (1982–93) raised the sociability of the drinking life to new heights. After a slow start, the show soon became a smash hit with its setting of a Boston neighborhood bar where a diverse group of regulars assemble to socialize over drinks. The characters who delight in jibing the bartender and waitresses as well as each other with sardonic one-liners were played against an ongoing series of subplots featuring the bar's womanizing owner (Ted Danson). Popular enough to win twenty-seven Emmy Awards, the *Cheers* spirit lived on in a spin-off starring one of the bar's regulars. The long-running *Frasier*, which started in 1993, had its psychiatrist title character (Kelsey Grammer) at the helm of a call-in radio show. Ironically, Grammer's real-life personal problems surfaced in his character, resulting in a more fully realized role that turned the show into another award-winning hit. Accordingly, it affirmed the fact that a sitcom's success now turned on how amusingly clever it could be in interpreting the widespread personal problems common to postmodern living.

## THE THEME OF RACE IN THE FAMILY SITCOM AND OTHER VARIATIONS

In the 1980s, a move toward portraying the nuclear family in a more positive light appeared in *The Cosby Show*, mentioned earlier, in which popular comedian Bill Cosby played the head of an upper-middle-class African American family. During an era when race relations were still problematic, it was somewhat ironic that a series about a black family's day-to-day concerns was so well received, winning four Emmys over the course of its long run. In breaking the stereotype of the conventional black-family ghetto image, though, this sitcom must have come across to many white viewers as a highly idealized interpretation of the black experience. But by this time, shows that avoided the American dilemma of race issues had come into vogue, as producers apparently reasoned that a valid way to circumvent the problems of race was through humor. Thus such series as *Benson*, *Different Strokes*, and *Webster* offered unique approaches to racial matters, particularly the latter two shows. They, in fact, dared to structure their series around the concerns of white parents who had adopted black children, with both amusing and surprisingly positive results. For a sitcom to take problems too seriously and not place them in a pervasively humorous context was to risk cancellation, which is what happened in 1987 to *Frank's Place*, whose all-black cast personally reacted to racist concerns. It would appear, then, that while the sitcom of this time had taken on an aura of realism, some issues were still considered too over the edge for the sitcom to portray. But to black viewers, a more real concern lay in the lack of black representation in mainstream programming.[10]

Demographics, of course, had a lot to do with whether a sitcom was successful or not, and networks, particularly Fox, recognizing that the mediated vision had now evolved into a diverse range of interests, were offering shows directed at select social groups, as noted. Nevertheless, some of the most popular still cut across the lines of age, gender, and ethnicity. For example, ABC's *Home Improvement*, in part a takeoff on technological gimmickry designed to aid the do-it-yourself male suburbanite, lasted from 1991 to 1998. Like *Cosby*, it succeeded in countering the cynicism of *Married . . . With Children* by showing that the middle-class family could be functional in spite of its problems. Though the macho poseur of the show's father figure (Tim Allen) belies his disastrous home maintenance escapades and ironically those on his own home improvement TV show, he has the best interests of his family and friends at heart. They, in turn, come across as the kind of people that appeals to a diverse television audience.

A more upscale show apparently aimed at urban professionals in the 25- to 35-year-old age group attracted a surprisingly strong following throughout its long run. *Seinfeld*, which started out in 1990, derived part of its appeal from the reputation of its title character, who transitioned his real-life role as a hip stand-up comedian into a TV show. In it, Jerry Seinfeld, even as a New York show-business celebrity, played off his own uncertainties about life against a lineup of neurotic hangers-on whose constant but frustrating search for meaningful social identities in multiple story lines generated the show's predominantly puerile male humor. Praised by critics who ironically labeled it "the show about nothing," *Seinfeld* might have symbolized to many the state of postmodern televised entertainment at the time. Nevertheless, it achieved a large cult following, as attested to by the viewing share of its final show in 1998.

Although the nostalgic ambience that still lingered in the '90s saw numerous reruns of 1950s–60s sitcoms appearing in syndication as well as on nostalgia-oriented networks like Nickelodeon's Nick at Nite and TV Land, a more realistic kind of nostalgia inspired the premise of Fox's *That '70s Show*, which started out in 1998. It, in fact, purported to reveal what

youths of the 1970s were really up to in their waking moments: mainly having a good time breaking the social code of
their parents, and looking to fulfill their sexual obsessions. If
this sitcom was a valid indicator, reality had now even infiltrated the long-fantasized province of nostalgia.

By century's end, then, the reality-oriented situation comedy was still finding ways to comment on postmodern life
through numerous variations, from HBO's *The Larry Sanders
Show* (1992–98), a brilliant lampoon of the late-night talk
show with Garry Shandling in the title role, to the quarrel-
some but amusing family members of Fox's *Malcolm in the
Middle,* the latest edgy take on the nuclear family, which
started in 1999. The sitcom's evolving focus on humor, no
matter how subversive in posture and content, still played to
viewers' realization that any problem was not so serious it
couldn't be laughed at. This understanding, in turn, enhanced
the sitcom's ongoing attraction as a reliable escapist outlet
sensitive to the mediated vision's longing for a lost sense of
community. Or, as Ed Papazian observes, sitcoms are "the
closest television comes to communicating with viewers as
human beings. Watching them, audiences let down their barriers and laugh; the very process is a release, which is triggered because the viewer sees something on the screen that
affects him as a person."[11] The most popular sitcoms, then,
have been those that have drawn viewers into a fabricated
world that, in spite of the intrusion of harsh social realities,
reaffirms a sense of communal belonging in an increasingly
fragmented society.

## OTHER APPROACHES TO DRAMATIZING THE REAL WORLD

By this time, though, the new sitcoms were facing stiff competition from compelling dramatic productions in the format
of seasonal series, as discussed earlier, and movies made for
television. After the positive reception of *Roots*, miniseries
continued to capitalize on the success of best-selling fiction
in such 1983 miniseries productions as Herman Wouk's novel
about World War II, *The Winds of War*, and James Clavell's
*Shogun*, about the political intrigues of seventeenth-century
Japan. Though some sponsors were fearful that viewing interest might wane in series that could last as long as twelve
hours, their redeeming quality was a reliance on a balanced

mixture of fact and fiction, resulting in a compelling sense of reality to maintain audience appeal. Like the made-for-TV movies, seasonal series were also taking on about any subject as fair game for dramatization, including homosexuality, the AIDS epidemic, drugs, racism, catastrophic disasters, and crime.[12] Meanwhile, the cable channels, through their more open approach to sex and violence, began producing docudramas and movies that derived ready-made subject matter from the nefarious deeds of serial killers, celebrity scandals/murders, and the tell-all biographies of celebrated figures that dwelled more on their shortcomings than their achievements. Indeed, as escapist entertainment, the problems of the real world were now perceived as a source that could be endlessly mined.

As broadcast networks scrambled to beat the competition from each other and the cable channels, doomsday and disaster films that had become a Hollywood staple in the '70s were now showing up more frequently on TV. An early example was ABC's *The Day After* (1983), a widely promoted made-for-TV movie that dealt with the aftermath of an atomic bomb attack on an ordinary American city. By seeming more fact than fiction, it was yet another example of television's power to induce viewers into accepting fiction as reality.[13] In this light, the highly popular horror fiction of Stephen King appeared tailor-made for the TV screen, which the 1994 production of *The Stand* chillingly demonstrated. This film version of King's 1978 apocalyptic novel told of the unleashing of a deadly virus capable of destroying civilization. By 1999 King's popularity as a master of postmodern gothic horror was such that he wrote a script especially for a television miniseries—*The Storm of the Century*, another of many takes on the apocalyptic mood at the end of the twentieth century.

## Presenting "Breaking" News as Entertainment

With TV news coverage becoming a more dominant source of information than the print media and, as such, a contributor to the demise of numerous daily papers, the mediated vision became mesmerized by its window on the postmodern world. Since the 1980s, in fact, the familiar faces of evening broadcast news anchors Peter Jennings (ABC), Dan Rather (CBS), and Tom Brokaw (NBC) had become directly associated with reportage of national and international import, not to mention that presented by the teams of cable newscasters on CNN and competing networks. While the evening broadcast programs had always been geared to outmaneuver each other in reporting the timeliest news, their two-hour morning shows now competed on an even fiercer basis in their mission of interpreting the news as compelling entertainment in spite of any downside to their lead reports.[14]

In 1996, the appearance of two more all-news cable channels, Fox News and MSNBC (a partnership of Microsoft and NBC), began to offer more competition to both the broadcast networks and Ted Turner's cable news outlets. To complement their barrage of periodic "breaking" news reports, the broadcast newsmagazine in the tradition of CBS's influential *60 Minutes* and *Sunday Morning*, with their retrospective, absorbing stories of an investigative or human-interest nature, continued to proliferate in the formats of ABC's *20/20*, NBC's *Dateline*, and CBS's *48 Hours*. In 1999 CBS even initiated *60 Minutes II*, a weeknight version of the highly acclaimed, long-running Sunday evening program that had made celebrities out of such insightful reporters as Mike Wallace, Morley Safer, Ed Bradley, and Andy Rooney.[15] Thus, programming newsworthy events and profiling those who figured in them made for compellingly entertaining viewing experiences and were now major missions of both the broadcast and cable networks.

## OTHER INNOVATIVE BROADCAST AND CABLE DEVELOPMENTS

By the mid '90s, two other broadcast networks, United Paramount (UPN) and Warner Brothers (The WB), were looking to cut into the viewing share of the established broadcast networks, while Cable TV was still adding to its ever-expanding number of channels addressing the special interests of a now vast and socially diverse audience.[16] In addition, many sites were being serviced by satellite signals with the potential to offer hundreds of specialized channels around the clock, from remote sporting events to X-rated adult movies. By century's end developments in digital technology promised even more viewing options, such as on-demand video with its capability to call up programs and movies at any time.[17]

A highly innovative marketing concept appeared in 1982 as

the Home Shopping Network, which not only attracted customers, but also competitors like the more successful QVC
channel in 1986. Through this electronic update of the Sears
catalog, credit card owners found it difficult to resist calling
in to order a desirable item displayed or modeled right before
their eyes. Further evidence of this seductive approach to attracting consumers, particularly women, appeared in the '90s
when retailers began experimenting with the trend toward
impulse buying through an interactive cable system that allowed the purchase of a televised item through the push of a
button on a handheld TV selector. Whereas the recently developed TV remote control allowed viewers to ignore commercial time and switch to another program in the interim,
this newer device was designed to respond directly to a home-
shopping commercial, ironically transforming the commercial into the program itself.

In the 1980s the marketing of television camera recorders
(camcorders) for making videos for personal use made possible the creation of one's own TV shows. This, in turn, provided the content for a highly popular family-oriented
program series called *America's Funniest Home Videos* on
which viewers saw the results of their efforts as a comical
mirror of middle-class social behavior. An offshoot of this innovation was the opportunity to record newsworthy events
that one might encounter unexpectedly—street violence,
plane crashes, automobile accidents, or some kind of natural
disaster. By selling such a scoop for viewing on either local or
national news, the amateur TV producer now had the means
to interpret reality for his/her own commercial ends as well
as personal entertainment.

## PUBLIC BROADCASTING'S ATTEMPTS
## TO TRANSFORM ITS ELITIST IMAGE

In this era, Public Broadcasting's elitist reputation that has
revered BBC programming grew more egalitarian and commercial by including in its traditional programming of scientific and humanistic subject matter more topics pertaining to
popular culture. Even in the area of science, Carl Sagan's attempt to clarify Einstein's theories of space and time in the
thirteen-part *Cosmos* series in the 1980s was a prime example of the updated PBS mission to entertain as well as inform

viewers. In the '90s, Ken Burns's multipart documentaries on the Civil War and baseball history revealed him as a master of this format. Displaying a natural talent for visualizing the cultural significance of subjects with mass appeal, he also applied his insights to shorter projects on figures of historical import. Burns's visual technique was supplemented in large part by close-ups of rare photographs and performers' voiceovers of personages integral to narrative development.

Equally as informative and entertaining were the subject matter of ongoing PBS series like *The American Experience*, which dealt with significant events from history, and *American Masters*, whose specials centered on important figures of American culture. To counter the competition generated by cable programming on the Arts & Entertainment (A&E), Discovery, Learning, and History channels, PBS broadened its audience appeal by moving in a variety of different directions. It not only televised opera and classical music concerts but reruns of the old Lawrence Welk Orchestra show.[18] In the late '90s a highly popular PBS series called *Antiques Roadshow* demonstrated that the mediated vision's interest in Americana and the lucrative hobby of collecting its artifacts was very much alive. Reality-based TV even showed up in 2000 in a BBC import, *The 1900 House*, in which a British family volunteered to live as its counterpart had 100 years before, discovering in the process that everyday life then was not nearly as easy as now.

The growing popularity of investigative programming like PBS's *NOVA* and *Frontline* series revealed both the democratization and specialization of the mediated vision's cultural awareness that such timely programming was responding to, and in this kind of factual focus, television was at its most visually compelling.[19]

## CELEBRATING THE PAST AND CULTIVATING ITS NOSTALGIC AURA

The History Channel, in particular, promoted its mission of bringing the historical moment alive by charging its offerings with stimulating narration. Capitalizing on a naturally endless source of subject matter to plumb, this channel was in a position to explore about any topic, from historically influential events and trends to those of nostalgic import.

Accordingly, nostalgia was the inspiration for many documentaries that appeared on the American Movie Channel (AMC), as attested to by its specials on Hollywood's filmmaking heritage. In this vein, Turner Classic Movies (TCM) offered periodic film festivals featuring the achievements of the most celebrated stars as well as interviews with those still living. The Arts and Entertainment channel (A&E) parlayed the mediated vision's fascination with famous people into a highly popular nightly series called *Biography* in which the lives of the famous from history and media culture were presented. The end of the decade saw a flurry of productions that surveyed significant events of the past 100 years. Heading the list was a twelve-hour documentary based on ABC newsman Peter Jennings's best-selling book *The Century*. But CNN sought to surpass them all with its ten-part series, *Millennium: A Thousand Years of History*. Clearly, the theme of the past's relationship to the present had become an entertainment staple of television programming.

## The Expanding Commercialization of the Electronic Church

Now even fundamentalist Christianity took on a show-business aura through cable television's expansive means to present its message to larger audiences. The Christian Broadcasting Network (CBN), for example, which had started up on a shoestring budget, grew into a highly profitable enterprise by the 1980s through periodic requests to viewers for support donations. Promoting its "born-again" posture and the promise of "life eternal" to believers and converts, numerous programs sprang up that revealed themselves as much more materialistically compromising in mission than the prototypal Billy Graham Crusade had been. During the late 1980s, in fact, abuses perpetrated by evangelical leaders resulted in both a temporary drop in ratings and revenue. Although the temptations of the real world had invaded the sacred province of those who professed to living the Christian life, many followers soon overlooked their leaders' misdeeds by continuing their support, hopefully to claim the ultimate reward of a celestial life.[20] While evangelical programs continued to spread the Gospel to a wide supportive audience, many of the faithful saw commercial television as a tool of the devil, whose abundance of godless programming was undermining the morals of the nation.

## LOOKING FOR ANSWERS TO THE PROBLEMS OF FANTASIZED REALITY

By the mid-1990s broadcast television had conceded the dominance of cable television and its power to respond to the special interests of social groups within the scope of the mediated vision. To keep pace with cable developments and hopefully reach all sectors of their viewing audience, the broadcast networks employed a variety of expedient strategies: twenty-four-hour programming, supplementary cable channels, on-site coverage of breaking news, expanded sports programming, and, of course, their annual deluge of comedy/dramatic series now laced with liberal amounts of violence and sexual content. It was this unregulated situation that created concerns among parents and watchdog groups who contended that America's youth was being exploited by the liberal posture of both network and cable TV.

In numerous opinion polls and surveys, parents, especially after the shock of rising school gun violence, called for changes in prime-time program content that would de-emphasize violence and sexual content. On occasion, their demands took on ironic overtones when conservative viewers objected to the depiction of sexual disease problems despite its educational import, as a critically praised *ER* episode did in dealing with the AIDS epidemic. In 1997, issues of religious concern, such as abortion and adultery, saw *Nothing Sacred* in the line of fire, as was the head-on confrontation with the social problems of race and drug abuse in Fox's gritty *Party of Five.* Though fictional TV of the '90s was intended primarily as entertainment, the question continued to be debated as to how far such fare should go in attending to the proliferating problems of the real world.

In early 1999, Scott Sassa, NBC's new entertainment head, announced that it would program "less sexual innuendo" and focus on "more racial diversity and traditional families," as opposed to the glut of ritualized shows about "white young professionals living in Manhattan without children."[21] Nevertheless, the fall 1999 season reflected a drop in ethnic diversity and a rise in vulgar language, violent behavior, and sexual content, almost as though these shows were attempting to emulate, if not surpass, the vulgarity of cable shows.

A parallel situation characterized the "reality" programming of syndicated talk shows on which it seemed no topic was considered too objectionable. While hosts such as Jerry Springer, Geraldo, and Jenny Jones introduced guests from marginalized areas of society who revealed intimate details of their aberrant lifestyles in combative sessions that often erupted in violent reactions, a great deal of controversy raged over the worth of such programming that many labeled "trash TV."[22] Though producers maintained that they were giving viewers what they wanted, parents countered that what they wanted was suitable entertainment the whole family could watch.

To justify dramatic series that dwelled on the harsh realities of life, defenders pointed to local and national TV news coverage in which real-life crime was by far the dominant news item. Moreover, a study released in late 1999 revealed that the new shows scheduled in the prime-time family hour contained as much and, in some cases, more vulgar language, sexual references, and violent content than in 1998.[23] In reaction to this development, major sponsors like General Motors, Proctor & Gamble, and IBM, fearful of what objectionable programs might do to their product advertising, made a pact in 1999 to attract more writers to create family-oriented scripts structured around traditional values in the vein of CBS's *Touched by an Angel* and the WB's *7th Heaven*.

To avoid the seemingly entrenched vulgarity of fin de siècle TV, many viewers found escapist solace in the traditional sitcom format of the 1950s–60s. To them, watching reruns of such old-time favorites as *The Andy Griffith Show*, *I Love Lucy*, and *My Three Sons* had a therapeutic effect through their depiction of apparently more stable times. Thus, the 1990s saw a resurgence of interest in old series syndicated on the broadcast networks and those scheduled on the Nick at Nite and TV Land cable channels. Significantly, in *TV Guide*'s 1997 listing of the 100 all-time best episodes of sitcoms and dramatic series, twelve of the top twenty were produced in the 1950s–70s era, with a 1975 *Mary Tyler Moore* episode at the top of the list and a 1952 *I Love Lucy* show second. Relevant here, too, is that of these twenty, fifteen were sitcoms.[24]

A prime example of a TV dramatic series of enduring appeal, due mainly to the sense of social values it imparted, was creator Gene Roddenberry's *Star Trek*. Though the show's initial reception in the 1960s was lukewarm at best, its later revival and popularity was periodically tested in syndication and new series appearing from the 1980s into the '90s. Largely due to the cult following that the series inspired, *Star Trek* became an entertainment industry unto itself, producing eight feature films since 1979 and spinning off collectibles, comic books, computer games, and Internet Web sites that cult followers generated. In the vein of New Wave science fiction, the TV series was hardly shy about offering stories that reflected contemporary topical issues, as some early shows' plots were influenced by such concerns as the Vietnam conflict and race relations. More recent programs dealt tastefully with drug addiction, homosexuality, and even euthanasia. In addition, the series featured a multiethnic makeup of the Starship Enterprise crew from the beginning, and through its openness toward minority roles, the ship's leadership evolved from the command of a white man to a black in 1993 to that of a woman in 1995. In its special way, then, *Star Trek* had an overall positive effect in helping revive the mediated vision's faltering faith in the future. Indeed, its visionary premise suggested that at some future time ethnic equality might be realized and most of humanity's social ills banished.

## TELEVISION'S IMPACT ON THE CHANGING VALUES OF YOUTH

Television's most dubious achievement during this era was the ease with which it continued to addict the nation's youth.[25] Vying for ascendancy in proselytizing children in the 1980s were two polar entities: the popular fantasized violence of the Saturday morning cartoons and the entertaining educational programs of PBS, in particular *Sesame Street*, which by 1999 had been on the air for thirty years. This kind of programming, with its focus on inculcating values and self-esteem, emphasized learning as fun, a concept also espoused by PBS's longer-running *Mister Rogers' Neighborhood*. With educational programming viewed as a viable force to counter television violence and vulgarity, Nickelodeon and the Children's Television Network, producer of *Sesame Street*, collaborated to create more innovative programs that promoted a positive attitude toward the learning process by making it entertaining. For example, Nickelodeon's new show, *Blue's Clues*, introduced preschoolers to the pleasures of engaging in problem-solving skills, and, as a result, it won an award as the top-rated children's show of 1998. Thus, at this earliest stage of formal learning, TV was indoctrinating children, who were now inundated by a deluge of media distractions, into the fantasized notion that education should be entertaining.

For youth's older television audience the prevalence of sex and violence in programming remained a very real issue, not so much to it as to parents who were beginning to realize the futility of monitoring their offspring's viewing habits. In the '90s, sex as a special province of the young made its mark in Fox's long-running *Beverly Hills 90210*. But competition heated up between Fox and the WB in the late '90s when the latter network began attracting large followings to the sexual content of *Dawson's Creek* and the fantasized violence that *Buffy the Vampire Slayer*'s self-reliant heroine encounters. Dramatic fare directed mainly at young viewers would remain a staple of TV programming into the new century, heightening the conflict between the media people who contended they were giving young viewers what they wanted to see and the critics who maintained that what they were getting was too much sex and violence.

## Signs of the Times: Technological Advances and Corporate Mergers

Aside from any social concerns that television viewing might have fomented, a major breakthrough in viewing it was high-definition TV (HDTV), which by the late '90s was being implemented into the national network/cable systems. For some time now TV aficionados had been enjoying the benefits of large-screen television and stereophonic sound systems that enhanced the viewing quality of both VCR movies and regular TV programs. Indeed, employing such a system was tantamount to owning one's own home theater. The main concern in this kind of arrangement was that the bigger the screen the less defined its image might appear. Now, HDTV's higher resolution promised a crystal clear, well-detailed picture that functioned literally as an open window through which the viewer could relate to both fantasized and real-life programming.

In the '90s, then, the ongoing expansion of the World Wide Web and rapid developments in computer technology were anticipating telecommunications' digital era and its impact on the whole realm of media entertainment. By 1997 the advent of WebTV's interactive mode resulted from the growing interrelationship between television and the personal computer, enabling one to request programming on demand.[26] Reflective of this transition, too, TV networks were establishing online identities that users could call up for further information on a news item or a program topic. Although publicized Web sites allowed users to download print and video items and even musical recordings, their future was uncertain due to the questionable legality of such procedures. One certain thing was the freedom the Internet provided the user to create one's own site through which he/she could barter and sell and submit online his/her own creative output, including fiction, music, or film, to a worldwide audience.

In addition to ongoing technological advances, certain corporate mergers were also expected to play a big role in the future of media-made entertainment. In late 1999 the media conglomerates of Walt Disney and Time Warner saw the advent of a powerful rival in the merger of Viacom, Inc. and CBS. The upshot of this move meant that Viacom, whose holdings included the MTV and Showtime networks as well as Paramount Pictures and the publishing house of Simon & Schuster, now owned CBS, the world's largest pure-play media company. Then, in January 2000, America Online announced that it was buying Time Warner, a union that, as the biggest corporate merger ever, was intended to enhance the cross-marketing potential of the visual media. While such mergers promised the mediated vision more opportunities to relate to escapist entertainment, they also revealed the powerful role that media culture had attained in the postmodern age, posing uncertainties about dictatorial control and cost factors that could devolve on the media consumer.

## THE MOVIES CAPITALIZE ON NEW WAYS TO ATTRACT VIEWERS

As television proved a boon to moviemaking in the long run, so the videocassette's role in providing a longer life for a first-run movie generated a financial windfall. By 1999 the rental and purchase of films on video were earning the movie business a sum approaching 20 billion dollars, an astounding amount of money for a subsidiary enterprise. Another boon to the business was the development of the digital versatile disc (DVD), which offered a high-quality tape of a movie and its outtakes along with critical commentary by its director and/or stars or film critics.

Even the initial fears that the VCR would steal theater patrons proved groundless. Many movie fans still preferred to see a first-run film at the multiplex theaters that had been cropping up in shopping malls since the 1980s. Despite signs of overbuilding in the '90s, teenagers, as the biggest ticket-buying group, were flocking to these cinema centers in record numbers, where they had a choice of films showing at separate theaters within a complex. Even older people, who now watched movies mostly on TV or videos, were attracted to the multiplex milieu where, in addition to seeing a first-run movie, they enjoyed free parking and the opportunity to shop and/or frequent a restaurant. In one fell swoop, three of the mediated vision's most cherished options were responded to: unhampered mobility, consumer opportunities, and, of course, movie escapism. Some theaters even coddled their patrons with the comforts of home, from cushioned lounge chairs to food/drink service.

Although by the '90s, tickets cost more than they ever had, many films exceeded two hours in length, as though to give moviegoers their money's worth. And with film realism enhanced by digital technology, the Roman epic *Gladiator* (2000), for example, was considered a memorable viewing experience, well worth the high price of admission. While some complained about the trend toward films' excessive length, the movie business was reaping huge profits at home and abroad, as well as from another thriving subsidiary outlet—licensed merchandise for the young in the form of various collectibles inspired by numerous fantasy films of the time.

## FANTASY AND NOSTALGIA AS INSPIRATIONAL SOURCES IN THE MOVIES

If television leaned toward interpreting reality as fantasy, then the movies helped transform fantasy into reality during this era. Throughout the 1980s–90s, numerous blockbuster films that were promoted as media events succeeded at the box office by capitalizing on the mediated vision's ongoing nostalgic inclinations. The flavor of the 1930s–40s movie serials was still being updated for a more sophisticated viewer, child and adult alike, in the continuation of George Lucas's *Star Wars* saga with the appearance of *The Empire Strikes Back* (1980) and *The Return of the Jedi* (1983). That the series had generated a nostalgic milieu of its own was borne out after sixteen years when the first episode of a new *Star Wars* trilogy was released—*The Phantom Menace* (1999). As the most hyped Hollywood production in history, it fomented a mood of eager anticipation among moviegoers, especially those intrigued by the earlier films. As a result, its box-office revenue, coupled with the inevitable merchandise spin-offs, turned *The Phantom Menace* into the movies' all-time leader in gross profits at the time. In Lucas's attempt to inspire as well as entertain, this film, like its predecessors, structured its plot around the timeless conflict between good and evil. Even more enhanced by the latest advances in computerized effects, *The Phantom Menace* was another example of postmodernism's quest to revitalize traditional values through a mass-directed medium.[27]

In *E.T.: The Extra-Terrestrial* (1982), another big-grossing fantasy film, Steven Spielberg drew on the innocence of childhood to suggest an underlying message of universal goodwill through the friendship that develops between a boy and an alien. But in his Indiana Jones series, beginning with *Raiders of the Lost Ark* (1981), made in collaboration with George Lucas, Spielberg was more intent on providing pure entertainment through his nostalgic feel for the action/adventure film of the 1930s–40s and Lucas's attraction to the Saturday matinee serial of the same era. The film's mood was intensified by special effects technology that created an exciting world of nonstop action. Both Spielberg and Lucas, through their sensitivity to the nostalgic impulse of the time, affirmed their filmmaking reputations with big box-office attractions that responded to the mediated vision's escapist desires in an era when film fantasy reigned.

Comic strips and comic books, whose visual influence George Lucas had retained from his youth, also contributed their fantasized focus to big movies in this era. Pulp fiction also became a reliable source, providing one of its most popular 1930s characters for *The Shadow* (1994) and inspiring futuristic science-fiction scenarios in *Blade Runner* (1982), *Terminator* (1987), and *RoboCop* (1996). But the comic book superhero proved a bigger attraction. Although two more Superman films appeared, the first Batman movie in 1989 was a greater box-office and merchandise spin-off success. Portraying the title character straight, *Batman* placed him in the same dark urban atmosphere of his early comic book appearances. Sequels were inevitable as this film's phenomenal reception spawned *Batman Returns* (1992) and *Batman Forever* (1995). But they fell far short of creating the same grim mood of the original, while *Batman and Robin* (1997), with its colorful array of villains, revived the camp style of the 1960s' television series.

Newspaper comics characters whose heyday had long passed also responded to the nostalgic mood. *Annie*, the long-running Broadway musical based on *Little Orphan Annie*, came to the movies in 1982, and with its imposing sets audiences were transported back to the days of the big Hollywood musical. Critically, though, *Annie* was not too well received, as was *Popeye* (1980), even with the inspired casting of Robin Williams in the title role. However, *Dick Tracy* (1990) had more big names to attract an audience: Warren Beatty as the great detective, Al Pacino as the lead villain, and Madonna as the femme fatale. The effective use of bold colors in the manner of the Sunday comics page's original look contributed to the setting's nostalgic but menacing air. Whether such technical efforts resulted in a hit like *Batman* or a flop like *The Phantom* (1996), the movies continued to look to the comic book and comic strip as dependable sources in their ongoing mission to satisfy the escapist as well as nostalgic yearnings of moviegoers. Indeed, with the box-office success of Marvel's *X-Men* in 2000 and planned films of popular characters Spider-Man, the Hulk, and the Fantastic Four, the future of the comic book superhero in film looked exceptionally bright.

Throughout this era, nostalgia also inspired numerous well-received dramatic films seeking to recapture the mood of place in an earlier time. In this light, director Barry Levinson was among the most adept at projecting a realistic sense of the recent past as well as its loss in such films as *Diner* (1982), *Avalon* (1990), and *Liberty Heights* (1999). The plot of many films turned on the postmodern sense of irony, as did *The Big Chill* (1983). In evoking memories of the 1960s, a group of former hippie types convene after the death of one of their own, only to realize that their disjointed lives could never recapture the sense of belonging they once shared during their counterculture days. The film version of E. L. Doctorow's best-selling novel *Ragtime* (1981), whose title recalled a nostalgic period of the nation's past, focused on the troubling problems of race and class in pre–World War I America. *Field of Dreams* (1989), based on W. D. Kinsella's novel *Shoeless Joe*, in its search for the country's lost innocence through the mythology of baseball's pastoral nature, related outright to the mediated vision's propensity to idealize the past. As its titular reference to a mythic baseball field suggests, this film reveals fantasy and nostalgia as complementary themes that inspired the mediated vision to see beyond immediate uncertainties.

## Mining the Past for the Movies' Subject Matter

That Hollywood was still attracted to reexamining the historical past in a spectacular way was attested to when director James Cameron drew on the Titanic's tragic shipboard setting that had haunted the century since 1912 to produce a film of blockbuster proportions, especially its length of over three hours. As the most recent film to focus on the doomed luxury liner that sank on its maiden voyage, *Titanic* (1997) won eleven Oscars to tie the mark set by its epic predecessor *Ben-Hur* in 1959. In dramatizing the tragedy of eighty-five years before, *Titanic* capitalized on the advances in computerized technology to create special effects that won awards for both their visual and sound dimensions. A much earlier time that the movies returned to was the Elizabethan period, which inspired films dealing with both the monarch for whom the era was named, *Elizabeth* (1998), and its world-renowned playwright. To critics the appeal of *Shakespeare in Love* (1999) as a romantic comedy lay in its treatment of the great dramatist as an ordinary person subject to human error and the follies of a painful love affair. Attracting a broad cross-section of moviegoers, this film and a postmodern version of the Bard's greatest play, *Hamlet* (2000), revealed that the movies' adaptation of traditionally highbrow subject matter for mass-mediated consumption was continuing unabated at the close of the century. In fact, a number of films based on the works of Shakespeare were released in the late '90s, among them *Romeo and Juliet* (1996) and *Titus* (1999).[28]

Another way Hollywood responded to the time's attraction to the past was through remaking or rereleasing some of its classic films, either for television or theater viewing. Thus, 1998 saw remakes of the Alfred Hitchcock thrillers *Rear Window* and *Psycho*. A remastered version of the 1973 horror hit *The Exorcist* appeared in 2000, including previously excised scenes for audiences now more accustomed to the movies' graphic fare. In large part, though, the fascination with old movies was being attended to by cable movie channels like American Movie Classics.[29]

## SPECIAL EFFECTS' IMPACT ON FANTASY AND SCIENCE-FICTION FILMS

In what amounted to an updating of B-movie escapism, many films made the most of computer-generated imagery (CGI) that could transform the most fantasized subject into the essence of reality. This process was a boon to the visual impact of a comedy-fantasy film like *Ghostbusters* (1984), about a team of misfits whose business is to exorcize haunted domains. Also profiting from the latest in CGI technology was *The Mask* (1994), in which Jim Carrey's role as a small-time loser is transfigured by the donning of a mythic mask into a swinging man about town whose wild physical gyrations are reminiscent of a Tex Avery animated cartoon chracter. Using CGI technology to bring prehistoric animals to life in contemporary times was the challenge Steven Spielberg faced in filming *Jurassic Park* (1993), succeeding admirably in this and its sequel, *The Lost World: Jurassic Park* (1997). In fact, these films' realistic depiction of computer-generated creatures helped them become big international box-office successes, demonstrating that CGI breakthroughs were seemingly unlimited in their power to create realistic fantasy for the mediated vision's edification.

A more visceral trend in the science-fiction film of this era was the merging of fantasy and horror through CGI to create an atmosphere of impending doom. This end was achieved to horrific effect in *Alien* and its sequels (1979–97). Their suspenseful episodes structured around rampaging but rarely seen extraterrestrial creatures aboard a spaceship are among the most terrifying ever filmed, winning an Oscar for surrealist designer H. R. Giger's efforts. At a time when box-office success was being measured in terms of multiple sequels, the basic premise of *Alien* was unique enough to inspire three more films. Also, the lead role of Sigourney Weaver as an intrepid spaceship commander was groundbreaking in her portrayal of a forceful woman rather than the usual victimized type in this kind of film.

By now the blockbuster SF film had become a dominant force in providing realistic fantasy for the mediated vision. In the genre's special take on what the future might hold, it seemed any concept, from the philosophical and "what if" situations to the comically absurd, could attract moviegoers. Aided by the latest advances in CGI technology were the spectacular version of SF's conventional alien invasion theme in *Independence Day* (1996), the international reaction to the discovery of intelligent life in outer space in *Contact* (1997), the extreme alien violence of *Starship Troopers* (1997)—an adaptation of Robert Heinlein's controversial novel—and even the comic send-ups of *Men in Black* (1997) and *Mars Attacks!* (1998), which carried on the spoofery that *Spaceballs* (1987) had initiated.

But the SF film that distinguished itself as the most experimentally influential of this era was *The Matrix* (1999). As a visionary film in the tradition of Fritz Lang's *Metropolis* (1926), it depicts a future world of virtual reality imposed on humans by machines to keep them in their thrall. In a complex, violence-filled plot structured around finding a "savior" to lead a revolt and free the enslaved, the film paradoxically blends philosophical, mythological, and theological references with media culture sources. In their revolutionary application of CGI technology, brothers Andy and Larry Wachowski, the film's creators, fashioned a mythic world of virtual reality that viewers could appreciate for its startling visual effects alone, particularly the comic book-inspired action scenes. To the mediated vision *The Matrix*'s strikingly original approach to fantasizing reality revealed that the science-fiction film could now utilize the technology of cyberspace both to entertain and make a powerful statement about the quest for self-realization in the postmodern age.[30]

## Other Uses of Special Effects in Film Fantasy

Like the SF film, the numerous horror and disaster movies that appeared in the 1980s–90s also responded to the mediated vision's fin de siècle mood of uncertainty. In this vein, horror emanating from a familiar context characterized certain films of this era. Stephen King's novel *The Shining* (1980), as an updated version of the conventional lonely old house setting in the guise of a vacated resort hotel, set the tone by involving a middle-class family in the psychic horrors engendered by its haunted milieu. That the real world was vying with a fantasized realm was evidenced in the recycling of the 1930s' movie monsters as psychological variations on the themes of their original models, as in *Bram Stoker's Dracula* (1993), a faithful remake of Stoker's original novel by Francis Ford Coppola; *Wolf* (1994), an updated version of the werewolf legend with Jack Nicholson in the lead role; and *Interview with the Vampire* (1994), in which Tom Cruise plays the title character of Anne Rice's novel that updated vampire mythology. Even Universal's original Mummy character, which England's Hammer studio had revived in the 1950s, was resurrected once again by Universal in *The Mummy* (1999), this time as a comic/shock version that benefited from CGI enhancement. The uncertainties engendered by the approaching new millennium also produced films with supernatural themes like *End of Days* and *Stigmata* (both 1999). Complementing *The Exorcist*'s revival in 2000 was the satanic presence that *Lost Souls* and even the comedy *Bedazzled* focused on. With the resources of CGI at their full disposal by the '90s, the movies emulated television news' power to convey the immediacy of such natural disasters as tornadoes, earthquakes, and volcanic eruptions. The trend peaked with *Deep Impact* and *Armageddon* (both 1998) in their depiction of desperate attempts to deter on-target meteorites from Earth's imminent annihilation.

From the '80s on, then, the mediated vision's demand for movie fantasy seemed insatiable, and filmmakers, armed with the tools of CGI technology, were only too happy to oblige. Among the leading directors of the genre was former child TV actor Ron Howard, who produced *Splash* (1984), about a romantically inclined mermaid come to the big city, and *Cocoon* (1985), whose senior citizen characters relate to an alien force that rejuvenates their lives. *Babe*, a fantasy sleeper of the 1995 film season, was a whimsical but inspirational tale about a farmer's pig who learns to perform like a sheepherding dog. It won an Academy Award for its unique effects that humanized the interaction of the animal characters, mainly through their dialogue.

Though black comedian Eddie Murphy's popular role in three *Beverly Hills Cop* capers since 1984 finally petered out, he found new life for his film career in two remakes: in the title roles of the 1963 Jerry Lewis comedy *The Nutty Professor* (1996) and the children's classic *Dr. Dolittle* (1998). In the latter film Murphy converses with animals who speak through the voices of other well-known comedians, while in a sequel to the former, *Nutty Professor: The Klumps* (2000), CGI allows him to continue playing the six different parts of the family members who made the original such a big hit.

A surprise hit of 1994 also bridged the gap between fantasy and reality through the ingenious use of startling visual effects. *Forrest Gump*, in which the title character shows up in some of the most momentous events of the 1950s–60s era while meeting many of the time's most celebrated figures along the way, radiated the inspirational appeal of a 1930s Frank Capra film. Tom Hanks as the simpleminded but well-intentioned Gump is perfectly cast in this throwback to a once-familiar film role—the dedicated innocent in search of meaning in a chaotic world. *Forrest Gump*'s manner of fantasizing reality, particularly in the computer-generated scenes in which Gump relates to Elvis Presley and President John Kennedy, evokes both humor and empathy, a unique achievement that accounted for this film's wide appeal at the time.[31]

The dominance of television in American society during this era was the theme of two satirical, timely approaches to its sociocultural impact. In *The Truman Show* (1998), Jim Carrey's role of a man whose daily life is being transcribed for a national TV audience symbolized the medium's pervasive, unavoidable presence in American life. However, the irony of Carrey's character is that he is initially unaware of his image's status as a media icon. Similarly, in *EDtv* (1999), versatile director Ron Howard produced a perceptive look at the rage for reality-based television. Here, an unknown named Ed Pekurny is chosen to have his daily life televised around the clock, resulting in his becoming an instant celebrity, but with all the personal annoyances attendant to such status. Reality-driven television could hardly have been any more tellingly satirized than in this film depicting TV's power to bestow immediate fame on an ordinary person. By the same token, the price of postmodern fame is effectively lampooned in the inventive surreal comedy *Being John Malkovich* (1999). Fittingly, this celebrity-obsessed era provided film a natural target for satire.

An ironic fantasy trend in the movies of the '90s revealed a fascination with the theme of death. But it was not so much portrayed in its dreaded finality as it was an event to be kept at a comfortable distance or even romanticized as another beginning. The 1934 role of Fredric March as the Grim Reaper in *Death Takes a Holiday* was reprised in the unlikely yuppie-type character of Brad Pitt in *Meet Joe Black* (1998). Robin Williams, whose wild comedic persona seemed to be the main requisite for assigning him to offbeat roles, enters the realm of the hereafter in *What Dreams May Come* (1998) to find himself in a Disneylike theme park version of heaven. Even when a character's life ceased to be, Hollywood was seemingly motivated to paint an idealized picture of the afterlife in accord with moviegoers' fantasy expectations at the time. A more compelling approach to transcending the finiteness of death was *The Sixth Sense* (1999), in which a young boy's psychic powers enable him to see and communicate with the ghosts of the dead. In fact, this film was popular enough to incite renewed interest in psychics as a way to reach loved ones in the afterlife.

## EXPLOITING VIOLENCE AND SEX IN THE MOVIES

Whether a film's dramatic mood was nostalgic or fantasized, Hollywood forged an intensely realistic interpretation of its subject matter during the last twenty years of the century. But no matter how sexually or violently graphic the content presented, Hollywood justified it as the kind of escapist entertainment viewers wanted. Nevertheless, the outcry of those concerned about excessive violent and sexual matter continued, especially during the late '90s when extreme violence among the young was attributed to the escalating attention to it in teen-targeted slasher films like the *Scream* series (1996–97) and the gross satire of them, *Scary Movie* (2000). Though many films were being edited by filmmakers to receive an R rating to avoid the dreaded NC-17 label that since

1990 had denied teens admission to this kind of movie, evidence showed that those under seventeen were now accessing the supposedly adults-only films. It was also revealed that adult moviegoers were becoming more desensitized to violent subject matter as presented in adult-directed features like *American Beauty, The Talented Mr. Ripley,* and *Fight Club* (all 1999).[32]

The movies' stance on graphic violence as integral to their realistic intent saw it more readily justified in the revival of the war film. Though the Vietnam conflict was now far enough distanced to be treated as suitable film fare, it generated polarized approaches to dramatizing it. From the right-wing viewpoint, a series of movies dealt with the plight of those deemed missing in action, who, if not dead, were felt to be imprisoned by the Communists. Thus came the cycle of movies built around the rescue mission, extending from *Uncommon Valor* (1983) through Chuck Norris's *Missing in Action* series (1984–85) to the second *Rambo* film (1985) in which Sylvester Stallone plays the indomitable John Rambo, self-styled symbol of America's revitalized image that countered the shameful pullout in Vietnam. Movie-minded Ronald Reagan was so taken by Rambo's violent heroics as a one-man army that he venerated the character to help bolster his administration's anti-Communist posture. Indeed, the popularity of the Rambo character was of such import that he instilled a new sense of confidence in the American psyche, similar to that which Stallone had fostered in the *Rocky* series' down-and-out professional boxer who rises to the top by virtue of his self-driven, dogged determination.

While *Top Gun, Heartbreak Ridge* (both 1986), and the grippingly realistic *Hamburger Hill* (1987) attempted to reaffirm the patriotic fervor that had died with the World War II films, 1986 also saw a film that bitterly denounced the Vietnam fiasco—Oliver Stone's *Platoon.* In winning an Oscar as best picture, this film played on the divisiveness that the war had imposed on the American people through its characterizations of dispirited soldiers engaged in the fearsome day-to-day realities of a murderous, seemingly meaningless struggle. Similarly, Stanley Kubrick's *Full Metal Jacket* (1987), in its antipatriotic vision of the military's transformation of raw recruits into brutal, merciless killers, implied that war was the ultimate factor in demoralizing the human spirit.[33]

What happens when a disenchanted paraplegic veteran returns from a Vietnam tour of duty that left him a cripple is the subject of Oliver Stone's next foray into the Vietnam terrain, *Born on the Fourth of July* (1989). The veteran, played by Tom Cruise, who ironically had also been cast as the gung-ho pilot trainee in *Top Gun*, represents the divisive conscience engendered by a war whose supposed purpose was to contain the spread of Communism and assert American nationalism, but at the expense of its young combatants. *Coming Home* (1978) had explored the same territory but from the perspectives of two combat-scarred veterans involved in a triangular romantic situation.

As it had been since the 1895 publication of *The Red Badge of Courage*, the question of why young men have to go to war and risk their lives in battle was still being asked, but more grippingly in film. It was again forcefully posed in the film of *The Thin Red Line* (1998), James Jones's novel about World War II, the last war when ostensibly men knew what they were fighting for. The same question arose again in the graphic combat violence depicted in Steven Spielberg's Academy Award film, *Saving Private Ryan* (1998). That war could inspire black comedy overtones, as had the World War II setting of *Catch-22* (1970), also informed *Three Kings* (1999), whose locale of the recent Gulf War satirized the insane nature of the combat experience. No matter the degree of violence presented, though, the war film played an ironic role in appealing to many viewers as compellingly intense entertainment.

### Dramatizing Social Concerns and Their Causes in the Movies

At home, the movies zeroed in on other battlefields where the problems of an increasingly fragmented social order were engaging the attention of moviegoers. In the ironically titled *Ordinary People* (1980), the self-oriented values of the time's upper middle class are dramatized in the uncharacteristic domineering mother role played by Mary Tyler Moore and a tragedy that tears her family apart. Roles of this type, whether in a matriarchal or feminist mode, naturally relied on strong female characterizations to underscore their overarching themes. Ironically, though, *Tootsie* (1982), one of the time's most popular films starred a man who, in assuming the role of a woman, makes a strong point about gender issues. Dustin Hoffman's masquerade as a TV soap-opera personality helps him realize what it's like to be a woman in a sexist society, suggesting that a better understanding between the sexes might result if men would become more open to the personal concerns of the opposite sex.[34]

In the wake of the feminist movement, the roles of women who crusade for a cause were played by some of Hollywood's most accomplished actresses: Meryl Streep in *Silkwood* (1983), whose cause is the safety of her coworkers in a nuclear power plant, and Sally Field in *Places in the Heart* (1984), which was structured around the struggle to save her Depression-era farm from foreclosure. Having won a Best Actress Oscar for her labor organizer role in *Norma Rae* (1979), Field received another for this film. In a career marked by her acting versatility, she also tried her hand at directing. In fact, during this time a number of women directors appeared who made films that focused on strong female roles. Barbra Streisand produced, directed, acted, and sang in *Yentl* (1983), about a nineteenth-century Jewish girl who dresses as a man to study the sacred religious writings denied women. Susan Seidelman directed *Desperately Seeking Susan* (1985), which, despite its comic perspective, intimated that the search for identity in postmodern society was a main concern of women. In the 1980s, lesbianism as an expression of feminist rebellion informed Donna Deitch's *Desert Hearts* (1985). In its attempt to project a sensitive, humanly realized picture of the lesbian lifestyle, this film avoided the usual stereotyping of such characters. Though this was a subject that still upset conservative moviegoers, a now more vocal gay/lesbian audience openly complained when homosexuals were cast in a negative light.

A shocking film to men that undermined a positive image of female transcendence in the movies was *Fatal Attraction* (1987). Its plot centers around a vengeful woman intent on breaking up the solid marriage of a successful attorney with whom she has had a weekend affair that promised more but left her spurned. The traditional home life of the American way and how a careless, adulterous affair can destroy it is the central theme here. Another offbeat version of women gaining revenge after being victimized by men was depicted in 1991 when the title characters of Ridley Scott's *Thelma and Louise* take to the road in an odyssey of violence. During this time, then, women, both on-screen and off as director or writer, had become a substantive force, reaffirming their contribution to filmmaking that dated from its early days.[35]

Recognizing that the marginalized older members of society now comprised a large part of the population, Hollywood began to draw on the life experiences of this longer-living age group for subject matter. Even though *On Golden Pond* (1981) looks squarely at the issue of impending death, as particularized in the crusty eighty-year-old character Henry Fonda plays, an appealing nostalgic aura pervades the idyllic setting of this film's lakeside retreat. The pairing of old favorites Fonda and Katharine Hepburn, whose roles won Best Actor Oscars, also triggered warm memories of Hollywood's golden years.

## The Youth Audience and Rating Problems

The youth sector of the media culture that had subdivided into the cult of well-heeled whites was now being courted through Hollywood's more liberal approach to sex and violence, resulting in a glut of movies directed at it. In addition to this era's violent slasher films, noted above, teen films of the 80s like *Fast Times at Ridgemont High* (1982) and *Ferris Bueller's Day Off* (1986) were much edgier in their approach to the experiences of suburban youth than those that had inspired the 1960s' beach surfing movies. In fact, the entrepreneurial pimp role that a high school student takes on in *Risky Business* (1983), the film that introduced Tom Cruise to moviegoers, anticipated even more "risqué" times in the teen genre. By this era, then, sex-obsessed films like *Porky's* (1982) and *American Pie* (1999) were as daringly permissive as their PG ratings allowed. Adults-only films with NC-17 ratings ironically presupposed (or ignored the fact) that teens seventeen and younger would be accompanied to the theater by a parent or another adult. But the realization that this situation prompted youths to find a way to view such films on their own (most readily through their release for VCR viewing) motivated a number of outspoken voices to question the ratings system as well as condemn PG films' increasingly gross content.[36] Clearly, the movies' rating system was in something of a muddle at this time and in need of an overhaul.

THE NEW AUTOCRATIC ROLE OF THE
DIRECTOR IN FILMMAKING

During this time there was no more effective practitioner of realism in filmmaking than Martin Scorsese, who made films ranging as far apart in subject matter as professional boxing in *Raging Bull* (1980) and New York high society of the late nineteenth century in his production of Edith Wharton's *The Age of Innocence* (1993). He moved as easily from treating the social impact of the TV celebrity talk show in *The King of Comedy* (1983) to taking on controversial religious fare in *The Last Temptation of Christ* (1988). While the former film was a box-office flop but well received by the critics for its convincing perspective on television as a postmodern societal force, the latter's humanizing of a holy figure proved too "realistic" for Christian fundamentalists who boycotted it. Scorsese seemed more at home in subject matter dealing with socially marginalized areas, such as the dark, alienated urban scene of *Taxi Driver* (1976) and the criminal misdeeds of *GoodFellas* (1990). Regardless of the subject, the hallmark of a Scorsese film was its honest rendering, which made it a highly compelling viewing experience.

Although Steven Spielberg was a proven master at turning fantasy into reality, by this time he had become versatile enough to direct mainstream films with a firm grasp on real-world issues. In *The Color Purple* (1985) his vision often dwells on idyllic rural scenes for dramatic contrast, but it never ventures too far from the film's central focus on the abuse that the story's Southern black women are subjected to. While this film's graphic realism was objectionable to some viewers, Spielberg never took on anymore disturbing a subject to film than the Jewish Holocaust of the World War II years. *Schindler's List* (1993), which won Oscars for best film and best director, reaffirmed the actuality of Adolf Hitler's plan to eradicate the Jews at a time when the historical memory of its horrors had begun to fade. Although this film countered the mediated vision's idealized sense of the past by reviving one of the twentieth century's darkest periods, it did so in a compellingly entertaining way.

As Spielberg's stark black-and-white cinematic vision of anti-Semitism's horrendous consequences complemented the harsh ambience of *Schindler's List*, so Oliver Stone relied on a semidocumentary film style in *JFK* (1991) to rekindle interest in the controversy surrounding the 1963 assassination of President John F. Kennedy. Contending that certain facts that had been suspiciously stored away could shed light on why Kennedy was murdered, a New Orleans district attorney, as the film's central figure, seeks to uncover a conspiracy by those in power to countermand the president's intention to bring an early end to the Vietnam War. But *JFK*, by creating more controversy than supplying any real answers, was essentially another version of Oliver Stone's personal condemnation of a government that fostered a war that had torn the nation apart. It was also a testimonial to the degree of mediated power and license that film directors now possessed in dramatizing their views on the ills of the postmodern world. Accordingly, extreme violence was a major player in such Stone films as *Natural Born Killers* (1994), a shocking account of an on-the-road serial-murder rampage, and even his film about professional football, *Any Given Sunday* (1999).

## Addressing the Problem of Racism in the Movies

Until this era, racism was considered too controversial and problematic an issue to be effectively addressed in the traditionally escapist framework of the movies. While a film like *Mississippi Burning* (1988), in depicting the South's violent reaction to its civil rights problems in the 1960s, was motivated to sensationalize its subject matter, certain directors at this time were compelled to dramatize the problems of race from a black point of view. Among them was a young black with the unpretentious name of Spike Lee. Like a number of other directors who had learned their trade in film school, Lee's movies were independently made. Nevertheless, many films of this type were good enough to attract the distribution of major studios. After producing two low-budget films that explored marginalized areas of black society, Lee made the highly controversial *Do the Right Thing* (1989), which focused on ethnic divisions in a Brooklyn community. Through its realistic attention to the language and behavior of street life, this film zeroed in on urban blacks' most prevalent concerns of the time: police brutality, the dominance of white entrepreneurship, and, more recently, the competitive encroachment of Asians and Hispanics. Although some felt the film's candid posture would precipitate urban violence, it succeeded instead in bringing needed attention to issues either ignored or romanticized. A case in point of the latter tendency was *Driving Miss Daisy* (1989) in which the amiable relationship between a white Southern lady of means (Jessica Tandy) and her black chauffeur (Morgan Freeman) reassured conservative moviegoers that the old social standards that divided race and class were still intact.

In the same year as *Driving Miss Daisy* and *Do the Right Thing*, the Civil War film *Glory* appeared, the story of an all-black Northern regiment (commanded by a white officer) that engages its foes courageously on the battlefield. Based on historical fact, this film was a not-too-subtle indictment of racism in its ironic depiction of a segregated unit recruited to represent the abolitionist North. A standout in its cast was young Denzel Washington, who won an Oscar for best supporting actor. While he went on to play a variety of roles in such films as *The Pelican Brief* (1993), *The Preacher's Wife* (1996), and three Spike Lee films, including *He Got Game* (1998), his most memorable part was the title role in *Malcolm X* (1992). Based on Alex Haley's biography of the Islamic leader who was assassinated in 1965, the film, under the direction of Lee, seemingly attempted to depict its fallen leader's controversial life as both an endorsement of black separatism and a reminder for blacks to generate a more proactive societal role if they would attain some measure of social equality.

Spike Lee, as a visually sensitive director who combined social realities and the tradition of film as entertainment, continued to dramatize incisive social statements about the downside of the black experience in America. In *Bamboozled* (2000) he again drew on irony to satirize whites' conventional expectations of the black entertainer that media culture had perpetuated since the days of vaudeville, revealing racism as an ingrained American disease. Nevertheless, by century's end, films structured around blacks' acceptance into the social mainstream of American life were appearing more frequently. For example, *Basketball and Love* (2000) was more concerned with its characters' personal problems in their daily lives than the social issues of race.

## COUNTERING HOLLYWOOD'S SUBVERSION OF ENTERTAINMENT

In his book about the ways in which popular (media) culture has undermined traditional values, Michael Medved labels Hollywood the "Poison Factory" because of the volume of films it has produced since the 1960s that promote not only sex and violence but depravity, vulgar behavior, foul language, and antipatriotism. It is as though, says Medved, the moviemakers are intent on an all-out, concerted effort to shock in order to attract audiences. The reason for this, he argues, is that Hollywood's creative people have lost touch with the country's traditional values, choosing to impose their own compulsions and wild fantasies upon moviegoers. Filmmakers, in contending that the extremes of violence and perversions of self-indulgence are what movie audiences want to see, justify their movies as a mirror of society's problems and not a contributor to their cause.

Medved traces the overt representation of antisocial and deviant behavior in mainstream movies to *Midnight Cowboy* (1969), the X-rated film that was named best picture. But a similar case could be made for *Bonnie and Clyde* (1967) and its rampant gun violence. The trend peaked in 1992 with another Academy Award film, *The Silence of the Lambs*, which sensationalized its protagonist's attraction to cannibalism. But, according to Medved, the truly successful films are those whose box-office staying power is rooted in Hollywood's mythmaking dreams. In other words, the movies that stand a better chance of becoming big hits are those designated for family audiences and not predicated on the intent of shock. Thus, Medved concludes, the moviemakers should take on the responsibility of promoting universal verities through their medium's unique power to "cultivate the best dreams" of the mediated vision.[37]

Relevant to Medved's critical posture was the American Film Institute's 1998 list of the 100 best American films from the beginnings to 1996. Of forty-nine cited films made since 1960, most of them, from *Psycho* (1960) and *The Manchurian Candidate* (1962) to *Pulp Fiction* (1994) and *Fargo* (1996), portray some form of extreme violence and/or strong sexual content. But a case could be made against the earliest film on the list, *The Birth of a Nation* (1915), as well as many other exemplary films whose subject matter ranged from the warmly inspirational to the socially transgressive. Reacting to the list, a newspaper report observed that even though some of its "honored films were dark and horrifying" while others were "affirmative and generous . . . almost all of them, . . . touched or excited audiences and fellow filmmakers." They, in fact, "most often reflected Hollywood's long-standing and sometimes contradictory tastes for social liberalism, political idealism, glamour and populist sentimentality."[38] To say, then, that such issues have been among the major concerns of mainstream movies is to realize that over the years the moviemakers have been both American media culture's major tastemaker and reflector in depicting sociocultural standards and any deviations from them.

The dual role of Hollywood as entertainer and social observer is perhaps better understood in the context of director Milos Forman's controversial film about a real-life publisher's personal war with the law over the right to publish a magazine many considered outright pornographic. The climactic court trial's outcome in *The People vs. Larry Flynt* (1997) not only shows that the sleazy career of a socially marginalized figure can make for compelling film fare, it also underscores the First Amendment's free-speech guarantee to Flynt to publish *Hustler*, even as degrading as its content might appear. Moreover, the fact that Forman also had the right to film such a subject for audiences to see, even though they might disagree with defendant Flynt's defense, revealed the First Amendment as the real hero of this film and not Flynt.

By this time, then, the mediated vision, conditioned as it had been by a liberal postmodernist milieu, had taken on a more tolerant attitude toward films that dealt with the realities of controversial subject matter. In general, critics had become more accepting of films grounded in morally transgressive matters, despite the conservative sector's continuing concerns, whose posture fueled a conflict that would persist into the new century.

## COMPUTER TECHNOLOGY'S IMPACT ON ANIMATION AND THE DOCUMENTARY

Ralph Bakshi, as a daring innovator who had demonstrated that even the animated cartoon could be controversial, as noted earlier, was criticized for his version of J. R. R. Tolkien's *The Lord of the Rings* (1978), mainly because its Rotoscoped characters came across to viewers as too realistic for a fantasized subject. Still contending that the future of animation lay in a realistic mode, Bakshi formulated plans in 1980 for *American Pop* as an animated epic based on the history of popular music. Featuring real-life characters performing in Rotoscoped animation, it would be, in Bakshi's words, "the most complex story ever attempted in animation."[39] But by this time, when studios were producing only animated feature films, Rotoscoping was obsolescent, as the animation process was now being enhanced by significant advances in computer technology, resulting in both improved animation techniques and faster production schedules.

By now, too, the Disney corporation was the dominant force in animation, even on TV, which saw the new cable Disney Channel releasing reruns of its classic cartoon features and shorts of the 1930s and '40s.[40] Although *Who Framed Roger Rabbit?* (1988) combined live action and animation with visually appealing results, a stream of wholly animated features in the 1990s carried on the established Disney tradition of bringing characters of fable, history, and fiction to life on the animated screen. With little disagreement, most were well received, and *Beauty and the Beast* (1991) was even nominated for a best picture award. Other popular releases during the decade included *The Little Mermaid*, *Aladdin*, *The Lion King*, *Pocahontas*, *The Hunchback of Notre Dame*, *Hercules*, and *Tarzan*, which in 1999 became the first animated version of Edgar Rice Burroughs's legendary character. Further success came with the appearance of *Toy Story* in 1995 as the first Hollywood feature to be totally animated by CGI technology.[41] To the family sector of the mediated vision, the magical world of animation still represented movie escapism in its purest form, and in looking ahead, the ongoing developments in digital technology, especially as they were utilized to depict the primeval times of *Dinosaur* (2000), boded well for the animated feature's future.

That computer technology had been rapidly evolving during the last two decades of the century was further evidenced by the advent of the personal computer (PC), home video games, videotape systems, CD-ROM software, the World Wide Web, the digital video disc (DVD), and, as mentioned, TV's high-definition picture. The movies' equivalent of this latter innovation was the IMAX viewing experience in which the projection of documentary subject matter onto a gigantic screen virtually enveloped viewers as part of what they saw.[42] In addition to PBS, such cable venues as the History Channel and A&E popularized the informative documentary as an intensely entertaining genre, as many of them were formulated to generate the dramatic impact of a fictional film. Because of filmmakers' postmodernist affinity for blurring fact and fiction, then, it appeared that their next productive venture could very well be in adapting the documentary format to new ways of viewing reality as entertainment.[43]

## THEATER AND THE POSTMODERN DRAMA OF SOCIAL AND INTERPERSONAL CONFLICT

Arthur Miller, now America's oldest living dramatist, continued to write social drama throughout this era, culminating in three plays in the '90s that attested to his enduring dramatic power. In fact, *The Ride Down Mount Morgan* (1991), *The Last Yankee* (1993), and *Broken Glass* (1994), in their poetic realism, all contain thematic echoes of Miller's earlier plays. In depicting how past problems can impact on his characters' conflict between the demands of their immediate communal circumstances and those of the private self, these plays imply that the failure to develop a sense of social responsibility can be a major barrier to cultivating meaningful interpersonal relationships. Though by this time Miller's career had long peaked, among the biggest Broadway events of the decade was the 1999 revival of *Death of a Salesman*, his most insightful play in dramatizing how past ambitions and the social realities of the present can conspire to destroy one's personal illusions about life. Even after fifty years since its first appearance, this work not only found more critical acclaim as one of best plays of the year but as a landmark of American drama.

Edward Albee, an occasional voice in the American theater since his Pulitzer-winning *Seascape* (1975), returned to New York after a period of presenting his plays abroad to offer *Three Tall Women* (1994). It not only won Albee a third Pulitzer but assured his rightful place in the pantheon of America's leading dramatists. In the vein of his experimental roots, this work centers on the physical decay of an elderly woman, whose character is admittedly molded after Albee's deceased adoptive mother. The three actresses who enact her life during its youth, middle, and old-age stages revealed her troubled, loveless persona through an interactive display of wit and ironic compassion. This play is yet another example of Albee's commitment to the examined life as a powerful metaphor for uncovering insights into the complexities of human relationships.

The experimental influence of Albee was still apparent in the plays of Sam Shepard, whose output Albee himself had championed from the start. Transcending his earlier spontaneous manner while maintaining an oblique vision, Shepard's plays like *True West* (1980), *Fool for Love* (1983), *States of Shock* (1991), and *Simpatico* (1995) were departures from his earlier emphasis on the breakdown of interpersonal relationships between family members to focus on that between his male characters and their female hangers-on. Haunted by their traumatic pasts, Shepard's characters are representative of the moral failure of the society in which they exist, a milieu in which declining traditional values have been supplanted by the escapist allurement of media culture, particularly that of rock music and movie icons. Shepard's intimate feel for the pervasiveness of the media and their dominance in postmodern life were undoubtedly a major influence on his film roles as a scriptwriter, director, and even an actor during this era.

The versatile David Mamet maintained a similar critical stance toward a morally bankrupt society in which self-aggrandizement now reigned supreme. In *Glengarry Glen Ross* (1983), for example, Mamet's acerbic comic vision, underscored by its scatological dialogue, centers on the intensely competitive practices of cutthroat real estate salesmen. Symbolic of the larger society's obsessive pursuit of material success, this play is another of Mamet's takes on how distorted the original meaning of the American Dream had become. From his first plays, cited earlier, to *The Old Neighborhood* (1997), Mamet's alienated urban world, through its comedic irony, reveals itself as terribly lacking in both individual and community commitment to traditional values. An updated posture shows up in his prolific output of Hollywood screenplays, from his remake of *The Postman Always Rings Twice* (1981) to a thriller like *The Edge* (1997). Also, his own plays that became films, such as *Oleanna* (1994) and *American Buffalo* (1996), offer further evidence of Hollywood's ongoing ties with the Broadway dramatic ethos in their reflection of the moral vagaries of postmodern American society.

In their quest for a stronger sociocultural identity in mainstream society, both the feminist and ethnic movements' continuing struggle against sexism and racism was effectively dramatized in well-received productions during this time. In her satirical commentary on society's ingrained sexist posture, Wendy Wasserstein, from the comedic tone of *Isn't It Romantic* (1981) and *The Heidi Chronicles* (1988) to her most important play, *An American Daughter* (1997), remained the ironic feminist voice of the time's large number of educated young women seeking a rewarding niche in a patriarchal job world but finding personal fulfillment a frustrating ordeal.

In the 1980s, dramatic theater found its strongest African American antiracist voice yet in a cycle of plays by August Wilson. Charles Fuller had presented a powerful indictment of institutionalized racism in the microcosmic setting of a segregated World War II army base in his Pulitzer Prize play *A Soldier's Pay* (1982). It was filmed as *A Soldier's Story* (1984) and nominated for an Academy Award. But Wilson, in his series of plays, dramatized the black American experience as the consequence of a cultural conflict fomented by blacks' struggle for social identity in the macrocosmic white world. In drawing on the natural rhythms of black speech and the heritage of African American culture, Wilson's plays, like *Ma Rainey's Black Bottom* (1982), *Fences* (1986), and *The Piano Lesson* (1987), render the social challenges peculiar to black life in America as formidable barriers to overcome. Winner of Pulitzers for the latter two works, Wilson helped sensitize the public consciousness to a long-needed revisioning of the black sociocultural experience in twentieth-century American history.

While the plays of such a postmodern experimentalist as Lanford Wilson were still focusing on the loss of a sense of community, the social issues of the gay liberation movement found their most brilliant proponent of its cause in Tony Kushner. As mentioned earlier, his Pulitzer-winning *Angels in America: A Gay Fantasia on National Themes*, staged in two parts during the early '90s, was a crowning achievement of the gay theater's emergence. Also reflecting the spread of minority concerns during this era in American theater was the representative output of Chicano, Native American, and Asian American dramatists. Each, in his/her own way, sought to express a unique cultural identity that had heretofore been denied and supplanted by the dominant culture's allegiance to the melting-pot or integrationist ideal. In this development, then, the mediated vision's inherent inclination to cross over any kind of sociocultural divide was clearly evident in the diverse voices of ethnic drama's attempts to preserve their respective cultural identities within the overarching sphere of the American social experience.

## THE THEATER REVIVES ITS PAST TRIUMPHS

Like Miller's *Death of a Salesman*, Eugene O'Neill's *The Iceman Cometh*, another American classic whose thematic impact derived from the failure of personal dreams, was also revived during the late '90s. Its positive reception pointed out the realization that American drama was looking increasingly to its past achievements for timeless themes that related to the concerns of postmodern life.

Some classic dramatic productions were revived to present their universal messages to contemporary audiences. In 1993, *Lysistrata*, the comedy by the Greek playwright Aristophanes, revitalized the original bawdy manner that saw its women characters conspiring to withhold sex from their men until war is outlawed. In 1998 Broadway also resurrected Henrik Ibsen's *A Doll's House*, whose late nineteenth-century plea for woman's social independence echoed the rising cry of Carrie Meeber's day. In the same year, *The Diary of Anne Frank*, a Broadway success in the 1950s, inspired theatergoers with its story of a Jewish family's brave, defiant stand against the oppression of the Nazi regime.

Reminiscent of the manner of a Eugene O'Neill play was a regional production that won the 1992 Pulitzer Prize before coming to Broadway in 1993, ironically, the first to do so. In deriving its dramatic power from dissenting factions in the past, Robert Schenkkan's *The Kentucky Cycle* sought to reveal the dark side of human nature through a series of nine playlets that encompassed two three-hour presentations. To achieve this end, Schenkkan centers on the scheming, murderous conflicts of seven generations of Kentucky families. As a microcosm of the larger historical sphere, this play is both a record and a rationalization of past contrapuntal forces from which the American nation was formed.

Also looking to the past for source material as a parallel to timely controversial issues, various playwrights of this era produced numerous works with polemic overtones. In 1998, their efforts culminated in such plays as *Gross Indecency: The Three Trials of Oscar Wilde*, an off-Broadway production whose central conflict centers around the artist's role as social rebel and society's intolerance of it; and *Corpus Christi*, a retelling of the Christ story that dared to depict his disciples as gay, which to many, of course, was considered outright blasphemy.

Not a few playwrights, including one of Broadway's most reputable, were caught up in the nostalgic mood of the time. While the witty plays of Neil Simon still attracted a loyal following to *Brighton Beach Memoirs* (1983), *Lost in Yonkers* (1991), and *Laughter on the 23rd Floor* (1993), his attempt in 1997 to recapture the atmosphere of the 1950s in *Proposals* seemed to suggest that the creative energy of this master of comedic drama might have spent itself. Even so, at century's end, the postmodern affinity for reviving the past, either in new subject matter or in the revived form of its big hits, was still a pervasive force in theater that responded to the nostalgic memories of the mediated vision.[44]

## The Influence of Nostalgia on Musical Theater

The pervasive nostalgic mood of this era played a significant role in regenerating the nation's musical heritage, most auspiciously in the big Broadway musical. One of the biggest appeared in 1980, *42nd Street*, which was inspired by the 1933 Busby Berkeley movie musical. But unique to the tradition of musical theater at this time was *Dreamgirls* (1981), which centered on the problems of a popular black singing group of the 1950s Motown type.

A revival of the legendary *Show Boat* first went to Toronto in 1993 where an opulently staged version could be presented less expensively, but where, ironically, it met with racist charges. In 1994, the 1950s baseball era that was dominated by the New York Yankees, was musically resurrected in a rerun of *Damn Yankees*, with the legendary George Abbott, the show's original director at the helm, defying his 100-years-plus age.[45]

In 1993, London theatergoers saw a musical version of Billy

Wilder's *Sunset Boulevard*, his 1950 satirical film that centered on a reclusive film star left over from Hollywood's silent era. It featured the music of British composer Andrew Lloyd Webber, who had built his career on such big Broadway hits as *Evita* (1979), *Cats* (1982), and *The Phantom of the Opera* (1988). *Cats*, in fact, was Webber's most popular and Broadway's longest-running show, finally closing in 2000 after 7,485 performances. It had run long enough to generate a nostalgic aura of its own.

Thus, from the '80s into the '90s, nostalgia continued to be a major inspiration for numerous musical productions. A return to the Ziegfeld years was captured in *Ziegfeld: A Night at the Follies* (1989) and the *Will Rogers Follies* (1991). Even the 1998 musical adaptation of E. L. Doctorow's novel *Ragtime* was nostalgically affective in evoking an America of the early twentieth century. In 1999's revival of Irving Berlin's *Annie Get Your Gun*, which was first staged in 1946, theatergoers were again transported back to the time of Buffalo Bill's Wild West Show with Bernadette Peters reprising Ethel Merman's role as the redoubtable Annie Oakley. Ten years after *Jerome Robbins's Broadway* (1989), a pastiche of the great choreographer's achievements, *Fosse* honored Bob Fosse's dance legacy in such big hits as *Sweet Charity*, *The Pajama Game*, *Damn Yankees*, and *Chicago*. It was a fitting tribute to a rich era of musical escapism that owed so much to the innovative dance stylings of one man. Fosse's influence lived on in 1996 with the revival of *Chicago*, which enjoyed a long run.

That one of America's most original art forms would go on into the new century responding to the nostalgic inclinations of the mediated vision was presaged by the acclaimed revival in 1999 of one of the 1950s' biggest hits. Indeed, Meredith Willson's *The Music Man*, with its small-town setting reminiscent of the century's early years, had inspired some notable numbers of the American songbook that now generated their own kind of nostalgia for those who recalled the original show or the 1962 film based on it.[46]

By the 1990s, even as Broadway faced an uncertain future, due mainly to mounting production costs that resulted in higher-priced tickets, more shows were being produced off-Broadway and off-off-Broadway, while the upsurge in alternative and regional/resident theater around the country continued unabated. With imported British productions growing more prevalent, theater historian Gerald M. Berkowitz observed that Broadway's role was now "no longer primarily as a creative force. It had evolved into a showcase, a central meeting place where Broadway expertise could contribute to the proud display of the best work of theatre artists from around America and the world."[47]

## THE NOSTALGIC MOOD INFILTRATES THE MUSIC SCENE

The music of the recent past also inspired responses from the musical subsectors of the media culture during this time. In 1994 the Woodstock rock festival of 1969 was revisited, though by nowhere near the number who showed up twenty-five years earlier. The main development this media-promoted event revealed since that time was a wide variety of rock music styles, evidenced by the numerous alternative bands that performed there. Then, in 1999, when Woodstock's thirtieth anniversary was celebrated on a vacated air force base in upstate New York, things turned more violent than nostalgic as disgruntled attendees went on a rampage to protest being overcharged for the three-day festival. But commercial rip-offs and disrupting riots by drug/alcohol-incited audiences were hardly new to rock concerts during these years.[48]

By the second half of the '90s the revival of earlier rock stylings was in full swing. Even the twentieth anniversary of punk rock in 1996 inspired a resurgence of interest in its ear-assaultive sounds, while 1997 saw a nostalgic fascination with collectibles associated with Kiss, the 1970s' most flamboyantly attired band. However, the nostalgic event of the time was the 1995 release of a highly promoted Beatles anthology, accompanied by a three-night television retrospective. As discussed earlier, both the collection and TV program revealed how the Beatles' music had evolved from its original pop rock style during its short but revolutionary life into a densely complex, even surrealistic manner to become a highly influential force in the realm of experimental rock. Ironically, this group's music, which was initially condemned by the mainstream sector of the media culture, had now attained widespread acceptance due to both its influence and a nostalgic aura reminiscent of the times that had produced it.[49]

In the late '90s, when a yearning for the New Wave rockers of the 1980s sprang up among older fans, recording companies and the Music Television (MTV) channel responded with revivals of such groups as Bon Jovi, Culture Club, Duran Duran, and the B-52s. In the tradition of the Beatles' studio experimentation, U2, Ireland's best-known rock band, in its 1998 CD release *The Best of 1980–1990*, was representative of the recording industry's attention to the nostalgic inclinations of those looking back to the personally definitive times of their younger days.

Derivative of the specials about deceased rock stars on MTV and the Video Hits One (VH-1) channel in the late '90s were CD resurrections of performers who had died since the 1970s. While the music of Jimi Hendrix, Jerry Garcia of the Grateful Dead, Jim Morrison of the Doors, Janis Joplin, and, of course, Elvis Presley held a nostalgic appeal for older rock fans, it also informed young viewers of the most influential forces of the rock tradition. Similar treatment was paid to early pop rock singers like Buddy Holley and later living legends Tina Turner, Little Richard, and Elton John, who in 2000 were featured in VH-1's series about the top TV rock events.[50]

The popularity of country music, too, saw a revival in CD collections of such old-time performers as Ernest Tubb, Patsy Cline, and yodeling pioneer Jimmie Rodgers. A monumental project in this trend was *The Complete Hank Williams*, a ten-CD collection of the short-lived singer's songs, released in 1998. Apparently, death was no deterrent to recording technology in bringing an iconic performer's music back to life and actually improving on its sound in the process.[51] In 1998, the passing of legendary vocalist Frank Sinatra sparked renewed interest in his legacy to popular music. In fact, his role as a singer in the big band era helped promote a revival of swing music and the exuberant dance style it inspired. After starting up in Southern California, where fittingly enough Benny Goodman's band had introduced the swing mode over sixty years before, clubs across the nation began to promote swing music dance nights.[52]

Another musical trend harkened back to the pop rock era of the 1950s when clean-cut teen idols like Ricky Nelson recorded sentimental romantic ballads directed at a predominantly teen-girl audience. In 1998, an updated style appeared in the young male groups, Backstreet Boys and 'N Sync, whose sold-out choreographed concerts were complemented by their best-selling recordings and MTV video appearances. A female counterpart arrived during this same time in the phenomenally popular teen singer Britney Spears, who would endure by adapting her style to youthful tastes that could change overnight as yet another trend appeared.

## NEW DIRECTIONS FOR POPULAR AND CLASSICAL MUSIC

During this era, singer/actress Madonna continued to hold her own by daring to challenge society's conventional image of the female entertainer. As a result, the media exploitation of her controversial impact on fashion and sexuality made her the female pop culture symbol of the postmodern music era.[53]

By 1999 another Ricky was having a big impact on the girls by way of a new musical style called Latin pop. Reflecting America's growing Hispanic demographic, the dynamic singing of Puerto Rican–born Ricky Martin, along with fellow Latin-style vocalists Marc Anthony and Jennifer Lopez, was indoctrinating American media culture into an unprecedented international connection. Earlier, the Latino sound, from that of bandleaders Xavier Cugat and Tito Puente to singers Richie Valens and Gloria Estefan, had played a marginal role in the course of American popular music. But now, the popularity of Martin and his peers was transcending previous social barriers to attract a mainstream audience that, in welcoming other musical influences from abroad, foreshadowed the global dimensions that popular music would achieve in the new century.

During the 1990s, the marketing of movie sound track recordings became more lucrative than ever before, especially those of blockbuster films like *Titanic*, whose poignantly expressive sound track made it one of the biggest sellers of all time. By this time, too, moviegoers had become attuned to not only the rock-oriented sound track but the symphonic aura of much film music and its power to charge the dramatic moment with emotional depth.[54] Producing such music for the movies had also made high-salaried "stars" of composers who had been traditionally considered lesser players in the filmmaking process. In addition to their efforts, another significant figure who helped introduce elitist-sounding music to wider tastes was composer/conductor Leonard Bernstein. Through his conducting showmanship he made classical music entertaining to concert audiences, leaving a legacy after his death in 1990 that revealed him as much at home composing in the Broadway musical form as in the symphonic or operatic.

Other salient signs of classical music's democratization were surfacing, too. Opera was attracting a more diverse audience to both its live on-site performances and PBS's televised productions. Thus, the operatic form, in updating its tradition of staging musical expression as melodrama, brought the fantasized emotional appeal of spectacular theater to the mediated vision. In addition to the well-attended concert appearances of popular tenors Placido Domingo and Luciano Pavarotti, rising American opera stars Dawn Upshaw and Audra McDonald, in their crossover recordings of Broadway musicals' popular songs, demonstrated that the classically trained voice could also generate mass appeal. The year 1993 found virtuoso pianist Van Cliburn back on the concert tour, playing the Tchaikovsky First Concerto in the grand manner that had won him first prize in Moscow's Tchaikovsky competition in 1958. It was this composition that Cliburn transformed into the most immediately recognizable and popular in the concerto repertoire. Even the dissonant sounds of once-controversial twentieth-century composers Igor Stravinsky and other pioneers of atonal music that had repelled earlier listeners, were appearing more frequently in concert programs. It wasn't too far-fetched to say that this acculturation into a new postmodern ambience of sound was attributable in some degree to younger listeners whose musical sensitivity had been conditioned by the strident sounds of hard rock music. It would appear, then, that the early twentieth-century elitist posture toward classical music that from George Gershwin and Paul Whiteman's introduction of "Symphonic Jazz" to the popularizing efforts of Leonard Bernstein and the Boston Pops concerts had evolved into a more publicly shared experience in the late twentieth century. But as the diverse musical forms of media culture revealed, classical music was only one of a variety of musical sounds and styles pervading this era, all of which appeared to be competing for an audience.

## THE SYMBIOSIS OF THE MUSIC SCENE, TECHNOLOGY ADVANCES, AND THE MEDIA

In 1981 the inauguration of the youth-oriented Music Television Channel (MTV), whose emphasis was on sight-and-sound stimulation, provided further evidence of the subdivision of popular music into a variety of styles. While MTV's music videos, through innovative filming techniques, continued to reflect the dominant role of rock in American music, they also included the hybrid stylings of groundbreaking groups, ballad singers, rappers, and pop rock. Actually, by 2000 the term "rock" had become broad enough for Cleveland's Rock and Roll Hall of Fame, which opened in 1995, to nominate for induction such diverse individual performers as Eric Clapton, Bonnie Raitt, James Taylor, Nat "King" Cole, and Billie Holiday, as well as groups like the Lovin' Spoonful, the Moonglows, and Earth, Wind & Fire.

The sociocultural impact of rock had also been significant enough to lead the recording industry into daring new directions, especially after significant technological advances. Following the development of digital recording in the 1970s came the greatest breakthrough yet—the compact disc (CD), which produced the purest listening experience ever. On the market in 1983, it had little difficulty in outselling the conventional LP album, though it lagged behind audiocassette sales. By the '90s, though, the CD had established itself as the preferred mode for music listening, and the end of the decade saw approximately 70 percent of American homes with CD players. The upshot of this development was to see the electronic media converge in a symbiotic relationship that profited from each form's unique but complementary role. An obvious example, which harkened back to the radio-record player console of the 1930s, was the home entertainment system, a self-contained unit that comprised not only a CD/tape player but a TV set, VCR, and radio.

By the 1980s the alternative styles of rock music had become entrenched in media culture. As reflected in TV advertising, movie sound tracks, MTV videos, and the growing number of FM stations that had converted to a rock niche, new variations were continually springing up, each striving to be more daringly different than their predecessors. The seeds for a culturally subversive style known as "grunge" had appeared in 1976 in a group of British punk rockers who called themselves the Sex Pistols. Their displays of outrageous, even violent behavior during performances were underscored by amateurish playing, vulgar, nihilistic lyrics, and their self-styled shabby clothes and extreme hairstyles.

While the general public either ignored or found itself repelled by punk rock's antisocial ways, its intentional shock effects influenced not a few rebellious youths as well as the later grunge style's overt theatrics. By the '90s, Nirvana, a popular grunge band led by rock icon Kurt Cobain, extended its countercultural style to other alternative groups whose esoteric names remained a mystery to the mainstream culture. Bands like Smashing Pumpkins and Pearl Jam, in their countering of the conservative entertainment traditions of media culture, were significant forces in cultivating the musical taste of the demographic sector that attended their concerts and purchased their recordings. It was this predominantly supportive youth audience that made these bands much wealthier than they could ever have imagined at their inceptions.

Moreover, a media force that had helped assure these bands' popularity, in addition to the growing number of narrowcast radio stations that played their recordings, was exposure on the MTV and VH-1 cable channels. By performing as actors in fast-cut minidramas derived from their music, their images were received in a manner akin to Michael Jackson's *Thriller*, a highly popular 1983 MTV video that became a runaway best seller. That MTV could also sell movies inspired by rock culture was evidenced by its videos featuring sequences from the musical *Flashdance* (1983), thus helping it become a box-office hit.

By century's end, rock music had firmly entrenched itself as a force of media culture heard by all its sectors in film, on TV as well as radio, and even over the intercom while shopping in a supermarket. Such music, from earlier pop and classic rock to the later alternatve and hard rock stylings, was programmed to suit the respective tastes of the media culture's niche audiences. But in the late '90s ongoing electronic advances, which were responded to by youthful experimentation with Ecstasy as the latest drug of choice, helped foment new psychedelic kinds of rock music—subgenres that the rave or club culture identified as the techno, trip-hop, and trance stylizations. In their computer-generated rhythms they anticipated ever-new ways of listening to and experiencing music in the twenty-first century.

The growing popularity of country music at this time was also attributable to its exposure and accessibility in all the media forms. Not only was it promoted on hundreds of independent radio stations around the nation, but country music was the primary program content of the Nashville Television Network (TNN), until 2000 when it began de-emphasizing its country-styled programming for a broader mission. Having evolved from its old-time roots through the interpretations of traditionalists like Johnny Cash, Merle Haggard, Waylon Jennings, and George Jones to the updated styles of Randy Travis, George Strait, Garth Brooks, Dolly Parton, and Reba McEntire, country music took off in many diverse directions, as radio programming began catering to such spin-offs as country-gospel, Western swing, and even country pop and rock.

On the cutting edge of media technology and country music recording trends, Nashville was the focal point for alternative styles and new faces to keep abreast of the times. Since women vocalists were now in great demand, not a few stylists of wide appeal came to the fore in the '90s, notably blues singer Kelly Willis and balladeers LeeAnn Rimes and Tricia Yearwood. Garth Brooks, the era's most popular country singer, profited from the latest media technology through a live concert beamed concurrently to Wal-Mart record departments around the nation, where shoppers were inspired to purchase his latest songs on the spot. Even in adapting country music's traditional outlook to the changing ways of postmodern life, it continued to reflect the old-time values of the mediated vision, thus reinforcing its more conservative role in the socially subversive ways of contemporary rock music.[55]

While rap music, a term many deemed an oxymoron, seemed to be the antithesis of country music, both forms' humble origins were the one thing they had in common. Derived from the earthy patois of hip-hop urban street culture and the stylings of Jamaican reggae music in the late 1970s, the conversational, rhyming delivery of '80s rappers like Ice-T and Run-DMC was charged with a hypnotic beat that reinforced their angry lyrics about urban blacks' social conditions. But the major criticism leveled at rap performers was their defiance of mainstream values by glorifying violence and the drug culture while treating women as degraded sex objects. As a black version of the punk/grunge stance, it achieved its most extreme expression of social rebellion in the gangsta rap that emerged from the urban ghettos of Los Angeles in 1987.

Pursuant to the empowered posture voiced in Public Enemy's CD, *Fear of a Black Planet* (1990), rap evolved in vari-

ous directions while generally maintaining its militancy.
After the explicitly vulgar lyrics tradition of gangsta rap elaborated on by Snoop Dogg's obsession with drugs, violence,
and casual sex, an exemplary rapper who rose from street
hustler to a millionaire performer by century's end was Jay-
Z, becoming something of a role model to other young blacks.
While his media-made image implied that escape from the
ghetto's grim life was not as impossible as one might think, it
also affirmed the widespread influence that rap now commanded, attested to by the riches its performers amassed.

But the mediated prevalence of rap's nihilistic messages
was highly disturbing to concerned parents and social critics.
Of special concern was the crossover impact on impressionable white males who bought 70 percent of the recordings.
There were also white rappers for them to identify with, from
the 1980s' Beastie Boys to the late '90s' Eminem, whose big
thing was fantasizing violence and vulgarity by vilifying
women and gays. In follow-up to the school violence outbreak
in the late '90s, concerted efforts were in the wind to regulate
the circulation of rap's calculated affront to traditional values. However, as this chronicle has demonstrated, remedies
for certain media forms' subversion of mainstream values
had been proposed before, with little or no results.[56]

Upon the drug-induced suicide of grunge band leader Kurt
Cobain in 1994, the moral vigilantes singled him out as yet another victim of the drug culture's glorification of self-
indulgence, attested to by a long line of deceased rock stars
dating back to the '60s. How, then, they wondered, could such
morally undermining forces among America's youth as rock
music and its drug milieu be justified? As though in response
to this question, another alternative musical style called
Christian or "praise and worship" rock had been operative
since the 1980s, promoting spiritual salvation and its reward
of eternal life. Although groups like Audio Adrenaline and
Jars of Clay emulated the sounds of the secular bands, the
main difference between secular and Christian rock lay in the
lyrics, which the latter used to promulgate the "born-again"
message of Jesus Christ. Since these bands recognized Jesus
as the greatest of all social rebels, they contended that rock,
as the quintessential rebellious musical form, was an appropriate medium to present the Christian message to youth. Of
course, not all adherents to the fundamentalist persuasion
agreed, arguing that supplanting traditional church music

with rock was not only a compromise with the things of this world but a form of blasphemy. Regardless of its professed intent, though, Christian rock represented yet another alternative spin-off striving to make its mark in the fragmented world of postmodern popular music.[57]

## African American Music's Legacy to American Media Culture

To review the development of American music in the twentieth century, particularly in light of its sociocultural influence, is to realize the dominant part that black musicians' unique contributions have played in both American and international music—from ragtime and blues at the century's beginning to the rap sounds of the urban hip-hop scene at its end. Yet, as the careers of ragtime composer Scott Joplin and composer/bandleader Duke Ellington reveal, the road to success had not been an easy one, impeded as it was by the social obstructions of a racist society. Not until 1955 did singer Marian Anderson break the color barrier of the Metropolitan Opera as its first black member, paving the way for Leontyne Price, who not only became a Metropolitan favorite but a performer of international renown. While slow progress was made across the cultural and social divides in the ensuing years, the most democratizing influence emanated from the energized improvisational style of jazz, whose impact was still being felt at century's end through this protean form's varied offshoots.

Of the early pioneers who challenged the elitist hierarchy of musical taste to transform jazz into an art form, trumpeter Louis Armstrong towered above all the instrumental soloists, influencing the improvisational and personalized styles of such masters of their respective instruments as Dizzy Gillespie, Coleman Hawkins, Charlie Parker, Miles Davis, and John Coltrane. The rediscovered recordings that revealed the Mississippi Delta roots of Robert Johnson's unique guitar skills and blues singing style extended to the rhythm-and-blues instrumental variations of Muddy Waters and B. B. King and the singular voices of James Brown, Marvin Gaye, and Sam Cooke. Similarly, the early female blues singers Ma Rainey and Bessie Smith bequeathed their sensitivity to women's concerns to the personalized jazz/pop stylings of Billie Holiday and Ella Fitzgerald, as well as the smoothly rendered ballads of stage and film stars Ethel Waters and Lena Horne. Along with the soul legacy of Mahalia Jackson and her gospel song background, Aretha Franklin combined the sacred and the secular to create a singing style passionate enough to earn her the undisputed title of Queen of Soul during the later years of the century.

As the Beatles had readily professed their debt to African American music styles like Chuck Berry's dynamics and Little Richard's flamboyance, so later alternative styles of electronic rock owed the success of their performance images to similar rock 'n' roll influences. The ongoing cross-fertilization process resulted in the rockabilly interpretations of a youthful Elvis Presley and his ilk, the astonishing electronic guitar technique of '60s hard rock star Jimi Hendrix, the dynamic choreographed productions of Michael Jackson, who became a performer of worldwide fame in the '80s, and the antiestablishment rappers of the '80s and '90s.

But the performer as the epitome of cross-fertilization was Ray Charles, whose voice and piano talents could relate to soul and gospel as readily as they could to jazz, pop, and country. The talents of composer and arranger also merged in another versatile black musician, Quincy Jones, who was equally at home in both the jazz and pop music idioms. However, the real genius of black American music, both as composer and performer, was Duke Ellington. His band's unique sound was original enough to outlast the big band era, while his visionary talent resulted in compositions that fused the best elements of jazz into symphonic suites and tone poems to capture emotional moods. Appropriately, jazz scholar/musician Wynton Marsalis set out to cultivate a cultural appreciation of Ellington's legacy through his own band's concerts and recordings of Ellington's music. In doing so, Marsalis contended that the era from Louis Armstrong to Duke Ellington is the province of America's own indigenous classical music.

Thus the heritage of African American music, from Scott Joplin through blues innovator W. C. Handy to Duke Ellington, was of such import as to assure a high international reputation. Moreover, this music has persisted as a bulwark against the social problems of race that haunted the twentieth century by helping bridge the sociocultural gulf between blacks and whites. A prime example of this intent was Aretha Franklin's contention that when she sang of women's concerns she was not just emoting about black women but all women. Also, in narrowing the breach between elitist tradition and the mediated vision's natural understanding of music as a humanizing force, black music never really forgot its humble roots. Though intensely escapist in its power to free the human spirit but down to earth in its sensitivity to life's frustrations and uncertainties, African American music's natural expressiveness, born of the racially divisive nature of American life in the twentieth century, also reflected the fragmented state of American media culture at century's end.

## The Newspapers' Transition Toward Media Convergence

By the 1980s the coverage of happenings in the world of music, both mainstream and subcultural, had become another important mission of newspapers who were eager to address the nation's lifestyle diversions in order to attract regular readers and build circulation. In 1982, the Gannett publishing chain, seemingly to compete with the *Wall Street Journal* and the *New York Times* as recognized "national" newspapers, began circulating a Monday-to-Friday daily called *USA Today*. As a product of satellite technology, its wide reportage of both national and international news, business, sports, and arts/entertainment developments turned it into a global newspaper. A timely feature that distinguished it from other papers was a captivating use of color and a makeup style modeled after the visual look of television. In deferring to the cultural image of TV as its main competitor, whose visual sensibility focused on news as entertainment, *USA Today* strived to emulate it through a visual style that, like TV, responded to readers' short attention span accruing from the ascendancy of the image over the word.

Although television had been a major factor in contributing to many urban/suburban newspapers' decline in circulation, another serious competitor appeared in the 1980s as an offshoot of computer technology. By the '90s, in fact, the newspapers' traditional print system of disseminating information was being challenged by the digitally electronic means of conveying information through Internet Web sites. To capitalize on this latest communications innovation as a way to en-

gage new readers in the journalistic process, many newspapers were motivated to supplement their daily print output
by creating their own Web sites for the online delivery of local
news reportage. Here again was another example of two diverse media forms realizing an opportunity to work symbioti-
cally rather than to avoid each other's specialized role.

While a number of same-city dailies owned by different
parent companies survived through joint operational agreements that allowed them to pool their resources, others were
absorbed into chains like those of Rupert Murdoch and Gannett that grew out of the era's oligopolistic trend. Exemplary,
too, of the move toward convergence was the appearance of
media empires such as that of the *Chicago Tribune*, which, in
addition to newspapers, now owned both radio and television
stations. As the corporate mergers of the big communications
entities had indicated, as noted earlier, the future promised
more of the same developments, but whose supposed mission
to expand the horizons of the mediated vision would really
prove more beneficial to corporate economic interests.

Although foreign-language and ethnic newspapers discovered growing audiences, as expected in a burgeoning polyglot
population, the mainstream urban dailies began to recognize
the growing Hispanic and Asian sectors as significant entities
in the media culture. This move was certainly good business,
as these social groups' rising economic status made them lucrative targets for attracting advertisers. Eager to respond to
the country's multicultural audience as another way to sell
more papers, then, the time's more liberal press was also receptive to reporting sensationalized news that was once the
province of the counterculture press and the exploitative tabloids. Then, too, the emphasis on pictorial orientation and colorful layouts to attract readers resulted in an intensely
competitive time for the print media. Like the magazine, the
newspaper had become highly dependent on an abundance of
visual imagery to promote its content.

Despite conservative reactions to its changing appearance
and new digital delivery mode, the newspaper's portable
print format still commanded widespread appeal to its longtime readers. Apparently, though, youth was a demographic
disappearing from the newspaper audience, due mainly to the
visually addictive power of both television and the Internet's
ready access to the so-called "information superhighway."

Yet the newspaper's history of adaptation to the threat of every new communications development that had arisen over the years assured the continuation of its traditional mission of conveying information and entertainment to meet the changing tastes of the media culture's socially diverse audience.

## THE COMICS REAFFIRM THE HUMOR OF SOCIAL/POLITICAL COMMENTARY

One newspaper tradition that had continued over the century was the syndicated daily features of both an informative and entertaining nature. Among the most anticipated were the columns and editorial cartoons of political opinion, the daily crossword puzzle, the advice/self-help columns, and, of course, that perennial mainstay that had reflected the changing social scene since the twentieth century's beginning—the comic strip. Although such longtime favorites as *Blondie*, *Beetle Bailey*, *Shoe*, and *Peanuts* were still running, the adventure strip was now practically nonexistent, a victim of television's more immediate manner of fantasizing reality in its dramatic series programming. By this time, too, the increasing cost of newsprint as well as a larger allotment to advertising space had resulted in the comic strip's most miniaturized format, both daily and Sunday. The upshot was the crowded page appearance of numerous humor strips, each espousing a fantasized approach to the realities of the postmodern world but nearly all typified by a minimalist, rubber-stamp style of drawing.

From a perspective that could detect humor in the most mundane activity, the panel cartoon was a highly popular format during this era. One of the most followed was Gary Larson's *The Far Side* with its bizarre take on contemporary social behavior. Though its creator periodically took time off from his work, *The Far Side* ran through the 1980s into the '90s until Larson ended it in 1995, much to the disappointment of his many fans. Other features similar to Larson's satirical manner that started up in the 1980s were David Wiley Miller's *Non Sequitur* and Mike Peters's *Mother Goose & Grimm*. Both Miller and Peters, like a number of other comics artists of this time, had backgrounds as political cartoonists, which helped explain their attraction to topical themes as well as why many comics of this time viewed real-life issues and concerns as sources of humor.[58] For many editorial cartoonists, the style to emulate was that of Pulitzer Prize–winner Herbert Block (Herblock). His *Washington Post* work, which was widely syndicated, featured a trenchant wit that skewered many a political leader of this era. His brand of acerbic humor was carried on in the output of other Pulitzer winners—notably that of Pat Oliphant and Jeff MacNelly.

One of the most admired strips with a humorous appeal all its own was Bill Watterson's *Calvin and Hobbes*, whose blending of reality and fantasy emanated from the interplay between the self-centered, hyperactive ways of the six-year-old Calvin and his stuffed tiger Hobbes, who in his owner's highly imaginative mind is both actively and intimately alive. Although Gary Trudeau had taken a two-year "sabbatical" from drawing *Doonesbury* in 1982, *Calvin and Hobbes'* fans were shocked to learn that Watterson was closing down his strip for good after a tremendously popular ten-year run since 1985.[59] On the other hand, it took Charles Schulz's death in early 2000 to end his much revered strip, though *Peanuts* continued in daily reprints selected from its fifty-year run.

The problems and issues of the real world cropped up in strips as varied as the highly fantasized ethos of Berke Breathed's *Bloom County* and the alienated characters of Bud Grace's *Ernie*, both of which capitalized on the period's penchant for loser types. The most successful "loser" of the time in terms of the strip's surprising popularity was the title character of *Dilbert*. In fact, since its start in 1989, this feature rewarded its creator Scott Adams with windfall returns on merchandise spin-offs and an animated TV series. In spite of his inferior draftsmanship, Adams attributed *Dilbert*'s appeal to the fact that many fans who had work experiences similar to the title character's day-to-day life in the corporate world identified with the humor implicit in his ongoing bureaucratic encounters.

Beginning in 1982, the familiar comic strip world of domestic life also took on the flavor of humorous social commentary, as, for example, Greg Howard's *Sally Forth* in its daily reactions of a young married couple to the routine of their life together. More significantly, by the '90s, everyday family life from an African American point of view had mellowed into *Jump Start*, Robb Armstrong's vision of a black urban family involved in the activities of mainstream American life. Thus, newspaper comics, after one hundred years since their inauspicious beginnings in the urban slum setting of New York that artist Richard Outcault called Hogan's Alley, had evolved from depicting the antic activities of the Yellow Kid and his fellow ghetto denizens to bring onstage another marginalized but now generally accepted minority group as paper actors playing a key role in the human comedy. *Jump Start* and Ray Billingsley's more socially conscious *Curtis* reflected their integration into the American social ethos, thanks in part to the TV sitcom's now receptive depiction of blacks. But signs in the late '90s of a more socially assertive posture toward racism were apparent in Aaron McGruder's *The Boondocks*—yet another example of the comic strip's ironic way of commenting on reality in the postmodern era.

To commemorate the centennial of one of the century's most influential and enduring forms of diversion, celebratory books and articles appeared in profusion.[60] Even the postal service issued a commemorative block of stamps featuring twenty of the century's most popular comic strip characters. With some strips starting to appear on Web sites, like that of the Universal Press Syndicate, this indigenously American art form looked ahead to continuing its long tradition of entertaining the mediated vision by adapting to the rapidly evolving digital technology of the twenty-first century.

## THE ONGOING SPECIALIZATION OF THE MAGAZINE

Whether it was considered a newspaper or a magazine, as the Audit Bureau of Circulation labeled it, the weekly tabloid was flourishing during this time. Even an occasional libel suit was hardly a deterrent, such as that, for example, filed by TV entertainer Carol Burnett against the *National Enquirer*, which won her a sizable amount of money. Clearly, celebrity indiscretions, whether true or fabricated, were still big news to a certain sector of the mediated vision. As though to thwart the competition from mainstream magazines like *People* and a multitude of entertainment/gossip publications as well as TV infotainment shows catering to such subject matter, American Media, which owned the *Enquirer*, the *Star*, and the *Weekly World News*, bought the *Globe*, the *Sun*, and the *National Examiner* in 1999. This transaction obviously substantiated tabloid media's ongoing show of faith in the reportage of exploitative subject matter that appealed to a talk-show mentality.

Like the newspaper, the magazine was still feeling the competitive pressures of TV's immediately realized entertainment focus. Unlike the newspaper, the magazine's propensity to specialize kept it in the forefront as a mirror of changing tastes revealed in the vast array of subcultural pursuits it covered. Thus, the magazine continued to reflect the ongoing cultural fragmentation of the media culture. By the middle of the '90s, in fact, hundreds of new magazines addressed to both specialized and general audiences were appearing annually on newsstands. (This output does not include the large number of irregularly scheduled alternative publications that addressed special topics and issues.)

While the subject matter of the specialty magazines ranged as far apart as the arts and the automotive, publications with established reputations naturally commanded the largest circulations. In 1993 the *Gale Directory of Publications* listed only such general-interest periodicals as *Reader's Digest* and *Time* in its top-ten circulation list along with eight directed at special interests: *TV Guide*, *National Geographic*, and five long-running women's magazines. However, at the top of the list was *Modern Maturity*, the magazine of the American Association of Retired Persons (AARP), whose growing membership all received copies.[61] The specialized magazine, still a viable medium for advertising the messages of consumerism, continued to reflect the escapist pursuits of its targeted audiences, deriving at least half its revenue from ads that mirrored the special tastes of readers.

The availability of more leisure time than ever before spawned numerous new publications dedicated to individualized sporting pursuits like golf, tennis, and boating as well as the newer subcultural activities of surfing, snorkeling, and skydiving, to name a few. The ever-expanding interest in sports saw the circulation of *Sports Illustrated* grow to the extent that it became the most successful magazine of its kind. Offering some competition, another magazine appeared in the '90s that capitalized on its popular TV counterpart. In fact, the oversized layout of *ESPN the Magazine* emulated the visual appearance of TV programming itself. Though the reality of abuses in organized sport and the natural environment often infiltrated *Sports Illustrated*'s pages, the leisure-emphasis magazines' compromise between productive work and escapist play was readily apparent, justifying the mediated vision's goal of fulfilling the self while relishing the means of doing so. One sure way was through travel, and as more people could now afford a trip to most any place in the world, more travel magazines appeared, even one appropriately named *Escape*.

Children's magazines were now emphasizing the important roles of play and education in their young readers' lives. Their approaches ranged from indoctrinating readers into the traditions of American sport in *Sports Illustrated for Kids* to inculcating the pleasures of learning about science and nature in *Odyssey*, *Ranger Rick*, and *Dolphin Log*. While *Cobblestone* magazine also found an audience for American history, *Sesame Street* brought its television mission of treating education as entertainment to the print medium.

By now, the sociocultural impact of media culture, as attested to by its sectors devoted to popular music, television programming, and movies, was being increasingly attended to by traditionally elitist journals like *Harper's*, the *Atlantic Monthly*, and the *National Review*, revealing that their readers' interests had now taken on a more democratized turn. Similarly, the urbane *New Yorker* was a force in keeping its readers informed of the latest media trends while satirizing them in its cartoons. Developments in the media culture were also attracting readers of magazines produced for ethnic audiences, since many of their own were now celebrities in the fields of entertainment and sports. Through its adulation of black entertainers and athletes, *Ebony* saw its circulation approach a million by the mid 1990s. And as the living standards of blacks rose, *Essence*'s attention to black culture functioned as a mirror of this end. With the increase in the Hispanic population, Spanish-language editions of magazines as disparate as *Cosmopolitan* and *The Ring* focused on popular topics of interest to their readers. The latter publication's new audience was an obvious reflection of the spreading fan interest in the numerous Hispanic boxers now active.

With the emergence of desktop publishing and the proliferation of Internet Web sites during the '90s, the publication of specialty fanzines exploded. As previously noted, the fanzine was geared to deal with any kind of topic, from the obscure to the popular, which in turn might appeal to a few hundred or several thousand. In 1994 *Time* reported that "the society of self-publishers is growing fast. This year alone, at least

20,000 titles have been produced in the U.S."[62] Ironically, the fanzine's popularity seemingly revealed a desire for communal identity amid an age of social fragmentation. As further evidence of the democratization of American culture, the varied subcultures now comprising it ranged in interest from the most mundane subject to the most esoteric.

Like newspapers, too, many mainstream magazines had fallen under the ownership of large corporations that oversaw the publication of an array of titles. While the long-established Hearst Corporation still published a variety of older titles such as *Cosmopolitan, Esquire,* and *Harper's Bazaar,* Time, Inc., now a subsidiary of Time Warner, had introduced new titles that included *Money, Parenting,* and *Entertainment Weekly.* The latter magazine, in covering the broad spectrum of popular culture's prolific output, from movies to comic books, mirrored the dominant status of the media culture at century's end.

Two developments at this time offered trendy insights into the entertaining appeal of the special interest magazine. In 1999, the conventional use of the cover as a sales device was exploited by the flurry of men's magazines whose covers revealed an obsession with female nudity. According to the editor of *Maxim,* a leading British publication of this kind, his magazine was simply promoting what men valued most—the hedonistic life as symbolized by an abundance of female sexuality and alcohol consumption. While the more staid American magazines like *GQ, Details,* and *Esquire* were quick to emulate this trend, *Playboy,* whose name more than its cover sold itself, had to wonder what all the fuss was about. Clearly, by the 1990s, female sexuality and the drinking life had become more open subject matter than when *Playboy* first exploited it in the 1950s.

The other notable development in magazine journalism reflected the ongoing appeal of celebrity lifestyle, as shown by the Hearst empire's secretive plans in 1999 for a new publication called *Talk.* It was rumored to be a "blend of gossip, pop culture, serious stuff—attention-grabbing."[63] In other words, more of the same kind of material that TV's infotainment and talk-show programs covered. Thus this magazine intended to carry on a media tradition that harkened back to the days of the Hollywood gossip columnist.

Although the corporately controlled magazines were expected to sacrifice their independent voices to the dictates of their ownership, they could look back on a long history of attending to the informational and entertainment needs of the mediated vision. In this light, the American magazine looked forward to the challenge of its future role as a democratizing media force in American life.

## THE COMIC BOOK AS LITERATURE: THE VISUAL APPEAL OF THE GRAPHIC NOVEL

The print form that has always defied categorization is the comic book. Neither the magazine nor the book publishing industry has laid claim to it as its own, so the comic book holds a unique position in a business that by the 1990s was some sixty years old. But because its anthology format offered adventure stories in the mode of the literary short story, and the book-length mini- and maxiseries were apparently modeled after the novel, the comic book could very well qualify in the book category. Its case was reinforced by the cultural transition that it underwent during this era, prompting *Entertainment Weekly* to include periodic reviews in its book section.

With Marvel and DC now in ascendancy, the 1980s–90s proved to be an eventful time for the comic book industry. The most maturely conceived artwork yet was being produced by artists on the order of Frank Miller, John Byrne, and Walt Simonson, to name only a few. Both the new realism and a direct distribution system to specialty comics shops around the country, as well as the collecting phenomenon, helped attract an adult readership of both older and newer fans. Also, the blockbuster movies depicting the exploits of Superman and Batman established a wider base of popularity for the comic book superhero. As the dominant fantasy figure of the genre, the superhero was now even more disposed to violent action in realistically rendered stories. In 1988, when the Superman character turned fifty, *Time* published a cover story that in exploring its mythical qualities revealed how institutionalized this popular icon had become in the American ethos.[64] As the ultimate fantasy figure, the Superman character had now expressed itself in all the media forms, including film, the Broadway stage, fiction, and advertising, not to mention merchandise spin-offs. And, of course, by century's end, his image was still going strong.

But like other media areas, the comic book industry found

the economic impact of technological and sociocultural change major forces to contend with. By the end of the '90s, Marvel was supplementing its comic book sales from the revenue generated by collectible character toys and action figures inspired by its lineup of superheroes in addition to their dramatized adventures on videocassettes and the marketing of video games that appealed to a new computer-oriented generation. As the superhero movies had realized, so the virtual reality of the computer presented Marvel and DC yet another challenging area to explore and add another dimension to their visions of fantasized reality. Moreover, other cultural perspectives had developed in the '80s that impacted the course of comic book realism and the cultural format it would take.

According to comics scholar Joseph Witek, the transition to a more mature rendering of realistic subject matter in comic book form, as evidenced by the historically based works of Art Spiegelman and Jack Jackson, was "an implicit rejection of the death grip that fantasy has long held on the medium. At the same time, as modern culture becomes less print-oriented and more visually literate, comic books become more attractive as a narrative form," or as Will Eisner termed it "sequential art."[65] Accordingly, his reality-based comics would afford the comic book a new aura of respectability, especially after his pioneering work in the graphic novel during the 1980s.

With realistic art an essential feature of the comic book, even in its most fantasized subject matter, DC began experimenting in the '80s with both the miniseries and maxiseries formats in which a story was extended over a number of issues to conclusion. As an expansive form that allowed for varying panel shapes and sizes to tell a story, the comic book proved a natural for this kind of visual narration. When, in 1986, artist Frank Miller returned the Batman character to his grim gothic origins in a four-part miniseries, *Batman: The Dark Knight Returns*, its reception was positive enough to merit reprinting the series as a graphic novel.[66] Around the same time, DC's twelve-part maxiseries, *Watchmen* (1986–87), was acclaimed a stunning tour de force in demonstrating how the graphic novel format could produce compelling visual narration. The product of writer Alan Moore and artist Dave Gibbons, *Watchmen* satirized the vigilante nature of the traditional superhero in a murder mystery that critics praised and fans consumed as a best-selling graphic novel. In

2000, DC looked to profit on the form's new literary status by hiring Will Eisner to continue creating his unique versions of the genre. Though now in his 80s, Eisner had lived long enough to see his serious treatment of comic book narrative achieve the status of an art form.

The flurry of independent publishers that arose in the wake of the comic shop direct-sales phenomenon led to the appearance of numerous iconic characters in the 1980s whose artists enjoyed much more creative freedom in depicting them than their corporate peers had. While the superb artwork of Dave Stevens infused a nostalgic flavor into the 1930s pulp fiction background of *The Rocketeer*, he also portrayed some of the sexiest women in the comics. Howard Chaykin's *American Flagg!*, a popular title of the First Publishing Company, pushed his artistic freedom to the limit in an adult-themed series depicting a hero whose adventures in a dystopic futuristic world of sex and violence borders on the pornographic. Capitalizing on this license, a number of independent publishers such as Eros Comix published series books that focused on the sexual adventures of a title character or characters, usually female, in hard-core detail.

Among the better defined of the maxiseries titles was Fantagraphics' *Love and Rockets*, which brothers Jaime and Gilbert Hernandez started in 1982 as a mixture of fantasized adventure and the personal problems of young Hispanic women in the punk rock era. Moreover, by appearing in the graphic novel format, or what the Spanish language terms *fotonovela*, this long-running series was, according to one critic, an example of postmodern realism that foreshadows a new kind of visual "narrative for the next society," presaging a form of virtual reality when "audience interacts with . . . performative artists."[67]

When this freer atmosphere prompted a reprint revival of the EC horror, crime, and science-fiction comics that had been suppressed in the 1950s, publishers continued to capitalize on the appeal of nostalgia, as Kitchen Sink Press did in reprinting such classic comic strip favorites from their origins as *Flash Gordon*, *Nancy*, and *Li'l Abner*. While comic books for children, like those published by the Archie and Harvey companies, still found a large audience, the Disney funny animal tradition was resurrected in an independent publisher's project to reprint the entire run of *Walt Disney's Comics and Stories*, in addition to comic books that featured

Carl Bark's classic work on Donald Duck. In 1999, to capitalize on the never-ending nostalgic mood, DC initiated its series
of Millennium Editions, reprints of notable comic books from
six decades of publishing. Transcending nostalgia by lending
dignity to the comic book as an art form, mainstream publications also continued to appear dedicated to its history, major
artists, characters, and genres as well as its sociocultural significance.[68]

By now, the comic book itself, printed in vivid colors on
quality interior paper and often on a cover of heavy stock,
was a high-priced item costing many times over its original
ten-cent tab. Helping publicize it as a cultural artifact during
this time were the collectors who published fanzines, attended annual conventions, and also kept up with the latest
developments through online Web sites. By now, too, the market for original comic books was drawing well-heeled investors to auctions at Sotheby's and Christie's East in New York,
where bids were offered in the thousands of dollars for rare
books of golden age vintage. The record at the time was the
reported $180,000 paid to a private dealer for a near-mint
first issue of *Superman* in 1996. Enhancing their worth as collectibles were critical discussions in publications such as the
*Comic Buyer's Guide*, the *Comics Journal*, and *Comic Book
Marketplace*. With the annual evaluations of editor Robert
Overstreet's *Comic Book Price Guide* making its thirtieth appearance in 1999, the future of the comic book as a collectible
continued to look bright—at least for those who could afford
to collect. Indeed, the collecting phenomenon, in according
such high value to a categorically ephemeral item, was yet
another sign of the postmodernist desire to connect with the
past's nostalgic icons and, by doing so, revive the seemingly
enchanted time they represented.

## The Book Challenges the Dominance
### of the Electronic Image

Whether in the form of comic books, newspapers, magazines, or fiction/nonfiction works, evidence revealed that
Americans were very much into reading as a pastime, despite
the predicted demise of print media due to the growing prevalence of the Internet and other visually oriented diversions.
In 1998, in fact, the fourth annual Harris Poll of U.S. leisure

activities rated reading number one, but television viewing came in a close second.[69] Undoubtedly, in responding to the entertainment demands of a highly mobile people, the print media's ready portability was a major factor for reading's top rank.

By now, too, the interdependence of the print and visual media had resulted in a relationship through which both sectors helped promote the other. Such an exchange often led to the popularization of a book originally deemed too academic or elitist for mass consumption. In 1988, for example, after Bill Moyers's PBS interview series with Joseph Campbell, author of *The Hero with a Thousand Faces* (1949), a comparative study of the world's mythologies, the book soared to the level of a best seller, dwarfing its earlier modest sales. Similarly, the appearance of an author on a reputable TV talk show like Oprah Winfrey's could boost the sales of a little-known novel, as it did for Toni Morrison's *Beloved* (1987), leading to a film version in 1998. For nonfiction in a specialized or scholarly vein, the interviews conducted on C-SPAN's *Booknotes* helped promote both well- and little-known authors' works that dealt with historical, cultural, and political subject matter. In retaining the book's reputation as a dominant sociocultural force, then, American publishers had achieved an output in 1992 of nearly 50,000 titles.[70]

The best-selling novel, by maintaining its longtime function as an escapist medium, was a valid indicator of this time's literary taste. Popular culture scholar James B. Twitchell has noted that of the top twenty-five best-selling novels in the 1980s, ten of thirteen that sold one million or more copies were by just three authors: Tom Clancy, Stephen King, and Danielle Steel. Moreover, he continued, the technothrillers of Clancy, the horror tales of King, and the romance stories of Steel had "found an audience that clearly wants more of the same," concluding that "this new audience is driving the machinery of publishing."[71] But this sameness of subject matter was not so much a new thing as it was the latest expression of the mediated vision's desire to be entertained in light of the postmodern escapist affinity for fantasized reality.

By this time, too, the media culture was fully acclimated to the interdependence of the print and visual media, as Twitchell remarks: "Movies are made from books, books are made from movies, television makes movies from books inspired by movies."[72] Conversely, the popularity of courtroom drama on television in the '90s was a factor in helping promote the best-selling and movie-made novels of Scott Turow and John Grisham that dealt with offenders of the justice system. As long as the mediated vision demanded the formulaic in its reading, it appeared that a popular author's name would continue to alert it to a particular brand of fiction. In this respect, Stephen King's horror fiction, which focused on the fears of ordinary people involved in extraordinary circumstances, was a leading "brand" in attracting a following large enough to make King the most successful writer of horror fiction in literary history.[73] By responding to the readers' of this genre's escapist expectations, then, the output of King, as well as others who wrote according to formula, was a cultural barometer of the time, pointing out the psychological uncertainties that inspired the escapist fantasies of the mediated vision.

Moreover, the bookstore as supermarket for promoting and selling the publishing industry's products and related merchandise proliferated during this era. Such chain stores as Walden, Barnes & Noble, and Books-a-Million popped up throughout the country, not only in shopping malls but as lone-standing edifices in diverse locations. These outlets, which offered a large variety of trade books as well as discounts on best-selling fiction and nonfiction, in addition to cheap remaindered selections, posed a serious threat to the traditional private bookstore. But it countered by turning to the old and rare book market in which the burgeoning worth of out-of-print books was enhanced by both the nostalgic milieu and the collecting phenomenon.

In response to the nostalgic mood and those who considered a book collection as a status symbol, certain publishers reissued leather-bound works of classic fiction and nonfiction, more to display than read. Although the Book of the Month Club and the Literary Guild were still making their monthly selections, newer operations like the Science-Fiction Book Club, the Mystery Guild, and the Stage & Screen Book Club for the Performing Arts reflected the ongoing trend toward specialization and diversification of reader interests. In addition, the magazine-based house of Time-Life Books offered books by mail order, promoting them as unique works that were generally unavailable in bookstores. Their subject matter embraced a wide variety of topics of historic and nostalgic appeal, especially as the new century approached.

Other, more unconventional, boons to book promotion

began to appear in the '90s. In 1995, the advent of Amazon. com on the Internet enabled bookselling to find its most direct outlet yet through which browsers could choose from a wide variety of selections. Best sellers were also being offered as "talking" books, that is, books on tape, in which an author or well-known personality reads a novel or nonfiction work, usually in an abridged form. As an edifying, entertaining way for a motorist to ease the boredom of a long drive as well as an aid to the blind and weakened vision of older readers, recorded books demonstrated another way to perpetuate their traditional image. In a report on the explosive popularity of audio books, *Time* reacted to the fear of purists that books on tape might deter interest in reading: "Just as Hollywood once feared the advent of videocassettes but later discovered that they fed rather than discouraged interest in movies, books on tape may actually promote the cause of literature."[74] Here again was strong evidence that a new form of media-oriented expression did not necessarily compete with an older form; rather, it could actually enhance the former through a kind of symbiotic relationship.

If adults had a variety of ways to satisfy their reading habits, one wondered what the young were reading—if anything, besieged as they were by the media competition of television, video games, and the growing appeal of the Internet. While the subject matter of children's magazines like *Cricket* and *Sesame Street* treated educational topics in a highly entertaining way, superhero comic books still sought to extend their perennial popularity through an abundance of violent stories, as noted. But teenagers of this time were also being exposed to a heavy dose of violence in the popular "thriller" fiction of Christopher Pike and R. L. Stine. The latter defended the violent content of his "Fear Street" series as escapist "safe scares . . . The books are not half as scary as the real world."[75] Their astronomical sales led to Stine's "Goosebump" series for preteens, which since 1992 found an avid following. All told, Stine had sold some 300 million of his books by 2000. Thus the thriller books, through their blend of horror and the supernatural, functioned as the print medium's answer to the popular teen horror movies of the time, revealing that tabloid reality had invaded the traditionally fantasized world of the series book. Even the Hardy Boys and Nancy Drew books yielded to the tastes' changing times as the social behavior of their characters was updated to meet readers' new lifestyle perceptions. Though their plots were charged with more violence, they were nowhere near the blood and gore featured in the thriller books.

The print rage for escapist thrills and suspense was no more sensationally exploited than in the Harry Potter books by British writer J. K. (Joanne) Rowling. By the late '90s her books' phenomenal appeal, emanating from the real-world concerns of their central character and his adventures in a fantasized realm of magic and wizardry, was sufficiently widespread to captivate both youth and adult audiences, as attested to by their ongoing appearances in the best-seller lists. In 2000, the fourth book in the series set an all-time publishing record for a first printing in the United States—nearly four million copies. Though the inevitable movie version was assured, a positive side to Rowling's books was a resurgence of interest in reading among youths who had been seduced by the visual appeal of TV and video games.

As though to honor the longtime fantasy tradition of children's literature, HarperCollins reissued one of its classics, *Charlotte's Web*, in 1999 on the 100th anniversary of author E. B. White's birth. Coincidentally, in the same year the National Education Association named this book, first published in 1952, its teachers' favorite children's book of the past 100 years. Like the intent of much adult fiction, children's literature, as it had since the days of *St. Nicholas* magazine, could entertain either through a nostalgic return to earlier times or by affording escape from or adjustment to the realities of changing times.

In this latter respect, the young adult novel, in which a more mature posture had been evolving since the late 1960s, achieved its maturest expression during this time. Instrumental in this kind of fiction's emphasis on the moral challenges to youth's social lives were the realistic novels of S. E. Hinton, Robert Lipsyte, David Guy, and Judy Blume. Whether dependent on the themes of sport and/or young love for a plot, their stories focused mainly on the personal (often sexual) and developmental concerns of both their male and/or female characters. While not strictly escapist in purpose, such fiction provided instructive entertainment for many a young reader uncertain about his or her social role in the rapidly changing postmodern scene.

THE NOVEL AS AN ONGOING SOCIOCULTURAL FORCE

In spite of the doomsayers' earlier prognosis that the novel was dead or dying, the last years of the century saw both the mainstream and popular novels maintain their prolific output, attracting attention in all the media forms. Attesting to the novel's status as a timely social document were the notable works of such established mainstream novelists as Gore Vidal, Philip Roth, and John Updike. In 1990 Updike completed his landmark Harry Angstrom saga about the problems devolving on American life since the 1960s with *Rabbit at Rest*, the fourth novel in the series. In *American Pastoral* (1997) the prolific Roth returned readers to the socially contested times of the 1960s in which youth was a major player for a not too very nostalgic read. Fittingly, in 2000 Vidal capped his series of historical novels with his seventh about the American scene—*The Golden Age*. In the postmodern manner, it focused on the interaction between both fictional and real-life characters during the World War II–postwar era, revealing the times as America's last period of sociocultural innocence.

Even the avant-garde novel of radical experiment that was defiantly different in characterization and narrative style, and thus marginal as far as popularity was concerned, continued to be widely reviewed if not widely read. Though the 1980s had seen a waning of this form's literary impact, Thomas Pynchon's *Vineland* (1990) and *Mason & Dixon* (1997) were promoted as publishing events. But the return to a more traditional kind of fiction had been prefigured in Don DeLillo's *White Noise* (1985), which merged the postmodern experimental approach to subject matter with a more conventional method of narrative exposition.

Since the counterculture trends of the 1960s, another kind of serious fiction had achieved a high level of critical respect by introducing fearless new voices who used fiction to address the problems and concerns that the minority sectors of women, gays, blacks, and other ethnics confronted in a culturally diverse national makeup. Thus, the postmodernist milieu, which had driven the novel in a variety of different directions, opened the way for writers as varied in their visions as Alice Walker's feminist portrayal of black life in the American South and John Rechy's graphic rendering of the

pursuit of gay hustling in the urban scene to create strong social statements from minority points of view.

But to be entertained rather than sociologically indoctrinated or intellectually challenged, as in the complex avant-
garde perspectives of Pynchon and his like, most readers
turned to writers who were attuned to relating a compelling
plot in a conventional narrative form, as in the highly popular
horror and romance genre cited above, as well as the best-
selling crime novels of writers like Elmore Leonard, Sue
Grafton, and John D. MacDonald. As though to serve the ends
of both enlightenment and entertainment, an exemplary best-
seller in the traditional mold of the novel was Tom Wolfe's *A
Man in Full* (1998). Through its evocation of social realism in
the narrative manner of classic nineteenth-century fiction,
Wolfe's writing countered the self-reflexive style of the experimental school to anticipate a resurgence of this kind of
fiction. Nevertheless, Wolfe's method of dissecting contemporary manners and mores was criticized by some of his peers
as pandering to best-seller interests and the entertainment
ends of media culture.

Obviously guilty of selling out to the time's obsession for
sensationalism that pays off in a big way was Thomas Harris's *Hannibal* (1999), the sequel to his earlier novel *The Silence of the Lambs* (1988), which introduced readers to the
gross excesses of a cannibalistic serial killer. The later book's
sales confirmed to publishers that gruesomely detailed violence was now a big draw to readers, thus assuring this novel's chances of becoming as big a hit movie as its controversial
predecessor. Similarly, Bret Easton Ellis's 1991 novel *American Psycho*, which depicted the gory, murderous rampages of
a yuppie-type Wall Street stockbroker, was initially considered unfilmable. But the movie version that finally appeared
in 2000 revealed that Hollywood now abided by its own rules
for making films.

So it went in the literary culture of the century's final two
decades—from novels of experimental bent to fiction in a
more conventional mode. In retrospect, perhaps a strong case
could be made for science fiction as the more representative
literary genre of the postmodern era in that since the 1970s a
talented, visionary cadre of writers had helped perpetuate it
as more than just a type of escapist literature. Appropriately,
in 1980 H. Bruce Franklin, in his biography of Robert Heinlein, wrote: ". . . science fiction [has] moved inexorably toward

the center of American culture, shaping our imagination . . . through movies, novels, television, comic books, simulation games, language, economic plans and investment programs, scientific research and pseudo-scientific cults, spaceships, real and imaginary."[76]

A major contributor to this transition in SF was the prolific Arthur Clarke, whose 1968 novel *2001: A Space Odyssey* and later works had foreshadowed New Wave science fiction. But while the visionary ventures of Clarke, the fantasized realism of Ray Bradbury, the robotic technology of Isaac Asimov, and the apocalyptic visions of Heinlein and Philip Dick have taken on classic stature, the perspective of Joanna Russ's feminist-oriented *The Female Man* (1975) and William Gibson's dystopic *Necromancer* (1986), in their hypothetical postures, prefigured SF's future potential as serious literature of social comment.

## NONFICTION'S LOOK AT THE PAST AND POSTMODERN ISSUES/CONCERNS

Much nonfiction of this era examined the fading character of the nation's past to analyze its worth in terms of present-day realities. Exemplary of this end was Tracy Kidder's *Home Town* (1999), whose subject is the New England township, showing how this idyllic image of America's past had undergone a postmodern transformation while attempting to retain its traditional sense of values. Kidder's insightful way of dealing with the impact of the new on the old distinguished much of his writing, beginning with *The Soul of a New Machine* (1982), a prescient analysis of the kind of sociocultural influence that the personal computer and its technology would have on the mediated vision.

Responding to the nostalgic mood at the end of the twentieth century, TV news anchorman Tom Brokaw looked back in *The Greatest Generation* (1998) to laud the idealism and durability of those Americans who weathered the Depression and sacrifices of World War II to bequeath their descendants a level of prosperity the nation had never known. Another TV anchor, Peter Jennings, collaborated with Todd Brewster to produce *The Century* (1998), a compelling narrative interspersed with a visual feast of photographs covering the political and sociocultural highlights of the past 100 years.

Unfortunately, in the rush to press, this book, as well as the equally visual import of Harold Evans's *American Century* (1998), were compelled to omit some significant events of the late '90s.

The big biography continued to attract a large following by relating the life stories of the century's famous figures, both living and dead, in a more down-to-earth light. Accordingly, A. Scott Berg's *Lindbergh* (1998) painted an unvarnished portrait of the most adulated personality of the 1920s—Charles Lindbergh—revealing how, after his celebrated solo flight, he was brought down to earth by a series of personally shattering events and his own complex makeup. In the tell-all biographical style of this era, then, the famous usually had to endure the selling power of personal indiscretions and scandal in a writer's attempt to humanize the mythical aura surrounding their lives. One's sex life was especially open to scrutiny, particularly if any kind of aberrant behavior was dredged up.[77] Even the celebrity authors (or ghostwriters) of autobiographies seemingly assumed that a bare-all posture was an essential element in the marketing success of their books.

While both sports and political figures were popular subjects to dissect, Hollywood still reigned as a favorite target for any writer seeking to exploit the rage for books about the transgressive side of celebrity culture. Thus the appearance of such works as Marlis J. Harris's *The Zanucks of Hollywood: The Dark Legacy of an American Dynasty* (1989), Gerald Clarke's ironically titled biography of Judy Garland, *Get Happy*, and David Stenn's *Bombshell: The Life and Death of Jean Harlow* (both 2000).[78] Some writers even sought to discredit established reputations through tabloid tactics, as Marc Eliot's *Walt Disney: Hollywood's Dark Prince* (1993) did, labeling the man who had parlayed traditional American values into commercialized escapist entertainment as an alcoholic and Nazi sympathizer, among other charges. Other writers delved into a celebrated figure's childhood to find the key to his/her success. Joseph C. McBride's *Steven Spielberg* (1997), for example, argued that the famous director's drive for success stemmed, in part, from a compelling desire to counter the anti-Semitic taunts he endured as a child. In painting a gossipy tabloid side to her years at 20th Century–Fox, Shirley Temple Black's autobiography, *Child Star* (1988), drew on events that publicists of her day had purposely avoided in order to present her Depression-era fans a highly positive picture of both her public and private lives.

By the '90s the traditional self-help book was finding a ready-made audience in the baby boomers of the postwar era who, now entering their fifties, were growing concerned about the aging process and its attendant problems. For a society obsessed with youth and appearance, to the extent that it had compartmentalized its citizens by age groups, with "senior" as the least appealing, publishers realized the profits to be made from books that offered plans to adjust to or deter aging. Thus, in addition to the scores of books on dieting and exercise to effect weight loss, a new wave of publications about ways to remain young and healthy was crowding bookstore displays, among them enticing titles like *Feel 30 for the Next 50 Years* and *Age-Proof Your Body: Your Complete Guide to Lifelong Vitality.*[79] Undoubtedly, reaching one's fiftieth birthday represented the great divide for many, particularly women, as a flood of books appeared on this topic, both humorous and inspirational. For the older end of the age spectrum, publications were structured around the concept of creative aging and even ways for the terminally ill to cope with the inevitable event of death itself.

Even though the mediated vision's inherent optimistic nature was still a factor in helping maintain a positive outlook on life, uncertainties still abounded. Psychotherapist Robert Gurzon, writing from his own clinical observations and experiences in *Finding Serenity in the Age of Anxiety* (1997), contended that the self-help movement itself had been a strong force in intensifying the uncertainties of the era. Paradoxically, at a time when living standards were at their highest level, people were turning inward to ask more questions of their personal lives and becoming more anxious in the process. As the new century drew ever closer, the future loomed ever more ominous, and as it had been since the beginning of the twentieth century, everyday life in the present tense still offered little solace except through the escapist modes of media culture.

## Debating the Future of the Book as a Cultural Force

Concerning the future of book publishing itself, one wondered if the prophets would ultimately prove correct in their prediction that Internet e-books or digital print on demand might supplant the print medium in the production of fiction and nonfiction. In early 2000 a sign of what could lay ahead was a new Stephen King novella serialized on the Internet for his many fans to download. In 1998, though, as if to assure the print book's future, the Modern Library recognized its cultural impact by announcing a ranked list of the century's 100 best novels in English and another for nonfiction. Although James Joyce's esoteric *Ulysses* was named best novel, undoubtedly more for its literary influence than readability, many works were listed that had achieved wide appeal. The same could be said of the nonfiction selections, particularly in the areas of biography and autobiography or personal memoirs, from *The Education of Henry Adams* (No. 1) to Annie Dillard's *Pilgrim at Tinker Creek* (No. 89). Such lists may have rankled many people more for what they left out than included, but the evidence was clear as to the book's longtime cultural influence. Whether its future lay in a print or digital version, the point of these lists was that book publishing would adapt to change as it always had, having survived the competition of the movies, radio, and television to play a key role in the media culture's intent of both informing and entertaining its democratized audience. The appreciative review of Jacques Barzun's scholarly study, *From Dawn to Decadence: 500 Years of Western Cultural Life* (2000), in an unlikely publication—*Entertainment Weekly*, the magazine of American media culture—attested to this ongoing process.[80]

## PROMOTING CONSUMER PRODUCTS AS EXPRESSIONS OF ENTERTAINMENT

The omnipresence of advertising signage in the waning years of the twentieth century had grown so pronounced as to overwhelm one's visual sensibility, for urban-sited advertising now competed in such mass profusion that it was now part of the milieu. While the ubiquitous outdoor billboard seductively informed motorists of consumer items essential to the good life or the best places to shop and entertain themselves, the proliferating nighttime locations of fast-food and established restaurants were identified by the garish allure of flamboyant neon lighting. The print medium's longtime dependence on advertising revenue promulgated its ads in a variety of ways. In addition to the Sunday newspaper sections devoted to automobile and real estate sales was a deluge of colorful inserts promoting sales at local stores, the newest products on the market, and grocery items supplemented by discount coupons. While magazines carried elaborate pullout ads for automobiles and even scented pages for women's perfume or men's cologne, the mails were cluttered with flyers publicizing everything from sweepstake contests to credit-card solicitations. Even moviegoers were now used to seeing familiar consumer items in popular films, a corporate sponsor's practice known as product placement. While NASCAR racing cars served as mobile ads for their sponsors' products, fans attending other sporting events were subjected to multiple advertisements sited around the playing area, including those for cigarettes, whose TV ads had been banned for twenty years but whose promotional imagery was now blatenly exposed to TV viewers. Now even users of the Internet found themselves subjected to a glut of commercials.

Ironically, though, technology, which had helped enhance the mission of consumer advertising throughout the century, was now favoring TV's targeted consumers with a remote control device that allowed them to switch to another channel or punch its mute button to avoid an annoying commercial. By the late '90s, in fact, the handheld remote control had become a household fixture, managing not only a TV set and a VCR but other electronically controlled fixtures. Some VCRs could even be programmed to omit advertising in the recording process. With the latest technology providing ways to circumvent advertising's invasion of viewer privacy, it was little wonder, then, that the advertising industry was compelled to come up with ever more seductive and entertaining ways to attract consumers.

Since the 1950s, the motivational research that ad agencies employed had evolved into the classification system of Values and Lifestyles (VALS), which, in reflecting the subcultural divisions of the media culture by the 1980s, helped agencies assess changing sociocultural values as a way to target potential consumers. In heeding their findings, then, advertising agencies deployed a variety of persuasive methods, both innovative and conventional. For example, as beer consumption had become popular among the young, its promotion often featured sexual implications. The sales pitch that had been around since advertising's earliest days, endorsement by a well-known personality, particularly those in entertainment and athletics, was updated for a more socially aware audience. Even before his amazing success on the professional golf tour, the fortuitous signing of sensational young golfer Tiger Woods to a multimillion dollar contract by the Nike sports shoe company turned out to be a highly profitable venture for both golfer and company, as golf had entrenched itself as a highly popular sport by now. For general audiences, the appealing images of children, pets, and plain ordinary people were also common in this era, lending TV ads a right-around-home air. While some ads played on the familiar quest to stay abreast of the times through products that enhanced social standing, the old curse of social insecurity still helped sell items intended to counter body odor, dandruff, or bad breath. Another proven way to address leisure-oriented consumers was by associating a product with a pleasant setting such as the healthy aura of the great outdoors, which, ironically enough, cigarette print ads tended to fix on. But a characteristic common to all this era's advertising was its intent to entertain, especially in television.

An innovative technique of future import appeared in the 1980s when TV commercials took a cue from MTV's jump-cut style of programming music videos for its youthful audience. As a result, the dazzling rush of images done in this manner commanded close attention to commercials in their mission to promote their products.[81] No matter the product, though, TV commercials were now highly sensitive to the need to be more entertaining in their attempt to capture the gaze of their diversified audience, which had now become more visually sophisticated than ever before.

TV advertising as entertainment even helped transform politics into a form of show business during this time, as candidates for public office took on the guise of theatrical performers in their campaign commercials. Thus, presidential hopefuls came across as actors in repetitive melodramas whose outcomes were determined by viewers' deciding which candidate presented the more winning performance. Significantly, in 1998 the election of a former professional wrestler as governor of Minnesota was convincing testimony to the fantasizing power of the television image to influence voters in an election's outcome.

Although consumers were attracted to any product associated with a celebrated real-life figure, his/her media-made image that endorsed a product projected something of a fantasized aura. To capitalize on the selling power of the fantasized image, then, agencies created TV commercials that featured popular fantasy characters whose huckster roles generated a high degree of entertainment value. Among the more popular were those starring humorous types, ranging from animal players like Taco Bell's spunky chihuahua and Budweiser's wisecracking frogs and lizards to the animated antics of Bart and Homer of *The Simpsons* in miniepisodes promoting Butterfinger candy bars. But whether staged as a comic scenario or minidrama in which real-life characters performed, TV commercials were primarily designed to entertain as they informed. In 1999, when the nostalgia-based cable channel TV Land ranked its "50 Greatest TV Commercials of All Time," twenty-nine of them had appeared during 1980–1999. Of them, the 1984 commercial ranked No. 1 was a prime example of the TV ad as minidrama. During that year's Super Bowl, Apple Computer's "1984" ad depicted an ironic Orwellian setting in which to introduce its new personal computer to the world, as well as set new standards for the art of television advertising.[82]

That TV commercials involve viewers more than they ever realize has been elaborated on by Jonathan Price. While admitting to how bad many of them are, he contends that the best commercials "are lively, very American minidramas, tiny films, high-speed epics" that offer us "a wild tour of our unconscious fantasies." In their promotional mission TV commercials elicit emotional responses from viewers while training the eye to absorb the rapid pace of fast cuts, spot imagery, and implied connections between scenes or concepts that create "a new style of visual entertainment." They are, Price concludes, "the pinnacle of our popular culture's artistic expression," starring its celebrity icons in highly expensive productions whose calculated design is more extravagant than that for "any movie, opera, stage play, painting, or videotape."[83]

## THE ONGOING SEDUCTIVE POWER OF ADVERTISING

As it had throughout the century, then, commercial advertising continued to exert a powerful spell over the mediated vision while fomenting not a few problematic issues in the

process. From children who immersed themselves in televised cartoon programs sponsored by products that held a
special appeal for them to older viewers whose obsession for
material success and maintaining a lifestyle of youth and
beauty dictated the kinds of ads directed at them, advertising
remained the prime mechanism for manipulating consumers
to the will of capitalistic enterprise.

In this light, one of this era's more successful innovations
in television advertising was the infomercial, usually a thirty-
minute program presented in an interview format or audi-
ence-participation show. In it, a supposedly successful entre-
preneur promoted a new household product or a get-rich plan
through real estate or sales. Usually offered in late-night fil-
ler slots, such programming attempted to attract viewers by
being as entertaining as a talk show. Another TV advertising
ploy was the 900-number call-in telephone line that sought to
sell goods or services (even sex talk), as opposed to the more
common practice of promoters directly calling a home phone.
Both systems created problems among impres_ionable contacts through the deceptive promotion of fraudulent products
and questionable services, seemingly recreating the conniving tactics of the old frontier medicine man. Even the educational system paid homage to the power of advertising when
in 1989 a number of public schools began showing Channel
One current events programming, whose commercials the
schools agreed to in exchange for expensive computer equipment. A similar practice was resorted to when certain school
boards, strapped for finances, subscribed to ways for advertisers to use the school campus as an outlet for product promotional purposes. One now had to wonder if the naming of
schools after sponsoring corporations would be far behind.

Health issues notwithstanding, people continued to over-
eat, consume alcoholic beverages, and smoke tobacco, despite the warning label that cigarette packages and their print
ads displayed. While teenagers viewed smoking as a form of
sophisticated rebellion, reformed older smokers, who had either experienced health problems or had a relative die from
a smoking-related illness, began instigating suits against the
tobacco companies in the 1990s, charging them with deceptive advertising.[84] But the images of desire that advertising
promulgated were often too strong to resist, as the mediated
vision fell prey to the deception behind the promise of an ad's
message. Children who coerced their parents into buying the
product spin-offs they saw on the Saturday morning cartoon

shows would learn in time, as their parents had, that the engineers of the advertising industry were masters in the art of product seduction. In 1998, when Mattel's Cool Shoppin' Barbie doll appeared equipped with a credit card, only parents sensitive to the exploitative dangers of credit buying objected to the implied message that going in debt to obtain a desirable item was an acceptable practice.

The social extremes that brand-name advertising could perpetrate was realized in the sneaker wars between the sports-shoe companies Adidas, Nike, and Reebok, whose ads induced youths into believing that their personal identities hinged on wearing these companies' high-priced, top-of-the-line shoes. It was a message powerful enough to entice economically deprived kids into committing violent acts to acquire such a socially desirable item. Tellingly, James Twitchell, in his study of the social impact of advertising on American culture, observes that not only Americans' but all peoples' love of material possessions had been a major factor in igniting the Industrial Revolution.[85] Since the emergence of nineteenth-century capitalism, then, the drive to acquire material possessions in America emanated from a desire to escape the pressing socioeconomic concerns of an agrarian society and pursue the opportunities that a growing urban milieu offered, a major premise of both this book and its predecessor.

Now, more than ever, the advertising industry capitalized on the escapist aura of annual holidays to promote and sell commercial products related to such disparate events as Christmas and Halloween. By inducing customers to commemorate these and other calendar events like birthdays, anniversaries, and even invented observances such as Secretary's Day. Such happenings were also a natural boon to the greeting-card business. Ever sensitive to the mediated vision's sentimental attachment to holidays and special occasions, commercial advertising, by adapting old customs to new ways of celebrating them, created a ritualized way for Americans to connect with a nostalgic past while hopefully anticipating a better day.[86]

## THE SHOPPING MALL AS A CENTER OF COMMERCIALIZED ENTERTAINMENT

The marketing institution that made the most of holidays and leisure time was the enclosed suburban mall, the era's most pervasive example of postmodern advertising as commercialized entertainment. Indeed, its escapist lure was promoted mainly by its acres of free parking, multiplex movie theaters, video game arcades, food courts, chain stores, and shops catering to a broad range of consumer desire. Though by the 1980s, signs of overbuilding were apparent, as some 1,500 regional malls had opened since the 1950s, most of them continued to compete as combined business and entertainment centers. In responding to the fantasy desires of the mediated vision, they staged seasonal events and planned self-indulgent activities to attract both parents and children. As the nation's largest, Minnesota's Mall of America, which opened in 1992, shared its business mission with entertainment venues by offering diverse shopping opportunities in over 400 stores amid a variety of entertainment attractions such as theaters, bars, and theme-park features. Because of its escapist milieu, Carole Rifkind has categorized mall culture as "America's Fantasy Urbanism" where citizens "think they can avoid the societal and civic responsibilities of the real world."[87]

Naturally, Christmas was always the big event of the malls' sales year, but by the late '90s the developing phenomenon of cybershopping on the Internet was making inroads into the annual ritual of shopping in overcrowded malls. With nearly 17 million customers expected to buy at least one item online during the 1998 Christmas season, this innovative shopping method appeared to be the wave of the future. But by isolating the potential consumer from the intimate contact of the on-site shopping experience, it remained to be seen what effect this new mediated process would have on the shopper and the face of retail sales.[88]

Retailing took on yet another escapist dimension in the '90s with the appearance of movie studio stores in malls and as lone-standing outlets that catered to the self-advertising wares of Walt Disney and the old Warner animation studios. As repositories of fantasized merchandise directed at the nostalgic as well as escapist inclinations of the mediated vision, they now concentrated the spin-off products of their entertainment empires in one place, which previously had been scattered in the diverse sites of theme parks, chain stores, and concession stands in theaters. Long established in the collective memory of American media culture, the Disney and Warner fantasy characters now profited from the intergenerational relationship of parent and child. Even though Warners' Bugs Bunny and Daffy Duck creations still retained a high level of popularity, those of the Disney organization, both old and new, held the upper hand due to their ongoing production of high-quality animated features like *The Lion King*, *Tarzan*, and *Dinosaur* that continued to generate spin-off merchandise and collectibles related to the films. As a result, the lucrative business of escapist entertainment promised an unceasing cycle of producing and marketing items of intrinsically nostalgic and escapist appeal to the mediated vision.

## The Marriage of Consumption and Entertainment

In the last decade of the century, then, advertising's campaign to equate consumption with entertainment was at its most predominant stage. The attention paid the commercials that aired during the annual Super Bowl game was a prime example of this end. With an astronomical price tag by the end of the decade of over two million dollars for a thirty-second spot, these ads were compelled to come across as entertaining as they could possibly be to attract and hold attention. Many of them, in achieving this end, were acclaimed as the best of their kind. The sports/corporate relationship also found alternative commercial outlets, as people nationwide seemed to revel in wearing T-shirts, caps, and other forms of regalia emblazoned with team names and logos as well as those of brands and corporations. Indeed, it was as though the products of leisure consumption had assumed a celebrity status of their own. Neal Gabler's explanation for the mass reception of such commercialism was that "entertainment and consumption were often two sides of the same ideological coin." Both offered "release, freedom, transport, escape." And both "often provided the same intoxication: the sheer, mindless pleasure of emancipation from reason, from responsibility, from tradition, from class and from all other bonds that restrained the self."[89] These words were also aptly applicable to the mediated vision's ongoing escapist affinity for fantasized reality in the closing years of the twentieth century, particularly in the realm of organized sports.

## THE RISE OF INDIVIDUALIZED SPORT

During this era, organized sports began to undergo a shift in participant interest that would have unique repercussions for their future and that of the media culture. Now, more independently minded male youths were avoiding traditional team sports for such self-challenging alternative activities as skateboarding, mountain biking, and snowboarding, labeled "extreme sports" by the media. As a growing spectator sport, NASCAR racing was also rising in popularity among youth. A sign of this ongoing transition was the Wheaties cereal box's adornment with pictures of both champion skateboarders and NASCAR drivers. With more TV cable time to fill, alternative sports were programmed that featured both male and female performers. For example, to reach the elusive 13- to 34-year-old male demographic, product sponsors found beach volleyball played by young women in skimpy swim attire a natural draw.

Various theories circulated as to why many high school boys were avoiding involvement in team sports, particularly football and basketball. One suggested that today's white youth, in particular, were too spoiled by soft living to meet the disciplinary demands of team sports. Another contended that because blacks were now dominating these games, whites felt inferior to their seemingly superior abilities. This surmise opened up an ongoing debate as to whether blacks were naturally skilled to achieve in athletics or more attracted to them as one of the few available ways to exchange a deprived background for an economically rewarding career, despite the overwhelming competitive odds against achieving it.

This was also a time when individualized sport and exercise became major components in the leisure activities of adults. Considered as not only ritualized escapism from the tedium of everyday life but as aids to fitness, participation in pursuits like golf, tennis, and even the physically demanding routines of jogging and health center regimens provided a sense of self-fulfillment not so readily realized through other, less physically demanding activities. Still, many found that watching the drama of sport unfold on television or on-site sufficed as vicarious leisure experience, especially those who were either not up to the demands of physical effort or were repelled by it. In the '90s a popular venue that came into its own promoting sports as leisure-time entertainment was the sports bar. With its variety of gaming diversions and multiple TV sets capable of pulling in any live sporting event by satellite, the sports bar cut across the barriers of gender relations as the ultimate democratic expression of the sports fan's escapist bent. Accordingly, his/her interest in televised sporting events as entertainment offered ongoing opportunities to party, through alcohol consumption, whether a favorite team or performer won or lost.

If institutionalized team sports lacked the humanizing qualities of individualized activities, as Robert Lipsyte had lamented in the '70s, the New Leisure was responding to the need to experience the heightened sense of self-fulfillment that its activities could bestow on a person's mental as well as physical well-being. Although one could participate in a noncompetitive activity of the New Games movement, in which the act of playing rather than winning was an end in itself, the competitive instinct was so ingrained in the American character that winning as the ultimate reward retained its persistent allure. Consequently, the inherent goal of winning had become integral to the coaching tactics of team sports for youth, which were now organized and controlled by adults. However, the phrase "out of control" was more aptly descriptive of the adult role, as with increasing frequency parents attending their children's games resorted to vulgar displays and even violent reactions to an official's decision or the chagrin of enduring a loss. Thus, even at its lowest entry level, organized sports had been infiltrated by the winning ethos that undermined the real purpose of youth sports—to provide participants the personal opportunity to enjoy themselves playing a game. The serious consequences of playing primarily to win were also showing up in other, more visible areas of the sports establishment.

## THE DECLINE OF THE HEROIC IDEAL IN SPORT

The Olympics of this era stand out as a showcase for both the good and the bad sides of American sports. From the underdog U.S. hockey team's stirring gold-medal victory in 1980 to the women's hockey team that also won a gold medal in 1998 (the first time this sport was allowed as an Olympic event for women), many triumphant moments were recorded. But numerous issues and concerns erupted that reflected the uncertainties of the postmodern era, as the problems of the real world continued to invade the once-hallowed realm of the Games. The stratagem of using the Olympics as a platform to express East-West political differences, as shown by the American boycott of the 1980 Moscow Summer Games and the Russians' of Los Angeles in 1984, continued until the breakup of the Soviet Union in the late '80s.

However, certain problems were internal to the Olympics' organization itself and the training of the athletes who participated. The process of selecting the site for the 2002 Winter Games uncovered the disturbing fact that members of the International Olympic Committee (IOC) had been bribed through a varied array of "gifts" from bidders and that such a practice dated back at least two decades. Then, too, the IOC had been growing more liberal as to the kinds of events introduced into the Games, even to the extent that professionalism was no longer a deterrent to the appearance of team sports, as when the United States' 1992 "Dream Team," made up of players from the National Basketball Association, crushed all its opposition as expected. But the 1998 hockey team comprised of NHL players, whose gross behavior off the ice outdid their losing performance on, revealed the self-centered athlete's errant ways as a festering problem in American sports as the century came to a close.

Among individual athletes in the sprint, strength, and endurance events was a significant number who relied on performance-enhancing drugs to excel. Thus, a big concern of Olympic officials was how to develop and administer ways and means for detecting and controlling drug usage. Also, sport's increasing commercialization through the promise to champion athletes of multimillion-dollar contracts and product endorsement rewards was another factor helping undermine the Olympic ideals. A sinister example of the power that attaining the ultimate prize now commanded was the violent attack on figure skater Nancy Kerrigan to prevent her from performing in the 1994 Winter Games. Investigation revealed that it had been perpetrated by her chief rival, who coveted the monetary rewards to be gained from winning a gold medal.

However, among the most remarkable accomplishments of this era were those of women athletes who, by overcoming both the stereotyping of females as physically inadequate for strenuous athletic competition and the social barriers to their participation, became role models for young women to emulate. The woman athlete's legacy was clearly evident in not only her achievements in the Olympics but in college and professional sports as well as the up-and-coming sport of soccer. In 1999, for example, the American World Cup team proved it could compete with the best when it won the championship. Though women had initially looked upon sport participation as primarily a self-fulfilling experience, ironic signs appeared during this era that women's athletics, on both the school and college levels, were falling prey to the same problem that had long plagued men's athletics, a pervasive force that cut across even gender differences—the pressure to win.

## PROBLEMS COMMON TO THE POSTMODERN COMMERCIALIZATION OF SPORTS

Dedicated sports fans long acclimated to the heroic ideal, or at least what they thought it should represent, now saw the hallowed sanctuary of American sport being corrupted by commercial interests—not only by the athletes but those who controlled the sports establishment, particularly the owners of professional franchises in the major team sports. In 1994, *Sports Illustrated* writer Steve Rushin identified five main areas that had transformed sports during the preceding forty years, and the bottom line for all of them was money: (1) Television, bolstered by advertising revenue, played a major role in conditioning audiences to the show-business aspects of sporting events; (2) Houston's Astrodome, as the first covered-dome site to provide an all-weather location for sports, initiated the domed-stadium trend; (3) The 1970s' World Football League, though of brief duration, revealed that professional football was ready for wider expansion; (4) The ascendancy of the minority athlete created a superior talent pool for professional sports as well as heated competition among team owners for their services; and (5) Commensurate with their popularity, sports-related merchandise and memorabilia generated windfall returns not only for its producers and sponsors but for the athletes themselves.[90]

Revelatory of how big money set the parameters for the way professional sport was organized and controlled were certain deceptive but accepted business practices. By the 1980s every city of any competitive marketing size was eager to obtain a big-time sports franchise, preferably football. Ironically, it was the taxpayers who had to foot the bill for a new sports facility, even as city authorities ignored projects of higher priority. In holding the upper hand in this arrangement, then, franchise owners were also afforded tax breaks and even an allowance for the appreciation of a player's salary, which since the '70s had been rapidly escalating in all the major team sports. Thus, due to free agency, the lack of a salary cap, and the competition for talented players to help build a winning franchise, it was not unusual by century's end for baseball teams to have several multimillionaire players on their rosters.[91] The fact that since 1972 there had been three player strikes, though they now made more money than ever before, did not set well with the fans either. Baseball's unionized labor issues and complex business side were now of such magnitude that the game's traditional image as an escapist refuge for fans had been subverted, thus denigrating its storied history as the populist game of American media culture.

Many disenchanted fans, rather than attend professional football games whose tickets and concession prices, like those for other sports venues, kept rising, elected to watch them on television. Here again, owners found another highly lucrative source of revenue. For example, for the television rights to NFL games during 1994–97, franchise owners shared a combined total of 4.38 billion dollars from the broadcast and cable networks, which in turn profited from the advertising bonanza that pro football programming generated. Even though the era was dominated by only four teams (the San Francisco 49ers, Dallas Cowboys, Green Bay Packers, and Denver Broncos), fans not only watched all their favorite teams on TV but filled the stadiums to make pro football the nation's most popular team sport.

Thus, those who could afford the outlay to attend a game still did, in spite of the owners' advantages and players' on-field tantrums and off-field antisocial behavior. Even a basketball players' strike prior to the 1998–99 season, which triggered angry accusations of greedy millionaire players seeking even higher salaries, did not deter fans from returning to the arena when an abbreviated season finally got under way. As a result, the mediated vision came to realize that what it was viewing, either on-site or on TV, was not sport in the truest sense of the word's meaning but high-priced entertainment. In this light, then, players, like celebrated film or rock stars, appeared to be justified in receiving their huge salaries. And many athletes actually performed as though they were celebrity entertainers, both in their game and away from it. Although many role-model athletes were extolled by the media, it was the self-centered antics and misdeeds of the subversive types that received the most coverage, reflecting the era's affinity for tabloid journalism.

But the most media-made sports event since Roger Maris broke Babe Ruth's home-run record in 1961 featured two of baseball's more heroic types. In 1998, when the media turned the home-run hitting duel between the St. Louis Cardinals' Mark McGuire and his nearest rival, the Chicago Cubs' Sammy Sosa, into something of a carnivalesque show, it held the country in thrall until McGuire finished with a total of seventy to best Ruth by ten and Maris by nine. Because so many on-field exploits came together to rescue the game from the rut it had been mired in during this problematic era, *Sports Illustrated* was moved to call the 1998 baseball season the "greatest ever."[92]

Although the Notre Dame setting of the inspirational movie *Rudy* (1993) helped perpetuate the mythology of college football and its traditions, real-world problems were increasingly endemic to intercollegiate sports during this time. Most of these issues stemmed from alumni pressure on coaches to produce winners in the revenue sports of football and basketball, resulting in the illegal recruitment of players and/or the exploitation of their athletic talent, which was generally far superior to their academic ability. At the cost of probation by the NCAA, many big-time programs devised deceptive ways and means to keep their players academically eligible, until those qualified left for the professional ranks. Drugs were also a pervasive problem that could result in a player's dismissal if he tested positive for their use. To the alumni and supporters of a team, though, each fall renewed the dream of winning a championship. However, the heroic ideal that had originated during the early days of the intercollegiate game had now been subverted by a win-at-all-costs posture and a show-business aura that the media exploited.

Thus, some saw the real enemy of sport as television in its proclivity toward overexposure. With twenty-four-hour cable channels like the two ESPN channels hungry for material to fill up their programming and attract advertising revenue, all kinds of venues from such alternative activities as those mentioned earlier, the derivative game of arena football, the staged melodramatic exploits of professional wrestling, and the national appeal of NASCAR racing to golf, boxing, and the traditional team sports in their seasons were not only responding to the escapist desires of the mediated vision but compelling it to endure a spiraling trend toward superfluous programming, and leaving not much to the imagination in the process.[93] As sports columnist Jeff MacGregor cynically commented on television's commercialization of sports and its ironic impact on the fan at the close of the century: ". . . you were a better fan back before your heroes came to you off the rack, prefabricated by the culture of celebrity, the latest and greatest striding to the first tee of his first tournament already clutching a fistful of endorsement deals and wearing the newest shoes, every moment of it manufactured by television for television, athletics as an act of product placement."[94]

### The Escapist Consolation of Sport's Nostalgic Past

As though to substantiate the notion that sport's nostalgic heritage had more positive appeal to the mediated vision, television began to program tributes to it during the late '90s, airing shows about the greatest athletes and teams of the century. While ESPN initiated a countdown series to name the greatest athlete of the century, *Sports Illustrated* featured photo-oriented articles that celebrated such topics as the best sports years, the greatest team dynasties, and, not to be outdone by ESPN, a list of superior athletes who competed for the honor of the century's greatest. Naturally, the upshot of both the television and magazine series helped spark endless arguments among viewers and readers as to which athlete or sporting event really was the greatest. But as the sporting achievements of the present evolved into nostalgic memories of the past, they in turn continued to inspire the mediated vision's enduring love affair with sports, despite the myriad problems common to the postmodern era that were mirrored in the microcosm of the sports world.

# 4

# Indulging the Self as a Way of Life at Century's End

Observers of the Webcam phenomenon say it's the logical next step for a society hooked on reality-based television shows. . . . People are already turning cameras on themselves; the Internet allows them to effectively broadcast those images, cheaply and continuously.
—"How the Internet is Changing America,"
*Newsweek*, Special Report (1999)

WITH THE AVAILABILITY OF LEISURE TIME AT AN ALL-TIME HIGH during the latter years of the twentieth century, many were taking advantage of the natural scene's escapist opportunities. This end was especially true of those who had the means to travel to high-scale skiing lodges and posh recreational sites or take to the water in a late-model powerboat, sailboat, or even a yacht. Although those who pursued the traditional outdoor activities of camping, fishing, and hunting to relate to the challenges of nature, they revealed their dependency on the latest conveniences to enhance the pleasures of what was once relished as a hardy experience. Hence, a common sight on the interstate highways during the '90s was the sport-utility vehicle (SUV) as well as the well-equipped recreational vehicle (RV) and the touring motor home, whose cell phone, computer, and satellite TV dish signified a reluctance to relinquish the familiar amenities of postmodern life.

However, the more daring youthful venturers were active in such physically demanding pursuits as backpacking, downhill or cross-country skiing, mountain climbing, snorkeling, surfing, and even skydiving. In fact, in this day of multiple subcultural leisure outlets, outdoor activities of the most esoteric kind were in high demand to meet the ongoing escapist desires of the adventurous. Regardless of the type activity, though, the main reason one became involved in these pursuits derived from the century-old ingrained quest to exchange the routine of urban life for the escapist release and self-realization of not only the natural environment but that of a fantasized milieu.

## The Packaged Vacation: A Popular New Self-Indulgent Activity

To those not so actively inclined during this economically flush time, exotic worldwide travel tours or the glamorous life aboard a cruise ship offered a more agreeable way to pamper the self. By the early '90s, the standard seven-day cruise had become a thoroughly democratized leisure experience, as travel agencies were offering economically priced family packages to such popular destinations as the Caribbean Islands, Mexico, Bermuda, and Alaska. Youthful travelers, from toddlers to teens, added a new social dimension to a kind of travel whose exclusiveness had been traditionally determined by class and age. Now, though, well-to-do senior travelers were even taking their grown offspring and grandchildren on cruises. With millions of Americans expected to escape the ordinary via this venue into the new century, cruise lines were launching larger ships whose attractions responded to a variety of interests, most creatively through theme-based itineraries featuring entertainment celebrities. In 1998 the Walt Disney Corporation introduced its version of the cruise experience with the inaugural sailings of its two fantasy ships—the Wonder and the Magic. From casino gambling and nightclub entertainment to video-game centers for youths, these vessels offered the latest in fantasized escape for all passengers.

Many families were structuring their vacations around an annual visit to a favorite theme park, whose popularity peaked during this period, attested to by the numerous new sites that opened their doors. While California boasted such attractions as Disneyland, Knott's Berry Farm, and Sea World San Diego, Florida blossomed into a theme-park mecca of international appeal during these years.[1] In 1996, when Walt Disney World in Orlando celebrated its twenty-fifth anniversary, those who had not been back since its opening in 1971 were treated to a plethora of new attractions: the Epcot

Center's cultural and science-oriented venues, the Disney-MGM Studios that featured attractions based on their animated films, a golf club, a new Hall of Presidents and Carousel of Progress, and Planet Hollywood's cuisine as well as Pleasure Island's jazz stylings. Later visitors beheld the planned living community called Celebration, the opening of Animal Kingdom, and the inception of the thrill ride Rock 'n' Roller Coaster, among a multitude of other attractions. Here, then, set apart from the routine demands of the outside world, was the latest version of Disney's self-contained magical realm that had paradoxically transformed fantasy into reality to become the epitome of self-indulgent escapism in the eyes of the mediated vision.[2]

In 1999, the aptly named Universal Studios Escape, Disney's biggest competitor in Orlando, expanded its operation to include Islands of Adventure. Billing itself as "The Theme Park of the 21st Century," Universal sought to transcend Disney's basic emphasis on the memories of childhood through attractions that appealed not only to a more sophisticated generation of children and teens but also their parents. To fulfill this mission, its new fantasy venues and rides inspired by the products of media culture such as comic books, science-fiction movies, Dr. Seuss tales, and cartoon characters were designed to provide the ultimate in escapist adventure. Their publicity, in fact, promoted the notion that here was a place where one could actually "Live the Movies" on thrill rides inspired by such disaster films as *Twister, Earthquake, Jaws*, and even the fantasy film *Back to the Future*. In addition, the escapist lure of nightlife was offered adults in the cafés and entertainment centers of CityWalk, while at the Portofino Bay Hotel, they were transported to foreign shores in the romanticized milieu of a quaint fishing village on the Mediterranean.

By the late '90s, though, the question of how many theme parks Orlando and its environs could support before reaching the saturation point was becoming a serious issue. Apparently the Disney philosophy of ever-evolving change and emphasis on the escapist theme concept were also the mutual intent of its competitors. Yet one had to wonder how much of a fantasy menu the mediated vision could digest, as after an extended stay at either Walt Disney World or Universal's Islands of Adventure, visitors might find themselves looking to escape from the inevitable reality of accounting for the ever-mounting cost of such a vacation.

## THE RISE OF GAMBLING AS RECREATIONAL ACTIVITY

While leisure-time outlets kept proliferating during this time, gambling, or "gaming" in euphemistic parlance, as a recreational attraction grew increasingly popular, both legally and illegally. However, for some the opportunity to gain instant riches proved more long-term addictive than temporarily escapist. By 1998, overall gambling revenues, to which casinos and lotteries provided the largest share, were up fivefold since 1992. In 1999, in fact, thirty-eight state-sponsored lotteries were operating around the country. Ignoring the downside of any attendant social problems, even some conservative states looking to augment tax revenues now supported instituting lotteries. Complementing the casinos of Las Vegas, Reno, and Atlantic City, gambling venues popped up in some unlikely places, in particular, Minnesota, which introduced its Indian-operated Mystic Lake casino, and the Mississippi Gulf Coast, which offered a bevy of hotel/casino attractions. More fittingly, nearby New Orleans added casino gambling to its varied points of interest in 1999 when Harrah's opened an atmospheric operation that attempted to relate gambling to an entertainment theme evocative of the city's Mardi Gras and jazz music heritage. By the late '90s, organized gambling was on the verge of providing the most open-ended opportunity yet to engage in it—online betting on the Internet. By inducing home-based gamblers to wager on anything from horse races to football games, such a practice resulted in many problems for the user. Just as online pornography had proven, the Internet's unregulated system had legislators puzzling over how to mandate ways and means to control the problems related to its user receptiveness.[3]

Las Vegas, as the nation's gaming capital as well as a center for show-business entertainment, was now taking notice of the success that the proliferating theme parks were enjoying. Indeed, the city where underworld activity had long been tolerated began implementing more family-oriented attractions as well as the fantasized replication of famous international tourist sites as featured venues. While adults indulged their gambling fantasies at the various casinos, their children were attended to by attractions designed especially for them. Many of these were in the form of sophisticated video games—in effect, gambling devices themselves. In the Vegas milieu, gambling and its offshoots helped promote the self-indulgent posture that whatever one did with leisure time was one's own business, simply because leisure activity had now become its own excuse for being.[4]

## THE FANTASIZED ALLURE OF ELECTRONIC GAME VIOLENCE

By the 1990s, a widespread subculture had developed around the computer technology of electronic games, inducing many youths into graphically violent role-playing experiences. Sited in shopping mall arcades since the '80s, the games were played mainly by males in their teens. The phenomenon had originated innocently enough in the late 1960s with the advent of simple video games that could be played at home on a television screen. Then, in 1972, with the appearance of the first successful commercial electronic game, Atari's *Pong*, computerized innovations began to proliferate, relegating the archetypal pinball machine and static board games to the realm of nostalgic recall.

Throughout the '70s, numerous enterprises contributed to the rapid development of this dynamic new industry that would explode in the 1980s. While an established toy company like Mattel began producing its popular handheld games, Coleco started out anew as a competitive provider in this area and later in the production of its home console player system. Though the advent of the Apple II personal computer proved a big boon to playing programmed games at home, Atari also came up with influential innovations during this time, in particular its Video Computer System (VCS) a cartridge-based game console. But the upshot of the competition between it and Mattel's Intellivision model would be an enduring marketing war in the home console business. More competition appeared in the late '70s when Japanese technology affirmed itself through the highly popular *Space Invaders*. Inherently designed to induce players to attain a high score for eliminating as many of the game's relentless aliens as possible, it was an omen of the violent kind of game tactics to come.

With the video arcade a popular venue in the 1980s, a large volume of archetypal games now responded to its young clientele's growing fascination with them. For one, the first games structured around original characters and media sources appeared. Pac-Man, whose quest was literally to devour his many enemies, became popular enough to inspire numerous merchandise spin-offs. Another popular character showed up as the heroic little Mario in Nintendo's chase game *Donkey Kong*. While Midway produced the first Hollywood licensed game in its popular version of the Disney science-fiction movie *Tron*, Atari came up with a big hit in *Star Wars*, due mainly to a player's involvement in the game's replication of the film's exciting aerial combat elements.

The '90s, when CD-ROM enhancement first became available for home computers, saw the advent of the *Myst* series, whose superior graphics anticipated many more technical advances. Whether the result of corporate competition or a reflection of the time's fascination with sensationalism, eidetic improvements would be increasingly utilized to intensify the violent three-dimensional scenarios of the chase/action games such as *Doom* and *Quake*. Then in 1996, the introduction of the Lara Croft character in Eidos's *Tomb Raider* equated sex and violence and helped promote Sony's PlayStation as the leading home console system of this time. But to most players sex appeal was secondary to a game's violent dimensions, which emanated from the vicarious thrill of tracking down a quarry and then utilizing lethal weapons to score points for each kill.

By 1998–99 the 5.5 billion dollar electronic games industry was churning out a multitude of products featuring violent content, inciting critics to charge that playing a gory game like *Mortal Kombat* desensitized youths to physical violence. Others countered that indulging in such play was merely another form of escapist fantasy common to the late twentieth century. And as the technology of computerized games kept advancing, they began to take on more of an adult appeal, so that by 2000, Nintendo was promoting its racy, adult-rated chase game *Perfect Dark*, structured around the comic book–like exploits of its sexy heroine. However, with violent behavior among the young on the rise, parents as well as social critics deduced that because the virtual world of video games involved a player on a more intimate basis than viewing television or movies did, there might very well be a connection between youths' antisocial activity and their exposure to simulated violence as escapist entertainment.

## THE SELF-INDULGENT VALUES OF YOUNG ADULTS

The proliferating movies and television series of this era focused on the self-centered lifestyle practiced by an age group ranging from around twenty-five to thirty-five. Labeled by the media as young urban professionals, or yuppies, they were primarily motivated to make money as rapidly as they could in the booming centers of finance and the computer technology industry. They were also inspired to spend their money just as fast as they made it, converting their earnings into the symbols of material success—luxury cars, designer clothes, and a high-rolling hedonistic lifestyle as well as leisure pursuits that involved them with lucrative business contacts.[5] The unrestrained wheeling and dealing that typified the 1980s' stock market negotiations, as well as yuppie greed, was the central focus of Oliver Stone's *Wall Street* (1987), while a pathological side was centered on in the controversial *American Psycho* (2000). But such films implied that though money might enhance material success, it did little to resolve the problems of one's personal life, a plot convention that ironically harkened back to the movies of the 1930s.

In contrast to these films' downside versions of urban high life, popular television series like the fictional *Dallas* and the real-world *Lifestyles of the Rich and Famous* offered a glorified look at the culture of self-aggrandizement by centering on the good life that only the very wealthy could afford. As the living standards of the average American reached their highest level during this time, many were induced into emulating the celebrity lifestyles of the so-called rich and famous. As usual, both television and the movies, as social barometers of the times, were highly influential in helping one keep up with the latest trends and fashion styles in order to appear successful, even if one were not. In particular, the movies' impact on male tastes was borne out by the trend to acquire as stylish a wardrobe as Richard Gere's in *American Gigolo* (1980). Accordingly, in the generally conservative decade of the '80s, such subtly resplendent designer clothes as dark business suits and colorful power ties for men, androgynous attire for professional women, and the essential designer accessories became the fashion rage. In fact, the modish styles of Italian fashion designer Giorgio Armani, who drew up the clothes for Gere's role as well as the stars of numerous other films, were still in vogue among the well-dressed at the century's end.

## FASHION TRENDS AS A SUBCULTURAL REFLECTION OF MEDIA CULTURE

However, ongoing social fragmentation also fomented a backlash to designer fashions in the veritable mishmash of anarchistic styles introduced by the trendsetting London houses of the early 1980s. Inspired by punk culture's radical emphasis on outrageous dress, some women even promoted underwear as outerwear after the shock style of the daringly inventive pop singer Madonna. But by the mid '80s, a reaction to punk's extremes appeared in the tradition of catwalk glamour fashion promoted by the images of celebrity models. On into the '90s, the faces of the so-called supermodels began to proliferate in product advertising and on magazine covers, making them as celebrated as movie/TV stars. Other notable media spin-offs of the supermodel class showed up in *Sports Illustrated*'s annual swimsuit issue and in the popular *Baywatch* TV series, which featured well-endowed young women in erotically styled swimsuits. While their erogenous areas radiated a natural appeal to voyeuristic males, impressionable females were inspired to descend on mass-market outlets in search of one-piece slenderizing swimsuits as well as brightly colored mix-and-match separates, hopefully to meet size requisites and enhance their beach-scene allure.

In the '90s, urban reality itself became a significant factor affecting fashion trends as TV costume designers, who had traditionally submitted to a democratized approach to style, derived much of their inspiration from what they saw worn on the street. To locate sources for such attire, they resorted to the mass-marketed brand names sold in department stores and even discount outlets. Now it seemed that both women's and men's styles depicted on prime-time television series were supplanting the movies' longtime influential role in dictating fashion.

By the mid '90s, the brand names of Ralph Lauren and Tommy Hilfiger, which had democratized the smart new sporting styles for men, gravitated toward an even more casual appearance. Pursuant to Lauren's dominance in the realm of men's informal fashion, Hilfiger also modified designer standards to produce styles that incorporated a colorful yet masculine look. In fact, urban males were now afforded a surrogate escape to the realm of the great outdoors simply by wearing such attire. Also, advances in fiber/fabric technology resulted in body-adaptive material that helped market jogging outfits. Along with the essential athletic footwear, this highly popular style became a fashion statement in itself, as acceptable for informal socializing as it was for its original sporting purpose. By the late '90s, casual dress had even invaded the workplace as businesses loosened their dress codes on what was called Funky or Free Friday when T-shirts, Levis, and sneakers were the mode. But this show of laxity was not without its critics concerning a potentially negative effect on traditional work standards.

In freeing itself from elitist dictates, then, fashion was now being inspired from below by the immoderate dress styles of youth, a trend that had been evolving since the 1960s. Consequently, some culture analysts were prompted to pronounce an end to traditional fashion as it had been known.[6] Nevertheless, the respective group members of society's subcultural sectors realized, as fashion taste had always dictated, that what they wore was a badge of social identity, whether in the conventional dress mode or the extreme casual manner of the hip-hop street look. The latter, commonly referred to in the '90s as the grunge style, actually amounted to no style at all, except among those who shared its slovenly code. Popularized by rebellious rap singers and inner-city youth, it harkened back to the antiestablishment dress of the hippies and rock music performers. As exhibited by males in their backward worn caps, oversized shirts, and underwear-exposing droopy pants, grunge was slobbish, even clownish in appearance. When young girls adapted to it by wearing revealing tank tops and brief, tight-fitting skirts or shorts, the style was considered extreme enough for some school systems to enact dress codes.

Like the counterculture dress of the hippies, then, grunge caught on as a collective signifying statement of the young that also promoted its own radical concept of "fashionable" accessories for both sexes. Accordingly, a common practice, in addition to the prominent bodily display of tattoos, was the piercing of one's ears, noses, and even tongues to display metal balls or rings. As the ultimate statement of this kind, the more daringly innovative utilized them to adorn their intimate body parts. Even college athletes were now brandishing tattoos and, more shockingly, wearing earrings, a practice once considered a sign of effeminacy. In this regard, college football coaches, traditionally the most conservative of authority figures concerning their players' off-field dress and behavior, had now given in to this new fashion and its seeming intent to reinforce one's personal identity within the collective posture of a team's competitive function.

Recognizing that most everyone aspired to his or her own

version of a hip identity, mass marketers saw any new trend in fashion or faddish behavior as worthy of commercial promotion, not only to the young, who naturally relished having their personal sense of social alienation pampered, but to those who desired to retain or regain their youth by emulating the ways of the young. From the 1970s' sex- and drug-charged ethos of the disco-dancing in-crowd to the 1990s' binge-drinking college students, social rebellion became a subcultural form of hip conformity. By this time, then, the 1960s' countercultural posture had been absorbed by the media culture, resulting in a paradoxical situation that blurred the distinction between the "cool" and what was considered square. The very thing that mainstream society had once adamantly rejected had now become culturally diffused through the pervasive power of the media, as magazines, radio, recordings, and television helped promote the dress, fads, and social attitudes of the hip-hop/grunge generation.[7]

Nevertheless, as new media developments in the postmodern era appeared and almost as soon disappeared, one had to wonder if anything of novel distinction could merit enduring interest anymore. But if novelty was exhausted, there was still the past to turn to, since nostalgia was still very much in the air. The acceptance by certain subcultural elements of what had been considered culturally square, as, for example, big band dance music and singers like Wayne Newton and Tony Bennett, once again revealed the postmodern affinity for resurrecting and promoting iconic images of past media culture as a buffer to the uncertainties of life in the present. Paradoxically, by the end of the century, the things that had once separated Norman Mailer's hipster from the conformist tendencies of the mainstream society had merged in a hybrid cultural identity.

## The Quest to Revive Both the Physical and Spiritual Self

Rather than adorning their bodies after the manner of the young crowd, many older health culture advocates were seeking to transform their ungainly physical appearances through participation in vigorous exercise regimens like bodybuilding and aerobics. But there were those more attracted to assuming the supine position of "couch potatoes," in the slang of the

time. In 1999 the announcement that half the nation's population was overweight should have been a wake-up call for the
obese sector to waddle down to the nearest health fitness
center and try out its Nautilus machines or various other exercise and weight-losing options that these places had introduced. Attempting to capitalize on this situation were the
often deceptive TV infomercials that publicized a myriad of
supposedly painless ways to either lose weight or build up
one's body.

Ironically, the media's periodic news releases and medical
breakthrough articles made Americans more health conscious than ever before at a time when many were not nearly
as physically active as they should have been. Especially sensitive to the dangers of cholesterol buildup, they reminded
themselves to check the content labels on food cans and packages, purchase low-calorie foods, ingest vitamin pills, drink
mineral water, and either quit or cut back on the smoking
habit. On the other hand, there were those who found escape
from their health problems through the personal use, or
abuse, of over-the-counter products and prescription drugs,
only to wind up aggravating their situations. For others, the
most popular escapist habit of drinking, both social and solitary, contributed to an alarming increase in alcoholism, not
only among the young but women and the elderly during this
time.

Naturally, the American obsession for maintaining a youthful appearance was the main motivation for staying in top
physical condition. Although those women looking for quick
results resorted to cosmetic surgery and liposuction, they
were not alone in their goal to retain the semblance of youth
through medical technology, as a number of men also underwent operations to improve their looks. Also, with male impotence diagnosed as more of a widespread problem than had
been thought, the appearance of a highly publicized answer
to erectile dysfunction called Viagra was considered a boon
to enhancing the sex life of many older men.

Although an AARP survey revealed that only one in four
older Americans desired to live to the age of 100, due mainly
to the debilitating health problems that could arise in the
aging process, statistics portended that many might live well
beyond 100 due to advances in medical science and improved
health care.[8] Nevertheless, the ingrained prejudices toward
aging in a youth-oriented society were readily apparent in

commercial advertising and the forms of media culture that ignored an integral social role for older citizens in favor of the more appealing interests and concerns of youth. Thus many news releases and magazine articles that dealt with the subject of older people were presented from more of a problematic point of view than a positive approach. The message was clear: Aging, because of its obvious attention to the natural decline from youth to the final stages of life, was not a topic conducive to the creation of favorable subject matter. The consensus was that either nostalgia for the good old days or the solace of an afterlife were appropriate panaceas for the aging sector.

Not so for longtime activist Betty Friedan, who at age seventy-two published *The Fountain of Age* (1993), in which she argued: "It is time to look at age on its own terms and put names on its values and strengths, breaking through the definition of age solely as deterioration or decline from youth."[9] To bolster her argument, she cites inspirational examples of older people who had continued to lead useful, vital and productive lives in the societal and cultural mainstreams. Taking Friedan's posture into account, advertisers and the creative people who responded to the segmented sectors that now comprised the media culture could ill afford to overlook this growing sector as a target and/or significant presence in their future planning.

In reaction to the personal emptiness spawned by the urban lifestyle's emphasis on material gain, the search for spiritual satisfaction found numerous outlets during this time. The 1980s' New Age movement, for example, represented an attempt to teach adherents how to relieve both physical and mental stress amid the social fragmentation of postmodern living by cultivating a sense of wholeness in one's physical and spiritual being. However, many of the movement's faddish offshoots were not so much signs of a "New Age" as they were a return to the traditional messages of astrology, yoga, and personal meditation. Along with the variations of Eastern philosophy designed to put the mind at ease, interest in such physically curative practices as acupuncture and finger pressure massage developed. While Christian fundamentalists looked askance at any such methods of offering solutions to one's spiritual and/or physical problems, they depended increasingly on the medium of television to generate financial support for their faith-healing programs and their scriptural-based plan of salvation and its reward of eternal life. Their message, they maintained, was especially timely as the new millennium approached, a time that many believers prophesied would see the second coming of Jesus Christ.[10]

Another, more earthbound way of realizing personal identity was through genealogy, which became a national obsession as the end of the century approached. Now, through ready access to archival sources on the Internet, the search process was made considerably easier, even though research problems persisted that only the most dedicated and determined users could resolve. From the perspective of the mediated vision, the natural desire to trace one's roots was fueled not only by a nostalgic fascination with the past but by a felt need to reinforce one's sense of self and place in the increasingly complex world of the present.

Numerous hopefuls even sought to transcend the finality of death as a barrier between past and present. Whether deceived or not by the practice of mediums who professed an innate ability to contact those who had passed on, the fact remained that there were many who believed, or wanted to believe, that a medium was sufficiently psychic to reach over to the Great Beyond and establish a relationship with their loved ones.

## THE MOVEMENT TO ESCAPE URBAN PROBLEMS FOR A BETTER LIFE

By contrast were those more concerned with finding ways and means to make the here and now a better time in which to make their lives more meaningful. For them, the fast-paced urban lifestyle dedicated to earning more money while enduring its encroachment upon their attempts to relish its benefits was playing itself out. As indeed it already had for those who renounced such a life for a slower-paced, more tranquil lifestyle in a rural setting or a small town. It is highly ironic, then, that the economic promise of a growing city like Chicago, which a hundred years before had attracted so many small-town/rural dwellers (as focused on in my earlier book dealing with the century's first half), was now repelling established city dwellers, motivating them in a real agrarian sense to look for greener pastures.

In 1997, a *Time* cover story, titled "The Great Escape," reported that many longtime city folk were moving to small towns not only to avoid the urban environment's crime, traffic, and cost of living but to take advantage of workplace change brought about by "powerful technological forces that [were] decentralizing the American economy."[11] Naturally, the Internet, cell phone, and fax machine, had been among the major players in this transition. In fact, the computer revolution had allowed many who relocated to retain their urban-based jobs simply because online connections had made geographical distance no longer the problem that it had been. A number of these venturers had even taken a cut in salary in exchange for a higher quality of life characterized by the self-realizing opportunities that outdoor leisure activities and the West's regenerative scenic wonders presented. Paradoxically, then, the "new" West, as it was represented by the states of Colorado, Idaho, Montana, New Mexico, Utah, and Wyoming, was now beckoning to those searching for the outdoor quality of life that had eluded them in an urban environment. Indeed, the territory of the Rockies as a vibrant symbol of this new West was now supplanting the myth of the golden West in which California had represented the Edenic future to many searching for it in the 1930s.

Even so, along with a continuing, unchecked population influx came the possibility that in time similar problems could ultimately develop that had undermined the mediated vision's urban dream of a better life—such issues and concerns as those Theodore Dreiser's *Sister Carrie* focused on in the growing urban centers of Chicago and New York toward the end of the nineteenth century. By 1999, the worldwide growth in population had exceeded six billion people, a statistic that boded ill for not only developing countries but also for the quality of life in wealthy, industrialized countries like the United States. In this light, then, the future of the beckoning hinterland as an escapist refuge was not nearly so promising as it would appear.

## THE INTERNET AND THE ADDICTIVE POWER OF VIRTUAL REALITY

Since the 1980s, a technological force of potentially greater sociocultural impact than television had been contributing to the mediated vision's ever-evolving social fragmentation. In less than a decade, software products like CD-ROM had made it possible for a personal computer to provide users specialized information as well as a menu of varied entertainment sources. Along with the Internet's rapid development as a communications medium, the online user had also uncovered an immediate way to transform his/her isolated self into a variety of social roles through relating online with others of similar interests. It was a relationship that would shortly involve users in some unique social problems.

By the '90s, parents of homes that had access to the Internet soon discovered that their young were being exposed to an even wider array of questionable diversions than just video-game violence. Chief among them were Web sites offering explicit sexual content and those catering to racist or radical political doctrine. Some even offered instructions for constructing homemade violence by disseminating bomb-making information behind the shield of free speech. Another problem arose from unsupervised youths using credit cards to make frivolous purchases from online auction and shopping sites—unbeknownst to parents until the charges came around. By the late '90s, then, with intraschool violence at an unprecedented level, the concerns about ready access to problematic Web sites and the potential influence of video-game violence were widespread. It would seem, then, that fantasy and reality had become interrelated to the extent that now the young, in particular, found it difficult to detect any rigid line of demarcation between the two.

Although teens were initially more knowledgeable about computer management than their parents, many adults soon acclimated to the Internet as an interactive medium that afforded a private means of escape from immediate concerns. In fact, the venture into virtual reality would become an addiction for many, at least according to a 1998 syndicated newspaper report that quoted a habitual Internet user: "With workaholics, gambling, alcoholism, it's escape. You also go to the world of the Internet and you escape. You don't have to deal with a lot of things. You can create a lot of safety. You're not looking face to face, not talking directly to people. It's more accessible, less risky than life."[12] Unfortunately, the open opportunity that the computer offered to initiate and carry on intimate dialogue with total strangers would lead to serious interpersonal consequences for not a few users, many stemming from the uninhibited initiation of sexual trysts.

Here, then, was shocking evidence of electronic technology's power to fantasize reality by transforming it into a seemingly more stimulating experience than what real life had to offer.

The user-friendly kind of service afforded by the personal computer had been developing rapidly since 1983, when *Time* named the computer as its "Man of the Year." By 1990, when corporate offices first had more desktop computers than typewriters, the information revolution had come into its own, providing immediate opportunities for interactive communication between sender and receiver. By the mid 1990s the Internet, which was originally established to transmit governmental and university research information, had become an international forum for general users through the organizational system of the World Wide Web, or what was popularly referred to as the "information highway." Capitalizing on the user's need for operational-system software, an enterprising young man named Bill Gates established his Microsoft empire and became fabulously rich as a result. Ultimately, for those who desired it, commercial subscriptions to such computer support services as CompuServe, America Online, and WebTV provided access to a variety of informational and entertainment sources. Now, the potential for what cyberspace had to offer appeared to be boundless, as worldwide users responded by creating their own Web sites, downloading popular music recordings and book excerpts, playing computer games, and communicating by electronic mail.

Paradoxically, though, the Internet's rapid growth as a democratizing media force, due mainly to its decentralization and lack of authoritarian control over who could access it, resulted in unexpected problems like those cited above as well as others to come. By directly relating to the interactive challenges of virtual reality, the isolated self now discovered the most intimately personal form of escapism yet in contrast with the more communally shared visual experience that the movies and television provided.

According to research scientist Sherry Turkle, the upshot of this revolutionary kind of sensibility was a new component of media culture that, in effect, enticed the user to substitute representations of reality for the real. Indeed, this unlikely process made it possible for one to indulge in fantasized experiences by assuming whatever identity one desired and play escapist "games" with other users, even to the point of extending one's physical presence to interact in sexual fantasies. By obviating face-to-face encounters through playing fictional roles and assuming multiple identities, a user could now escape real-world concerns by engaging in "chatroom" dialogue that could result in the fabrication of a self-determined fantasy world.

However, such a process raised many concerns, as, for example, the kind of psychological and sociological effects that the creation of fictional identities could have on the user's sense of his/her true self. Thus, Turkle contended that the virtual reality of cyberspace was not only changing the way users thought about themselves but the nature of their sexuality, their personal identities, and their communal relationships.[13] But Turkle also argued that the virtual realm of cyberspace should be understood as more than a place of "escape and meaningless diversion," for as she concludes; "Without a deep understanding of the many selves we express in the virtual we cannot use our experiences there to enrich the real."[14] By knowing our virtual selves, then, such knowledge could be used positively for "personal transformation" in the "real." As though anticipating an integral social role for the computer in the new century, Turkle's findings opened up a whole new realm of thought about the nature of the self in terms of what virtual reality had revealed about it.

## PREDICTING THE TRIUMPH OF THE IMAGE OVER THE WORD

But the most momentous communications achievement has yet to be realized, according to Mitchell Stephens's brave prophecy—the potential for the moving image to augment and possibly supplant the printed word as the dominant language of the future.[15] The instrumental factor in this transition, he contends, will be the new digital technology of the computer, the latest development in his argument (and this book's) that each established mass-media form of communication, from the printing press through radio, the movies, and television to the computer, had been reluctant to concede its established status to a newer form that threatened its dominance. Ultimately, though, each medium, in realizing its limitations, either yielded to or compromised with the more advanced techniques of the newer form.

In the novel, the communication problems that the printed

word encountered in visually expressing abstract concepts and inner thought processes had required the avant-garde modernist vision of a James Joyce or William Faulkner and later the self-reflexive postmodernist style of a John Barth or Thomas Pynchon that formulated its own private vision. Even the more visually expansive form of film had to rely on such technical devices as montage, crosscutting, and even the complementary components of color and music to express complex visual meaning. But, according to Stephens, the advent of the New Video in the 1980s, through its computer-generated graphics and visual techniques of fast- or jump-cutting, rapid transition, and continuously changing camera angles, anticipated a more efficient and challenging way of viewing and absorbing information. Pioneered by TV commercials, fast-paced television shows, such as *Rowan and Martin's Laugh-In* (1967–73), and, beginning in 1981, the hyperactivity of MTV videos, the moving image's visual energy not only related complex information, it created new patterns of communication to stimulate the viewer's visual sense. According to Stephens, then, the digitalized image would continue to evolve as a major force in sensitizing viewers' visual capability to ingest more information in rapid fashion. Moreover, in contrast to the conventional narrative style of movies and television, he argued that the New Video's ability to communicate complex concepts would involve audiences on a higher intellectual plain, ultimately leading to new theories about the visual process itself.[16] At century's end, then, it would appear that the mediated vision was being subtly conditioned to the moving image as a revolutionary new creative language to interpret the varieties and complexities of human experience.

## The Downside of Postmodern Media Culture at Century's End

If the visual primacy of the image over the reflective role of the word was a dominant characteristic of postmodern media culture toward the end of the twentieth century, there were those who saw it as a cultural failing and not so much as an achievement. In fact, the very sameness of the media forms' respective responses to the subcultural demands of the mediated vision incited conservative critics to voice their acerbic opinions on the "trashing of taste" in American culture. As one of the most outspoken, James B. Twitchell echoed Neil Postman's satirical perception of Las Vegas's fantasized milieu in *Amusing Ourselves to Death* (1985) as "a metaphor of [America's] national character and aspirations" to demonstrate how vulgarity had triumphed in an "Age of Show Business."[17]

Because of the mediated vision's commercially proven demand for formulaic reading matter, it continued to be rewarded with more of the same kind of fare, as Twitchell contended. Accordingly, publisher Kent Carroll observed that as a result of fiction's obsession for the formulaic, today's publishing "no longer creates a market for its goods" but "responds to public demand."[18] In the area of nonfiction, for example, even the perennial self-help advice/inspiration book had yielded to a widespread interest in come-on titles that instructed the reader how to become more self-serving rather than self-achieving in this genre's tradition as a guide to cultivating a meaningful life. Another postmodern trend, Carroll noted, was the blurring of the line between fiction and nonfiction in the celebrity biography in order to make such reading more compellingly entertaining.[19] Here again, it appeared, standards were being compromised to present readers with what they would seemingly like to read rather than what good editorial taste dictated they should.

While publishers justified their commercial posture by contending that they were merely giving readers what they wanted, the moviemakers and TV programmers were still letting themselves off the hook with a similar argument. In this light, Twitchell observed that the huge success of the blockbuster movies of the 1980s, along with the merchandizing and aftermarket bonanza these films generated in videocassettes and cable/network TV runs, assured ever more of the same. Along with the ongoing emphasis on sex and violence flavored with vulgar language and antisocial behavior in the gross manner of many youth-directed films, advances in computerized effects promised moviegoers more sensational action scenarios in the violently explosive manner of *The Terminator* series. Even the ratings system now played into the hands of movie producers as a film's R rating assured its box-office appeal to sensation-seeking audiences, especially youth who found ways to exploit the rating system.[20]

To Twitchell, the medium that most flagrantly showcased

the "carnival culture of modern life" during this era was television, primarily through its mindless repetition. Even with the advent of cable TV and niche programming, the result was a multiplicity of sameness, mainly because TV programming demanded that it offer what the largest audience wanted to see and then repeat it until interest in it died out. Because of the saturation of highly hyped attractions like professional wrestling, auto racing, tabloid exploitation, combative talk shows, and crime reality programming, Twitchell concluded that the average TV viewer's power of mental reflection had grown decidedly passive.[21]

Most critics of media culture concurred that the root cause for the "triumph of vulgarity" in this era was a widespread liberalism that could be traced back to the antiestablishment movement of youth in the 1960s. Film critic Michael Medved, whose charges against Hollywood's seeming attempt to undermine traditional American values were discussed earlier, argued that, by sensationalizing their films as an inducement to seeing them, the new wave of writers/directors who comprised the entertainment elite were still lost in the time warp of the 1960s when shock was a way of life. Robert H. Bork, in his book on the effects of liberalism on postmodern American mores and social behavior, also traced what he termed the "Collapse of Popular Culture" to the vagaries of youth in the 1960s.[22] As the first generation not subject to want, Bork charged that its affluence had resulted in boredom, incurring the need to seek out sensation as a "palliative" through sex, rock music, drugs, and other extreme measures. Thus, as the forms of media culture clearly demonstrated, the intense search for escapist release continued to manifest itself in a society addicted to the pursuit of pleasure for its own sake. Consequently, as Bork lamented, the sense of belonging that communal institutions traditionally venerated had largely disappeared.[23] Due to this liberal drift toward unrestrained hedonism and personal license, as well as the loss of a strong sense of communal values, Bork painted a grim picture of media culture's status at this time and its implications for the nation's future.

Conservative newspaper columnists of the '90s struck similar postures, singling out the media culture as a conspiratorial force to be reckoned with, particularly television and the movies. Charley Reese, writing for King Features Syndicate, contended that the veritable deluge of culturally deviant entertainment produced in the late twentieth century had caused American society to lose contact with reality. In one of his columns, Reese even took the Walt Disney Corporation to task for its increasing dedication to making money at the expense of debasing the values of its traditional approach to entertainment. This situation, along with crime, political corruption, and other social deviations, Reese warned, was yet another sign of the nation's moral collapse. After the murderous gun rampage of two Colorado high school students in 1999, Reese again took aim at the media as partly responsible. The nation's youth, he said, was being compelled to fantasize life through a "commercialized culture of violence, death, and nihilism" in "the form of films, videos, video games and music" produced by the entertainment corporations—all in the name of making more money.[24] Another conservative columnist, Mona Charen, charged that youth entertainment, especially that presented by the concerts of touring rock music groups, had seduced naive audiences into believing their performers' gross behavior and rebellious posture represented reality. Was anyone condemning such tasteless antics? she asked. Those in an authoritative position, such as responsible adults and culture critics, had seemingly reneged on their responsibility, Charen concluded, for there was "apparently nothing, no matter how debased, degraded, disgusting or contemptible, that will elicit censure from them."[25] Shortly, in 2000, syndicated columnist Leonard Pitts and *Entertainment Weekly* film critic Lisa Schwarzbaum concurred on why there was little or no outcry. Wrote Pitts: "We've become a people too cool to take offense, too jaded for questions of decency." And Schwarzbaum: "So eager are we not to be the kind of rubes unsettled by . . . anything that at least doesn't bore us that we're *unnecessarily* tolerant of raunch. The notion of indecency has become obsolete."[26]

In light of all these comments, one of the more original assessments of media culture's status at the end of the twentieth century was Neal Gabler's *Life the Movie* (1998) that compared contemporary life to that of an ongoing movie inspired by the celebrity ethos that had engulfed it. Following up on Philip Roth's supposition that entertainment might be the purpose of life and Daniel Boorstin's contention that Americans were now living in a "world where fantasy is more real than reality," Gabler argued that "life itself was gradually becoming a medium all its own, like television, radio, print and film, and that all of us were becoming at once performance artists in and audiences for a grand, ongoing show."[27] Thus, Gabler's "Republic of Entertainment" represented a way of life in which value was measured by either the self-indulgence or notoriety of celebrity. As such, it was a way of life exploited by not only entertainers and sports figures but political leaders and even certain criminals whose deviant acts placed them in the media limelight.

Although by the close of the century the sociocultural consequences of celebrity entertainment as a primary focus of American life were still to be determined, what was clear was that its theatrical techniques had infiltrated such preeminent sectors of American society as business, politics, law, sports, and the fine arts, as discussed below. Even the traditional experiences of attending church services or engaging in the classroom learning process were often made less tedious through the media-oriented techniques of entertainment.

## THE MUSEUM'S MEDIA-MADE ENTERTAINMENT ROLE

By the end of the twentieth century the 1893 Chicago Exposition's high-culture milieu of the White City that was symbolically divorced from the popular attractions of the Midway Plaisance (as discussed in my earlier book) had become culturally diffused in the eyes of the mediated vision. Among the most telling signs of this development was the democratization of that sacralized repository of the fine arts—the museum. Indeed, by the late 1990s it had become something of a center of entertainment itself, billing itself as the "new public square," where people from all walks were being enticed to peruse its holdings.[28] Drawing on the promotional ploys of media culture, the nation's mushrooming museums, with new ones still popping up and adding to the more than 6,000 in existence, were exploiting highly appealing themes and exhibits as "blockbuster" shows. While many of these were dedicated to diverse fields other than the arts, the mass marketing of the fine arts institutions incited considerable criticism from purists who saw it as akin to the practice of publicizing a theme park or shopping mall. Ironically, both private and public-supported museums of the arts, which once purposely ignored the masses, were now being accused of outright pandering to them.

However, such criticism paled in comparison to the feeling of outrage generated by those museum visitors whose traditional values were demeaned by the subversive content of exhibits that tended to shock and offend their sense of decency and moral respectability. In 1999, for example, New York's one-hundred-year-old Brooklyn Museum of Art aroused the furor of patrons who contended that part of its exhibit was religiously blasphemous. In fact, it was controversial enough for the city's mayor to threaten cutting off the museum's annual operational funds. Once again the old questions of how far freedom of creative expression should go and what should determine the cultural definition of art were raised, as in the eyes of a socially segmented society what might be considered a work of art in one sector could be looked upon as outright sham in another. But if art had the prerogative to counter the status quo, no matter how morally questionable a work might be, then the Brooklyn exhibit was a big success in capitalizing on such notoriety, for curious thousands continued to show up to see what all the media publicity was about. Ironically, the event was something of a throwback to the more artistically conservative time of 1913 when crowds came to view New York's much ballyhooed Armory Show, which introduced modern art to a public largely baffled by such shocking avant-garde visions that contrasted with the kind of commercial art the popular magazines featured in that day.

More evidence that the American museum had become a place of diversionary appeal according to its new public image was showing up on Internet Web sites that began displaying notable museum collections during the '90s. In responding to the subdivided spectrum of the mediated vision, site exhibits ranged from the early modernist influences of New York's Museum of Modern Art to the postmodern music icons honored at Cleveland's Rock and Roll Hall of Fame and Museum, demonstrating that now even a once marginalized form of entertainment could secure an honored place in the American cultural scene. Thus the new public museum, with its complements of library, media hall, shop, and café, functioned as a kind of miniature fair unto itself—as both an escapist haven from a troubled world but, due to the controversies certain exhibits elicited, a reminder of its uncertainties.

# Epilogue: Looking Back While Looking Ahead to a New Century

> Our past is a subjective fantasy and the future which the
> revolutionaries pledged to create has still not arrived.
> That leaves us with only the tenuous present.
> —Peter Conrad, *Modern Times, Modern Places*

IN RANKING THE TECHNOLOGICAL FORCES OF THE PAST 100 YEARS that have had the greatest sociocultural impact on the development of a media-made culture—from the communally based escapist offerings of the movies at the century's beginning to the individual's fantasized indulgence in the virtual reality of cyberspace at its end—the achievements of electronics technology, particularly that of the computer, stand at the top of the list.[1] But during the second half of the century, prophetically oriented books warned of technology as a force of cultural change to be reckoned with, as did Alvin Toffler's best-selling *Future Shock* (1970). Another, like William Strauss and Neil Howe's cyclical study of history, *The Fourth Turning* (1996), contended that the coming millennium would see the beginning of the latest historical cycle and with it the promise of a new social order; that is, if citizens could cultivate a sense of renewed communal responsibility and the proper use of technological advances to bring people together for this purpose.

Among the most positive-inclined of these manifestos about technology's role in preparing the way for the future was John Naisbitt's *Megatrends* (1982), which focused on the role of the computer as a major force in the shift from an industrial to an informational society. Concomitant with this development, Naisbitt identified the implications of key societal trends that were intended to make the future "more real, more knowable," especially to those who preferred the well-knownness of the past to the uncertainties of the future.[2] By

362

the '90s, though, despite the optimistic insights of a seer like Naisbitt, the media's unrelenting reportage of the postmodern world's daunting events had become ominous enough to trigger new fears of what the future might hold.

## THE SOCIOCULTURAL IMPORT OF MEDIA CULTURE'S ASCENDANCY

Although modernist views in the arts during the early years of the century had identified technology as the root cause of society's problems, it ultimately proved to be the main reason for the triumph of modernism's prime adversary. In fact, as this book has attempted to show, technological advances played a major role in establishing popular or media culture as the dominant sociocultural force of the postmodern era. In the late nineteenth and early twentieth centuries, signs of this development had appeared in the mediated vision's receptivity to the developing forms of media culture as antidotes to the alienating ills of urban life, discussed at length in the first volume of this project. City dwellers found escapist solace not only in such communal attractions as theatrical venues, sporting events, and the diversions of the print media but, due to timely technological breakthroughs, in musical recordings and the movies. Even the most technically dependent of the new entertainment forms, the movies became the most culturally influential in closing the gap between the popular and elitist approaches to creative expression in the first half of the century, especially after critics accorded film the stature of an art form. Then, in the 1920s–30s, radio, by captivating listeners through a nationally homogenized conduit of entertainment and information, became the first medium to provide the mediated vision a simultaneous sense of immediacy, thus prefiguring the visual sensibility of television and its status as the most widespread and dominant entertainment venue of the century's second half.

Since the 1950s–60s' rock music revolution, which, of course, owed much of its aural impact to electronic innovations, the upshot of youth's rebellious but trendsetting lifestyles that promoted immoderate dress and self-referential behavior as forms of hipness was a socially extreme put-down of fashion and civility. By the latter years of the century, this paradoxical situation was manifested in the multiple celebrity images of media-made entertainers, many of whose day in the sun was brief but whose influence on fashion styles and social behavior was widespread.

As American culture splintered into subcultures of alternative musical styles, along with a multitude of other special-interest sectors that were a defining criterion of the postmodern era, the times also saw the arts take a variety of directions in which both the creative act and its product often revealed the dominant influences of technology and media culture. As a prominent example in the 1960s–70s, pop art, by integrating the democratizing elements of media culture into its varied forms of creative expression, overtly acknowledged the role of technology in its mission, revealing that traditional art had seemingly conceded its elitist authority to the ascendancy of media culture. During this era, then, the media-made products of the commercialized world of consumerism and celebrity were accepted as fit subject matter for the arts.

By this time, too, the most visible evidence of postmodernism's enshrinement of the image lay in the architectural style of pastiche that countered the modernist concept of "less is more" by celebrating the iconography of ornament and the pictorial. Such a lavish style directly addressed the mediated vision's attraction to spectacle as escapism, particularly as it was epitomized in the excesses of electronic signage and baroque flamboyance of the Las Vegas scene's technological glitz and glitter.[3]

Since the 1970s, the electronic media also responded to postmodernism's nostalgic affinities by preserving and reproducing both the sounds and images of the past. While old-time popular music was recycled through radio's "golden oldies" niche programming and CD recordings, vintage movies were readily accessed on videocassettes and cable movie channels. In fact, "The Great Nostalgia Kick" that a 1982 *U.S. News & World Report* cover story had featured was still pervading the national scene in the 1990s, affirming the article's summation that the nostalgic mood "could go on indefinitely—contributing even more, perhaps, to reality's displacement."[4]

Through "specials" that evoked the achievements of the past as well as through niche programming, television also played a key role in responding to this ongoing phenomenon. Accordingly, collectible shows revealed the mediated vision's enduring fascination with antique artifacts of both elitist and popular significance. As new subcultural interests arose, cable TV functioned as the primary conduit for special-interest programming, prompting TV historian Ed Papazian's opinion that to compete successfully with cable, the broadcast networks needed to develop programs directed at postmodern society's "fragmented constituency" of "self-focused interest groups."[5] But they seemed more inclined toward programming their usual fare of situation comedies and crime dramas while expanding on the "news magazine" concept that investigated current topics of the day, many of whose sensational, tabloidlike content had wide viewer appeal.

## MEDIA CULTURE'S ROLE IN THE DEMOCRATIZATION OF THE ARTS

Both the democratization of American art's elitist role and its intent of inciting visual pleasure as well as consternation were explored by art critic Robert Hughes in *American Visions: The Epic History of Art in America* (1997) and the eight-part PBS television series based on it. Fittingly, the inspirational origins of American art that Hughes identifies paralleled the mediated vision's inherent sensitivity to the nostalgic lure of the past and the promise of a once idealized future. For, as Hughes argues, the creation of the nation's art was stimulated by both the American people's reverence for the past, as defined by their immigrant origins, and their faith in "the idea of progress and newness."[6]

Yet, for a people whose main motivation had been the pursuit of dreams, the realities of the present engendered by the alienation of life in an urban industrialized society fueled an ongoing debate between the realists and the abstract expressionists about the visual arts' true mission. Relevant to this argument that had earlier found symbolic focus in the 1913 Armory Show, Hughes devoted a significant part of his book to the evolution of twentieth-century art. Pursuant to the paradoxical relationship of a materialistic society with the late nineteenth-century views on the fine arts as high culture, Hughes showed how the elitist sensibility gradually eroded to become more democratized, culminating by the 1960s in the pop art movement's recognition of mass-media culture as a pervasive force that had increasing relevance in revealing the material obsessions of postmodern life.

Though Hughes had earlier criticized museum authorities

for staging art exhibits as highly promoted spectacles, he was obliged to modify his posture after viewing the Whitney Museum of American Art's timely 1999 exhibit titled "The American Century." Ten years earlier the Whitney had presaged a sociocultural shift in evaluating the media's role in influencing the arts with its presentation of "Image World: Art and Media Culture." Now, as the new millennium approached, it sought to do for the arts what the mass media were doing to commemorate the century's end by looking back to look ahead. Planned in two parts, the first covering the years 1900–1950, the show, as Hughes's *Time* review noted, focused mainly on painting and photography to present "a straightforward trot through art and social history, aimed at a general, nonspecialist public."[7] Supplemented by computer-generated tributes to the nongallery roles of music, film, and dance, the exhibit, as a sign of the times, was underwritten by Intel, which also offered a relevant Web site dedicated to art history.

If a dominant modernist temperament had characterized American art's first half-century, viewers who anticipated the show's postmodern component would see how art, in continuing to express the sociocultural contradictions of the American experience, also reflected the expectations and uncertainties attendant to the arrival of a new century. To Hughes and most visitors, though, the original Whitney exhibit was an unadulterated visual triumph in its mission to capture and project the nation's self-image—from the early years of the media culture's pervasive faith in the American way to a more disillusioned time when its fragmented spectrum viewed life through escapist venues of fantasy masquerading as reality; and, conversely, through escapist renderings of reality posing as fantasy.

## THE PEOPLE'S "EXPRESSIVE LIFE" AS A DETERMINER OF CULTURE

Since the merging of working-class escapist entertainment venues with middle-class communal values in the early years of the century, then, mainstream American culture ultimately evolved into what Lawrence W. Levine has termed a "shared public culture," a democratized composite of elitist and popular tastes. In his reaction to the elitist notion of marking off culture into "rigid hierarchical divisions" of high and low, as it had been by the arbiters of taste in the late nineteenth century, Levine contended that "culture encompasses all genres and modes of a people's expressive life." Thus my book's central metaphor of the mediated vision that, in focusing on the ways in which the media culture has helped the American people adjust to life's discontentments, reflects this "expressive life," most prevantly today in its subcultural expressions, revealing a people's universal dreams, hopes, and fears as well as their petty, self-aggrandizing concerns. In viewing culture as an ongoing dynamic process, then, this book concludes that people, rather than "intellectual abstractions" of hierarchical divisions, determine what culture is.[8] If the escapist venues of media culture have been a prevalent sociocultural force in the past 100 years, then the ways in which these forms have expressed themselves reveal a great deal about the American people's sociological or psychological state of being during a given time.

In this light, the heirs of Carrie Meeber, the late nineteenth century's prototype of the New Woman, have played a prominent role in the twentieth century's changing "expressive life," particularly as the media culture has depicted women's persistent strivings to transform their escapist dreams into reality. Thus, from Carrie's quest in the urban milieu of her day for what Theodore Dreiser termed "dreams become real" up to the late twentieth-century search for self in the virtual reality of cyberspace, this book and its predessor, by tracing the ever-changing ways in which an increasingly democratized media culture reflected American life, has been an attempt to understand this complex process. And despite the so-called progress that resulted in higher living standards and improved social harmony, the times, as they stood at the brink of the twenty-first century, appeared not to have changed much for the better. Yet, through its attempt to transform reality into fantasized entertainment, American media culture looked to continue responding to the mediated vision's desires and dreams during the even more challenging times of the twenty-first century.

# Notes

## PROLOGUE

For the momentous sociocultural changes in American life that occurred during the postwar era, see Robert Sobel, *The Great Boom, 1950–2000* (New York: St. Martin's Press, 2000), chapters 1 and 2, from which the prologue's opening epigraph is suggested.

## CHAPTER 1: 1946–1963—LIVING THE AMERICAN DREAM IN A TIME of NEW UNCERTAINTIES

1. Karal Ann Marling, *As Seen on TV: The Visual Culture of Everyday Life in the 1950s* (Cambridge, Mass.: Harvard University Press, 1994), 5.
2. In 1950 more than 7.5 million TV sets were purchased by Americans in contrast to only 10,000 in 1946. See Sobel, *The Great Boom*, 162.
3. David Marc has assessed the basic appeal of the 1950s family sitcom in terms of the mediated vision's communal values: "Public affection for [the sitcom] can easily be attributed to a romantic folkish yearning on the part of the audience for a return to a stable, divorce-free, two-parent household in which father ventures out into the world to hunt for a paycheck while mother stays at home enforcing physical and spiritual cleanliness." See *Comic Visions: TV Comedy and American Culture*, 2nd ed. (Malden, Mass.: Blackwell, 1997), 43. Sex as part of married life was tactfully avoided until 1953 when *I Love Lucy* aired episodes about its title character's pregnancy. For this show's media impact, see Louis Chunovic, *One Foot on the Floor: The Curious Evolution of Sex in Television from* I Love Lucy *to* South Park (New York: TV Books, 2000), 33–37. The antiseptic world of the '50s family sitcom is incisively satirized in the film *Pleasantville* (1998).
4. By this time, the socially realistic plots of *The Dick Van Dyke Show* (1961–65) contrasted with the formulaic story lines of the popular family sitcoms of the 1950s like *Father Knows Best, The Trouble with Father*, and *Leave It to Beaver*, anticipating group-bonded sitcoms like *The Mary Tyler Moore Show* and *M*A*S*H*, which were structured around more realistic humanized relationships. See Marc, 70.
5. Disney's profitable venture into television and its impact on media culture is analyzed in Steven Watts, *The Magic Kingdom: Walt Disney and the American Way of Life* (Boston: Houghton Mifflin, 1997). See, in particular, chapter 16.
6. As a major force underscoring the subtitle of his book, Neal Gabler

points out television's propensity for heightening reality as entertainment. See *Life the Movie: How Entertainment Conquered Reality* (New York: Knopf, 1998), 88. For the early development of TV's morning news programming, see Gerry Davis, The Today Show: *An Anecdotal History* (New York: William Morrow, 1987).

7. Quoted in David Halberstam, *The Fifties* (New York: Villard, 1993), 732.

8. Jeff Greenfield, *Television: The First Fifty Years* (New York: Crescent Books, 1981), 203.

9. Halberstam, 475.

10. Other notable Broadway productions of the era that also appeared as films during this time were *Gentlemen Prefer Blondes* (1953), *Guys and Dolls* (1955), *The Pajama Game* (1957), *Silk Stockings* (1959), *Can-Can* (1960), and *Flower Drum Song* (1961). For a survey of leading Broadway musicals made into movies from the 1930s to the '70s, see Robert Matthew-Walker, *From Broadway to Hollywood: The Musical and the Cinema* (London: Sanctuary, 1996).

11. As the playwright who brought international attention to American drama, Eugene O'Neill won his fourth Pulitzer Prize posthumously for *Long Day's Journey into Night* in 1956. A movie version appeared in 1962. Other noteworthy plays of the time made into well-received films were *State of the Union* (1948), *Born Yesterday* (1950), *The Seven Year Itch* (1955), *The Teahouse of the August Moon* (1956), and *Inherit the Wind* (1960).

12. Producer Darryl Zanuck was the leading proponent of controversial, reality-derived subject matter and themes offered as provocative entertainment. His productions of *Gentleman's Agreement* (1947), *The Snake Pit* (1948), and *Pinky* (1949) extended his posture of such daring films for their time as *The Grapes of Wrath* (1940) and *The Ox-Bow Incident* (1943).

13. *The Day the Earth Stood Still* (1951) was the best-received science-fiction film of this era due to its timely message of goodwill among people as the key to world peace. The film's significance for the cold war era is discussed in Kim Newman, *Apocalypse Movies: End of the World Cinema* (New York: St. Martin's Griffin, 2000), 137–43.

14. In discussing Darryl Zanuck's promotion of CinemaScope, George F. Custen says his adamant stand against television "was designed to remind Americans how puny their small black-and-white sets were." See *Twentieth Century's Fox: Darryl F. Zanuck and the Culture of Hollywood* (New York: Basic Books, 1997), 320–22.

15. Quoted in J. Philip di Franco, ed., *The Movie World of Roger Corman* (New York: Chelsea House, 1979), 31. For further discussion of Corman's venture into science fiction, see Newman, *Apocalypse Movies*, 104–9.

16. Eddie Muller and Daniel Faris, *Grindhouse: The Forbidden World of "Adults Only" Cinema* (New York: St. Martin's, 1996), 59.

17. By 1999, nineteen films in the James Bond series had been made, while periodic TV showings kept the older films alive. Even though Sean Connery was succeeded by several others in the lead role, he would remain typed in the eyes of fans as the authentic James Bond.

18. The prime venue for these kinds of cartoons was the Saturday morning children's shows. They enticed their youthful audience into a fantasized world whose seductive commercials also indoctrinated viewers into the world of consumer enterprise.

19. During this era, Disney produced a number of live-action films, such as the classic adventure stories *Treasure Island* (1949), *20,000 Leagues Under the Sea* (1954), and *Swiss Family Robinson* (1960). Disney also turned out the True Life Adventure series about the natural scene that included documentary-type films like *The Living Desert* and *The Vanishing Prairie*. But none of the above productions was as popular with children as 1954's three-part television series about the legendary Davy Crockett. In extolling the virtues of the frontier spirit during a time of cold war politics, Disney hoped to reaffirm traditional American values and ideals. See Watts, *The Magic Kingdom*, 287–95.

20. As best-selling novels, both *The Caine Mutiny* and *Mr. Roberts* were transcribed into long-running Broadway plays as well as successful films, substantiating the ongoing interdependence of the media culture's creative forms. Other best sellers of the time were less than appealing as films, e.g., Carson McCullers's play and novel, *The Member of the Wedding* (1952), Irwin Shaw's *The Young Lions* (1958), Robert Penn Warren's *Band of Angels* (1957), and James Gould Cozzens's *By Love Possessed* (1961).

21. The best seller's preoccupation with the theme of entrepreneurial success during the years 1945–65 is a central focus in Elizabeth Long, *The American Dream and the Popular Novel* (Boston: Routledge & Kegan Paul, 1985).

22. But this film proved Wright a better writer than an actor. Paving the way for the day of the black actor in serious dramatic roles was Sidney Poitier, who from the '50s to the early '60s appeared in such well-received films as *No Way Out* (1950), with Richard Widmark; *The Blackboard Jungle* (1955), with Glenn Ford; *The Defiant Ones* (1958), with Tony Curtis; *A Raisin in the Sun* (1961), based on the prize-winning play; and *Lilies of the Field* (1963), for which he won an Academy Award as best actor. Other films of this era that sensitized moviegoers to racist problems were *Home of the Brave* (1949), which changed the original play's focus on a Jew to a black man, and *Sergeant Rutledge* (1960). Both films' ironic implications of military settings enhanced their dramatic conflict.

23. Philip Roth, "Writing American Fiction," *Commentary* 31 (March 1961): 223–33. But Elizabeth Long contends that novelists were closer to the mark than social critics like William H. Whyte Jr. and C. Wright Mills, whom she takes to task for "failing to grasp the complexity of the cultural developments that best-selling novels reveal." See *The American Dream and the Popular Novel*, chapter 6.

24. J. Edgar Hoover, *Masters of Deceit* (New York: Pocket Books, 1959), foreword, v.

25. The research of Dr. Alfred C. Kinsey, its findings about the nature of human sexuality, and their social impact are examined in John Heidenry, *What Wild Ecstasy: The Rise and Fall of the Sexual Revolution* (New York: Simon & Schuster, 1997), chapter 1 and passim; and in James R. Petersen, *The Century of Sex: Playboy's History of the Sexual Revolution, 1900–1999* (New York: Grove Press, 1999), 196–200, 222–28.

26. Eberhard and Phyllis Kronhausen, *Pornography and the Law: The Psychology of Erotic Realism and Pornography* (New York: Ballantine, 1959), 23. The key players in countering society's restrictive edicts against pornographic subject matter are discussed in Heidenry, chapters 2 and 3.

27. Elizabeth Long makes a relevant point concerning a theme common

to best-selling fiction during these years, observing that even in novels with a biblical setting, like *The Big Fisherman*, key characters are depicted as enterprising men dedicated to earthly success as well as spiritual salvation. See *The American Dream and the Popular Novel*, 69–71.

28. The fantasized aura that the flying saucer's contribution to media culture had taken on by century's end is entertainingly discussed and illustrated in Eric and Leif Nesheim, *Saucer Attack! Pop Culture in the Golden Age of Flying Saucers* (Los Angeles: General Publishing Group, 1997).

29. Ostensibly, the dearth of female writers of science fiction was attributable to the understanding that the genre had been mainly a prescribed male province from its beginnings. But this sexist posture would change in the '70s with the recognition of highly talented women writers on the order of Ursula K. Le Guin, Anne McCaffrey, Octavia Butler, and Joanna Russ. For the rise of the woman SF writer, see Brooks Landon, *Science Fiction after 1900: From the Steam Man to the Stars* (New York: Twayne, 1997).

30. Heinlein clearly recognized science fiction's pervasive influence on American culture in commenting that "it can be felt in such diverse realms as industrial design and marketing, military strategy, sexual mores, foreign policy, and practical epistemology—in other words, our basic sense of what is real and isn't." New Wave pioneer Thomas M. Disch elaborates on this observation in his introduction to *The Dreams Our Stuff Is Made of: How Science Fiction Conquered the World* (New York: Free Press, 1998). He also expounds at length on Heinlein's solipsistic stance and its effects on his ideas about race, politics, the military, nuclear war, religion, sex, and the space program as they relate to his fiction's conceptual framework of a future history.

31. The controversies concerning the sociocultural import of horror comics since the late 1940s are focused on in Stephen Sennitt, *Ghastly Terror! The Horrible Story of the Horror Comics* (Manchester, UK: Headpress, 1999).

32. For a study of the Code's impact on comic book publishing at the time, see Amy Kiste Nyberg, *Seal of Approval: The History of the Comics Code* (Jackson: University Press of Mississippi, 1998). Publisher James Warren's alternative was the magazine route. In 1958 he found an eager audience for *Famous Monsters of Filmland*, whose articles featured explicit photos that kept the classic horror-movie creatures alive. But in the 1960s Warren resurrected the original horror comics in the adult format of the black-and-white magazines *Creepy* and *Eerie*. They in turn spawned numerous imitations into the 1970s. See Sennitt, 64–128.

33. It is not so surprising that Bradbury's works would appear as comic book versions in that he had always professed a strong attraction to the comics as an expressive art form, attested to by the visual sensibility of his fiction. For Bradbury's personal opinions about his lifelong love affair with the comics, see his introduction in *The Ray Bradbury Chronicles*, vol. 1 (New York: Bantam, 1992)—the first in a series of authorized adaptations of his stories in the comics' format by multiple artists.

34. In his analysis of the comic book's reaction to postwar social change, William W. Savage Jr. has demonstrated that the sociopolitical concerns of the time supplied the primary subject matter for the comic book as a unique merging of reality and fantasy. See *Comic Books and America, 1945–1954* (Norman: University of Oklahoma Press, 1990), chapter 6. Ac-

cording to Savage, "comic books did their most memorable work at a time when American society was experiencing intense and prolonged stress stemming from problems of postwar adjustment" (preface, ix). For a more comprehensive study of the comic book's sociocultural influence since 1945, see Bradford W. Wright, *Comic Book Nation: The Transformation of Youth Culture in America* (Baltimore: Johns Hopkins University Press, 2001).

35. The collecting mania that started up in the 1960s would continue throughout the rest of the century. It was enhanced by the appearances of an annual price guide in 1970, fanzines, newspapers, and a monthly magazine marketing update, as well as other publications that determined the value of character spin-off merchandise. Two publications that reveal how the comic book fan movement grew are Bill Schelly, *The Golden Age of Comic Fandom* (1995) and Roy Thomas and Bill Schelly, eds., *Alter Ego: The Best of the Legendary Comics Fanzine* (1997). Thus, from the mediated vision's postmodern perspective, the fan publications had willed a return to the comic book's past by recreating it.

36. Robert C. Harvey asserts that the comic book medium challenges artists "to realize a greater range of possibilities" than the newspaper comic strip. "Comic books can tell their stories all at once with no repetition (and therefore with greater dramatic impact), can exploit varying panel sizes and shapes to embellish stories with special narrative-enhancing effects, can manipulate time over longer periods to create mood, and can do it all in color." By the 1980s, with the advent of the adult-directed graphic novel, these elements would come to full fruition. See *The Art of the Comic Book: An Aesthetic History* (Jackson: University Press of Mississippi, 1996), 24.

37. The anticipation of Milton Caniff's new adventure feature was of such magnitude at the time that *Time* (13 January 1947) carried a cover story on Caniff and *Steve Canyon* the very day the strip started. As a master of cinematic drawing style in his serialized storytelling, Caniff continued to employ it to great advantage until the strip's end in 1988, when his patriotic hero's conservative values were in decline. For a detailed analysis of how comic strip art developed over the century along with examples of five distinct movements that Robert C. Harvey ascribes to it, see *Children of the Yellow Kid: The Evolution of the American Comic Strip* (Seattle: Frye Art Museum, 1998).

38. Even after *Casey Ruggles* ended, Tufts went on to outdo his earlier efforts in 1955 with *Lance*, another historically based but short-lived Western strip whose illustrative realism was magnificently enhanced by the color of a large Sunday page.

39. Through his dedication to making the world a better place for humanity, Ben Bolt was also unique as a comic strip character in winning the Nobel Peace Prize. In 1978, this event, along with his death by an assassin's bullet, closed out this strip in tragic but momentous fashion. By this time, real-world issues and concerns were regular topics in the traditionally fantasized realm of the comic strip.

40. Exemplary reprints of Al Capp's evolving satirical posture appeared in *The World of Li'l Abner* (New York: Ballantine Books, 1953). But Kitchen Sink Press took on the monumental task of publishing the strip's entire run (1934–77), the first volume of which appeared in 1988. For an insightful

analysis of Al Capp's and Walt Kelly's respective methods of satirizing the social and political scenes of their times, see Harvey, *Children of the Yellow Kid*, 141, 143–46, 149–50, 154, 156.

41. See John A. Lent, "Pogo," in *100 Years of American Newspaper Comics*, ed. Maurice Horn (New York: Gramercy Books, 1996), 244.

42. In 1964, theologian Robert L. Short surmised in *The Gospel According to Peanuts* that the strips are "wonderfully imaginative parables of our times" (quoted in Horn above, 238). But according to Thierry Groensteen, "the *Peanuts* characters don't so much pose the great [theological] questions . . . as treat little problems as if they were great questions." See "The Schulz System: Why *Peanuts* Works," *Nemo: The Classic Comics Library* 31 (January 1992): 28. Whether or not one concurs with this opinion, *Peanuts* would have momentous influence on the comic vision and minimal drawing style of future newspaper strips.

43. If any comic strip strived to be self-consciously religious at times, it was *B.C.*, as since the 1980s Johnny Hart often allowed his primeval characters to pose and ponder theological questions and the mysteries of existence. Though most fans delighted in such uplifting fare, some felt that the comic strip is an improper vehicle to convey messages inspired by Christian convictions.

44. Jules Feiffer has been among the most versatile of creative forces in the second half of the twentieth century. In addition to the satirical cartoon series he began drawing for *The Village Voice* in 1956, he has excelled in the novel, play, and screenplay genres. Feiffer's interest in the comics as a theatrical format developed early when he worked as a youthful assistant to Will Eisner on the visually innovative comic book feature *The Spirit*.

45. With the advent of Barbie, precocious preteen girls rejected the traditional doll for the grown-up world of their new social icon who even had her own car. By 1961 Barbie also had a boyfriend that promised a relationship of even more maturely conceived social dimensions.

46. The era covered in Rick Polizzi and Fred Schaefer, *Spin Again: Board Games from the Fifties and Sixties* (San Francisco: Chronicle Books, 1991) represents the end of the board game's family-oriented popularity before the video games designed for a solitary player began to take over. Along with the Pac-Man mania, the age of high-tech electronic games arrived in the 1980s when the mall arcades became awash with video games that attracted teenage males. But undoubtedly those fallout shelters of the 1950s were stocked with an ample supply of board games.

47. ENIAC was an acronym for Electronic Numerical Integrator and Computer, and, of course, it would not be the last such designation, as the nation was on the brink of a virtual world that would be dominated by developments in the electronics industry.

48. Loudon Wainwright, *The Great American Magazine: An Inside History of* Life (New York: Knopf, 1986), 179. For the American magazine's early role in democratizing the mediated vision, see Wiley Lee Umphlett, *The Visual Focus of American Media Culture: The Modern Era, 1893–1945* (Madison, N.J.: Fairleigh Dickinson University Press, 2004).

49. Wainwright, 267.

50. In 1978, *TV Guide*'s editorial director Merrill Panitt attributed the growth of its circulation and advertising revenue to the simple fact that this magazine "covers—and criticizes—a communications medium that has be-

come an important force in our lives." See introduction in TV Guide: *The First 25 Years*, ed. Jay S. Harris (New York: Simon & Schuster, 1978), 15–18.

51. Such a high-rolling lifestyle naturally mandated articles on men's fashions, automotive gadgetry, cuisine/drink, and household accessories like high-fidelity record-play systems; in short, all the information a young man needed to know to attract the opposite sex. In the more liberal times of the 1960s, *Playboy* even assumed a receptive, though controversial, posture toward the use of drugs as a recreational activity. For *Playboy*'s influence on the New Morality of the 1960s, see Petersen, *The Century of Sex*, 264–70.

52. As Alan Betrock points out, the *Enquirer* later defied its competition when it "decided to go more upscale—color covers and interiors, fashion and diet advice, heartwarming human interest stories and the like." See the introduction in *Sleazy Business: A Pictorial History of Exploitation Tabloids, 1959–1974* (Brooklyn, N.Y.: Shake Books, 1996), 4–5.

53. *Mad*'s sociocultural import is a main theme in Maria Reidelbach, *Completely* Mad: *A History of the Comic Book and Magazine* (Boston: Little, Brown, 1991). See chapter 10, in particular.

54. For an analysis of teen magazines' social impact on the youth culture of the time, see Michael Barson and Steven Heller, *Teenage Confidential: An Illustrated History of the American Teen* (San Francisco: Chronicle Books, 1998).

55. The DJ's social impact on youth culture is analyzed in depth in Susan J. Douglas, *Listening In: Radio and the American Imagination* (New York: Times Books, 1999), chapter 9.

56. The sociocultural import of the TV commercial on viewing habits is discussed in Jim Hall, *Mighty Minutes: An Illustrated History of Television's Best Commercials* (New York: Harmony Books, 1984). The entertaining role that specially created characters and images have played in appealing to both adult and child is the central focus of Warren Dotz and Jim Morton, *What a Character! 20th Century American Advertising Icons* (San Francisco: Chronicle Books, 1996).

57. For an insightful and wide-ranging look at the media roles that cereal companies have played in promoting their products to both young and old, see Scott Bruce and Bill Crawford, *Cerealizing America: The Unsweetened Story of American Breakfast Cereal* (Boston: Faber and Faber, 1995).

58. The influential role of the universal credit card in changing the purchasing habits of the American consumer is analyzed in Sobel, *The Great Boom*, 188–93.

59. For the contributions of both Les Paul and Leo Fender to the development of the electric guitar, see Mark Prendergast, *The Ambient Century: From Mahler to Trance; The Evolution of Sound in the Electronic Age* (New York: Bloomsbury, 2000), 187–88. See also James Miller, *Almost Grown: The Rise of Rock* (London: William Heinemann, 1999), 39–43.

60. Bob Merlis and Davin Seay, *Heart and Soul: A Celebration of Black Music Style in America, 1930–1975* (New York: Stewart, Tabori & Chang, 1997), 48. During this time, too, the new relationship between artist and technician saw the recording itself become a more dominant cultural entity in comparison to the earlier time of sheet music prevalence, discussed in my earlier book.

61. Television's *American Bandstand* played a significant role in not only making rock music popular to youth in the late 1950s and early '60s but in nurturing black doo-wop and R&B styles. The popularity of black-styled music accounted for the show's attention to both white and black couples socializing and dancing together, a unique sight at the time. Also, showing what the dancers were wearing helped keep style-sensitive viewers informed of the latest dress styles in a growing youth culture. Little wonder, then, that this show harbored the power to build the image of a singer or group and send their songs to the top of the charts. Host Dick Clark's role in making his show a color-blind force in the popularization of rock music is recounted in Miller, *Almost Grown*, 145–51.

62. Benjamin Fine, *1,000,000 Delinquents* (Cleveland, Ohio: World Publishing Company, 1955), 26.

63. See "The Leisured Masses," *Business Week*, 12 September 1953, 142. This article also states that "there seems to be a major trend away from passive, crowd amusements toward active pursuits that people can carry on independently." According to this observation, then, leisure pursuits played a significant role in countering the conformist behavior of the time.

64. John Kenneth Galbraith, *The Affluent Society* (Boston: Houghton Mifflin, 1958), 345. David Brooks has traced the origins of a postmodern class he labels "Bourgeois Bohemians," or "Bobos," to the 1950s when the college degree in itself began to be prized as a badge of social identity rather than a sign of scholarship. See *Bobos in Paradise: The New Upper Class and How They Got There* (New York: Simon & Schuster, 2000), chapter 1.

65. Marling, *As Seen on TV*, 98. Steven Watts also contends that "in a larger sense, Disneyland was a unique embodiment of prosperous, middle-class, postwar America. As nothing else quite did, it stood, literally, as a monument to the American way of life." See Watts, *The Magic Kingdom*, 384. In effect, then, Disneyland encapsulated in the present the mediated vision's longtime attraction to both the nostalgic aura of the past and the promise of fulfilling future aspirations.

66. Nevertheless, the efficacy of the good life that corporate abundance had afforded always shone through the park's fantasized attractions. Watts observes that Disneyland "allowed visitors to revel in the fantasy life of their culture during the halcyon days of the American century and ritually reaffirm an idealistic view of themselves." See *The Magic Kingdom*, 396. Here again is evidence of the media culture's fantasized power to generate a positive conception of self.

67. By the waning years of the century, the Football Hall of Fame would take on a quasi-religious significance, akin to that the earlier established (1939) Baseball Hall of Fame at Cooperstown, New York, had acquired. Indeed, by now these places had become nostalgic reminders of the hallowed pasts of the mediated vision's favorite team sports and the most outstanding players.

68. Symbolically, in 1951, America's first great woman Olympic athlete, golfer Babe Didrikson Zaharias, was named "Woman Athlete of the First Half Century" by the Associated Press.

69. Mary Ellen Hanson, *Go! Fight! Win! Cheerleading in American Culture* (Bowling Green, Ohio: Popular Press, 1995), 52.

70. "10 Amazing Years: 1947–1957," *U.S. News & World Report*, 27 December 1957, 53. Also see Sobel, *The Great Boom*, chapters 1–6.

71. Invented in 1950 by a Detroit graphics designer, the paint-by-number system soon developed into a thriving business called Craft Master, which by 1954 had sold more than 80 million dollars worth of paint-by-number kits. Its fiftieth anniversary in 2000 inspired an art exhibit at the Detroit Historical Museum and a later show at the Smithsonian Institution's National Museum of American History.

72. The cultural problems that Midcult presented as a more sophisticated form of Masscult are addressed in Dwight MacDonald, "Masscult and Midcult," in *American Literature, American Culture*, ed. Gordon Hutner (New York: Oxford University Press, 1999), 398–404.

73. Gilbert Seldes, *The Great Audience* (New York: Viking, 1950), 250.

74. Ibid., 269.

## CHAPTER 2: 1964–1979—ADJUSTING TO POSTMODERN SOCIAL CHALLENGES

1. In the 1950s the term "Negro" was still culturally acceptable, but by the mid '60s "Black" as a racially descriptive term began to gain favor, followed by "African American."

2. An instrumental force in this pursuit was the National Organization for Women (NOW), whose leaders—Gloria Steinem, editor of *Ms.* magazine, and Betty Friedan, author of *The Feminine Mystique*—fostered a defiant new militancy. For *Ms.*'s role in the feminist movement, see Mary Thom, *Inside Ms.: 25 Years of the Magazine and the Feminist Movement* (New York: Henry Holt, 1997).

3. Accordingly, Rachel Carson's *Silent Spring* (1962) was a timely warning against the use of pesticides. By 1999, the Modern Library saw fit to list this book among the top five of the 100 "best" works of nonfiction in the twentieth century, while *Time* magazine, 29 March 1999, ranked its mild-mannered but stubbornly determined author among the "Greatest Minds" of the century. To environmentalists in the 1960s–70s, Carson's efforts to make the natural world a better place were a major influence on their goals.

4. However, the British attempt to reveal the "real self" through an antifashion look was countered by Pierre Cardin's French line that focused on a "label" of annual collections for those still governed by the dictates of mainstream fashion. Ironically, mass production was a democratizing factor on the "exclusive" women's wear labels, such as those of celebrity icons Gloria Vanderbilt and Joan Collins. But it was youth's experimental influence in the 1960s that carried over into the 1970s in the self-expressive modes of Ralph Lauren's sportswear for men, Calvin Klein's designer jeans for women, and even Yves St. Laurent's esoteric attempts to "liberate" women's fashions.

5. The probable source of the epithet "hippie" is "hipster," which signified the self-assertive urban lifestyle of the African American male in the 1950s. Though Caroline Bird first identified this lifestyle in a 1957 *Harper's Bazaar* article, it was popularized by Norman Mailer's essay "The White Negro." See Mailer, *Advertisements for Myself* (New York: Signet Books, 1959), 302–22.

6. Julian Robinson, *Body Packaging: A Guide to Human Sexual Display* (Los Angeles: Elysium, 1988), 11.

7. For the evolution of swimsuit fashion and its impact on social mores, see Lena Lencek and Gideon Bosker, *Making Waves: Swimsuits and the Undressing of America* (San Francisco: Chronicle Books, 1989).

8. Bob Dylan's early involvement in folk music is a central focus in Robbie Tolliver, *Hoot! A 25-Year History of the Greenwich Village Scene* (New York: St. Martin's Press, 1986), 62–91.

9. For Dylan's influential role in the development of rock music, see James Miller, *Almost Grown: The Rise of Rock* (London: William Heinemann, 1999), 218–25; and Mark Prendergast, *The Ambient Century: From Mahler to Trance; The Evolution of Sound in the Electronic Age* (New York: Bloomsbury, 2000), 196–98.

10. Dylan's influence on the Beatles' development of a more mature sound is discussed in Miller, *Almost Grown*, 225–31. The Beatles' achievements in their brief meteoric career are summed up in Prendergast, *The Ambient Century*, 190–96. For their legacy to later bands, see Miller, chapter 6.

11. Radio's growing attention to airing "progressive" rock music during this time is discussed in Susan J. Douglas, *Listening In: Radio and the American Imagination* (New York: Times Books, 1999), 269–78.

12. André Millard, *America on Record: A History of Recorded Sound* (New York: Cambridge University Press, 1995), 305.

13. For a survey of important technological breakthroughs that affected the development of electronic music in the late twentieth century, see Prendergast, *The Ambient Century*, 81–88.

14. A provocative study of popular music's transition from vitality into vulgarity is Martha Bayles, *Hole in Our Soul: The Loss of Beauty and Meaning in American Popular Music* (New York: Free Press, 1994). In this light, see also Donald Clarke, *The Rise and Fall of Popular Music* (New York: St. Martin's Griffin, 1995), 199.

15. Plato's Retreat's extreme, open receptiveness to liberated sex is candidly described in John Heidenry, *What Wild Ecstasy: The Rise and Fall of the Sexual Revolution* (New York: Simon & Schuster, 1997), 211–12.

16. For the extent and social influence of Hugh Hefner's sexually oriented empire, see ibid., 58–61.

17. Male homosexuality, which was becoming more of an open lifestyle during this time, was generally thought to be a main contributor to the spread of AIDS, an acronym for Acquired Immune Deficiency Syndrome. But the disease soon became widespread among heterosexuals, rising to alarming proportions near the century's end. For the coming out of the gay lifestyle and the backlash to it, see James R. Petersen, *The Century of Sex: Playboy's History of the Sexual Revolution* (New York: Grove Press, 1999), 311–13, 370–72.

18. Quoted in Eddie Muller and Daniel Faris, *Grindhouse: The Forbidden World of "Adults Only" Cinema* (New York: St. Martin's Griffin, 1996), 129.

19. Or, to paraphrase this comment, as "appearances and hype" have always beguiled and ruled the mediated vision. See Leonard Quart and Albert Auster, *American Film and Society Since 1945*, 2nd ed. (Westport, Conn.: Praeger, 1991), 115.

20. In fact, by the end of the 1970s, according to Ed Guerrero, "Hollywood's construction of blackness was concentrated . . . on one comic 'superstar,' Richard Pryor." See *Framing Blackness: The African American Image in Film* (Philadelphia: Temple University Press, 1993), 110. For a discussion of the "blaxploitation" film's import in the early '70s, see S. Torriano Berry and Venise T. Berry, *The 50 Most Influential Black Films* (New York: Kensington, 2001), 113–24, 141–43. A more fully realized take on the African American experience was Gordon Parks's *The Learning Tree* (1969), which was the first film directed by a black and produced by a major studio (Warner Brothers). It represented a major advance toward the strong characterizations of the socially oriented films that would appear in the 1980s–90s. Other films of this era that presaged a growing attention to the big problems and minor triumphs of black life in America were *Nothing but a Man* (1964), *Guess Who's Coming to Dinner* (1967), *Claudine* (1974), and *Cooley High* (1975).

21. Fred Davis, *Yearning for Yesterday: A Sociology of Nostalgia* (New York: Free Press, 1979), 135. Davis's observation suggests Fredric Jameson's ironic assessment of the postmodern affinity for the nostalgic film as "Nostalgia for the Present." See *Postmodernism or, The Cultural Logic of Late Capitalism* (Durham, N.C.: Duke University Press, 1999), chapter 9.

22. For new directions in movie sound track music influenced by electronic sound, note Prendergast's opinion of Greek composer Vangelis's scoring output in *The Ambient Century*, 184.

23. On Woody Allen's personal approach to filmmaking, see Julian Fox, *Woody: Movies from Manhattan* (Woodstock, N.Y.: Overlook Press, 1996), 19–23.

24. Danny Peary, a devotee of the cult movie, has selected one hundred films that fans feel are deserving of this category and discussed their import in *Cult Movies: The Classics, the Sleepers, the Weird, and the Wonderful* (New York: Delacorte, 1981). His foreword (xiii) states that "Cultists believe they are among the blessed few who have discovered something in particular films that the average moviegoer and critic have missed—the something that makes the pictures extraordinary." As a leading example, Peary cites *The Rocky Horror Picture Show* (1975), which, he says, "cannot even be discussed without mentioning its fans." For the ritualized reactions of this film's cult following, see 302–5.

25. In 1956, the robotic character Robby in MGM's *Forbidden Planet*, which was the first SF film accorded A-movie status by a major studio, prefigured the more advanced technology for depicting such a character. Both this film and the earlier *Destination Moon* (1950), based on a Robert Heinlein novel, anticipated the movies' more realistic interpretation of SF subject matter. The later films would reflect the scientifically based approach of "hard" SF and/or the speculative concepts of the New Wave movement, particularly in their dystopic visions of the future.

26. In assessing film as the dominant art form of the twentieth century, Norman K. Denzin implies that nostalgia is another manifestation of the "mass-mediated, cinematic postmodern world where the boundaries between images and reality have blurred." See his preface in *Images of Postmodern Society: Social Theory and Contemporary Cinema* (London: Sage Publications, 1991).

27. According to Stefan Kanfer, Bakshi presaged "a new direction for

animation; it was no longer cute or even beautiful. It was candid, challenging, unlimited in its power." See *Serious Business: The Art and Commerce of Animation in America from* Betty Boop *to* Toy Story (New York: Scribner, 1997), 205.

28. Pursuant to the visual impact of *Yellow Submarine*, youth's psychedelic orientation in the 1960s viewed *Fantasia* as a sensory high that helped raise it to cult status. See Kanfer, 201. See also Peary, *Cult Movies*, 92, 93.

29. Quoted in Leonard Maltin, *Of Mice and Magic: A History of American Animated Cartoons* (New York: McGraw-Hill, 1980), 78. Even such an iconoclastic book as Richard Schickel's *The Disney Version: The Life, Times, Art, and Commerce of Walt Disney* (1985) failed to undermine the popular appeal of the Disney mystique, which sought to recreate the world in the way it thought the mediated vision wanted it to be.

30. One of the more influential of recent film studies on this book is Robert Sklar, *Movie-Made America: A Social History of American Movies* (New York: Random House, 1975), revised and updated in 1994. For a bibliography of other notable works published before and since 1975, see the revised edition, 399–404.

31. David Marc has observed that the 1960s sitcom was into a mood of "deep escapism," one that "seemed utterly indifferent toward verisimilitude, preferring instead to explore and allegorize the turgid daydreams of American mass culture." See *Comic Visions: TV Comedy and American Culture*, 2nd ed. (Malden, Mass.: Blackwell, 1997), 106. But in the '70s, when the fantasized world of the sitcom gave way to the real-world issues of *All in the Family*, not a few viewers were upset by this shocking shift toward focusing on the realities of family life.

32. For an overview of Wolper's achievements in transforming reality into entertainment, see David Marc and Robert J. Thompson, *Prime Time, Prime Movers: From* I Love Lucy *to* L.A. Law; *America's Greatest TV Shows and the People Who Created Them* (Boston: Little, Brown, 1992), 285–300.

33. But the police drama's main appeal to the mediated vision lay in its "uncompromising law-and-order aspect [that] made it palatable to more conservative audiences concerned about the breakdown of American society." See Ed Papazian, *Medium Rare: The Evolution, Workings, and Impact of Commercial Television* (New York: Media Dynamics, 1991), 278.

34. Edith Efron, "Does TV Violence Affect Our Society?" in *TV Guide: The First 25 Years*, ed. Jay S. Harris (New York: Simon & Schuster, 1978), 229.

35. Marc and Thompson, 49–50. In *Comic Visions* Marc contends that *All in the Family*, along with *The Mary Tyler Moore Show* and *M\*A\*S\*H*, by creating a unique version of the storytelling tradition of the novel and the movies, raised the sitcom to the level of an art form.

36. Bruce J. Schulman has observed how a popular sitcom like *The Jeffersons* ironically promoted racial diversity rather than equality, denoting the "beginning of the end of the integrationist ideal." See *The Seventies: The Great Shift in American Culture, Society, and Politics* (New York: Free Press, 2001), 53–54.

37. Jeff Greenfield, *Television: The First Fifty Years* (New York: Crescent Books, 1981), 92.

38. As many of Serling's stories had a pulp/comic book flavor to them,

Tom Engelhardt notes that with *The Twilight Zone*'s "fear of the unknown" premise and its effect on the viewer, "television, for the first time, knowingly slipped into the territory of the science fiction film and horror comic" that had appealed more to a youthful audience. See *The End of Victory Culture: Cold War America and the Disillusioning of a Generation* (New York: Basic Books, 1995), 153.

39. *Saturday Night Live*, as a vehicle for stand-up comedy and satirical skits, proved popular enough to still be running at the century's end, having reflected the mediated vision's changing tastes in humor since its beginning. It seemingly left no stone unturned in spoofing everything and everybody, from celebrities to politicians in the news.

40. As most children readily connected with the likable personalities of cereal-sponsored characters like Cap'n Crunch, Tony the Tiger, and Trix Rabbit, they were naturally receptive to the commercial roles that helped sell the products they promoted. The deceptive side of advertising cereals is revealed in Scott Bruce and Bill Crawford, *Cerealizing America: The Unsweetened Story of American Breakfast Cereal* (Boston: Faber and Faber, 1995).

41. Concerning the rationale for the program's "magazine" format, producer Don Hewitt indicated that it derived from the intent of featuring an investigative report in its entirety without any commercial interruption.

42. Richard K. Doan, "Public Television: Is Anybody Watching?" in Harris, ed., TV Guide: *The First 25 Years*, 188.

43. Garff B. Wilson, *Three Hundred Years of American Drama and Theatre*, 2nd ed. (Englewood Cliffs, N.J.: Prentice-Hall, 1982), 306. For developments since the 1970s, see "A Changing Theatre: Broadway to the Regions," in *The Cambridge History of American Theatre: Post–World War II to the 1990s*, vol. 3, ed. Don B. Wilmeth and Christopher Bigsby (Cambridge: Cambridge University Press, 2000), 163–83.

44. Gerald M. Berkowitz, *New Broadways: Theatre across America, 1950–1980* (Totowa, N.J.: Rowman & Allanheld, 1982), 161–62. For an overview of developments in the stage musical during this era, see John Degen, "Musical Theatre since World War II," in *The Cambridge History of American Theatre*, vol. 3, 435–54.

45. While David Marc, in *Comic Visions*, has pointed out the influence of stand-up comedy on the sitcom, columnist Laurie Stone has analyzed its iconoclastic tradition in the styles of later stand-up comedians toward the century's end. In their more liberal times, she asserts that no topic or individual was immune from the merciless posture of quick-witted, irreverent performers like Robin Williams, Joan Rivers, Whoopi Goldberg, and Chris Rock. See *Laughing in the Dark: A Decade of Subversive Comedy* (Hopewell, N.J.: Ecco Press, 1997).

46. The various ways in which theatrical sex was presented in this era are addressed in Jack Boulware, *Sex American Style: An Illustrated Romp through the Golden Age of Heterosexuality* (Venice, Calif.: Feral House, 1997), 48–51.

47. The origin, development, and sociocultural impact of *Ms.*, the first feminist magazine, are detailed in Mary Thom, *Inside Ms.: 25 Years of the Magazine and the Feminist Movement* (New York: Henry Holt, 1997).

48. Gerald Clarke, "The Meaning of Nostalgia," *Time*, 3 May 1971, 77.

49. A sampling of *American Heritage*'s 1970s' essay and photo feature

titles speak for themselves as to their nostalgic flavor: "I Remember Grandpa's Village," "The Great Bicycle Delirium," "The Age of the Trolley," "Games People Played," "Growing Up in Newport," and so on. Another rationale for the mediated vision's special focus on nostalgia in the 1970s is Michael Kammen's observation: "Nostalgia is most likely to increase or become prominent in times of transition, in periods of cultural anxiety, or when a society feels a strong sense of discontinuity with its past." See *Mystic Chords of Memory: The Transformation of Tradition in American Culture* (New York: Vintage Books, 1993), 618.

50. Larry Flynt's daring approach to publishing raunch is discussed in Petersen, *The Century of Sex*, 353–54, and his run-ins with the law, in Heidenry, *What Wild Ecstasy*, 205–9.

51. An educational program whose success attests to the high educational level of its participants is Elderhostel, which started out in the 1970s. Generally, host institutions, that is, colleges receptive to the idea that learning can be enjoyable, offer a week of course work and related tours to those fifty-five and over. For many enrollees, the experience of going back to school became a nostalgia trip in itself.

52. For the evolving approaches to magazine cover and interior design since the 1960s, see Steven Heller and Teresa Fernandes, *Magazines Inside and Out* (New York: PBC International, 1996), 6–9.

53. Richard Kluger, *The Paper: The Life and Death of the* New York Herald Tribune (New York: Knopf, 1986), 673.

54. The proactive role of the underground press in representing the counterculture views of youth at this time is noted in Petersen, *The Century of Sex*, 286–87.

55. Despite his ability as a master storyteller, Caniff "realized that Vietnam could not inspire the idealism of WW II: 'There's no Hitler today . . . There's no Hirohito. There's none of that. Just a big fat nothing to get killed for, just because you got in the wrong place.'" Quoted in R. C. Harvey, "Caniff's Private War to Save *Steve Canyon,*" *Nemo: The Classic Comics Library* 32 (Winter 1992): 19. But as an adventure strip, *Steve Canyon,* like others of the genre, was also a victim of television's series programming that responded to the mediated vision's ever-changing fantasy moods.

56. See Harold Gray, *Arf! The Life and Hard Times of Little Orphan Annie* (New Rochelle, N.Y.: Arlington House, 1970). Ironically, in this collection's introduction, Al Capp, whose *Li'l Abner* had satirized Harold Gray's conservatism, admits that *Annie*'s creator was right on target concerning the nation's growing loss of respect for law and authority.

57. For an analysis of the *Annie* phenomenon and its media-made spin-offs over the years, see Bruce Smith, *The History of Little Orphan Annie* (New York: Ballantine, 1982).

58. Among the more noteworthy publications were Pierre Couperie and Maurice C. Horn, *A History of the Comic Strip* (New York: Crown, 1968); Jerry Robinson, *The Comics: An Illustrated History of Comic Strip Art* (New York: G. P. Putnam's, 1974); and Maurice Horn, ed., *The World Encyclopedia of Comics* (New York: Chelsea House, 1976). Recognizing the comic strip's sociocultural import, Hyperion Press began publishing its Library of Classic American Comic Strips in 1977, which included such old-time favorites as *Buster Brown, Happy Hooligan, Barney Google,* and *Skippy.* Of relevance here, too, was the establishment in 1974 of the International

Museum of Cartoon Art, dedicated to the preservation of original comics art. Under the leadership of longtime cartoonist Mort Walker, the continually expanding holdings found a new location in 1996 in Boca Raton, Florida.

59. Attesting to the significant but unheralded role of women cartoonists in the twentieth century is Trina Robbins and Catherine Yronwode's, *Women and the Comics* (Forestville, Calif.: Eclipse Books, 1985).

60. This book's popularity prompted a sequel, *The Comic Book Book* (New Rochelle, N.Y.: Arlington House, 1973). Other nostalgic publications about comic books and their heroes included the reprint collections of Batman and Superman, each subtitled *From the '30s to the '70s* (New York: Crown, 1971), and Hubert H. Crawford, *Crawford's Encyclopedia of Comic Books* (Middle Village, N.Y.: Jonathan David, 1978). The special interests of collectors were represented in Robert Lesser, *A Celebration of Comic Art and Memorabilia* (New York: Hawthorn Books, 1975), while the nostalgic appeal and escapist fantasy of the comic book's cover art found another source in Richard O'Brien, *The Golden Age of Comic Books, 1937–1945* (New York: Ballantine, 1977).

61. For the contributing factors to the revival of the horror comics, see Stephen Sennitt, *Ghastly Terror! The Horrible Story of the Horror Comics* (Manchester, UK: Headpress, 1999), 169–80. Horror as popular subject matter for not only the comics but fiction and film since the 1950s is presented in visually impressive fashion in Robert Weinberg, *Horror of the Twentieth Century: An Illustrated History* (Portland, Ore.: Collectors Press, 2000).

62. Gerald Clarke, "The Comics on the Couch," *Time*, 13 December 1971, 70. Social relevance as a contemporary theme in the comic book is addressed in Gerard Jones and Will Jacobs, *The Comic Book Heroes* (Rocklin, Calif.: Prima Publishing, 1997), 146–51.

63. The earliest book study of the comix phenomenon is Mark James Estren, *A History of Underground Comics* (San Francisco: Straight Arrow Books, 1974). But earlier, Les Daniels devoted a chapter to it in *Comix: A History of Comic Books in America* (New York: Outerbridge & Dienstfrey, 1971), 165–93. Robert C. Harvey contends that the underground comix phenomenon has resulted in a more socially open posture in the contemporary newspaper comic strip. A prime example of this trend is Bill Griffith's Zippy character, whose strip was picked up for national syndication in 1986. See *Children of the Yellow Kid*, 158, 161.

64. A colorful photographic survey of hippie culture's visual influence is James Henke and Parke Puterbaugh, eds., *I Want to Take You Higher: The Psychedelic Era, 1965–1969* (San Francisco: Chronicle Books, 1997).

65. Indeed, by the 1990s, such reputable New York art dealers as Christie's East and Sotheby's were conducting periodic auctions of vintage comic books and comic art collectibles that generated astronomical sales.

66. For biographical analyses of these and other artists' contributions to comic book art, see Ron Goulart, *The Great Comic Book Artists* (New York: St. Martin's, 1986). A second volume appeared in 1989. Comics historian Mike Benton narrowed the list of the greatest comic book artists to thirteen in *Masters of Imagination: The Comic Book Artists Hall of Fame* (Dallas: Taylor Publishing, 1994).

67. Kitchen Sink Press's venture into reprinting vintage comic strips

began in the early '80s with the publication of the *Steve Canyon* magazine, continuing in series of such notable strips as *Li'l Abner, Alley Oop, Flash Gordon,* and *Nancy,* as well as the syndicated newspaper version of *Batman.* For its many publishing achievements in the comics field, see Dave Schreiner, *Kitchen Sink Press: The First 25 Years* (Northampton, Mass.: Kitchen Sink Press, 1994). During this time, Fantagraphics Books also published "classic" comic strip reprints, such as *Popeye, Little Nemo in Slumberland, Pogo,* and *Little Orphan Annie.*

68. Robert C. Harvey, *The Art of the Comic Book: An Aesthetic History* (Jackson: University Press of Mississippi, 1996), ix. Substantiating Harvey's opinion is Roger Sabin's focus on the rise of the graphic novel in the late 1980s in *Adult Comics: An Introduction* (London: Routledge, 1993), 235–48. Also, Joseph Witek has argued that "the potential has always existed for comic books to present the same kinds of narratives as other verbal and pictorial media." See *Comic Books as History: The Narrative Art of Jack Jackson, Art Spiegelman, and Harvey Pekar* (Oxford: University Press of Mississippi, 1989), 11. Thus, the basis for Witek's contention that such comic books "merit serious critical analysis" lies in their shift from pure fantasy to historical and contemporary realism that entertains as it informs. Significantly, Scott McCloud has utilized the comic book format itself to present his in-depth analysis of the comics as a serious cultural form of expression in *Understanding Comics: The Invisible Art* (New York: HarperPerennial, 1994).

69. Robert Bowden, "Stan Lee: The Marvel of the Comic World" in the *St. Petersburg* (Fla.) *Times,* 3 May 1978.

70. See Merrill Panitt, "Television Today: The State of the Art," in Harris, ed., TV Guide: *The First 25 years,* 271.

71. Wilson Bryan Key, *Media Sexploitation* (New York: New American Library, 1976). This book complements Key's earlier work, *Subliminal Seduction: Ad Media's Manipulation of a Not So Innocent America* (Englewood Cliffs, N.J.: Prentice-Hall, 1973).

72. Respecting this observation, Mitchell Stephens has pointed out how fast-cut visual developments in TV commercials since the 1970s conditioned the public eye—or the mediated vision—to the nonverbal demands of the "photographic instant." See *The Rise of the Image, The Fall of the Word* (New York: Oxford University Press, 1998), 129. For the potential implications of Stephens's views, see chapter 3.

73. Jim Hall, *Mighty Minutes: An Illustrated History of Television's Best Commercials* (New York: Harmony Books, 1984), 11.

74. Morris Dickstein, *Gates of Eden: American Culture in the Sixties* (Cambridge: Harvard University Press, 1997), 189.

75. Elizabeth Long, *The American Dream and the Popular Novel* (Boston: Routledge & Kegan Paul, 1985), 107.

76. For critical analyses of King's compelling postmodern manner of transforming everyday life into horrific ordeals, see Jonathan P. Davis, ed., *Stephen King's America* (Bowling Green, Ohio: Popular Press, 1994).

77. The college classroom, in fact, was where not only postmodern literature was studied during this era but the output of media culture as well, particularly as it was manifested in film studies. A move toward democratizing the curriculum in the 1960s, when enrollments began to drop, led to the introduction of interdisciplinary programs of more contemporary rele-

vance in many schools, hopefully to attract students and maintain needed enrollments. For readers outside the classroom, however, experimental fiction's esoteric vision of a postmodernist realm in which fantasy and reality are merged remained a marginalized reading experience. John M. Unsworth has commented on the ironic status of this kind of writing: "'Serious' fiction that is nonrealist in its aesthetic orientation is prestigious but unprofitable, and those who write it tend to be men confined to the academy, which is the only place that their professionalism does have a market value." See his essay on the book marketplace in *The Columbia History of the American Novel*, ed. Emory Elliott (New York: Columbia University Press, 1991), 679–96. For an illuminating interpretation of both experimental and traditional variations in postmodernist fiction since the 1960s, see Wendy Steiner, "Rethinking Postmodernism," in *The Cambridge History of American Literature: Prose Writing, 1940–1990*, vol. 7, ed. Sacvan Bercovitch (Cambridge: Cambridge University Press, 1999), 427–50.

78. Thomas L. Bonn, *Undercover: An Illustrated History of American Mass Market Paperbacks* (New York: Penguin Books, 1982).

79. For the rise of feminist criticism since the '60s and its militant posture on gender issues, see Evan Carton and Gerald Graff, "The Canon, the Academy, and Gender," in *The Cambridge History of American Literature: Poetry and Criticism, 1940–1995*, vol. 8, ed. Sacvan Bercovitch (Cambridge: Cambridge University Press), 324–53.

80. Gay Talese's adventurous role in exploring the extremes of the sexual revolution is discussed in Heidenry, *What Wild Ecstasy*, chapter 12.

81. In examining the theme of male toughness in American culture, Rupert Wilkinson says its postmodern manifestation surfaced in the balanced qualities of physical courage and bureaucratic competence in the astronaut's makeup. See *American Tough: The Tough-Guy Tradition and American Character* (New York: Perennial Library, 1986), 19–20, 160–61.

82. Both Rich and Bly, as poet-critics, were representative of a new sociocultural role for the poet in the postmodern era. Though Rich was a product of the academic tradition, her involvement in radical politics saw her become a spokesperson for women's causes. Similarly, the nonacademician Bly, in his best seller *Iron John* (1990), sought to awaken the American male to a new sense of his diminished masculinity. As media icons, both achieved a degree of celebrity usually denied the contemporary poet.

83. Art's gravitation toward the function of entertainment is yet another development that supports Neal Gabler's thesis in *Life the Movie: How Entertainment Conquered Reality* (New York: Knopf, 1998).

84. Michele H. Bogart, *Artists, Advertising, and the Borders of Art* (Chicago: University of Chicago Press, 1995), 298–99. For Andy Warhol's overall impact on postmodern art, see Tilman Osterwold, *Pop Art* (Cologne: Taschen, 1999), 167–78.

85. Marco Livingstone, *Pop Art: A Continuing History* (New York: Abrams, 1990), 118. Livingstone also points out the paradox of Warhol's technique: ". . . it was through such seemingly mindless repetition that Warhol proposed his own concepts of transcendence, involving a heightening of perception through concentration on minor variations of apparently identical things" (116). Neal Gabler notes, too, that in blending art and popular culture Warhol saw art as a "product of culture's collective sensibility," which at the time was under the sway of consumerism and media culture's pervasive visual impact. See *Life the Movie*, 133.

86. In this regard, comic book historian Les Daniels has commented: "By putting a frame around comic book images, Pop Art simultaneously exalted and debased the medium. It was a way of looking at the work as an artifact of an obsolete culture, as a museum piece." See *DC Comics: Sixty Years of the World's Favorite Comic Book Heroes* (Boston: Bulfinch, 1995), 149.

87. For the revolutionary contributions of John Cage and Karlheinz Stockhausen to the development of electronic music, see Prendergast, *The Ambient Century*, 44–49, 51–57.

88. Quoted in Richard Marshall, ed., *Great Events of the 20th Century: How They Changed Our Lives* (Pleasantville, N.Y.: Reader's Digest Association, 1977), 467.

89. See Ileen Sheppard, "Icons and Images: The Cultural Legacy of the Fair," in *Remembering the Future: The New York World's Fair from 1939 to 1964* (New York: Rizzoli, 1989), 170.

90. According to the technicians who produced them, the "fact that the Disney shows proved to be so popular at the [New York] fair was a prime factor in the decision to proceed with a new project called Walt Disney World." See The Imagineers, *Walt Disney Imagineering: A Behind the Dreams Look at Making the Magic Real* (New York: Hyperion, 1996), 31.

91. The antiseptic appearance of Walt Disney World emanated in large part from Disney's own reformist reaction to the urban blight that had perennially plagued the nation's cities. See Steven Watts, *The Magic Kingdom: Walt Disney and the American Way of Life* (Boston: Houghton Mifflin, 1997), 440–41. Beth Dunlop has considered the architectural designs of the Disney theme parks as contemporary triumphs in *Building a Dream: The Art of Disney Architecture* (New York: Abrams, 1996). But Ada Louise Huxtable criticized the Disney style for what she terms its "unrelenting commercialism" and "uninspired design." See *The Unreal America: Architecture and Illusion* (New York: New Press, 1997), 49–55.

92. The visual achievements as well as the foresight of the Imagineers have been documented in *Walt Disney Imagineering*. Clearly, their main mission has been to create their projects in light of Walt Disney's personal entreaty: "I don't want the public to see the world they live in while they're in the park. I want them to feel they're in another world." Quoted from p. 90.

93. Quoted in Jeff Kurtti, *Since the World Began: Walt Disney World; The First 25 Years* (New York: Hyperion, 1996), 18.

94. Lipsyte's thoughts about the commercialized problems of organized sports are summarized in "Varsity Syndrome: The Unkindest Cut" in which this quote appears. See this essay in Wiley Lee Umphlett, ed., *American Sport Culture: The Humanistic Dimensions* (Lewisburg, Pa.: Bucknell University Press, 1985), 111–21.

95. See Lasch, "The Corruption of Sports," in ibid., 50–67. Neal Gabler, too, has contended that the show-business aspects of sports have transformed athletes into performers/entertainers with clearly defined personas to maintain. A key player in programming sports as entertainment was innovative ABC-TV executive Roone Arledge who, in 1960, exhorted: "We are going to add show business to sports!" For his achievements in this transition, see Frank Deford's tribute to Arledge upon his death: "Roone Arledge, 1931–2002," *Sports Illustrated*, 16 November 2002, 121–26.

96. The growing dominance of African American athletes during these

years fueled a debate that would last the rest of the century: whether black dominance in sport was due to genetic traits or was socially determined due to lack of opportunity in traditional career areas other than entertainment and sports. But in identifying with sports as escapist experience through the ultimate goal of winning, the mediated vision maintained its color-blind outlook as opposed to the larger society's inclination toward a racist posture.

97. In motor sports this era saw the annual Indianapolis 500 race maintain its popularity while the major events of the National Association of Stock Car Auto Racing (NASCAR) continued to attract fans. They and the drivers who competed in them would rise to their greatest period of popularity in the last years of the century, thus perpetuating the automobile as an iconic symbol of escapist adventure in the eyes of the mediated vision.

98. Greenfield, *Television*, 213. By 1979 the mediated vision's seemingly insatiable appetite for a variety of sports as escapist entertainment was responded to by the most saturated coverage in sports journalism yet—that of the aptly named Entertainment and Sports Programming Network (ESPN), which televised sporting events and relevant news on a twenty-four-hour daily schedule.

99. James A. Michener, *Sports in America* (New York: Random House, 1976), 451.

## CHAPTER 3: 1980–2000—FANTASIZING REALITY AS A REFUGE FROM REAL-LIFE UNCERTAINTIES

1. Neal Gabler, *Life the Movie: How Entertainment Conquered Reality* (New York: Knopf, 1998), 109.

2. The beguiling power of celebrity may have been a key factor in Clinton's political survival, as to many he came across as something of a movie personality starring in his own blockbuster production. Art imitating life was clearly evident in the 1998 film *Primary Colors* and the popular 1999 television series *The West Wing*, both seemingly inspired by the goings-on in the Clinton administration. That celebrity could suffice as a qualification for high office was intimated in 1999 when longtime movie actor Warren Beatty declared his interest in becoming a presidential candidate.

3. Jerome Tuccille, introduction, in *Rupert Murdoch* (New York: Donald I. Fine, 1989).

4. In the late '70s and early '80s, the daring advent of sexually explicit content in public-access cable programming and the outcry against it are noted in Louis Chunovic, *One Foot on the Floor: The Curious Evolution of Sex on Television from* I Love Lucy *to* South Park (New York: TV Books, 2000), 77–78, 89–90.

5. Mark Fishman and Gray Cavender, eds., *Entertaining Crime: Television Reality Programs* (New York: Aldine de Gruyter, 1995), 14.

6. By the late 1990s, the Fox broadcast network had led the way in legitimating violence and offensive language in such shows as the long-running, SF-oriented *The X-Files* and both the short-lived *Harsh Realm* and *Action*. The latter was a behind-the-scenes satire of the Hollywood filmmaking industry in which obvious profanities were bleeped out. While critics gener-

ally praised these shows, a 1999 Parents Television Council survey reacted negatively to such programming, concluding that violent content, foul language, and sexual references had become unwarranted fixtures in the fantasized world of television drama. The postmodern fascination with violence as entertainment is addressed from various viewpoints in Jeffrey H. Goldstein, ed., *Why We Watch: The Attractions of Violent Entertainment* (New York: Oxford University Press, 1998).

7. The enduring popularity of the soap-opera genre was substantiated in 2000 with the advent of a cable channel called *SoapNet*, whose main purpose was to rebroadcast programming for a nighttime audience.

8. David Marc, *Comic Visions: Television Comedy and American Culture*, 2nd ed. (Malden, Mass.: Blackwell, 1993), 192.

9. Voice-overs were a key factor in enhancing TV's animated cartoon humor, as a number of celebrity figures who made animated appearances on *The Simpsons* contributed to the show's longtime popularity. Other animated shows of the '90s like *Futurama*, a takeoff on life in the thirtieth century, and *Dilbert*, which transitioned its satire of the corporate world from the newspaper comic strip, looked to compete with the new wave of fantasized reality series. The cable channels' freedom of expression resulted in MTV's *Beavis and Butt-head*, structured around two antisocial middle schoolers, whose misadventures had a surprising seven-year run in the '90s, while Comedy Central's *South Park*, with its cast of scheming, pottymouthed elementary schoolkids, created an outrageous world all its own. Thus the deviant ways of reality had now invaded the traditionally inviolable world of the animated cartoon. Ted Turner's Cartoon Network countered the trend by offering less offensive new features and reruns of the old studio cartoons that were an integral part of theater programming in the 1930s and '40s.

10. After numerous complaints and protests from minority groups in the late '90s, the major networks, including Fox, which had been the leader in black characterization, began adding minorities to their casts. A newly formed multiracial coalition asserted that appropriate minority representation was essential to television's growing attention to reality programming, thus attesting to the cross-racial power of the mediated vision in a pluralistic society. Accordingly, by 2000 the Showtime cable channel was offering shows that catered to both black and Hispanic viewers.

11. Ed Papazian, *Medium Rare: The Evolution, Workings, and Impact of Commercial Television* (New York: Media Dynamics, 1991), 224.

12. The criminal element's strong attraction to TV viewers was evidenced in 1999 by critics' rave notices for HBO's *The Sopranos*, which later received four Emmy awards. Indeed, the show was popular enough to offer its initial thirteen episodes in reruns and return for a second season in 2000. The humanized but graphic attention to the psychological turmoil of the show's lead character and his mafiosa dealings turned out to be surprisingly appealing stuff to most viewers. Competition from the judicial side of the law appeared in the form of such well-received series as *The Practice*, *L.A. Law*, and even the juvenile court world of *Judging Amy*, an unexpected hit of the 1999 season. The scheduling of actual cases tried by real judges in such daytime shows as *The People's Court*, *Divorce Court*, and *Judge Judy* also found large audiences. By this time, then, both sides of the law were offering their respective versions of reality programming as entertainment.

13. Benefiting from the advances in computer graphics and special-effects technology by 1999, CBS offered its take on the current rage for the disaster movie in *Aftershock: Earthquake in New York*. In it, a four-minute quake convincingly wipes out the familiar landmarks of the New York skyline, an ominous omen of a major real-world terrorist act soon to come.

14. Another, more visible sign of television's feel for news as entertainment was the three network morning shows' creation of indoor-outdoor window studios that attracted out-of-town visitors by the score, brandishing signs and waving at the camera to realize their own brief moment of televised fame. NBC's *Today Show* initiated the practice at Rockefeller Center, and in 1999, ABC opened its new studios at Times Square while CBS set up at East Fifty-Ninth Street.

15. By the end of the century, news as entertainment ranged from Jeanne Moos's humorous coverage of offbeat subject matter for CNN to MSNBC's *Headliners & Legends*, with its focus on "the sights, sounds and stories of the people that change our world . . . and shape our lives." The competition for novel approaches to news as entertaining fare had become fierce enough that a late 1999 segment on ABC's *20/20* reported that certain supposedly real happenings were being acted out to "create" news, unbeknownst to receptive TV stations and networks on the lookout for sensational material to attract viewers.

16. In 1998, the Warner Brothers network (the WB) surpassed the program ratings of its main broadcast competitor, the United Paramount Network (UPN), mainly with programs geared to youth audiences—*Dawson's Creek*, *Buffy the Vampire Slayer*, and the family-oriented *7th Heaven*. Among the most popular cable services in the 1990s was the Weather Channel, which had been on the air since the early 1980s. To the mediated vision its continuously updated information was essential to personal well-being, especially in times of severe weather threats. Other specialized channels appeared in the forms of Fox's FX, which by 1999 was targeting the special interests of young males; the Food Network, whose New York studio offered passers-by the opportunity to view its appetizing cooking segments; and a variety of all-movie channels, some catering to specific themes and subject matter. The backlash to vulgarity in programming appeared in late 1999 as PAX TV, a broadcast network that promised programs devoid of foul language, unjustified violence, and explicit sexual behavior. Niche programming in a number of other areas was a sure sign of more to come in TV's seemingly endless attempt to address singular interests in a nation whose ongoing social fragmentation generated such demand.

17. Indeed, in the new century the viewing options of digital television would offer programming choices that numbered in the hundreds.

18. As broadcasts of the NBC Symphony Orchestra were to its time, so PBS's *Great Performances* series sensitized viewers to the glories of classical music, both operatic and symphonic. PBS also leaned toward the popular in presenting Broadway musical highlights. To purists, however, the Lawrence Welk series, as well as the scheduling of rock and country music, could have been well avoided. But such programming was yet another sign of PBS's postmodern intent to respond to all tastes.

19. As it quietly celebrated its thirtieth anniversary in 1999, PBS, despite its critics, looked confidently ahead to the new century. Now comprising a network of over 300 stations, PBS was revered by many as a pioneer

in its own right, having been on the cutting edge of TV technology. Although commercial cable outlets like the History Channel now competed with its documentary efforts, PBS continued to offer well-received, high-quality programming. In 1999, for example, notable specials appeared, such as *Crucible of Empire*, which portrayed America's imperialistic role in the Spanish-American War. While *America 1900* focused on the country's sociocultural status at the beginning of the twentieth century, a twelve-hour history of New York City, like the others, anticipated the coming of the new century by looking back at where the nation had been.

20. How televangelism was transforming church-based religion into a form of entertainment is described by Edwin Diamond in "God's Television," *American Film*, March 1980, 30–32, 34–35. That there was a show-business side to television ministry was demonstrated most exploitatively in the 1980s in evangelists Jim and Tammy Bakker's Disneyesque theme park scheme called Heritage USA. The Bakkers's shocking misuse of their followers' membership funds brought about their downfall. For analyses of the varied programs and personalities that have appeared in electronic evangelism, see Hal Erickson, *Religious Radio and Television in the United States, 1921–1991* (Jefferson, N.C.: McFarland, 1992).

21. Sassa was responding to criticism of the network's "overused, unrealistic formula" for its sitcoms. Reported in an article syndicated by the *Cincinnati Enquirer*, 18 January 1999.

22. As a popular reality entertainment mode that radio had developed through the likes of Larry King, Rush Limbaugh, Don Imus, and Howard Stern, all of whom gravitated toward the television medium, daytime TV talk shows proliferated in the early '90s. At night were the established shows of David Letterman and Jay Leno (Johnny Carson's successor), as well as numerous cable talk-show hosts. But the daytime shows created the most controversy, particularly that showcasing the permissive style of Jerry Springer, whose problem-beset guests were evidently encouraged to say whatever they wanted as well as behave as outrageously as they dared before their studio audiences. By the '90s, too, sleazy subject matter on talk radio shows was in vogue. For an overview, see Peter Laufer, *Inside Talk Radio: America's Voice or Just Hot Air?* (New York: Birch Lane Press, 1995), chapters 8 and 11. At a time when sensationalized subject matter, such as the O. J. Simpson murder trial, was endlessly discussed on cable talk shows with plenty of time to consume, Oprah Winfrey's TV show, which had started out in 1986, devoted itself to timely topics of more socially redeeming value, especially to women. Its host was the first black to succeed in a format that Phil Donahue had pioneered for the serious exposition of topical matters.

23. The study, conducted by the Center for Media and Public Affairs, was reported by the Gannett News Service, 23 September 1999.

24. The *TV Guide* rankings were reported by the Associated Press, 26 June 1997. Concurrently, the rerun programming of Nick at Nite and TV Land as a nostalgic haven from contemporary concerns revealed a resurgence of interest in the game shows of TV's early days. The success of ABC's *Who Wants to Be a Millionaire?* triggered various spin-offs, while CBS sought to revive its once highly popular *What's My Line?* While such shows as *Jeopardy* and *Wheel of Fortune* had been running for years, syndication saw a racier version of *Hollywood Squares* appear in 1999. The tal-

ent show also reappeared in host Dick Clark's *Your Big Break*; and wrestling, once a mainstay of 1950s TV, was again enjoying widespread popularity, prompting the president of the UPN network to go after it in a big way to recharge its failing fortunes. Even the topical humor of the long-running *Saturday Night Live* came across nostalgically when it celebrated its twenty-fifth anniversary in 1999 with clips from its earlier shows.

25. According to a study by the independent Kaiser Family Foundation, watching television was the favorite pastime of children, ranking ahead of involvement with computers, video games, music, and reading, as reported by the Associated Press, 18 November 1999. Despite Surgeon General David Satcher's urging, earlier that year, that children turn off TV and engage in outdoor activities, his advice apparently fell on deaf ears. Clearly, by the end of the century watching television had become too ingrained a cultural habit among both adults and children to abruptly refrain from watching it. But for those parents wishing to monitor the kind of subject matter their children might watch, the program-blocking V-chip was supposed to be optional with new TV purchases by 1 July 1999. The device was designed to monitor a program's suitability for young viewers according to the industry's new labeling system.

26. Interactive television, though still in an experimental stage, as reported by the Associated Press, 11 December 2000, was designed to allow a viewer to access favorite programs, play along with game shows, purchase products, check bank accounts, print out news reports, and surf the Web, among other options.

27. *Time*, 26 April 1999, devoted a cover story to the release of *The Phantom Menace*, which, as the first film in the new series, was intended to provide the background leading up to the events of the earlier films. The magazine also included Bill Moyers's interview with George Lucas that focused on the director's theory of cinema as an updating of universal myths offering insights into the human experience. To Lucas, film, as a visual composite of all the arts, has the power to turn dreams into virtual reality. But, according to *Time* reviewer Richard Corliss, Lucas's latest attempt to convey his message was overwhelmed by a veritable deluge of visual effects—yet another sign of the dominant role computer graphics were assuming in the moviemaking process at this time, exemplified in such SF films' focus on virtual reality as *Existenz* and *The Matrix* (both 1999).

28. The movies' infatuation with Shakespeare near the close of the century was reported in an article syndicated by *USA Today*, 29 January 1999.

29. The videocassette also made available vintage films that ranged from the classics to B movies, as well as animated cartoons and serials, either through rental from video shops, chain stores, and supermarkets or outright purchase.

30. A comparison between this film and the 1982 Disney film *Tron* reveals how advanced the field of computer-generated imagery had become. As a reflector of postmodernist trends beholden to the pervasive power of the computer, it was reminiscent of William Gibson's cyberpunk novel *Necromancer* (1984), which explored the high-tech challenges of cyberspace in a dystopic future. *The Matrix* undoubtedly anticipated both a sequel and a flurry of similar films dependent on computer technology as an essential aid to making films that visualize complex concepts.

31. A great deal of the credit for *Forrest Gump*'s success went to Tom

Hanks, who came into the top of his form as a movie actor in the 1990s. Playing roles as varied as a gay lawyer in *Philadelphia* (1993), an astronaut in *Apollo 13* (1995), and a World War II army officer in *Saving Private Ryan* (1998), Hanks brought the personal, immediate sense of television drama to the big screen. For this reason, as well as his versatility, he was the mediated vision's most representative film actor of the 1990s.

32. In the wake of escalating school violence, a 3 July 1999 Associated Press poll measuring attitudes toward violence in the movies revealed that most adult moviegoers did not appear unduly disturbed by violent content. They had either become inured to it or accepted it as fabricated for the purpose of a film's plot.

33. Among the movies' most versatile and respected directors, Kubrick died in 1999, bequeathing a legacy of filmmaking that included such influential and thematically varied films as *Spartacus* (1960), *Lolita* (1962), *Dr. Strangelove* (1964), *2001: A Space Odyssey* (1968), *A Clockwork Orange* (1971), *The Shining* (1980), and *Eyes Wide Shut* (1999).

34. In 1993, Robin Williams assumed a similar role in *Mrs. Doubtfire* but for a different purpose—to be a nanny to his children after a bitter divorce. That movies based on cross-gender situations were more attuned to comedy was attested to by the American Film Institute's 1998 list of the 100 funniest movies, ranking *Some Like It Hot* (1959) as number one. The list was syndicated by the Associated Press, 14 June 2000.

35. For the influential roles of women in film's early development, see Anthony Slide, *The Silent Feminists: America's First Women Directors* (Lanham, Md.: Scarecrow Press, 1996).

36. For example, a review of *Drive Me Crazy* (1999), another racy comedy about teenage social life, uncovered a basic problem about movies ironically rated for parental guidance—their permissiveness toward youthful misbehavior. This film, it noted, "includes more than one scene in which high school students take over a house and swill booze like sailors on leave, without a parent in sight" (review syndicated by the *Cincinnati Enquirer*, 30 September 1999). This, of course, was the kind of film that teenagers flocked to see, and, as a result, opportunistic movie producers kept stretching the limits of the PG rating accorded such films. Teen life as a sociocultural force in the movies is examined in Jon Lewis, *The Road to Romance and Ruin: Teen Films and Youth Culture* (New York: Routledge, 1992).

37. Michael Medved, *Hollywood versus America: Popular Culture and the War on Traditional Values* (New York: HarperCollins, 1992), 343. But even the G and PG ratings that Medved supported had taken on a more liberal interpretation of their subject matter, as noted above. In 2000, the Directors Guild of America termed the NC-17 rating an "abject failure," as films that should have been denied admission to minors, for example, the controversial *Natural Born Killers*, were recut to receive a "hard" R rating. Report syndicated by the *New York Daily News*, 20 September 2000.

38. Report syndicated by the *Chicago Tribune*, 19 June 1998. The American Film Institute revealed its list of the century's best films in a CBS TV special, 16 June 1998.

39. Rex McGee, "All That Jazz . . . Swing . . . Pop . . . and Rock," *American Film*, July–August 1980, 26. Moreover, Bakshi argued that he was striving for realism in animation, what he termed a "realistic painting in motion" (27). But it was Bakshi's striving after realism in a medium more conducive

to fantasy that ultimately undermined his career. See Stefan Kanfer, *Serious Business: The Art and Commerce of Animation in America* (New York: Scribner, 1997), 202–5.

40. Conversely, even the TV cartoon series directed at children proved it had sufficient appeal to cross over into the movies, as in 1998 the popular Nickelodeon Rugrat characters made it to the big screen in *The Rugrats Movie*. Seemingly, each year produced a new media-made visual phenomenon for children. In 1999 a Japanese import called Pokemon caught their fancy, as its fantasized characters inspired a collectible trading-card mania that morphed into a television series, a video game, and, of course, a movie. From Power Rangers, Teenage Mutant Ninja Turtles, and Rugrats to Pokemon, the 1990s was big for both children, merchants, and the creators of animated cartoons.

41. *Toy Story*'s box-office success resulted in the equally successful *Toy Story 2* in 1999. Both films were products of the inventive Pixar studio's tie-in with Disney. A survey of the film's audiences in six cities showed that the largest groups attending were in the age ranges of 35–49 (28 percent), 21–34 (26 percent), and 1–11 (24 percent), revealing that such films could turn moviegoing into a family experience once again. Survey report syndicated by *USA Today*, 3 December 1999.

42. Scheduled to open on IMAX screens around the world in January 2000 was Walt Disney's *Fantasia 2000*, a remastered sequel to the 1940 classic and the first animated film made expressly for IMAX viewing.

43. The blurring of fact and fiction was integral to the making of *The Blair Witch Project* (1998), an improvised horror tale filmed by some enterprising college students as a documentary. Surprisingly, it was such a big box-office hit, a sequel soon appeared.

44. For an overview of developments in the American theater during this complex era, see Arnold Aronson, "American Theatre in Context: 1945–Present," in *The Cambridge History of American Theatre*, vol. 3, ed. Don Wilmeth and Christopher Bigsby (Cambridge: Cambridge University Press, 1995), 87–162.

45. George Abbott, who lived to be 107, was a Broadway mainstay for over eighty years. His versatility as a director, producer, and writer was evidenced in over 120 shows, winning in the process a Pulitzer Prize and four Tony Awards.

46. For developments in musical theater during this era, see John Degen, "Musical Theatre since World War II," in *The Cambridge History of American Theatre*, 454–65.

47. Gerald M. Berkowitz, *New Broadways: Theatre Across America; Approaching a New Millennium*, rev. ed. (New York: Applause Books, 1997), 215.

48. Riots and antisocial behavior as an ongoing problem at rock concerts since the '50s are pointed out in James Miller, *Almost Grown: The Rise of Rock* (London: William Heinemann, 1999), passim. Concerning the high price of concert tickets, an Associated Press story (14 July 1999) reported that not only rock groups like the Rolling Stones were charging more for tickets (nearly $110 average per seat on a 1999 U.S. tour), but that opera star Luciano Pavarotti took in around $130 average for four shows. Apparently, most music fans felt the escapist experience provided by these revered performers was well worth the inflated ticket prices.

49. In 1999 the Recording Industry Association of America reported that the Beatles were "the most successful recording act of the 20th century," with sales of more than 106 million albums. Singers Garth Brooks and Barbra Streisand were a distant second and third, respectively. The report, based on statistics compiled since 1958, the period when the majority of record sales occurred, was syndicated by *USA Today*, 11 November 1999.

50. In a 25 July 2000 report, the Associated Press cited the top TV rock events that VH-1 planned to highlight, beginning with the Beatles' American debut in 1964.

51. Country music icon Patsy Cline, who died in a 1963 plane crash, was "revived" by a technological process that allowed her to make duets of her songs with singers like Glen Campbell and Crystal Gayle. There had also been the recording of "Unforgettable" by Natalie Cole along with the voice of her deceased father Nat "King" Cole, and despite the objections of purists, a move was under way to resurrect the voices of Elvis Presley and Roy Orbison in similar fashion.

52. Lyle Lovett and his "Large Band" went on tour in 1999 to popularize as well as capitalize on the swing revival. Also, the effervescent sounds of the Lawrence Welk orchestra's "champagne music" was recreated for a new generation as well as older fans at the Welk Resort's Champagne Theatre in Branson, Missouri, a place devoted to the nostalgic affinities of the mediated vision.

53. Madonna's rapid rise to fame through the music video medium and the controversies that marked her career are discussed in Scott Nance, *Music You Can See! The MTV Story* (Las Vegas: Pioneer Books, 1993), 143–48.

54. The popularity of symphonic music as a source for movie sound tracks is discussed in a syndicated *USA Today* report, 1 May 1998. Beginning in the '80s, synthesizer-generated music also added a new aural dimension to movie sound tracks, as in the breakthrough scores that Vangelis composed for *Chariots of Fire* (1981) and *Blade Runner* (1982).

55. As a role model, for example, Garth Brooks emphasized family values and genuine emotion in an updated context. See Bruce Feiler, "Country Music's New Values," *USA Weekend*, 3–5 April 1998, 24. Vince Gill, another traditionalist, attributed country music's popularity to the fact that it has something for everybody.

56. Despite its critics, rap music, with Eminem leading the pack, was still going strong in the late 1990s. From a socially critical perspective, popular music historian Donald Clarke contended: "Rap is an illustration not just of what pop music has come to, but of what a nation has come to." See *The Rise and Fall of Popular Music* (New York: St. Martin's Griffin, 1995), 552–53. As a reflector of the times, then, many considered rap as a sign of the media culture's decadent status. In 1999, black syndicated columnist Leonard Pitts of the *Miami Herald* called rap "a death-affirming music of scabrous explicitness and coarse joys" and termed its performers exemplars of gangsta rap's code of violence. As a perverse expression of fantasized reality, according to Pitts, rap represented "the triumph of a cynical, values-free vision exploited and mass-marketed so effectively that it becomes possible for a sheltered suburban kid . . . to adopt its hopelessness." However, there were those who analyzed rap as a timely reflector of social significance, as Tricia Rose did in *Black Noise: Rap Music and Black Cul-*

*ture in Contemporary America* (Middletown, Conn.: Wesleyan University Press, 1994).

57. For an informed analysis of the moral conflict between Christian ministry and secular entertainment that this kind of music confronts, see Jay R. Howard and John M. Struck, *Apostles of Rock: The Splintered World of Contemporary Christian Music* (Lexington: University Press of Kentucky, 1999).

58. In counterpoint to *Doonesbury*, whose politically liberal posture qualified it to appear on the editorial page, was Bruce Tinsley's *Mallard Fillmore*. Its title character was a duck whose conservative outlook made the strip no less a fit for the editorial page. The fact that Johnny Hart occasionally used *B.C.* to espouse some of his Christian views offended some readers and editors alike who felt that a newspaper comic strip was hardly an appropriate medium for the issues and concerns of personal religious convictions.

59. In a rare move for the creator of a popular comic strip, Watterson turned down all proposals for spin-off agreements during *Calvin*'s entire run, contending that "merchandising the strip would destroy the relationship that must exist between a creator and his creation, if the work is to have a life of its own." This special relationship was evidenced in Watterson's unique approach to interpreting Calvin's private world, accounting in large part for the strip's humor. See Robert C. Harvey, *The Art of the Funnies: An Aesthetic History* (Jackson: University Press of Mississippi, 1994), 232.

60. The most notable of these books published in the centennial year 1995 were Bill Blackbeard and Dale Crain, eds., *The Comic Strip Century: Celebrating 100 Years of an American Art Form*, 2 vols. (Englewood Cliffs, N.J.: O. G. Publishing, 1995) and Bill Blackbeard, ed., *R. F. Outcault's The Yellow Kid: A Centennial Celebration of the Kid Who Started the Comics* (Northampton, Mass.: Kitchen Sink Press, 1995). Another timely book was Maurice Horn, ed., *100 Years of American Newspaper Comics: An Illustrated Encyclopedia* (New York: Gramercy, 1996), which analyzed the import of the century's popular strips and their creators' contribution to the comics' development. Horn predicted that the comic strip would continue to exert a sociocultural force in the coming century. See his introduction, 19. For the potential impact of the digital revolution on the comics, see Scott McCloud, *Reinventing Comics: How Imagination and Technology are Revolutionizing an Art Form* (New York: HarperCollins, 2000), 200–237.

61. For a listing of magazines with the highest circulation in the '90s, see Stan Le Roy Wilson, *Mass Media/Mass Culture: An Introduction* (New York: McGraw-Hill, 1994), 131.

62. See D. M. Gross, "Zine but Not Heard," *Time*, 5 September 1994, 68–69. The trend toward creating minicommunities of like-minded specialists was expected to continue, as realized by the appearance of Penguin's *The World of Zines* (1994), a do-it-yourself guide to publishing one's own fanzine.

63. See R. Turner, "All That Talk about Tina," *Newsweek*, 8 February 1999, 54–55. With Tina Brown, the shrewd former editor of *Vanity Fair* and *The New Yorker*, recruited to head up the new magazine, the inside scoop on celebrity culture was assured as a major feature.

64. See Otto Friedrich, "Up, Up and Awaaay!!!" *Time*, 14 March 1988,

66–72. Anticipating Superman's fiftieth anniversary, Dennis Dooley and Gary Engle edited a collection of essays in *Superman at Fifty: The Persistence of a Legend* (Cleveland, Ohio: Octavia Press, 1987). In the book's preface the editors contend that the *Superman* stories, even in their intent of providing nothing more complicated than "entertainment and some basic human yearnings," have presented "a rich lode of pop cultural lore [that] say so much about the character and values of America" (12).

65. Joseph Witek, *Comic Books as History: The Narrative Art of Jack Jackson, Art Spiegelman, and Harvey Pekar* (Oxford: University Press of Mississippi, 1989), 153. For Eisner's insights into sequential art or graphic narration, see Will Eisner, *Graphic Storytelling and Visual Narrative* (Tamarac, Fla.: Poorhouse Press, 1996). This book's attention to the influence of film and electronic techniques updates his earlier *Comics and Sequential Art*. On confronting the problem of prejudicial attitudes toward the comics as "art," see McCloud, "Setting Course: A 'Low' Art Takes the High Road," in *Reinventing Comics*, 26–55.

66. To evoke the understanding that comics had grown up, Miller depicted Batman as a middle-aged "brooding psychopath" still bent on vengeance for the death of his parents many years before, as Roger Sabin observes in *Adult Comics: An Introduction* (London: Routledge, 1993), 87. For Miller's emphasis on the social realities of the time as a source of fantasized realism and its impact on the comic book audience, see Gerard Jones and Will Jacobs, *The Comic Book Heroes* (Rocklin, Calif.: Prima, 1997), 296–97. The growing attention to minority representation in the comics, particularly in those directed at an adult audience, is discussed in McCloud, *Reinventing Comics*, 96–110.

67. José David Saldivar, "Postmodern Realism," in *The Columbia History of the American Novel*, ed. Emory Elliott (New York: Columbia University Press, 1991), 540.

68. Some of these works were cited earlier, but one of the most outstanding in its intent to set critical principles for judging the comic book's artistic achievements is Robert C. Harvey, *The Art of the Comic Book: An Aesthetic History* (Jackson: University Press of Mississippi, 1996). Also, for their unique insights into the nature of the comics medium are Scott McCloud, *Understanding Comics: The Invisible Art* (New York: HarperPerennial, 1994) and *Reinventing Comics*, cited above. A work that examines the cultural import of both the comic strip and the comic book is M. Thomas Inge, *Comics as Culture* (Jackson: University Press of Mississippi, 1990). For an insightful analysis of the comic book spectrum's diverse makeup, from collectors to investors, see Matthew J. Pustz, *Comic Book Culture: Fanboys and True Believers* (Jackson: University Press of Mississippi, 1999), 66–109.

69. The results of the poll were reported by the Gannett News Service, 18 July 1998.

70. For the profitable status of book publishing in America in the '90s, see Wilson, *Mass Media/Mass Culture*, 96–98.

71. James B. Twitchell, *Carnival Culture: The Trashing of Taste in America* (New York: Columbia University Press, 1992), 73.

72. Ibid., 81.

73. King's popularity and critical stature as both a writer and film source are assessed in Don Herron, ed., *Reign of Fear: The Fiction and the Films of Stephen King* (Lancaster, P.A.: Underwood-Miller, 1992).

74. Richard Zoglin, "A Real Tape Turner," *Time*, 29 August 1994, 74.

75. Quoted in Paul Gray, "Carnage: An Open Book," *Time*, 2 August 1993, 54. Stine's contention that the real world needs embellishing to attract young readers bored with the routine of their lives is yet another postmodern take on reality offered as escapist fantasy.

76. H. Bruce Franklin, *Robert A. Heinlein: America as Science Fiction* (New York: Oxford University Press, 1980), 3.

77. That so-called "aberrant" sex had become a promotional feature of the book market was exemplified by author Paul Alexander's intimation that James Dean was homosexual in *Boulevard of Broken Dreams* (New York: Viking, 1994). But in Hollywood mythology and the eyes of the mediated vision, Dean, even in death, remained the perennial media-made image of the 1950s' rebellious youth.

78. Sports figures, considered entertainers and celebrities as well, provided an endless source of autobiographies, biographies, and memoirs during this era. They were either of the old-style heroic success story or the sensationalized self-revelatory exposé. The latter commanded more attention in a tradition that extended from baseball's Jim Bouton in *Ball Four* (1970) to basketball's Dennis Rodman in *Bad as I Wanna Be* (1996). For an analysis of the autobiography's sociocultural import as well as a listing of the most notable during 1975–88, see Mary McElroy, "Athletes Displaying Their Lives: The Emergence of the Contemporary Sports Autobiography," in Wiley Lee Umphlett, ed., *The Achievement of American Sport Literature: A Critical Appraisal* (Madison, N.J.: Fairleigh Dickinson University Press, 1991), 165–83.

79. Sex as essential to a long and healthy life, both physically and mentally, was the thesis in Thomas Moore, *The Soul of Sex: Cultivating Life as an Act of Love* (New York: HarperCollins, 1998). With a subtitle suggesting that one's sex life should be a vital, fulfilling experience to ensure the basic human need of belonging, Moore's posture ran counter to many books of the 1970s that promoted the notion of sex as a primarily recreational activity.

80. The review appeared in *Entertainment Weekly*, 28 July 2000, 176.

81. According to Mitchell Stephens, such techniques had been evolving in TV commercials since the 1970s, culminating in the New Video in which fast-cut computerized editing was helping "solve the image's intelligibility problems." See *The Rise of the Image, The Fall of the Word* (New York: Oxford University Press, 1998), 69.

82. For a complete list of the commercials' rankings, see Dottie Enrico, "The Fifty Greatest TV Commercials of All Time," *TV Guide*, 3–9 July 1999, 2–34.

83. Jonathan Price, *Commercials: The Best Thing on TV* (New York: Viking Penguin, 1978), excerpted in Edward Jay Whetmore, *Mediamerica, Mediaworld* (Belmont, Calif.: Wadsworth, 1993), 292–93.

84. To the mediated vision during Hollywood's golden age, smoking by male movie actors was considered a sign of manliness, as evidenced in the roles of Humphrey Bogart and John Wayne, both of whom later succumbed to lung cancer. In later years smoking by movie actors was limited to subversive types and rebellious youth, which according to a 1997 study was influencing the young's attraction to smoking. Its findings were syndicated in a report by Gannett News Service, 18 June 1997.

85. For an informative as well as entertaining survey of the role of advertising in postmodern America, see James B. Twitchell, *AdCult USA: The Triumph of Advertising in American Culture* (New York: Columbia University Press, 1996).

86. The role of the mass media in promoting the commercial import of the American holiday is well documented in Jack Santino, *New Old-Fashioned Ways: Holidays and Popular Culture* (Knoxville: University of Tennessee Press, 1996).

87. Carole Rifkind, "America's Fantasy Urbanism: The Waxing of the Mall and the Waning of Civility," in *Dumbing Down: Essays on the Strip-Mining of American Culture*, ed. Katharine Washburn and John Thornton (New York: Norton, 1996), 262.

88. For an overview of things to come in the area of online shopping, see Steven Levy, "Xmas.com," *Newsweek*, 7 December 1998, 50–56. Naturally, the credit card, which would mark its fiftieth anniversary in 2000, was a key player in this kind of transaction.

89. Gabler, *Life the Movie*, 205.

90. See Steve Rushin, "1954–1994: How We Got Here," *Sports Illustrated*, 16 August 1994, 35–49.

91. Syndicated columnist George Will, a longtime observer of the game, assessed the downside of this situation as it affected the fans of teams whose comparatively low salary base put them at a disadvantage in contending for a pennant: "Baseball fans are experts at the willful suspension of disbelief, but there are limits to even their credulity." Clearly, the mediated vision's longtime love affair with sport was being put to its strongest test during this era. Will's column was syndicated by the *Washington Post* Writer's Group, 3 March 1999.

92. In 1998, Cal Ripken Jr. also set the record for consecutive games played (2,632). For an inspired summing up of the '98 baseball season, see Tom Verducci, "The Greatest Season Ever," *Sports Illustrated*, 5 October 1998, 38–44. The magazine later named Mark McGuire its "Hero of the Year."

93. In this regard, the made-for-TV sports, or the so-called "trash" sports, that had been appearing since the 1970s *Superstars* series, continued to find an audience. As weekend TV diversions that proved more entertaining than sporting, they mirrored the escapist fantasies of a leisure-oriented audience. For a lively discussion about such programming's socio-economic import, see David A. Klatell and Norman Marcus, *Sports for Sale: Television, Money, and the Fans* (New York: Oxford University Press, 1988), 151–60.

94. Jeff MacGregor, column in *Sports Illustrated*, 5 April 1999, 24.

## CHAPTER 4: INDULGING THE SELF AS A WAY OF LIFE AT CENTURY'S END

1. During this time, too, the Disney Corporation expanded its interests overseas, and in addition to the parks opened in Paris and Tokyo, it announced in 1999 that a third overseas theme park would be built in Hong Kong. Since this area had become a part of mainland China, the fact that

the Disney mystique could even enchant the Chinese Communists demonstrated the universal power of the mediated vision. And in accord with this capability, it appeared that the Disney dream would continue to be a major exemplar of this sensibility. Thus, Jeff Kurtti commented: "Walt Disney World will without a doubt continue growing into the next century, enlarging and expanding—as Walt Disney himself stated—'as long as there is imagination left in the world.'" See *Since the World Began: Walt Disney World; The First 25 Years* (New York: Hyperion, 1996), 186.

2. But architecture critic Ada Louise Huxtable was not nearly as taken with the Disney style as most, calling it more technologically commercial than imaginative in effect. See *The Unreal America: Architecture and Illusion* (New York: New Press, 1997), 48–55.

3. The big boom in casino gambling and the attempt to control online sports betting were reported by Knight Ridder, 10 October 1999.

4. The astonishing growth, glitz, and glamour that typified postmodern Las Vegas were graphically captured in the photographs displayed in Isabella Brega, *Las Vegas: The Brightest Star of the Desert* (Vercelli, Italy: White Star, 2000). But to Huxtable, the Vegas escapist milieu persisted as the epitome of an ersatz architecture that offered its fake images of famous landmarks as another form of fantasy and reality. See *The Unreal America*, 75–81.

5. To David Brooks, though, yuppie culture was only a phase before the ultimate merging of the 1960s counterculture bohemians with the bourgeois values they had rebelled against. Hence his label "Bobos" (bourgeois bohemians) for what he terms "The New Upper Class." See *Bobos in Paradise* (New York: Simon & Schuster, 2000).

6. From 1994 to 2000, an end to traditional fashion was being reported on various fronts. Martha Duffy, in "Fashion's Fall," *Time*, 25 April 1994, saw the extremes in fashion as an "epidemic of cynicism passing for wit." Teri Agins, in *The End of Fashion: The Mass Marketing of the Clothing Business* (New York: William Morrow, 1999), observed that the democratization of brand-name clothes marketed at mall stores was a major factor in this process. By 2000 the trend culminated in the ultimate casual style that critics labeled "slob chic," a sign to them that it was time for conservative fashion to reassert itself.

7. Note P. David Marshall's comments on this social change as it has evolved since the 1950s and '60s: "The division of the social world into patterns of consumption generally configured around the concepts of style and lifestyle has become naturalized and is no longer in opposition to a morality of work and production." By the 1990s, then, these patterns were labeled by Marshall as "market fragmentation or segmentation," as reflected in the media culture's subcultural fragmentation. See *Celebrity and Power: Fame in Contemporary Culture* (Minneapolis: University of Minnesota Press, 1997), 161.

8. The AARP survey (27 May 1999) that revealed an ambivalent attitude toward living longer also pointed out that the senior years were now more rewarding than for those who lived earlier. And as far as outstanding accomplishments are concerned, it noted, older people could point to Senator John Glenn, who, as the first person to orbit the earth in 1959, returned to space in 1998 at the age of seventy-seven.

9. Betty Friedan, "My Quest for the Fountain of Age," *Time*, 6 September 1993, 64.

10. In 1979, a more proactive political stance had been initiated by fundamentalist minister Jerry Falwell. Referring to his followers as the Moral Majority, he allied the movement with the rise of New Right political conservatism. For a penetrating analysis of the conservative Right that set the stage for the Reagan era, see Bruce J. Schulman, *The Seventies: The Great Shift in American Culture, Society, and Politics* (New York: Free Press, 2001), chapter 8.

11. Eric Pooley, "The Great Escape," *Time*, 8 December 1997, 54.

12. Quote is from the report, syndicated 26 June 1998. A later Associated Press report (27 August 1999) of a study by the American Psychological Association revealed Internet addiction as a growing problem. In fact, it indicated that more participants in the study responded "yes" to a question about using the Internet as an escape than any other about why they used it.

13. For an insightful discussion of the problems inherent in escapism via the Internet, see Sherry Turkle, "Virtuality and Its Discontents," in *Life on the Screen: Identity in the Age of the Internet* (New York: Simon & Schuster, 1995), 235–54.

14. Ibid., 269. For further elaboration, see Turkle's chapter on "Identity Crisis," 255–69.

15. See Stephens, *The Rise of the Image*. For examples of the trend toward the dominance of the image over the word in television, print, and Internet advertising, see Lazar Ozamic, *No-Copy Advertising* (Celigny, Switzerland: Rotovision, 2001).

16. Stephens, 193–94. A main contention of Stephens here is that this new way of seeing "enables artists to think new thoughts and . . . us to see more clearly what they are thinking."

17. Twitchell, *Carnival Culture*, 3.

18. Kent Carroll, "The Facts of Fiction and the Fiction of Facts," in *Dumbing Down*, 231.

19. In this light, biographer Edmund Morris, in his attempt to create a real person out of the elusive character of President Ronald Reagan, injected himself as a fictional observer in *Dutch: A Memoir of Ronald Reagan* (1999). While most readers relished the book, it was generally berated by the critics for its semifictional elements, yet another example of the postmodernist literary tendency to merge nonfiction and fiction.

20. In 1999, following outbreaks of violence in the nation's high schools, Hollywood was again targeted for its focus on unwarranted violence. But controversial films still strived for an R rating, as the NC-17 rating was considered box-office poison. And so the ratings war continued, with no end in sight. See John Cloud, "Taking Aim at Show Biz," *Time*, 21 June 1999, 42–43.

21. See Twitchell, *Carnival Culture*, 193–97.

22. Robert H. Bork, *Slouching Towards Gomorrah: Modern Liberalism and American Decline* (New York: Regan Books, 1996), 123–39.

23. A persuasive argument for the essential communal role that popular social institutions still play is Ray Oldenburg, *The Great Good Place: Cafés, Coffee Shops, Community Centers, Beauty Parlors, General Stores, Bars, Hangouts, and How They Get You through the Day* (New York: Paragon House, 1989).

24. Charley Reese, "Media, Government Support Killing Message," King Features Syndicate, 19 May 1999.

25. Mona Charen, "Culture's Melting, Grownups on the Run," 14 May 1997. Syndicated by the Gannett News Service.

26. In his 12 August 2000 column, Pitts responded to Schwarzbaum's commentary in "Lewd Awakening," *Entertainment Weekly*, 11 August 2000, 20–26.

27. Gabler, *Life the Movie*, 4, 6.

28. See Mark Morrison, "The New Public Square," *USA Weekend*, 12–14 December 1997, 6–7. On the proliferation and democratization of museums since the 1960s, see also Charles Mathes, introduction, in *Treasures of American Museums* (New York: M&M Books, 1991).

## Epilogue: Looking Back While Looking Ahead To A New Century

1. A survey of 100 U.S. college history professors ranked the computer first among the century's most socioculturally innovative inventions, followed in order by nuclear energy, television, the airplane, and the automobile. Reported by the Gannett News Service, 24 November 1997. But a later Knight Ridder report (3 January 2000) identified splitting the atom as "the most profound event of the century because it embodies the hope and the terror of technological innovation."

2. John Naisbitt, *Megatrends: Ten New Directions Transforming Our Lives* (New York: Warner Books, 1984), 279. Most futurists, that is, those who study the future's sociocultural implications, were in agreement by century's end that technology would wield the greatest impact on the human condition. Alvin Toffler seemed especially mindful of this end, as since *Future Shock* in 1970 he published a new book every ten years: *The Third Wave* (1980), a treatise on the information age's impact, and *Powershift* (1990), which assessed its effects on the struggle for ascendancy among postmodern institutions near the century's end. Still, the past retained its attraction to the mediated vision because one could be personally selective in looking back to the appeal of its nostalgic side, while the rapid change that the future boded took on an ominous, even perilous aspect.

3. John Docker cites Robert Venturi, et al., *Learning from Las Vegas* (Cambridge, Mass.: MIT Press, 1977) as the "manifesto" of "architectural postmodernism," one that promotes a playful mixture of all styles that had preceded it, thus suggesting an architecture designed to meet new sociocultural and commercial requisites. See *Postmodernism and Popular Culture: A Cultural History* (Cambridge: Cambridge University Press, 1977), 82–89. Similarly, Marxist critic Fredric Jameson assessed contemporary urban architecture as "a kind of aesthetic populism," a form symbolic of the breakdown of "the older . . . frontier between high culture and so-called mass or commercial culture." See *Postmodernism or, The Cultural Logic of Late Capitalism* (Durham, N.C.: Duke University Press, 1999), 2. For a more pointedly critical analysis of the Las Vegas brand of architectural illusion, see Huxtable, *The Unreal America*, 75–79.

4. *U.S. News & World Report*, "The Great Nostalgia Kick," 22 March 1982, 60.

5. Papazian, *Medium Rare*, 571.

6. Robert Hughes, "American Visions," *Time*, Special Issue, Spring 1997, 9.

7. Hughes, "A Nation's Self-Image," *Time*, 10 May 1999, 78–81.

8. See Lawrence W. Levine, *Highbrow/Lowbrow: The Emergence of Cultural Hierarchy in America* (Cambridge, Mass.: Harvard University Press, 1988), 233–34, 243, 256. To some, though, the meaning of a democratized culture itself had come into question. In 2001, for example, syndicated columnist George Will criticized the National Endowment for the Humanities for its broadening of the traditional standards that had supported the understanding of culture as the pursuit of excellence in the arts (see bibliography for source of Will's argument). Earlier, Allan Bloom had attacked the higher-education establishment in a best-selling book whose lengthy title reflected his posture: *The Closing of the American Mind: How Higher Education Has Failed Democracy and Impoverished the Souls of Today's Students* (New York: Simon & Schuster, 1987). But Levine countered Bloom's enshrinement of education's cultural traditions with *The Opening of the American Mind: Canons, Culture and History* (Boston: Beacon Press, 1996). And so the debate, as it had since the nineteenth century, continued on into the twenty-first century.

# Bibliography

Agins, Teri. *The End of Fashion: The Mass Marketing of the Clothing Business*. New York: Morrow, 1999.

Aronson, Arnold. "American Theatre in Context: 1945–Present." In *The Cambridge History of American Theatre*, vol. 3, edited by Don Wilmeth and Christopher Bigsby, 454–65. Cambridge: Cambridge University Press, 1995.

"Aversion to Violence in Movies Drops." Syndicated report of Associated Press poll results, 3 July 1999.

Barrett, Greg. "Reading is No. 1 Pastime in America." Report of Harris Poll results syndicated by Gannett News Service, 18 July 1998.

Barson, Michael, and Steven Heller. *Teenage Confidential: An Illustrated History of the American Teen*. San Franciso: Chronicle Books, 1998.

Bauder, David. "*Mary [Tyler Moore]* Crowned Best TV Show Ever." Report syndicated by the Associated Press, 26 June 1997.

———. "Turn off the Tube: Surgeon General Says Kids Should Do Other Things." Report syndicated by the Associated Press, 23 April 1999.

———. "VH-1 Revisits Rock 'n' Roll Revolutions." Report syndicated by the Associated Press, 25 July 2000.

Bayles, Martha. *Hole in Our Soul: The Loss of Beauty and Meaning in American Popular Music*. New York: Free Press, 1994.

"The Beatles are Best Seller of the Century." Report syndicated by *USA Today*, 11 November 1999.

Benton, Mike. *The Illustrated History of Horror Comics*. Dallas: Taylor Publishing, 1991.

———. *Masters of Imagination: The Comic Book Artists Hall of Fame*. Dallas: Taylor Publishing, 1994.

Bercovitch, Sacvan, ed. *The Cambridge History of American Literature: Prose Writing, 1940–1990*. Vol. 7. Cambridge: Cambridge University Press, 1999.

———, ed. *The Cambridge History of American Literature: Poetry and Criticism, 1940–1995*. Vol. 8. Cambridge: Cambridge University Press, 1996.

Berkowitz, Gerald M. *New Broadways: Theatre across America, 1950–1980*. Totowa, N.J.: Rowman & Allanheld, 1982.

———. *New Broadways: Theatre across America; Approaching a New Millennium*. Rev. ed. New York: Applause Books, 1997.

Berry, S. Torriano, and Venise T. Berry. *The 50 Most Influential Black Films*. New York: Kensington, 2001.

Betrock, Alan. *Sleazy Business: A Pictorial History of Exploitation Tabloids, 1959–1974.* Brooklyn, N.Y.: Shake Books, 1996.

Blackbeard, Bill, and Dale Crain, eds. *The Comic Strip Century: Celebrating 100 Years of an American Art Form,* 2 vols. Englewood Cliffs, N.J.: O.G. Publishing, 1995.

Bogart, Michele H. *Artists, Advertising, and the Borders of Art.* Chicago: University of Chicago Press, 1995.

Bonn, Thomas L. *Undercover: An Illustrated History of American Mass Market Paperbacks.* New York: Penguin Books, 1982.

Bork, Robert H. *Slouching Towards Gomorrah: Modern Liberalism and American Decline.* New York: Regan Books, 1996.

Boulware, Jack. *Sex American Style: An Illustrated Romp through the Golden Age of Heterosexuality.* Venice, Calif.: Feral House, 1997.

Bowden, Robert. "Stan Lee: The Marvel of the Comic World." *St. Petersburg* (Fla.) *Times,* 3 May 1978.

Bradbury, Ray. Introduction. In *The Ray Bradbury Chronicles.* Vol. 1. New York: Bantam, 1992.

Brega, Isabella. *Las Vegas: The Brightest Star of the Desert.* Vercelli, Italy: White Star, 2000.

Brooks, David. *Bobos in Paradise: The New Upper Class and How They Got There.* New York: Simon & Schuster, 2000.

Bruce, Scott, and Bill Crawford. *Cerealizing America: The Unsweetened Story of American Breakfast Cereal.* Boston: Faber and Faber, 1995.

Capp, Al. *The World of Li'l Abner.* New York: Ballantine, 1953.

Carroll, Kent. "The Facts of Fiction and the Fiction of Facts." In *Dumbing Down: Essays on the Strip-Mining of American Culture,* edited by Katharine Washburn and John Thornton, 224–33. New York: Norton, 1996.

Carson, Rachel. *Silent Spring.* Boston: Houghton Mifflin, 1962.

Charen, Mona. "Culture's Melting, Grownups on the Run." Column syndicated by Gannett News Service, 14 May 1999.

Chunovic, Louis. *One Foot on the Floor: The Curious Evolution of Sex in Television from* I Love Lucy *to* South Park. New York: TV Books, 2000.

Clarke, Donald. *The Rise and Fall of Popular Music.* New York: St. Martin's Griffin, 1995.

Clarke, Gerald. "The Comics on the Couch." *Time,* 13 December 1971, 70–71.

———. "The Meaning of Nostalgia." *Time,* 3 May 1971, 77.

Cloud, John. "Taking Aim at Show Biz." *Time,* 21 June 1999, 42–43.

Corliss, Richard. "Ready, Set, Glow! A Look at the New Episode in the *Star Wars* Saga." *Time,* April 1999, 79–89.

Couperie, Pierre, and Maurice Horn. *A History of the Comic Strip.* New York: Crown, 1968.

Custen, George F. *Twentieth Century's Fox: Darryl F. Zanuck and the Culture of Hollywood.* New York: Basic Books, 1997.

Daniels, Les. *DC Comics: Sixty Years of the World's Favorite Comic Book Heroes.* Boston: Bulfinch Press, 1995.

Davis, Fred. *Yearning for Yesterday: A Sociology of Nostalgia.* New York: Free Press, 1979.

Davis, Gerry. The Today Show: *An Anecdotal History.* New York: William Morrow, 1987.

Davis, Jonathan P., ed. *Stephen King's America.* Bowling Green, Ohio: Popular Press, 1994.

Deford, Frank. "Roone Arledge, 1931–2002." *Sports Illustrated,* 16 December 2002, 121–26.

Degen, John. "Musical Theatre since World War II." In *The Cambridge History of American Theatre,* vol. 3, edited by Don Wilmeth and Christopher Bigsby, 454–65. Cambridge: Cambridge University Press, 1995.

Denzin, Norman K. *Images of Postmodern Society: Social Theory and Contemporary Cinema.* London: Sage Publications, 1991.

Diamond, Edwin. "God's Television." *American Film,* March 1980, 30–32, 34–35.

Dickstein, Morris. *Gates of Eden: American Culture in the Sixties.* Cambridge, Mass.: Harvard University Press, 1997.

Di Fate, Vincent. *Infinite Worlds: The Fantastic Visions of Science Fiction Art.* New York: Penguin, 1997.

di Franco, J. Philip. *The Movie World of Roger Corman.* New York: Chelsea House, 1979.

Disch, Thomas M. *The Dreams Our Stuff Is Made of: How Science Fiction Conquered the World.* New York: Free Press, 1998.

Doan, Richard K. "Public Television: Is Anybody Watching?" In TV Guide: *The First 25 Years,* edited by Jay S. Harris, 188–89. New York: Simon & Schuster, 1978.

Docker, John. *Postmodernism and Popular Culture: A Cultural History.* Cambridge: Cambridge University Press, 1977.

Donn, Jeff. "Addicted to the Net? You Have Company." Report syndicated by the Associated Press, 27 August 1999.

Dooley, Dennis, and Gary Engle, eds. *Superman at Fifty: The Persistence of a Legend.* Cleveland, Ohio: Octavia Press, 1987.

Dotz, Warren, and Jim Morton. *What a Character! 20th-Century American Advertising Icons.* San Francisco: Chronicle Books, 1996.

Douglas, Susan J. *Listening In: Radio and the American Imagination from Amos 'n' Andy and Edward R. Murrow to Wolfman Jack and Howard Stern.* New York: Times Books, 1999.

Duffy, Martha. "Fashion's Fall." *Time,* 25 April 1994, 76–80.

Efron, Edith. "Does TV Violence Affect Our Society?" In TV Guide: *The First 25 Years,* edited by Jay S. Harris, 226–29. New York: Simon & Schuster, 1978.

Eisner, Will. *Graphic Storytelling and Visual Narrative.* Tamarac, Fla.: Poorhouse Press, 1996.

Elber, Lynn. "'Family Hour' a Little too Spicy, Study Shows." Report syndicated by the Associated Press, 21 August 1999.

Elliott, Emory, ed. *The Columbia History of the American Novel.* New York: Columbia University Press, 1991.

Engelhardt, Tom. *The End of Victory Culture: Cold War America and the Disillusioning of a Generation.* New York: Basic Books, 1995.

Enrico, Dottie. "The Fifty Greatest TV Commercials of All Time." *TV Guide*, 3–9 July 1999, 2–34.

Erickson, Hal. *Religious Radio and Television in the United States, 1921–1991.* Jefferson, N.C.: McFarland, 1992.

Estren, Mark James. *A History of Underground Comics.* San Francisco: Straight Arrow Books, 1974.

Feiffer, Jules. *The Great Comic Book Heroes.* New York: Bonanza, 1965.

Feiler, Bruce. "Country Music's New Values." *USA Weekend*, 3–5 April 1998, 24.

Fine, Benjamin. *1,000,000 Delinquents.* Cleveland, Ohio: World Publishing, 1955.

Fine, Marshall. "Smoking in Films Seen as Enticing Teens." Report syndicated by Gannett News Service, 18 June 1997.

Fishman, Mark, and Gray Cavender, eds. *Entertaining Crime: Television Reality Programs.* New York: Aldine de Gruyter, 1995.

Fox, Julian. *Woody: Movies from Manhattan.* Woodstock, N.Y.: Overlook Press, 1996.

Franklin, H. Bruce. *Robert A. Heinlein: America as Science Fiction.* New York: Oxford University Press, 1980.

Friedan, Betty. *The Feminine Mystique.* New York: Norton, 1963.

———. *The Fountain of Age.* New York: Simon & Schuster, 1993.

———. "My Quest for the Fountain of Age." *Time*, 6 September 1993, 61–64.

Friedrich, Otto. "Up, Up and Awaaay!!!" *Time*, 14 March 1988, 66–74.

Gabler, Neal. *Life the Movie: How Entertainment Conquered Reality.* New York: Knopf, 1998.

Galbraith, John Kenneth. *The Affluent Society.* Boston: Houghton Mifflin, 1958.

Germain, David. "Film Institute Lists 100 Funniest Movies." Report syndicated by the Associated Press, 14 June 2000.

Goldstein, Jeffrey, ed. *Why We Watch: The Attractions of Violent Entertainment.* New York: Oxford University Press, 1998.

Goulart, Ron. *The Great Comic Book Artists.* Vol 1. New York: St. Martin's, 1986.

Gray, Paul. "Carnage: An Open Book." *Time*, 2 August 1993, 54.

Greenfield, Jeff. *Television: The First Fifty Years.* New York: Crescent Books, 1981.

Groensteen, Thierry. "The Schulz System: Why *Peanuts* Works." *Nemo: The Classic Comics Library* 31 (January 1992): 26–41.

Gross, D. M. "Zine but Not Heard." *Time*, 5 September 1994, 68–69.

Guerrero, Ed. *Framing Blackness: The African American Image in Film.* Philadelphia: Temple University Press, 1993.

Halberstam, David. *The Fifties.* New York: Villard, 1993.

Hall, Jim. *Mighty Minutes: An Illustrated History of Television's Best Commercials.* New York: Harmony Books, 1984.

Hanson, Mary Ellen. *Go! Fight! Win! Cheerleading in American Culture.* Bowling Green, Ohio: Popular Press, 1995.

Harris, Jay S., ed. TV Guide: *The First 25 Years.* New York: Simon & Schuster, 1978.

Harvey, Robert C. *The Art of the Comic Book: An Aesthetic History.* Jackson: University Press of Mississippi, 1996.

———. *The Art of the Funnies: An Aesthetic History.* Jackson: University Press of Mississippi, 1994.

———. "Caniff's Private War to Save *Steve Canyon.*" *Nemo: The Classic Comics Library* 32 (Winter 1992): 4–21.

———. *Children of the Yellow Kid: The Evolution of the American Comic Strip.* Seattle: Frye Museum, 1998.

Heidenry, John. *What Wild Ecstasy: The Rise and Fall of the Sexual Revolution.* New York: Simon & Schuster, 1997.

Heller, Steven, and Teresa Fernandes. *Magazines Inside and Out.* New York: PBC International, 1996.

Henke, James, and Parke Puterbaugh, eds. *I Want to Take You Higher: The Psychedelic Era, 1965–69.* San Francisco: Chronicle Books, 1997.

Herron, Don, ed. *Reign of Fear: The Fiction and the Films of Stephen King.* Lancaster, P.A.: Underwood-Miller, 1992.

Hoover, J. Edgar. *Masters of Deceit.* New York: Pocket Books, 1959.

Horn, Maurice, ed. *100 Years of American Newspaper Comics.* New York: Gramercy Books, 1996.

———, ed. *The World Encyclopedia of Comics.* New York: Chelsea House, 1976.

Howard, Jay R., and John M. Struck. *Apostles of Rock: The Splintered World of Contemporary Christian Rock.* Lexington: University Press of Kentucky, 1999.

Hughes, Robert. "American Visions." *Time,* Special Issue, Spring 1997, 9.

———. "A Nation's Self-Image." *Time,* 10 May 1999, 78–81.

Hutner, Gordon, ed. *American Literature, American Culture.* New York: Oxford University Press, 1999.

Huxtable, Ada Louise. *The Unreal America: Architecture and Illusion.* New York: New Press, 1997.

The Imagineers. *Walt Disney Imagineering: A Behind the Dreams Look at Making the Magic Real.* New York: Hyperion, 1996.

Inge, M. Thomas. *Comics as Culture.* Jackson: University Press of Mississippi, 1990.

Jameson, Fredric. *Postmodernism or, The Cultural Logic of Late Capitalism.* Durham, N.C.: Duke University Press, 1999.

Jones, George E. "The Great Nostalgia Kick." *U.S News & World Report,* 22 March 1982, 57–60.

Jones, Gerard, and Will Jacobs. *The Comic Book Heroes.* Rocklin, Calif.: Prima Publishing, 1997.

Kammen, Michael. *Mystic Chords of Memory: The Transformation of Tradition in American Culture.* New York: Vintage Books, 1993.

Kanfer, Stefan. *Serious Business: The Art and Commerce of Animation in America from* Betty Boop *to* Toy Story. New York: Scribner, 1997.

Key, Wilson Bryan. *Media Sexploitation.* New York: New American Library, 1976.

Kiesewetter, John. "NBC President Wants to Take Network in New Direction." Report syndicated by *Cincinnati Enquirer,* 18 January 1999.

Klatell, David A., and Norman Marcus. *Sports for Sale: Television, Money, and the Fans.* New York: Oxford University Press, 1988.

Kluger, Richard. *The Paper: The Life and Death of the* New York Herald Tribune. New York: Knopf, 1986.

Kronhausen, Eberhard, and Phyllis Kronhausen. *Pornography and the Law: The Psychology of Erotic Realism and Pornography.* New York: Ballantine, 1959.

Kurtti, Jeff. *Since the World Began: Walt Disney World; The First 25 Years.* New York: Hyperion, 1996.

Landon, Brooks. *Science Fiction after 1900: From the Steam Man to the Stars.* New York: Twayne, 1997.

Lasch, Christopher. "The Corruption of Sports." In *American Sport Culture: The Humanistic Dimensions,* edited by Wiley Lee Umphlett, 50–67. Lewisburg, Pa.: Bucknell University Press, 1985.

Laufer, Peter. *Inside Talk Radio: America's Voice or Just Hot Air?* New York: Birch Lane Press, 1995.

"The Leisured Masses." *Business Week,* 12 September 1953, 142–45.

Lencek, Lena, and Gideon Bosker. *Making Waves: Swimsuits and the Undressing of America.* San Francisco: Chronicle Books, 1989.

Lent, John A. "Pogo." In *100 Years of American Newspaper Comics,* edited by Maurice Horn, 244–45. New York: Gramercy Books, 1996.

Levine, Lawrence W. *Highbrow/Lowbrow: The Emergence of Cultural Hierarchy in America.* Cambridge, Mass.: Harvard University Press, 1988.

Levy, Steven. "Xmas.com." *Newsweek,* 7 December 1998, 50–56.

Lewis, Jon. *The Road to Romance and Ruin: Teen Films and Youth Culture* (New York: Routledge, 1992).

Lipsyte, Robert. "Varsity Syndrome: The Unkindest Cut." In *American Sport Culture: The Humanistic Dimensions,* edited by Wiley Lee Umphlett, 111–21. Lewisburg, P.A.: Bucknell University Press, 1985.

Livingstone, Marco. *Pop Art: A Continuing History.* New York: Abrams, 1990.

Long, Elizabeth. *The American Dream and the Popular Novel.* Boston: Routledge & Kegan Paul, 1985.

Lupoff, Dick, and Don Thompson. *All in Color for a Dime.* New Rochelle, N.Y.: Arlington House, 1970.

MacDonald, Dwight. "Masscult and Midcult." In *American Literature, American Culture,* edited by Gordon Hutner, 393–404. New York: Oxford University Press.

Mailer, Norman. "The White Negro." In *Advertisements for Myself,* 302–22. New York: Signet Books, 1959.

Maltin, Leonard. *Of Mice and Magic: A History of American Animated Cartoons*. New York: McGraw-Hill, 1980.

Marc, David. *Comic Visions: Television Comedy and American Culture*. 2nd ed. Malden, Mass.: Blackwell, 1997.

————, and Robert J. Thompson. *Prime Time, Prime Movers: From* I Love Lucy *to* L.A. Law; *America's Greatest TV Shows and the People Who Created Them*. Boston: Little, Brown, 1992.

Marling, Karal Ann. *As Seen on TV: The Visual Culture of Everyday Life in the 1950s*. Cambridge, Mass.: Harvard University Press, 1994.

Marshall, P. David. *Celebrity and Power: Fame in Contemporary Culture*. Minneapolis: University of Minnesota Press, 1997.

Marshall, Richard, ed. "Technology and Art." In *Great Events of the 20th Century: How They Changed Our Lives*, 462–67. Pleasantville, N.Y.: Reader's Digest Association, 1977.

Mathes, Charles. Introduction. In *Treasures of American Museums*. New York: M&M Books, 1991.

Mathews, Jack. "Directors Guild Gives Movie Ratings System an F." Report syndicated by *New York Daily News*, 20 September 2000.

Matthew-Walker, Robert. *From Broadway to Hollywood: The Musical and the Cinema*. London: Sanctuary, 1996.

Matthiessen, Peter. "Environmentalist Rachel Carson." *Time*, 29 March 1999, 187–90.

McCloud, Scott. *Reinventing Comics: How Imagination and Technology are Revolutionizing an Art Form*. New York: HarperPerennial, 2000.

————. *Understanding Comics: The Invisible Art*. New York: HarperPerennial, 1994.

McElroy, Mary. "Athletes Displaying Their Lives: The Emergence of the Contemporary Sports Autobiography." In *The Achievement of American Sport Literature: A Critical Appraisal*, edited by Wiley Lee Umphlett, 165–83. Madison, N.J.: Fairleigh Dickinson University Press, 1991.

McFarling, Usha Lee. "Many Ambivalent about Longer Life." Report syndicated by Knight Ridder, 27 May 1999.

McGee, Rex. "All That Jazz . . . Swing . . . Pop . . . and Rock." *American Film*, July–August 1980, 26–31, 65.

McGurk, Margaret A. "*Drive Me Crazy* is Yet Another Standard Flick about High School." Syndicated by the *Cincinnati Enquirer*, 30 September 1999.

Medved, Michael. *Hollywood versus America: Popular Culture and the War on Traditional Values*. New York: HarperCollins, 1992.

Merlis, Bob, and Davin Seay. *Heart and Soul: A Celebration of Black Music Style in America, 1930–1975*. New York: Stewart, Tabori & Chang, 1997.

Michener, James. *Sports in America*. New York: Random House, 1976.

Millard, André. *America on Record: A History of Recorded Sound*. New York: Cambridge University Press, 1995.

Miller, Frank. *Censored Hollywood: Sex, Sin and Violence on Screen*. Atlanta: Turner Publishing, 1994.

Miller, James. *Almost Grown: The Rise of Rock*. London: William Heinemann, 1999.

Moore, Frazier. "TV Reigns as Media King in Lives of Today's Kids." Report syndicated by the Associated Press, 18 November 1999.

Moore, Thomas. *The Soul of Sex: Cultivating Life as an Act of Love*. New York: HarperCollins, 1998.

Morrison, Mark. "The New Public Square." *USA Weekend*, 12–14 December 1997, 6–7.

"Movies, TV, Music Videos Chock-full of 'Serious' Violence, Study Says." Report of Center for Media and Public Affairs study syndicated by Gannett News Service, 26 September 1999.

Moyers, Bill. "Of Myth and Men." *Time*, 26 April 1999, 90–94.

Muller, Eddie, and Daniel Faris. *Grindhouse: The Forbidden World of "Adults Only" Cinema*. New York: St. Martin's, 1996.

Naisbitt, John. *Megatrends: Ten New Directions Transforming Our Lives*. New York: Warner Books, 1984.

Nance, Scott. *Music You Can See! The MTV Story*. Las Vegas: Pioneer Books, 1993.

Nesheim, Eric, and Leif Nesheim. *Saucer Attack! Pop Culture in the Golden Age of Flying Saucers*. Los Angeles: General Publishing, 1997.

Newman, Kim. *Apocalypse Movies: End of the World Cinema*. New York: St. Martin's Griffin, 2000.

North-Hager, Eddie. "Internet is New Escape." Report syndicated by *Tucson Citizen*, 26 June 1998.

Nyberg, Amy Kiste. *Seal of Approval: The History of the Comics Code*. Jackson: University Press of Mississippi, 1998.

Omicinski, John. "Summing Up the 20th Century—The Great, the Good, the Bad." Report syndicated by Gannett News Service, 24 November 1997.

Osterwold, Tilman. *Pop Art*. Cologne: Taschen, 1999.

Ozamic, Lazar. *No-Copy Advertising*. Coligny, Switzerland: RotoVision, 2001.

Panitt, Merrill. Introduction. In TV Guide: *The First 25 Years*, edited by Jay S. Harris, 15–18. New York: Simon & Schuster, 1978.

———. "Television Today: The State of the Art." In ibid., 267–75.

Papazian, Ed. *Medium Rare: The Evolution, Workings, and Impact of Commercial Television*. New York: Media Dynamics, 1991.

Peary, Danny. *Cult Movies: The Classics, the Sleepers, the Weird, and the Wonderful*. New York: Delacorte, 1981.

Petersen, James R. *The Century of Sex: Playboy's History of the Sexual Revolution, 1900–1999*. New York: Grove Press, 1999.

Pitts, Leonard. "Elvis' Hips Set up Pop Culture for a Fall." Column syndicated by the *Miami Herald*, 12 August 2000.

———. "Gangsta Rap's Insidious Lie: Life is Useless." Column syndicated by the *Miami Herald*, 20 November 1999.

Polizzi, Rick, and Fred Schaefer. *Spin Again: Board Games from the Fifties and Sixties*. San Francisco: Chronicle Books, 1991.

Poniewozik, James. "The Culture Comes Home." *Time*, 19 November 2001, 126–27.

Pooley, Eric. "The Great Escape." *Time*, 8 December 1997, 52–65.

"Pop Concert Ticket Costs are Hitting a High Note." Report syndicated by the Associated Press, 14 July 1999.

Powell, Richard J. *Black Art and Culture in the 20th Century*. New York: Thames and Hudson, 1997.

Prendergast, Mark. *The Ambient Century: From Mahler to Trance; The Evolution of Sound in the Electronic Age*. New York: Bloomsbury, 2000.

Price, Jonathan. *Commercials: The Best Thing on TV*. New York: Viking Penguin, 1978.

Puig, Claudia. "*Toy Story 2* Could Reign through Holidays." Report syndicated by *USA Today*, 3 December 1999.

Pustz, Matthew J. *Comic Book Culture: Fanboys and True Believers*. Jackson: University Press of Mississippi, 1999.

Quart, Leonard, and Albert Auster. *American Film and Society since 1945*. 2nd ed. Westport, Conn.: Praeger, 1991.

Reese, Charley. "Media, Government Support Killing Message." Column syndicated by King Features, 19 May 1999.

Reidelbach, Maria. *Completely* Mad: *A History of the Comic Book and Magazine*. Boston: Little, Brown, 1991.

Reisner, Neil. "Lawmakers Fight the Odds to Control Online Casinos." Report syndicated by Knight Ridder, 10 October 1999.

Rifkind, Carole. "America's Fantasy Urbanism: The Waxing of the Mall and the Waning of Civility." In *Dumbing Down: Essays on the Strip-Mining of American Culture*, edited by Katharine Washburn and John Thornton, 261–69. New York: Norton, 1996.

Robbins, Trina, and Catherine Yronwode. *Women and the Comics*. Forestville, Calif.: Eclipse Books, 1985.

Robinson, Jerry. *The Comics: An Illustrated History of Comic Strip Art*. New York: G. P. Putnam's, 1974.

Robinson, Julian. *Body Packaging: A Guide to Human Sexual Display*. Los Angeles: Elysium, 1988.

Rose, Tricia. *Black Noise: Rap Music and Black Culture in Contemporary America*. Middletown, Conn.: Wesleyan University Press, 1994.

Roth, Philip. "Writing American Fiction." *Commentary* 31 (March 1961): 223–33.

Rushin, Steve. "1954–1994: How We Got Here." *Sports Illustrated*, 16 August 1994, 35–49.

Sabin, Roger. *Adult Comics: An Introduction*. London: Routledge, 1993.

Saldivar, José David. "Postmodern Realism." In *The Columbia History of the American Novel*, edited by Emory Elliott, 521–41. New York: Columbia University Press, 1991.

Santino, Jack. *New Old-Fashioned Ways: Holidays and Popular Culture*. Knoxville: University of Tennessee Press, 1996.

Savage Jr., William W. *Comic Books in America, 1945–1954*. Norman: University of Oklahoma Press, 1990.

Schelly, Bill. *The Golden Age of Comic Fandom.* Seattle: Hamster Press, 1995.

Schickel, Richard. *The Disney Version: The Life, Times, Art, and Commerce of Walt Disney.* New York: Touchstone, 1985.

Schulman, Bruce J. *The Seventies: The Great Shift in American Culture, Society, and Politics.* New York: Free Press, 2001.

Schwarzbaum, Lisa. "Lewd Awakening." *Entertainment Weekly,* 11 August 2000, 20–26.

Seldes, Gilbert. *The Great Audience.* New York: Viking, 1950.

Sennitt, Stephen. *Ghastly Terror! The Horrible Story of the Horror Comics.* Manchester, UK: Headpress, 1999.

Sheppard, Ileen. "Icons and Images: The Cultural Legacy of the Fair." In *Remembering the Future: The New York World's Fair from 1939 to 1964,* 167–92. New York: Rizzoli, 1989.

Sklar, Robert. *Movie-Made America: A Social History of American Movies.* Rev. ed. New York: Random House, 1994.

Slide, Anthony. *The Silent Feminists: America's First Women Directors.* Lanham, M.D.: Scarecrow Press, 1996.

Smith, Bruce. *The History of Little Orphan Annie.* New York: Ballantine, 1982.

Sobel, Robert. *The Great Boom, 1950–2000: How a Generation of Americans Created the World's Most Prosperous Society.* New York: St. Martin's Press, 2000.

Steiner, Wendy. "Rethinking Postmodernism." In *The Cambridge History of American Literature: Prose Writing, 1940–1990,* vol. 7, edited by Sacvan Bercovitch, 470–50. Cambridge: Cambridge University Press, 1999.

Stephens, Mitchell. *The Rise of the Image, The Fall of the Word.* New York: Oxford University Press, 1998.

Steranko, James. *History of Comics.* 2 vols. Reading, P.A.: Supergraphics, 1970–72.

Stone, Laurie. *Laughing in the Dark: A Decade of Subversive Comedy.* Hopewell, N.J.: Ecco Press, 1997.

"10 Amazing Years: 1947–1957." *U.S. News & World Report,* 27 December 1957, 42–53.

Thom, Mary. *Inside Ms.: 25 Years of the Magazine and the Feminist Movement.* New York: Henry Holt, 1997.

Thomas, Roy, and Bill Schelly, eds. *Alter Ego: The Best of the Legendary Comics Fanzine.* Seattle: Hamster Press, 1997.

Toffler, Alvin. *Future Shock.* New York: Random House, 1970.

Tolliver, Robbie. *Hoot! A 25-Year History of the Greenwich Village Scene.* New York: St. Martin's Press, 1986.

"Top 25 Innovations of the 20th Century." Report syndicated by Knight Ridder, 3 January 2000.

Tuccille, Jerome. *Rupert Murdoch.* New York: Donald I. Fine, 1989.

Turkle, Sherry. *Life on the Screen: Identity in the Age of the Internet.* New York: Simon & Schuster, 1995.

"TV Meets Internet, But Future is Fuzzy." Report syndicated by the Associated Press, 26 April 1999.

Twitchell, James B. *AdCult USA: The Triumph of Advertising in American Culture*. New York: Columbia University Press, 1996.

———. *Carnival Culture: The Trashing of Taste in America*. New York: Columbia University Press, 1992.

Umphlett, Wiley Lee, ed. *The Achievement of American Sport Literature: A Critical Appraisal*. Madison, N.J.: Fairleigh Dickinson University Press, 1991.

———, ed. *American Sport Culture: The Humanistic Dimensions*. Lewisburg, P.A.: Bucknell University Press, 1985.

———. *The Visual Focus of American Media Culture: The Modern Era, 1893–1945*. Madison, N.J.: Fairleigh Dickinson University Press, 2004.

Unsworth, John M. "Book Marketplace." In *Columbia History of the American Novel*, ed. Emory Elliott, 679–96. New York: Columbia University Press, 1991.

Venturi, Robert, Scott Brown, and Steven Izenour. *Learning from Las Vegas: The Forgotten Symbolism of Architectural Form*. Cambridge: MIT Press, 1972.

Wainwright, Loudon. *The Great American Magazine: An Inside History of Life*. New York: Knopf, 1986.

Washburn, Katharine, and John Thornton. *Dumbing Down: Essays on the Strip-Mining of American Culture*. New York: Norton, 1996.

Watts, Steven. *The Magic Kingdom: Walt Disney and the American Way of Life*. Boston: Houghton Mifflin, 1997.

Whetmore, Edward Jay. *Mediamerica, Mediaworld*. Belmont, Calif.: Wadsworth, 1993.

Wilkinson, Rupert. *American Tough: The Tough-Guy Tradition and American Character*. New York: Perennial Library, 1986.

Will, George. "First of All, We Need to Define Culture." Column syndicated by *Washington Post* Writers Group, 1 January 2001.

———. "Only Rich Teams Play on Field of Dreams." Column syndicated by *Washington Post* Writers Group, 4 March 1999.

Wilmeth, Don B., and Christopher Bigsby, eds. *The Cambridge History of American Theatre: Post–World War II to the 1990s*. Vol. 3. Cambridge: Cambridge University Press, 2000.

Wilmington, Michael. "Top 100 Movies Present a Striking Portrait of America." Report syndicated by the *Chicago Tribune*, 19 June 1998.

Wilson, Garff B. *Three Hundred Years of American Drama and Theatre*. 2nd ed. Englewood Cliffs, N.J.: Prentice-Hall, 1982.

Wilson, Stan Le Roy. *Mass Media/Mass Culture: An Introduction*. New York: McGraw-Hill, 1994.

Witek, Joseph. *Comic Books as History: The Narrative Art of Jack Jackson, Art Spiegelman, and Harvey Pekar*. Jackson: University Press of Mississippi, 1989.

Wloszczyna, Susan. "Hark! Moviemakers and Shakespeare in Love." Report syndicated by *USA Today*, 29 January 1999.

Wright, Bradford W. *Comic Book Nation: The Transformation of Youth Culture in America.* Baltimore: Johns Hopkins University Press, 2001.

Zoglin, Richard. "A Real Tape Turner." *Time*, 29 August 1994, 73–74.

# Index

Page numbers in boldface refer to figures, pictures in the text.

414